Playing Across a Divide

PLAYING ACROSS A DIVIDE

Israeli-Palestinian Musical Encounters

Benjamin Brinner

OXFORD
UNIVERSITY PRESS
2009

OXFORD
UNIVERSITY PRESS

Oxford University Press, Inc., publishes works that further
Oxford University's objective of excellence
in research, scholarship, and education.

Oxford   New York
Auckland   Cape Town   Dar es Salaam   Hong Kong   Karachi
Kuala Lumpur   Madrid   Melbourne   Mexico City   Nairobi
New Delhi   Shanghai   Taipei   Toronto

With offices in
Argentina   Austria   Brazil   Chile   Czech Republic   France   Greece
Guatemala   Hungary   Italy   Japan   Poland   Portugal   Singapore
South Korea   Switzerland   Thailand   Turkey   Ukraine   Vietnam

Published by Oxford University Press, Inc.
198 Madison Avenue, New York, New York 10016

www.oup.com

Oxford is a registered trademark of Oxford University Press

Publication of this book was supported by the Gustave Reese Publication
Endowment Fund of the American Musicological Society.

Library of Congress Cataloging-in-Publication Data
Brinner, Benjamin Elon.
Playing across a divide : Israeli-Palestinian musical encounters / by
Benjamin Brinner.
    p.   cm.
Includes bibliographical references and index.
ISBN 978-0-19-517581-3; 978-0-19-539594-5 (pbk.)
1. Music—Israel—History and criticism. 2. Palestinian
Arabs—Music—History and criticism. 3. Music—Social aspects—Israel.
I. Title.
ML3754.B75 2009
780.95694'09049—dc22   2009003323

Recorded audio tracks (marked in text with 🔊) are available online
at http://www.oup.com/us/playingacrossadivide
Access with username Music1 and password Book5983

9 8 7 6 5 4 3 2 1
Printed in the United States of America
on acid-free paper

Acknowledgments

This book emerged from a complex network of connections among people, institutions, ideas, and music. It was made possible by the generosity of the musicians—cited throughout the book—who invited me to rehearsals, to concerts, and to their homes, who spoke with me candidly and often at great length about their work, their aspirations, and their frustrations, sharing their views of a musical scene that they had helped to create as well as press clippings, recordings, and photos. In particular I would like to thank Taiseer Elias, Jamal Sa'id, Shoham Einav, Yair Dalal, Avshalom Farjun, Miguel Herstein, and Amir Milstein for years of friendship, conversation, and hospitality. Invitations from Scott Marcus, Tim Rice, Philip Schuyler, and Veit Erlmann to present parts of this project at their universities stimulated my thinking and helped the book along. The manuscript benefited from readings by Lisa Gold, Michael Tenzer, Eliot Bates, Christina Sunardi, Jihad Racy, and my colleagues at Berkeley, Jocelyne Guilbault and Bonnie Wade, with whom I consulted at many stages of the project. Among the numerous current and former students who helped me to refine my thinking, Matthew Rahaim, Louisa Wong, Rita Lindahl, and John-Carlos Perea made especially helpful comments.

Grants from the Center for Middle East Studies and the Committee on Research at the University of California at Berkeley supported research trips and the Gustave Reese Publication Endowment Fund of the American Musicological Society provided support for the publication of the book. I also thank the staff of Oxford University Press, including Suzanne Ryan, Kim Robinson, Norm Hirschy, Madelyn Sutton, and Gwen Colvin, for their assistance in bringing this book to completion.

Finally, to my parents for their continuing support, to my siblings and their spouses (Leyla and Yacov, Rafi and Danielle) for their hospitality in England and Israel that smoothed the travels back and forth, and especially to my wife Lisa Gold, and my children Maya, Omri, and Devon, I offer my heartfelt thanks for their support and love throughout this long journey.

Contents

PART I

Setting the Stage

1

First Encounters

A Time of Hope—The Mid 1990s

Not long after the signing of the 1993 Oslo Peace Accords between Israel and the Palestinian Liberation Organization, a ceremony was held on the West Bank to mark one of the first stages in the implementation of those accords. Representatives of the Israeli military government met with representatives of the newly constituted Palestinian Authority to hand over the administration of health services in the West Bank and Gaza Strip. This was a closed event, marked by considerable tension. Most of the people present probably had had few peaceful or pleasant encounters with members of the other side, certainly not on a more or less equal footing.

The musicians of Alei Hazayit, a band hired by the Israeli organizers to provide entertainment, felt saddled with the added task of breaking the ice between the two sides. This small band of male Arab instrumentalists and a female Jewish singer presented a mixed program of songs in Hebrew and Arabic. Although the songs came from different sources, the musicians unified them with the driving rhythms of the *darbukkah* (goblet drum), the melodic elaboration of Arab violin and *'ud* (fretless lute), the timbre of the singer's voice, and the mingling of languages within a song. Songs sung in Hebrew were paraphrased in poetic Arabic, dramatically recited by the drummer, while the singer prefaced Arabic songs with a Hebrew paraphrase.

The musicians told me that they softened the tension with melodies and rhythms familiar to those present. They said they felt the tension melting away as people on both sides of the room heard "their own" musics mixing and found that they had common ground with those on the other side of the divide.[1] By their actions these musicians modeled the possibilities

---

1. As I was not present I cannot corroborate this account.

for peaceful coexistence and collaboration, embodying the symbolism of their band's name, "The Olive Leaves."

A few years later, on a warm summer night in Jerusalem, an audience gathered at a crafts fair below the walls of the Old City to hear another band, Bustan Abraham. The outdoor stage was situated in a park that lies between the centuries-old stone walls and the modern city. A no-man's-land between Jordan and Israel from 1948 to 1967, this is still a border area but now it is relatively convenient and safe for everyone. Seated on rocks, grass, and plastic chairs, this mixed group of Arabs and Jews, coming from the Old City and the new, responded with enthusiasm to the virtuoso performance of the six young men, Arabs and Jews. The program of original compositions was purely instrumental, without words to divide or bind the disparate audience. The musical language was a new synthesis, drawing on common Middle Eastern musical elements, but not situated centrally in an Arab or Turkish style. Elements of other musical styles, ranging from Indian *sarod* playing to hard-edged jazz flute were equally prominent. By their enthusiastic responses, the audience demonstrated that this stylistic mixture spoke to them. They called out for the band's signature encore, an arrangement of the Turkish tune "Tini Mini Hanem." As each member of the band took a rhythmically emphatic solo that helped to drive the performance inexorably toward a cathartic finish, the audience clapped along. On this sensuous night, playing on relatively neutral ground in a hotly contested holy city, this group lived up to its name, too. Bustan Abraham, the Garden of Abraham, links the common ancestor of Jews and Arabs to an image of fertility and tranquility.

Neither of these performances garnered as much attention as the Peace Concert held in Oslo on September 13, 1994, to mark the anniversary of the signing of the Oslo Peace Accords and the awarding of the Nobel Peace Prize to Israeli and Palestinian leaders.[2] Seizing the moment for its symbolic value, a relatively unknown Israeli musician, Yair Dalal, brought together Israeli and Palestinian musicians to perform "Zaman es-Salaam" (Time of Peace) with choirs of Palestinian, Israeli, and Norwegian children singing in Hebrew and Arabic to the accompaniment of the Norwegian Philharmonic under the baton of Zubin Mehta.[3] Yet this most explicit and public use of music to evoke the peaceful coexistence of Palestinians and Israelis, while an impressive accomplishment in terms of public relations and logistics, was not the only or even the most successful attempt at musical collaboration between Israeli Jews and Palestinian Arabs. Though singular in many respects, this performance also represented an emerging phenomenon.

A Time of Disillusionment—The Twenty-First Century

These three vignettes stem from a time of hope, when more signs pointed to a future of peaceful coexistence than to a return to the days of violence.

2. The Accords were signed on September 9, 1993.
3. See Kahan 1995, a documentary about this performance.

The assassination of Israeli Prime Minister Yitzhak Rabin by a right-wing Israeli Jew in late 1995 dealt a blow to the euphoria that had already begun to dissipate due to killings and delays in implementation of the peace accords. Even so, when Bustan Abraham played in Jerusalem in 1997 there was still considerable optimism about the future. Just a few years later, at the dawn of the twenty-first century, this optimism was only a distant memory. The horrors of the second Palestinian *intifada* (uprising) had crippled hopes for a peaceful settlement. Yet these musicians continued to collaborate, in one way or another, across deepening sociopolitical divisions in a time of disillusionment, and new bands followed in their footsteps.

Returning to Israel at the beginning of 2002, after an absence of more than two years, I found the members of Alei Hazayit working hard on new repertoire. Although their plans were constantly in flux due to the unpredictable political situation, they were particularly enthusiastic about one daring arrangement of "Shabehi Yerushalayim" (exalt Jerusalem), a Hebrew song with a biblical text. By far their most ambitious undertaking, this was a self-conscious evocation of the three monotheistic religions. Dramatic declamation in Arabic and Hebrew, already featured in their earlier work, was augmented in the studio with the sounds of thunder, church bells, *shofar* blasts, and the Muslim call to prayer. Jamal Sa'id, one of the leading forces in the group and the key arranger of its repertoire, vividly described to me his vision for a video clip to accompany the song, claiming that it would surpass all the professionally produced promotional spots because as a native of the Old City he knew Jerusalem best. He and his co-leader, the singer Shoham Einav, stressed the need for secrecy at this time. They felt that they had hit on something original and potentially successful that they did not want to have stolen, as they felt had happened to their earlier combinations of Hebrew songs with Arabic arrangement. They also feared for the safety of the Palestinian members of the group should the mixing of the sonic icons of the three religions be viewed as blasphemous.

It is not only religious zealots who oppose such efforts. Several months later the left-leaning Israeli newspaper Ha'aretz published an interview with Khaled Jubran, a Palestinian musician, teacher, and composer who has come to reject all artistic collaboration between Jews and Arabs. He dismissed Jewish-Arab ensembles as cooptation, as a pursuit of the exotic, and as a form of prostitution, claiming further that music is incapable of overcoming mutual hatred between two nations.[4] This is a particularly bitter statement by an unusual figure: an Israeli Arab, born, raised, and educated through graduate school in Israel. Abandoning various joint

---

4. Ben Ze'ev 2002. Jubran buttressed his argument with a radically nationalist and essentialist view of music: "Some say music is an international language. It isn't. It is the most culturally dependent thing I know. Beethoven is German, and Debussy is the embodiment of Frenchness just like the Italianness of Verdi—and Abdul Wahab is Egyptian. And that is how their music is as well." Jubran's views were echoed with nearly the same severity by his former student, Amer Nakhleh, who claimed that only bands featuring coexistence received support and decried such efforts as exploitation (Ben Ze'ev 2004).

performances with Jews, Jubran moved to Ramallah, in the West Bank, established a music school there, and joined Sabreen, a Palestinian band featuring his sister Kamilya Jubran that championed Palestinian culture and national aspirations.

While many other Israeli Arab musicians are not enchanted with their situation, they do not go to such extremes. The Arab members of Bustan Abraham did not feel that they cheapened or betrayed their cultural heritage by mixing elements of it judiciously with other musical practices that they and their band mates had mastered. They are highly discerning composers, arrangers, and performers who do not accept every attempt at musical mixture uncritically as a "good thing." Their music was not thrown together in one rehearsal in order to exploit a passing fad or to salve the consciences of left-wing intellectuals as Jubran imagined (Ben Ze'ev 2002). Working in a highly egalitarian ensemble, the members of Bustan Abraham crafted a new type of musical expression, one that was neither embarrassed by its sources nor disrespectful of them, but used them as a basis to move in new directions. This type of artistic cooperation should not be equated with selling out or, worse, with collaboration in the sense of betrayal. Nonetheless, by 2003 the ensemble had disbanded and I found one of the former members playing in an all-Arab ensemble at a ten-concert festival of peace and coexistence that did not include a single performance where Jews and Arabs shared the stage.[5]

Clearly some radical changes had occurred in the course of ten years. It would be a mistake to believe that trends might not change again or that these few examples paint a complete picture. I have chosen a stark contrast to show the extent of difference in opinions and deeds. A few days after the Tel Aviv festival that featured coexistence in name only, I attended a Jerusalem concert by Joseph and One, a band that presented Israeli Jews and Arabs on stage together without any fanfare. Politics and social engineering need not always occupy center stage. It was heartening to see that the legacy of Bustan Abraham, which placed musical goals above political ones, was being maintained.

Musical Missions

What goals did these musicians set themselves in the early 1990s as they embarked on their journey? Before turning to what they said in interviews and conversations, it is instructive to examine the published "mission statements" of groups such as Bustan Abraham. Most of these performers recorded on their own labels or were involved in production in other ways so it is reasonable to assume that they exerted considerable, if not complete, control over the statements made about their goals. Such statements can be taken as indications of creative intentions as well as attempts at effective merchandising.

5. This was held in mid-June at the Tsavta Club in Tel Aviv.

On their eponymous first recording (1992), Bustan Abraham made strong claims to originality in creating a new type of music that was superior to earlier attempts at East/West fusion and would appeal to Eastern and Western audiences while leading the way for other collaborations between Jews and Arabs.[6] Shoham Einav, founder of Alei Hazayit, took a different approach on the cover of a demo recording self-produced in the mid-1990s:

> The Olive Leaves Band includes an Israeli soloist singer and six Arab musicians playing authentic Arabic instruments. The repertoire focuses on the relations between people, on love, fraternity and peace. They express themselves through musical sounds, rhythms and melodies which originated widely in Arab countries as well as in Israel. All unfold through melodies of love, sounds of the desert, tranquility of peace, and the pulsating rhythm of life, characteristic to both cultures. (The Olive Leaves Band, 1996)

This concoction of high-minded values (love, peace, fraternity), musical genres, and sounds aims straight at the consumer's heartstrings. A similar message is conveyed in the liner notes to Yair Dalal's album *Silan:*

> Like the timelessness of the traditions and rhythms of Dalal's compositions, Yair Dalal and the Al Ol ensemble's music is inescapably about coalescence, about shared traditions, shared instrumentation, the vastness of desert time and space and about peace. The ensemble truly embodies in their music and composition the changing spirit of the Middle East. They are a fine example of artists whose music transcends both art and politics to promote cultural understanding and peace. (Dalal, 1997)

Crafted in English to appeal to the imagined tastes of an international market these statements raise numerous questions. What is involved in creating a new type of music? What might a new Israeli music mean in cultural, social, political, and historical terms? Why would musicians want to create such a thing, for which market, and at what level of engagement with audiences, institutions, and the music industry? The musicians' commitment to cooperation and peaceful coexistence between Jews and Arabs is fairly explicit, although the particular Dalal album quoted here did not embody such collaboration.[7] What can they hope to accomplish and gain by such efforts?

These musicians do not necessarily share the same motivations or place the same importance on sounding peaceful coexistence. Nor do they necessarily perceive themselves as belonging to a movement or some other large group. Despite this lack of social cohesion and uniformity of purpose there are good reasons to consider them as participants in a single, stylistically

6. The liner notes are quoted and analyzed in chapter 5.
7. Many of Dalal's other efforts do; see chapter 7.

heterogeneous musical scene in which tensions inherent to Israeli and Palestinian existence are played out. The musical focus of the scene may limit its political effectiveness in practical terms but endows it with considerable emotional power. Putting themselves in the spotlight, the performers model sociopolitical as well as cultural possibilities for the future.

Genesis and Structure of This Book

The truism that all books are products of their time is particularly apt for this one. Like so much else connected with Israelis and Palestinians it has not been impervious to the ups and downs of the "peace process." Had I written it in the late 1990s when a large chunk of the fieldwork was done, relations between Israel and the Palestinian Authority were not utterly smashed on the rocks, and the second Palestinian uprising had not yet begun, the conclusions would doubtless have differed. Delaying publication another ten years would produce a significantly different book.

While teaching in Jerusalem and Tel Aviv in the late 1980s, I began ethnographic research on Arab musicians in Israel and the West Bank, hoping to produce an account of rapidly changing current practice based on musicians' life histories.[8] It appeared to be a time of considerable tension between old and new, as great external pressures entwined with internal changes in patronage, taste, repertoire, and performance practice. Musicians told me that their situation was frustrating on various levels. Occupying seemingly contradictory positions, they lived and worked as musicians at the geographical center of the Middle East, acutely aware of its various musical trends yet completely peripheral to the larger flow of Middle Eastern musical life.

Continuing the theoretical interest in musical competence and interaction that I had first developed in a dissertation on Javanese music, I sought to learn how musical competences were shaped by proximity to Egyptian, Lebanese, Syrian, and Jordanian music, to analyze the interaction of these musicians in performance, and to study the conflicting desires of musicians and audiences, especially in light of changing performance contexts and technologies. Arab musicians' interaction with Jewish musicians was not on my horizon. Not only was the investigation of musical hybridity still uncommon in ethnomusicological research, such interactions had not yet appeared on the Israeli musical scene in any significant way other than occasional performances of mainstream Arab music by mixed ensembles of Jews and Arabs.[9]

---

8. I was unaware that Israeli sociologist Motti Regev was working on a similar project around that time (Regev 1993).

9. The Israel Broadcasting Authority orchestra for Arab music included Jews and Arabs who sometimes performed together for private concerts, too. In 1986 two Israeli Jewish and Arab musicians performed a song about peace together (Perelson 1998: 118), but such collaborations were not yet a trend.

This situation changed almost as soon as I left Israel in 1988 to teach at Berkeley. Returning in the early 1990s I found that almost all of the Arab musicians I knew were entering into partnerships with Jewish musicians. It was striking that this occurred during the first Palestinian uprising (*intifada*), which had begun in late 1987. Arab musicians in Jerusalem and the West Bank, who had found their performance opportunities financially rewarding but artistically unsatisfying, saw their primary source of livelihood dry up almost overnight when the underground Palestinian leadership declared a ban on live music at weddings and other celebrations.[10] Cross-cultural collaborations offered an opportunity to break out of an artistically limiting situation, to continue to perform, and, perhaps, to make a living. Arab musicians living within Israel were not constrained by the *intifada* but were also genuinely excited to be opening up new aesthetic ground in contrast to the relative stagnation of the local Arab musical scene and what they perceived as the constrained and imitative nature of much other Israeli music, which took—and to a large extent continues to take—its cues from American and European trends.

This phenomenon became the focus of my research because of its inherent interest and obvious importance for the field of ethnomusicology and the study of music in Israel and the Middle East in general. As I studied the intersecting paths of Jewish and Arab musicians in Israel a host of new issues arose. Hybrid musical ensembles, styles, forms, and performances are not only of great intrinsic musical interest but offer excellent opportunities for examining interaction. There were so many social and cultural divides to bridge, so many opportunities for misunderstandings and for making explicit the assumptions that are often hidden from view in more conventional settings. My focus shifted again, from foregrounding the Arab/Jew divide to viewing it as merely one of several types of difference to be bridged in the musical endeavors I encountered. Musicians differed in the types of music they knew how to play, their formal training, the directions they wanted to explore, their ability and desire to use notation, their engagement with or distaste for popular music or religious music, and so on. Here was a challenging, new kind of field.

This was neither a long-established musical tradition, with a body of theory to explicate or conventions awaiting deduction and precise formulation, nor a highly mediated popular music driven by the music industry, though elements of both were present. The extent of the phenomenon also defied easy delimitation, as it tended to "bleed" into related musical endeavors in other parts of the world. For me the "challenge of coming to terms with the changed context of ethnographic work" (Gupta & Ferguson 1997a: 3) consisted of retooling and engaging with a broad range of music and writing in search of tools and perspectives, comparative cases, any insights I could gain elsewhere. I began with what I knew best, studying

10. Overtly political songs were permitted by the leaders of the *intifada* but did not provide a means to earn a living. The musicians studied here rejected such songs.

competence and interaction, then followed what seemed most important about the musicians and what they were doing. It helped greatly that the musicians were consciously engaged in forging new music and directing their attention to aspects of composition, rehearsal, and performance that tend to be part of the habitus, the taken-for-granted business of a musician's everyday, in established musical practices. But because it was so new, I sometimes wondered what would be the larger significance of the actions and thoughts of a handful of musicians. Despite the disbanding of Bustan Abraham and an indefinite hiatus in Alei Hazayit's work, the larger scene in which these musicians worked continues and the issues that turned out to be of particular importance there have implications for music, musicians, and audiences elsewhere.

This book is about particular people, the situations in which they find themselves, and the paths that they make for themselves in this far from perfect world. It is also a book about that world, as seen from the passionate viewpoints of the participants. It is only fitting that in writing about so fraught a situation my own perspective is brought under scrutiny, that I give readers a sense of how my coordinates of being relate to my horizons of knowing, to paraphrase one of the pithier formulations of the new ethnographic imperative.[11]

With the juxtaposition of hope and disillusionment that opens this book I have made clear much of my own position. I write this as an American who has spent some eight years in Israel at various times from the late 1960s to the present, who has family and friends (both Arabs and Jews) in Israel, who has studied and taught in Israeli universities, and who has been dismayed and disgusted by the callousness, zealotry, and violent actions of those who would set the terms by which all shall live or die. Neither Palestinians nor Israelis are going to pack up and move away or acquiesce in their own disappearance. Some compromise is imperative. Still hoping for a resolution other than walls of separation, I believe that the people who are the subject of this book have contributed to the possibility of a better future. By the very act of collaborating artistically they pointed to the possibility of compromise and coexistence. It is premature to judge their efforts a failure. That they did not succeed in the short term should be taken as evidence of the limits of musical action in the face of deeply seated prejudices and power bases that thrive on conflict.

This is almost an eyewitness account: I was there at the beginning and have had the privilege of following firsthand the careers of some of the prime movers in this scene for twenty years. This time span offsets the intermittent nature of the research, conducted in intense bursts on an annual basis rather than concentrated in the more traditional year of fieldwork, and gives insights and perspective that would be difficult or impossible to attain in the span of a single year. This same depth means that I am not a completely neutral observer. I write here about people for whom I care a great deal and music that I enjoy and value highly. They have earned

11. Handelman and Shamgar-Handelman 1993: 446.

my respect for choosing the difficult path of collaborative bridge building across some of the deepest sociocultural chasms in the world. I have advocated for them and some of them have attempted to draw me into their internal arguments.

All of the above has put me in a difficult position more than once in the course of researching and writing this book. The scene is too small and the performers are too individualized to disguise identities. To do so would be unfair, in any case, for these musicians deserve wider recognition.

I have hesitated to lock in print an analysis that might thereafter limit readers' perceptions of musicians who have the right, even the need, to continue to shape their careers and images. My respect for them as people and artists also suggests a limit on analysis that would descend into psychoanalysis. Thus, I have aimed for balance and some distance, weighing the claims, both overt and tacit, of the various parties to this absorbing cultural marketplace while trying to steer clear of hagiography, authorial omniscience, and the elevated podium of the infallible critic and arbiter of musical taste.

My ties to several people who figure centrally in this book are complex. I taught ethnomusicology in Israel from 1985 to 1988. During the same period I also directed the Workshop for Non-Western Music, a program that presented concerts, lecture-demonstrations, occasional workshops, and ongoing classes. Various musical practices were included in our programs, but the centerpiece was always Arab music, primarily the Egyptian-centered mainstream of twentieth-century Middle Eastern music. Thus, before the research period for this book I stood as teacher, student, presenter, or supervisor in relation to several of the key figures in this book, and had looser links to others. But when I embarked on the research I opted for the role of interlocutor over participant performer. This was due to the brevity of my research trips and to a desire to maintain some distance and perspective. A participant researcher might have excessive influence in a field so small and new. All this contributes to a subject position that is more complex than the already complex norm of ethnomusicological research.

My primary purpose in writing this book is to call attention to an important phenomenon in which issues that I believe fundamental to any study of music—questions of musical competence, interaction, and composition/improvisation—are brought into prominence due to the many sociocultural divisions that must be bridged. But I write also in the belief that what these people have done makes a difference in both artistic and sociopolitical terms. Once I might have described the focus of this study as the liminal area in which cultures rub against each other, but the unraveling of the "peoples and cultures" paradigm as an analytic framework precludes that possibility (Gupta and Ferguson 1997a: 1–3). I do not offer a comprehensive portrait of Israeli or Palestinian music, culture, or people. Gupta and Ferguson, whose writings I found helpful to think with, argue that it is time for anthropology (and, by extension, ethnomusicology) to move away from cultural-territorial entities, to the "ongoing historical and political processes" on which cultural, ethnic, and national territorializations are contingent (ibid. 4). For this purpose I know of no better approach than an ethnography of micropractices, a study of musicians as individual actors operating within existing cultural configurations and building new bridges between these configurations.

This book is also unusual in that its topic is not a particular genre or style, but a group of musicians who are united by common challenges to which they have responded in diverse ways. Like these musicians, this book does not have clear precedents or a ready-made home. It does not fit within the field of popular music studies both because of its subject matter and its method. These musicians pursue success, but not on the terms of the popular music industry which hardly notices their existence. Mass mediation figures far less centrally in their work than it does in mainstream Israeli popular music, for instance. Nonetheless, they have made choices shaped to a large degree by the industry—sometimes in conscious opposition to it, sometimes in tacit acceptance of its dominance—including patterns of distribution, audience expectations, performance venues, and so on.

The participants in these exchanges vary greatly in training, experience, assumptions, and expectations. The professional situations of Arab and Jewish musicians contrast in crucial ways, in socioeconomic and political spheres as well as in the realms of aesthetic values, musical competence and interaction. To put it more concretely, opportunities for musical employment in the Arab "sector" of Israeli society differ greatly from those in the Jewish sector, as do training possibilities, professional conventions, and the value accorded musicians' efforts. Working with musicians so unlike themselves, the subjects of this book have been forced to figure out how to communicate and collaborate across gaping social, political, and cultural divides and how to create an exchange that is rewarding for all the participants. While the most obvious gap is that between Jews and Arabs, it is by no means the only division. Some of the differences between these musicians have little if anything to do with social identity and everything to do with musical training and interests.

Due to this complexity I begin by sketching a sociocultural map in order to show how individuals navigate this terrain as musicians, listeners, and human beings. To do so is to speak in terms of paths, convergences, and borders to be crossed. One map will not suffice as the physical terrain intersects with the spiritual, political, social, and musical/stylistic in various ways. The social terrain must be understood not only in terms of the ethnic, religious, and regional identities of musicians and audiences, but also in terms of social networks, some of which are transnational in scope. The next part of this chapter offers an orientation to this complexity of people, politics, and place. Ascribed identities are a basic fact of life that must be recognized in order to make sense of people's actions, choices, and interactions. This is particularly true in Israel and neighboring areas where so much depends upon identity. Every Arab musician discussed in this book has basic things in common with millions of other Arabs, including language and many aspects of cultural heritage. In no other way do they form a coherent group—they are not all Muslim, they are not all opposed to Israel's existence, they did not grow up in the same circumstances—yet they are constantly taken to be representative of Arabs as a whole by concert promoters, reviewers, and audience members, both in Israel and abroad. Much the same could be said of the musicians who are Israeli Jews. Each one is an individual with particular views on political and cultural issues, particular allegiances, and so on. Thus while analysis of identity is not my primary goal, the subject must be addressed in order to problematize common labels and dispel the assumptions that they embody.

In the next two chapters I discuss the working life of musicians to give sufficient depth to understand the actions and positions of the performers reacting against the status quo. Chapter 2 concerns Palestinian musicians playing Arab music in Israel and the West Bank in the last decades of the twentieth century, while chapter 3 is a summary of other musical options within Israel in that same period.

Musicians are the focus of part II, with particular attention given to three clusters: Alei Hazayit, Bustan Abraham, and Yair Dalal's various collaborations. These provide three reference points around which to chart larger networks of musicians, institutions, and audiences. They are dissimilar enough to demonstrate the variety of initiatives and responses possible in the circumstances of this time and place, but they share the aforementioned challenge of discovering ways to bridge some of the same sociocultural divides. Their trajectories reveal much about the workings of Israeli society, not only as it bears on the arts, but as it shapes the possibilities for musicians from particular social backgrounds. Chapters 4 and 5 outline the histories of Alei Hazayit and Bustan Abraham, with some basic observations about each group, leading to a comparison of the two bands in chapter 6. The discussion of the larger network of musicians within which these performers work begins in chapter 7, with the numerous connections forged by Yair Dalal, expanding in chapter 8 to the larger network in which Alei Hazayit and Bustan Abraham were also enmeshed.

The pair of chapters in part III offers a closer examination of the creative processes of these musicians from two perspectives. Chapter 9 concerns the musical resources that Alei Hazayit, Bustan Abraham, and Yair Dalal utilized, their methods for combining elements of various musical practices, and the mediation and reception of their efforts by promoters and critics. The second perspective concerns the relationship between composition and improvisation, a central issue in this field of music making. As the cumulative output of these musicians is sufficiently large to render a detailed analysis unmanageable in size for this book I have limited the discussion in chapter 10 to aspects of Bustan Abraham's unusually large and varied body of work.

Part IV begins with issues of representation in chapter 11, which concerns the meanings that musicians and others in the production network have conveyed through recordings, texts, and visual aspects of representation. This leads, in the final chapter, to a discussion of the social, political, and cultural significance of these musical collaborations, ranging from reasons that this phenomenon arose in Israel in the 1990s, through a discussion of transnational circulation, to conclude with the transformative effects and potential of these musicians and their music.

People, Places, Politics

> The dynamics of collaboration, representation, and appropriation create new, complicated political and subject positions that shift with increasing frequency.
>
> —Taylor 1997: 197

Complications of subject positions and interactions could hardly be more apparent than in the musical scene discussed in this book. Like almost everything else in Israel and the Palestinian territories, terminology is hotly contested. Place names, the labels used to characterize and categorize people, even the defining historical events, differ depending on one's perspective. As Gupta and Ferguson noted, "All associations of place, people, and culture are social and historical creations to be explained, not given natural facts" (1997a: 4). The following sections are intended to give the reader unfamiliar with the area an overview of population groups, places, and recent history sufficient for this book.[12]

Identifying Labels

The people at the center of this book, coming from different social groups and musical backgrounds, converged to create new music. Just as their music is difficult to label, the people involved also resist facile labeling. Saying that one person is an Israeli, another a Palestinian, for instance, is to resort to stereotypical categories that evoke sets of largely unquestioned characteristics and to imply stark divisions. Evaluating the actions of these musicians and the claims to authenticity and representation made by and for them requires a more detailed and refined understanding of identity than the handful of common stereotypes affords us.

When it comes to mapping multiple identities, interests, and allegiances, the reality of contemporary Israel/Palestine is dauntingly complex. Yet it is precisely this complexity that is reduced to stark black and white contrasts, with few shades of gray, when broadcast to the outside world. One has but to delve a bit into individual social, political, and cultural selves to encounter a wide, finely differentiated spectrum of identities and subject positions, ascribed, claimed, and inferred. Although many people maintain rigidly categorized views of themselves and others, the

---

12. It is not my intent to settle the differences or discuss exhaustively the labels, only to clarify my own usage in these pages. Numerous books and articles address these issues from many points on the political spectrum.

situation is far from static. In later chapters we shall see how particular musicians shape and present themselves in relation to varying contexts, fellow performers, and audiences. This chapter introduces some of the basic distinctions and groups through which people construct identities.

Ethnic, religious, and national labels present the thorniest conundrum. Palestinian, Arab, Israeli, Israeli Arab, Israeli Jew, Sephardi, Mizrahi, Ashkenazi, Christian, Druze, Arab Jew, secular, orthodox, nationalist, *sabra*, immigrant, refugee[13]—the list of identifying labels is long, particularly if one includes all the sectarian divisions within the major religious groups and the ethnic groups identified primarily by country of origin (particularly for Jews), region (particularly for Palestinian Arabs), or sociocultural background. As it is impossible to elucidate all of these differences in a single chapter, I will sketch the dimensions of identity here, leaving it to later chapters to demonstrate how complex and variable this can be for an individual, while examining its relevance to musical choices and understandings.

The label "Palestinian" has both nationalist and ethnic connotations, implying solidarity with an aggrieved population with aspirations for sovereignty, as well as identification with a cultural group defined by territory. "Arab," on the other hand, is a broad identifier that speaks to fundamental linguistic and cultural commonalities that reach from the western end of North Africa to the eastern border of Iraq. Palestinians are a minority in Israel, but as Arabs they are part of an encompassing majority. Thus, the label Palestinian plays down the latter strength in favor of a highly localized identity, while Arab asserts a large-scale ethnic identity but denies or downplays Palestinian nationalist aspirations. Palestinian is a newer identity, as George Bisharat notes: "Palestinian national identity . . . developed in the crucible of violent contestation between Arab residents of Palestine and the Zionist movement for control of that land" (1997: 205). Bisharat's particular bias as a Palestinian scholar is evident in the juxtaposing of individuals on one side and a monolithic movement on the other, when in fact both individuals and sociopolitical organizations were active on both sides of the dispute. Bisharat notes the instrumentality of Palestinian identity as a means to an end rather than an end in itself. While self-identification as Palestinian can underscore an oppositional stance of resistance to Israel, the label Arab may be deployed to invoke a broader, highly valued cultural heritage, implying at the same time the political obligation of other Arabs to come to the aid of Palestinians.

To say that someone is an Israeli often implies that she or he is a Jew, yet over one million Israeli citizens are not, including non-Jewish immigrants from the former Soviet Union. Arab citizens of Israel are referred to as Israeli Arabs by the Israeli government and by most Jewish Israelis; some

13. Most of these terms do not lose much by translation into English from Arabic and Hebrew, though a complete linguistic analysis would surely turn up some important exceptions. Sabra (Hebrew *tsabar*) is the term for native-born Israeli Jews.

may self-identify with this label in certain circumstances while using Palestinian or Arab in others. To some the term Israeli Arab denotes acceptance of Israeli dominion and should therefore be avoided; to others it is a simple statement of citizenship and social milieu. Roda Kanaaneh, daughter of a Palestinian Arab man, writes in her book on Palestinian women in Israel, "Palestinian Arabs in the Galilee largely refer to themselves as either Palestinians or Arabs . . . The state of Israel has historically chosen not to use the term 'Palestinian' because its use would imply recognition of Palestinians as a national group that has rights" (2002: 11). She cites a 1989 survey by Nadim Rouhana in which Palestinian university students in Israel, asked to self identify, chose various combinations of the words Palestinian, Arab, Israel, and Israeli.[14]

To be an Israeli citizen is to be identified by religion. The ministry of religious affairs and the interior ministry, which control many aspects of an individual's life, are organized along those lines. Even the most outspoken atheist, if born a Jew, will be categorized as such on identity papers. The labels Christian and Muslim are likewise applied to whole communities, only some of whose members actively practice their religion with any degree of orthodoxy. Thus, to say that someone is a Jew or an Israeli Jew need not imply that the person is pious or even religious at all. The lives of most Israelis are secular most of the time in most ways. External forms of religious observance are common—recognition of the main holidays, perhaps Friday night candle lighting, even superstitious invocation of the name of God[15]—but there is a huge gulf between such people and the orthodox, who have been a politically powerful minority since the foundation of the state and have recently grown greatly in number and strength. As most of the people central to this book are secular in outlook, I shall use the term Jew as an ethnic label, referring to a basically secular outlook informed by a Jewish background. The few religious Jews in this scene will be noted as such where pertinent.

Distinctions among Jews are based on origins, culture, and religious practices. European Jews were the first to return in large numbers to Palestine, the land of Israel, beginning in the late nineteenth century. Although the predominantly socialist, secular, and Eastern European early immigrants differed greatly in sociopolitical outlook both from the religious Jews already living in Palestine and from the Central and Western

14. Kanaaneh conveniently ignores the fact that Jews living in Palestine prior to 1948 were labeled as Palestinians in all official documents. She also writes that "the Israeli preference for the term 'Arab' to refer to Palestinian Arabs . . . conveniently erases the existence of other Arabs in the country—Arab Jews. These identity politics lie under the surface of such terms in the Galilee and should be kept in mind" (2002: 11), but many Arab Jews reject that appellation (see below).

15. I have noticed a marked increase in the use of the formula *im yirtze hashem* by secular Jews. This expression is equivalent to "God willing" but literally means "if the Name wishes," thus reflecting an Orthodox interpretation of the biblical commandment against taking God's name in vain.

European Jews who followed in the period between the two world wars, they have all been lumped into the category of Ashkenazim (sing. Ashkenazi). This label has traditionally distinguished Jewish religious practice concentrated in Central and Eastern Europe from other Jewish sects. Its utility as a social category in Israel has severe limitations. The Jews who came to Israel, mainly in the 1950s, from North Africa, the Middle East, and Central Asia are similarly lumped together in large categories: Sephardi and Mizrahi.

Sephardim (literally Spanish Jews) are the descendants of the Jews expelled from Spain when Christians completed their reconquest of the Iberian Peninsula at the end of the fifteenth century. These refugees settled in North Africa and around the rim of the Mediterranean all the way to Greece, Turkey, and the Balkans. Today the term Sephardi is often used loosely and ahistorically to denote all non-European Jews. Mizrahi (literally Eastern, often translated as Oriental) technically designates Jews from the Middle East, but has also lost its specificity as it is often conflated with Sephardi. More specific distinctions are commonly made according to country or area of origin or descent: e.g., North African, Moroccan, Kurdish, Babylonian (Iraqi), Persian, and even the bizarrely anachronistic use of Anglo-Saxon to denote those who come from English-speaking countries.

The identity Arab Jew (or Jewish Arab) recognizes Jews' long-term presence in Arab lands, sharing language and many other cultural practices with Muslim and Christian Arabs. "We are actually Jewish Arabs, just as there are Christian Arabs and Circassian Arabs . . . I am Middle Eastern both due to my parentage and the ancient origins of my people," Yair Dalal told an interviewer.[16] This positioning sidesteps the Mizrahi/Sephardi conflation, but its principal use today appears to be an expression of affinity and solidarity with Palestinians in particular and with Arabs in general.[17] Given the protracted state of enmity with Arab countries and early efforts by Israeli state institutions to suppress the Arab–ness of Jewish immigrants from Arab countries, the label Arab Jew is not widely favored.

Perhaps the biggest problem with the use of these labels is the rendering of Jewish Israeli society in terms of an opposition between two monoliths: Ashkenazim opposed to a bloc composed of Sephardi, Mizrahi, and/or Arab Jews. This ignores the large number of Israelis whose parentage is mixed, making them "both/and," as well as the considerable number on either side of the divide who are fully integrated with one another. Such inaccuracies are further compounded by the equation of Ashkenazi/

16. Lev-Ari 2003. Dalal took this position when I first interviewed him in 1994. Musician Nitzan Peri expressed the same position: "Do you think my [Iraqi-born] father isn't an Arab? The fact that we are Jews by religion doesn't matter. In cultural terms, my father is an Arab" (Davis 2002a). See also Lee 2008 for a moving account of a conference on Iraqi Jews convened at Tel Aviv University in 2008.

17. In a pro-Palestinian journal, Ella Shohat has explored the construction of Mizrahi by the Israeli establishment as a category to cut Arab Jews off from their roots in Arab lands (1999). See also Kanaaneh 2002: 44.

Mizrahi with a class distinction (upper/middle versus lower class) that oversimplifies to the point of caricature.

It is clear that many immigrants from North Africa and the Middle East and their children have suffered from discrimination, particularly in the first decades after coming to Israel. But we should not accept uncritically the bifurcation of Israeli Jews into "Eastern" Jews, torn from the loving embrace of their native Arab culture to be oppressed by the "European" Jewish establishment. This simplistic reading of Israeli society has been furthered by scholars such as Swedenburg[18] and by figures such as the outspoken Israeli musician Avihu Medina, whose statements are directly linked to the furthering of his own career. It ignores the large number of second, third, or fourth generation Israeli Jews of mixed descent and the differentiation of Jews of Middle Eastern, North African, and European origin according to time and conditions of immigration and absorption into Israeli society, not to mention political and religious orientation. Moreover, it fails to take into account the "us against them" mentality of Israeli (Jewish) solidarity that tends to unify otherwise contentious foes when Jews are attacked. But this misrepresentation of Israeli Jewish society as consisting of two ethnically distinct blocs locked in a relationship of oppressed and oppressor aligns well with the essentialist East/West dualities that pervade cultural discourse in the area.[19]

Religious affiliation figures prominently among the Arab population, too. Christians and Druze[20] set themselves apart from the vastly more numerous Muslim majority. Such distinctions are far more than a matter of semantics as they are ensconced in Israeli law and policy. Druze men serve in the Israeli military but Christian and Muslim Arabs do not. While Muslim, Christian, and Druze musicians do perform together and for one another's communities, there are experiential differences among them, not the least of which stem from the different ritual musical practices to which they are exposed. Distinct from the rest of the Arab population are Bedouin who, until recently, have lived a different life from sedentary Palestinian farmers and city dwellers, developing distinctive cultural practices and speaking a different dialect of Arabic. As with other categories, this last is in flux, with the cessation of nomadic life and recent calls by some Bedouin for jettisoning that label in favor of unity with other Palestinian Arabs.

Citizenship, with its attendant rights, delineates a third dimension along which affiliation and identity are measured. Both Jews and Arabs

18. See Swedenburg 2000, e.g., or the same author's characterization that the singer Natacha's "Middle Eastern "genetic" background, therefore, is Sephardi (or, to use the more politicized term, Mizrahi)" or his invoking of a "Eurocentric/Ashkenazi perspective" later in the same paragraph and his offhanded statement later in the same article "the majority second-class Mizrahi Jews" (2001:65).

19. The mistake is further compounded by equations with other binary oppositions. See Khazzoom (2000).

20. The Druze religion developed in the eleventh century as an offshoot of Islam.

distinguish Palestinian Arab citizens of Israel from Palestinian Arabs living in the occupied territories and in other countries, many of whom are refugees or the descendants of refugees. While they may be treated as second-class citizens in some regards, the privileges of Israeli Arabs are significant compared with the latter group in terms of education, health care, social security payments, and the all-important identification papers that give them far greater freedom of movement. In recent years some people have used the term Israeli Palestinian to acknowledge the political aspirations, sociocultural identity, and citizenship that set these people apart from Palestinians living in the occupied territories, neighboring Arab countries, and other parts of the world. Among non-Israeli Palestinian Arabs, residents of Jerusalem are accorded special status by the Israeli government.

The Israeli government, like the governments of neighboring Arab countries, has exploited schisms in the Arab population. Young Bedouin and Druze men born in Israel not only serve in Israel's armed forces, unlike all other Arab citizens of Israel, but often do so in specialized capacities that bring them in direct confrontation with other Arabs. Bedouin trackers have been important in the ongoing battle to intercept those infiltrating Israel's borders from Egypt and Jordan, while many Druze serve in the Border Police, which is notorious for its rough handling of Palestinians in the occupied territories. Bedouin did not join forces with Palestinians in the first or second *intifada,* but concerns have been growing in recent years that the onset of a separate Bedouin *intifada* is imminent.[21]

Numerous other types of identity come into play in the constitution of Israeli society, including gender, class, and political ideologies. Socialism, capitalism, individualism, collectivism, and communism all have their adherents and their visible effects on Israeli life. The highly fragmented political spectrum is divided along these and other lines. Strong age-group bonds are formed and maintained through the school policy of keeping a class of children together from one grade to the next and stimulating social cohesion within that group. As none of these give rise to terminological controversies like those surrounding Israeli and Palestinian identity, the reader should have no problem understanding the mobilization of such affiliations when noted here.

Regional identities appear to be most significant for the Arab population, at least as regards musical practices. The life and concerns of village dwellers are markedly different from those of urbanites on the one hand and the steadily shrinking nomadic population on the other.[22] Similarly, residents of the Galilee, the West Bank, and the Gaza Strip differ significantly in sociocultural terms from one another and from the Arabs of Haifa, Jaffa, or Jerusalem. Even the widespread availability of mass media and the extensive contacts between these segments of the population have not

21. See, e.g., Barzilai 2004, Nir 2002, and "Unbenign neglect," an editorial in *The Jerusalem Post* (January 11, 2002).

22. These last enter the framework of this book only marginally, through Yair Dalal's work with members of the Azazme tribe of Bedouin.

erased all the differences in musical taste and experience associated with such divisions.

Identity is multifaceted, relational, and situational. This is probably true for anyone, anywhere, but it is particularly crucial to acknowledge in the case of Israelis and Palestinians in light of the one-dimensional identities portrayed in the media and implied or directly asserted in daily conversation. With the intense hatred often expressed by members of one group for all the members of another, the widespread demonizing and posturing, it is too easy to lose sight of the individual human beings who are being pigeonholed and the relational nuances that may be played out among these people in a wide variety of contexts. Those who identify both as Israeli Arabs and as Palestinians (in addition to Christian, from the Galilee, teacher, performer, father, son, and so on), depending on context, navigate treacherous waters, foregrounding particular affiliations in response to differing pressures. Israeli Jews, too, can find that alternate ways of presenting themselves work better in particular situations.

Politics and Place

A series of place names imposed by successive rulers designates this land. The biblical land of Canaan, conquered by the Jews, was later divided into the kingdoms of Judea and Samaria. Fought over by a series of great powers, including Egypt, Assyria, Greece and Rome, it was first called Philistia by Greek writers after the Philistines who inhabited some of the southern coastal region around 1200 BCE, and then Palestina by the Romans as part of a larger administrative area, Syria-Palestina. The Jewish inhabitants, exiled by the Romans after an unsuccessful revolt, called their ancestral homeland the land of Israel throughout centuries of diaspora. Conquered by Arabs in 640 CE during the spread of Islam from the Arabian Peninsula, much of this land was ruled by European Crusaders from 1100 to 1291, reconquered for Islam by the Mamluks and then incorporated in the Ottoman Turkish Empire, which grew to control most of the Middle East. The British took this area from the Ottoman Turks in 1917, receiving a mandate from the League of Nations after World War I to administer it under the name of Palestine. During this period (1917–1948) all residents—Jews, Arabs, and others—were classified as Palestinians.

The Jewish population of Palestine had increased greatly by the end of this period due to Zionism, a sociopolitical movement originating in Europe in the late nineteenth century and dedicated to the reestablishment of a Jewish homeland in Palestine. Waves of immigration came principally from Eastern Europe (beginning in the 1880s) and Central Europe (increasing after the rise of Hitler in the 1930s). Predominantly socialist and secular in outlook, the early immigrants set the tone for the nascent state. Those who came from Central Europe transplanted European high culture and greatly influenced the infrastructure for cultural activities and education that persists to the present.[23]

23. See Bohlman 1989 and Hirshberg 1995 and 2002.

Intense Arab opposition to Jewish immigration and the proposed establishment of a Jewish state led to growing tensions and violence, as well as British restrictions on further immigration. In 1947 the United Nations ratified a partitioning of Palestine between Arabs and Jews that satisfied no one. From 1948 to 1949 the Jewish state, newly named Israel, fought a war against the invading armies of the neighboring Arab countries, a war known to Israeli Jews as the War of Independence. Palestinians call it *il-naqba* (the disaster) and stress the eradication of villages and creation of large refugee populations. At the end of this war, Israel controlled substantial parts of the area that had been under the British Mandate while the rest was controlled by Jordan (the West Bank) or Egypt (the Gaza Strip). Jewish refugees from Arab countries and post-Holocaust Europe arrived in large numbers over the next few years. The Arab population of Palestine suffered several fates: those remaining within Israel's new boundaries lived under military rule until 1965, but became Israeli citizens; those whose homes were in areas outside Israel's boundaries became subjects of Jordan or Egypt; and others who had fled homes now inside Israel became refugees in Gaza, the West Bank, and elsewhere in neighboring Arab countries. It was in the mid-1960s that Palestinian resistance and nationalism began to become more organized with the foundation of groups such as the Palestinian Liberation Organization (PLO).

During the Six Day War, fought between Israel, Syria, and Jordan in 1967, Israel captured the Gaza Strip and the Sinai Peninsula from Egypt, the West Bank from Jordan, and the Golan Heights from Syria. Egypt and Syria attempted to reconquer the Sinai and the Golan Heights in the Yom Kippur War of 1973. The near success destroyed Israel's post-1967 euphoria. The first peace treaty between Israel and an Arab state led to the return of the Sinai Peninsula to Egypt, and the opening of the border to travel in 1979. Palestinians in the Gaza Strip and the West Bank remained under Israeli military rule and suffered increasing expropriation of land for the establishment of Jewish settlements. They staged an uprising in late 1987 that petered out in the early 1990s.

Accords signed by Israel and the Palestine Liberation Organization in 1993 and 1994 established mutual recognition and began a process of turning over parts of the Gaza Strip and the West Bank to the newly constituted Palestinian Authority. Normalization of relations with Jordan ensued in the wake of these agreements, King Hussein relinquishing his claims to the West Bank and agreeing to open the border with Israel. This greatly lessened the isolation of Israel in the Arab and broader Muslim world, opening up possibilities for travel and trade as agreements with various other Arab and African states followed. But further negotiations between Israel and the Palestinian Authority were disrupted and then halted by continuing controversy over pacing and terms as well as terrorist attacks (including a Palestinian campaign of suicide bombers and the slaughter of Muslims at a holy site by a Jewish settler) and the assassination of Israeli Prime Minister Yitzhak Rabin. A second, much bloodier Palestinian uprising began in September 2000 and continues at the time of writing.[24] All of these events have shaped the outlook and activities of musicians, as we shall see throughout this book.

The importance of the land to both Jews and Palestinians cannot be too strongly emphasized. Whether it is expressed in terms of agricultural roots and village loyalties or narratives of reforestation, reclamation of the swamps, and making the desert bloom this sense of connection is powerful. The state and its educational apparatus nurture this sense of Jewish belonging by marking biblical sites and by extensive archaeological activity. A large repertoire of songs also strengthens it. Palestinians, too, have songs and literature celebrating the land and expressing eternal loyalty to it.[25]

The actual area of Israel and the Occupied Territories is quite small, yet it contains some significant regional differences, geographically, culturally, and politically. The Galilee (*hagalil* in Hebrew, *il-jalil* in Arabic) with its largely rural landscape of hills and fertile valleys encompasses the northern portion of the country (see figure 1.1). It is typified by a strong Arab presence on the land in numerous villages and small towns, but also includes the ancient city of Safed (*tsefat* in Hebrew), historical center of Jewish mysticism and site of a significant Jewish presence through the centuries. It is also emblematic of Israeli pioneering and includes most of the *kibbutzim* (collective farms) established in the early twentieth century. In the late twentieth century, the Israeli government sought to counter the increasing Arab population by the establishment of rural Jewish townships. The area also became a magnet for Israelis seeking to lead alternative lifestyles focused on a return to the land and, in some cases, a new spirituality, expressed musically by performers such as George Sama'an (an Israeli Arab) and the members of Sheva (a band of Israeli Jews), who will figure peripherally in this book.

The southern portion of Israel, the Negev and Aravah, is mainly desert, in striking contrast to the green farmlands and tree-topped hills of the Galilee. The South also contains the Israeli cities of Beer Sheva and Eilat, as well as townships in which previously nomadic Bedouin have been settled. The significance of this area for this book would be almost nil were it not for the strong bond to the southern desert that Yair Dalal professes throughout his work.

Jewish population is densest on the coastal plain around the metropolis of Tel Aviv, the cultural center of the country. Most of this area is urban and suburban, rapidly replacing the rich agricultural lands that once predominated, and little Arab presence is left other than in the ancient city of Jaffa, on the southern edge of Tel Aviv. Just to the east of these plains, the

24. The course of events was, of course, more complex than this, but this outline should suffice for present purposes. The interested reader will find numerous accounts of this history.

25. They have also produced schoolbooks that deny Jewish historical connections to the land and identify Palestinians as direct descendants of the original historic inhabitants of the area.

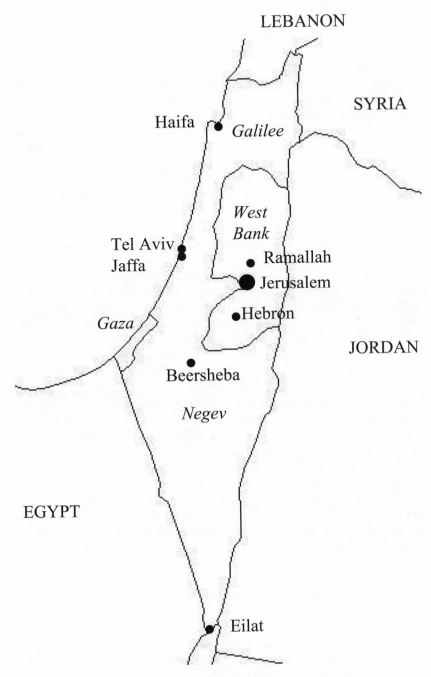

Figure 1.1. Map of Israel and the West Bank

West Bank extends from rocky hills eastward into the valley of the Jordan River, which marks the boundary with Jordan. Several major Palestinian cities and numerous villages lie close to Israel's urban centers. This has political and military ramifications, but also means that local radio and television coverage easily crosses the border. Dotted among the villages and cities of the West Bank are small settlements and a few cities established by Jewish settlers and connected by an exclusive set of new roads intended to keep them safe from Palestinian attacks. Palestinians in the Gaza Strip, on the southwest coast, are far more cramped and cut off from Israel than their brethren in the West Bank. Until the beginning of the second *intifada*, many Gaza residents worked in Israel, but access was severely restricted due to the numerous suicide bombers entering Israel from the Strip. The situation radically changed when Israel withdrew its settlers and soldiers unilaterally in 2005. It changed again when the militant Muslim organization Hamas won local elections, forcibly overcame its rivals, and began to fire missiles on Israel.

Surrounded on north, east, and south by the West Bank, the city of Jerusalem (*Yerushalayim* in Hebrew and *al-Quds* in Arabic) has been at the center of the conflict. Divided into Jordanian East Jerusalem and Israeli West Jerusalem from the end of the 1948 war until the 1967 war, it has since been the object of successive national and municipal government efforts to fully incorporate all parts of the city and a large swath of surrounding communities and land into one metropolis. This has been accomplished through massive construction projects, including housing, roads, public buildings, and parks, and by granting the Palestinian residents of East Jerusalem special status (including greater freedom of movement and eligibility for various sorts of economic aid). While the city includes substantial Arab and Jewish populations living not far from one another, there is relatively little mingling compared with Haifa or Jaffa, cities in which a substantial Arab population lives side by side in relative harmony with Jewish residents. One of the few places in Jerusalem where Israeli Arabs and Jews have mingled extensively is the Hebrew University, the premier institution of higher education in Israel, which draws students from all over the country. This institution's Department of Musicology and the loosely affiliated Jerusalem Academy of Music and Dance are important sites for this book where many of the musicians I will discuss have trained, taught, and forged new musical partnerships.

While some of the musical activity to be chronicled here has roots in rural areas, most of it is urban. The cities contrast greatly in significance and cultural life. Jerusalem is the holy city, a site of longing for Jews, Christians, and Muslims. With the Dome of the Rock and al-Aqsa mosque located just above the Wailing Wall, and the Church of the Holy Sepulcher only a few minutes' walk away, members of the three faiths worship very close to one another. Jerusalem is the capital of the Jewish state and the desired capital of a Palestinian one. In cultural terms it is considered by many Israelis and Palestinians to be a provincial backwater despite considerable secular cultural life. At the same time, many—including those who are not religious in a traditional, mainstream sense—see it as a site of intense spirituality. Tel Aviv is the urbane antithesis of Jerusalem, the center of secular Israeli culture. Where international diversity in Jerusalem is to be found mainly in the mix of religious representatives, tourists and pilgrims who come from almost every nation, Tel Aviv is more flamboyantly cosmopolitan. Haifa, Israel's third largest city, is the secular, proletarian capital of the north and, as already noted, a city of peaceful coexistence.[26] For many Arab musicians of the north, it has been the first place to go to study European music. Ramallah is the cultural and political center of the Palestinian Authority. It is home to a conservatory (supported by Daniel Barenboim and Edward Said, among others) and other cultural activity despite years of armed conflict in its midst.

Power

Power relations intertwine with many of the issues to be discussed here, particularly interaction among musicians. Within Israel, as a Jewish state, people identified as Jews enjoy greater freedom, political clout, and less harassment due to that official identity. Yet most of those who collaborate musically with Arabs do not exploit that difference and, as far as I have observed, actively try to right the balance. As Israeli citizens, Palestinian Arabs born inside Israel may choose to work against or within the system with far less difficulty and personal danger than Palestinians in the West Bank or Gaza. There are Arab political parties and Arab members of the parliament (Knesset). By contrast, Palestinians in the occupied territories have lived, on the whole, a much more difficult life, their movement constrained by the military, with permits constantly required. This was an issue of central importance to relations within Alei Hazayit and it affected Yair Dalal's collaborations, too.

If knowledge is power, then imbalances between Israeli Jews and Arabs are not one-sided. Israeli Arabs often know more about Israeli Jewish cultural life than vice versa, as is common for minority communities elsewhere. The curriculum in Israeli Arab schools includes not only Hebrew language instruction beginning in second or third grade, but units on Jewish history and Israeli literature. Taken together with exposure to the mainstream, Hebrew-language mass media this offers intimate knowledge of Jewish Israelis that is not balanced by similarly widespread knowledge of Arabic and Israeli Arabs among the Jewish population.[27] This difference carries over into the musical world we are about to enter. Some of the Arab musicians involved have greater knowledge of European music than any

26. This is only enhanced by the presence of the central shrines and institutions of the Bahá'í faith.
27. See, for instance, the attitudes displayed in a review of a Hebrew anthology of Palestinian literature (Atamna 1994). Some Israeli Jews with particular interest in Arab affairs (including but not limited to military intelligence personnel who constitute a high proportion of Middle East specialists at the universities) acquire deep knowledge in this area. A recent article by a former head of Israel's secret service is an example of this phenomenon (Melman 2004).

of their Jewish counterparts have of Arab music. They almost invariably have greater knowledge of Arab musical practice, training Jewish musicians and lending authority and credibility to collaborations in which they are involved. I shall return to this point in subsequent chapters.

Further asymmetries should also be kept in mind. In many ways, Israeli Jews constitute a multiethnic group forming a single nation while Palestinian Arabs are part of a multinational ethnic group. Though Jews are defined by religious affiliation, most of the musical mixes to be discussed here have little if anything that is identifiably "Jewish."[28] Palestinian musicians generally bring music that is defined as "Arab" into the mix, but nothing explicitly Muslim or Christian and little, if anything, that is exclusively Palestinian. Arab music is both too broad and too narrow a label. It is too broad in that it encompasses the related, but strikingly diverse, musical traditions of North Africa, the culture area stretching from Egypt to Syria, the Arabian Peninsula, and Iraq. It is too narrow because it implies an ethnic/racial/linguistic uniformity that ignores the active participation of Armenians, Greeks, Jews, Turks, and others in musical practices shared with the Arab majority. "Middle Eastern music" is useful in a general, ethnically inclusive sense, but it ignores the dominant Arab presence —especially the centrality of Arabic song texts—and glosses over the differences between Turkish and Arab practices.[29]

Finally, I must stress once again that this Arab/Jew matrix is only one way of looking at human relations in the area. Alliances shift with context, and differences of gender, class, general education, and musical background can be just as important. Strong cosmopolitan tendencies among a significant proportion of the population—and musicians in particular—further complicate the picture.[30]

Theoretical Concepts and Models

This multifaceted phenomenon fairly bursts with possibilities for interpretation and calls for a variety of theoretical perspectives. Musical analysis offers a central entry point, but clearly there is much more to analyze than the synthesis of a new musical style. The collaboration between Israelis and Palestinians, Jews and Arabs, in the invention of new forms of musical expression at this particular time, is rife with intriguing angles. It has specific social and cultural aspects that set it apart from superficially similar musical activities by bands consisting solely of Israeli Jews (such as the East/West Ensemble or Eyal Sela's Darma) or by mixed groups in Europe and North America.[31]

28. A few works by Yair Dalal are an important exception to this.
29. For further discussion see chapter 3.
30. See chapter 3.
31. Such experimentation has increased greatly in frequency over the past decade, not only in Israel where numerous all-Jewish groups have been joining

In the course of the book numerous issues surface that are the subject of extensive writings and sometimes heated debate in ethnomusicology and related fields, such as popular music studies, cultural studies, and anthropology. These include tradition, identity, authenticity, hybridity, and representation; all of which are linked to questions of authority, itself entwined with competence and interaction. Since the Israeli scene is connected to the larger world music scene, with musicians frequently traveling abroad and collaborating with guests at home, it is also necessary to consider transnational links, cosmopolitan attitudes, and the effects of increasing globalization as the circulation of people, ideas, and commodities has accelerated over the past few decades. The Israeli-Palestinian imbroglio, with its tortured history and various power imbalances, suggests the pertinence of colonial and post-colonial power structures and patterns of interaction to present social interaction. I have not found it possible to do all of these issues justice in one book. Some I treat at length, leaving others as topics for further research. Here I will point briefly to some of the writings I have found most helpful.

This is, in some ways, a highly localized manifestation of a phenomenon that appears to be broadly dispersed around the world. The musicians discussed here feel deep roots in a particular place and express that in their choice of songs, the titles they give their instrumental compositions, and in their decision to stay in Israel even when their personal circumstances are rotten. But the sense of place is also a commodity to trade in an international marketplace—the world music circuit—that values roots and authenticity. Therefore, the local scene also feeds into a much larger international network that is constituted from a round of international festivals (on themes such as world music, roots music, and Mediterranean music), other touring opportunities, collaborations at home and abroad with musicians from other countries, contracts with foreign labels, stints in foreign countries, and so on. The list of reasons to travel is long (including teaching, studying, performance) and the circulation of recordings to radio stations, stores, and individual consumers is manifold. The sort of international comings and goings that figure centrally in the careers of Alei Hazayit, Bustan Abraham, and Yair Dalal would have been nearly unthinkable twenty years earlier, in terms of both economic feasibility and audience interest—the two are, of course, integrally related. The study of Indian music in India by members of Al Ol would also have been highly unlikely. The awareness of musical fusion occurring elsewhere and of particular localized musical practices also depends on these heightened global connections.

A considerable body of work is relevant to understanding these complexities. Arjun Appadurai's "flows" and "scapes" have intrigued ethnomusicologists because they capture the fluid interconnectedness of phenomena

this stream, but also in Europe and North America. Simon Shaheen has been a particularly visible Arab proponent of this trend in the U.S. In England, Israeli Gil Atsmon and Palestinian Adel Salameh are active along these lines, as are Rabih Abou Khalil in Germany and Sara Alexander in France.

so multifaceted and widespread that prior theoretical tools are insufficient. Appadurai's ideas inspired Mark Slobin to propose super-, intra-, and subcultures (1993) as a framework for theorizing the diversity and interrelations of communities, cultures, and musical styles in late twentieth-century America. The micromusical worlds described by Slobin offer many nooks and crannies to be explored. Ingrid Monson (1999) has argued that it is fruitful to play Slobin's ideas against Veit Erlmann's. Arguing for inescapable commodification, Veit Erlmann links world music to the global imagination and rapidly shifting patterns of identity and cultural practice (1996a: 468). While I find Slobin's ideas stimulating, the music scene I discuss in this book does not easily fit his tripartite scheme. I hope to show that this scene overlaps with or partakes in the international world music scene, but is neither as rootless nor as commodified as the cases discussed by Erlmann. Monson uses the shorthand characterizations "culture as text" and "culture as commodity" to accentuate differences between these viewpoints.

Here I am chiefly concerned with a third viewpoint: *culture as action*. Some products of these actions, e.g., commercial recordings, clearly are commodities, but they can also be read as texts. Others, such as feelings that people have toward one another in the wake of performing together or hearing a joint performance, cannot. Processes can also become commodities: Staging a world music jam session at a festival, for instance, is a commodification of action—usually centering on the processes of groove and improvisation.

One of Monson's key concerns is the pervasiveness of power relations: "However good various types of groove might make us feel . . ." she writes, "they cannot be presumed to be innocent of power" (1999: 52). Power imbalances are a major concern in writings about international collaborations, particularly between First World and Third World musicians. Among the numerous recent writings on questions of appropriation and exploitation, the oft-cited work by Steven Feld on "pygmy pop" (1996) and by Louise Meintjes on Paul Simon's *Graceland* (1990), stand out for their focus and clarity. Timothy Taylor's *Global Pop* (1997) examines some of the same questions over a much broader swath. Jocelyne Guilbault's discussions of lateral collaborations and flows in a transnational scene that spans the Caribbean, North America, and Europe (1997b, 2001) offer a corrective to an overemphasis on North-South or First World-Third World interactions. Though it differs in many ways from Guilbault's work, my project also calls into question the utility of these dichotomies, arguing that they cannot be mapped directly onto the music or the musicians and their production network.

Some of the basic concepts of network theory are useful for making sense of the myriad connections that link the musicians within this scene to one another and to other scenes in Israel, the Palestinian territories, and abroad. I applied the concept of network in my earlier investigations of musical interaction in Javanese, Balinese, and Middle Eastern music, which focused on musicians, their interaction, and their knowledge (Brinner 1995). There I proposed that musical performance be analyzed in terms of musicians' competence (what they know) and how they use this knowledge in interacting with one another. I suggested further that we study the interactive networks that form in any performance, as a set of links joining particular people (each with his or her own competence, motivations, and so on) filling particular roles in accordance with the conventions associated with specific styles, genres, and contexts. In a study of Javanese *pathetan* performance (1985) I had already demonstrated that such networks have strong social components, with considerations of status, relative competence, and other sociocultural concerns affecting the interaction in any given instance. I was working with such small networks (four or five musicians) that most of the network characteristics and effects now being explored would not have stood out or had much import. While working on the present book and tracking all the people involved in relevant recordings, I became aware of the presence of individuals whose many connections make them hubs in a larger network of musicians and of the high degree of connectivity throughout that network.[32] I extended my earlier analysis of interpersonal networks to include the patterns of association among musicians that bridge ensembles and connect most of the musicians within this small, tightly knit scene.

I argue that one of the main networks linking these musicians is a scene, working from Will Straw's definition of scene as a "cultural space in which a range of musical practices coexist, interacting with each other within a variety of processes of differentiation, and according to widely varying trajectories of change and cross-fertilization." This scene also exhibits the "ongoing exploration of one or more musical idioms said to be rooted within a geographically specific historical heritage" that Straw attributes to community (Straw 1991: 273). But the people active in this scene are only loosely affiliated with one another, despite numerous links, and they valorize a wide and shifting array of "ethnic" music without being bound to tradition or invested in its preservation. Despite this looseness it was possible, at the beginning of the twenty-first century, to discern the emergence of an art world (Becker 1992) as a broader circle of people became involved in this musical scene and institutions were created or incorporated in it.

Scene is a more appropriate term than community for describing the affiliations that formed in the 1990s because it indicates something that people can flow in and out of without necessarily feeling bound to one another by communal ties.[33] In other words, the character and strength

32. It was serendipitous that Barabasi's survey of the ever-widening applications of network analysis (2002) was published shortly after I realized the need to look into networks further. From there I proceeded to the network theory writings cited in chapter 8.

33. Mark DeWitt has provided a useful discussion of community and scene, with a brief history of some of the problematic connotations that community has accrued (1998: 13–17).

of links within these two types of network differ. Each of these musicians is also embedded in longer-lasting—and often more tightly knit—social networks that constitute communities. This distinction between scene and community helps us to recognize the risks taken and the support garnered in these communities when a musician steps "outside" to work with members of another community, particularly one that may be perceived as antagonistic toward one's "own kind."

An imagined community, that near ubiquitous formulation proposed by Benedict Anderson (1983), forms around the notion of something shared. Insofar as that shared something has some foundation in the past, it is often conceived as "tradition." But we know, thanks to Hobsbawm and Ranger (1983) and the host of scholars who have extended their work to virtually every corner of the world, that many so-called traditions are invented or constructed after the fact. Writing about Malta, Sant Cassia clarifies the possibility, perhaps even necessity, of construction even for long-standing practices when he notes "'Tradition' is neither self-evident nor transparent. It needs to be identified, packaged, and made the subject of discretion and taste" (2000: 291). Chris Waterman, taking a cue from Marcus and Fischer's formulation of the challenge for ethnography—"how to represent the embedding of richly described local, cultural worlds in larger impersonal systems of global economy"—suggests shifting from clichéd juxtapositions of continuity and change to an "analytical framework concerned with global networks, the creation of nation-states and peoples, and the invention of tradition" (Waterman 1990: 367, citing Marcus & Fischer 1986: 77). This suggestion is particularly appropriate for the project at hand, one in which a relatively new nation-state, Israel, is locked in an ongoing struggle with the would-be Palestinian nation-state. Uncritical narratives of rejuvenation and return to sources abound. Waterman's warning about the danger of projections into the past—assuming that the ancestors of oysters are also oysters (1990: 368)—is à propos (substituting goats or camels for oysters).

Israelis and Palestinians invent and reinvent traditions, not only within local frames of reference for local audiences, but also on the world stage with reference to global concerns. These constitute part of an argument for each people's long-standing right to sovereign existence. In Israel's public discourse, the content and status of older musical practices varies in a dialectic between diasporic Jewish "roots" and newer Israeli "traditions," between the ancient and the contemporary. Among Palestinians specific village practices vie with contemporary Arab popular music for prominence in representing the nation (Poché 2001, Van Aken 2006). Against and across these separate trends stand the efforts of Yair Dalal and a few others to emphasize the common musical expression of Middle Eastern Jews and Arabs.

Awareness of invented traditions should not blind us to phenomena that can reasonably be considered traditional. Although many scholars now appear to be leery of using the word with anything other than ironic distance, tradition is still useful to designate cultural knowledge that has been developed and shared by a group for a considerable time. Whether we are talking about specific songs or ways of performing and listening, it is an appropriate term without a ready substitute. We just need to be skeptical of claims for great antiquity or fixity and to question the goals that tradition is being mobilized to serve.

Recuperating and promoting heritage—the sum total of a group's traditions, some invented, some not—are distinctive facets of Yair Dalal's work as a performer and composer. In this he differs from the members of Bustan Abraham and Alei Hazayit. Such activity raises questions of authority and representation. Who has the authority to claim and interpret that heritage? Who really knows it? And how is it to be presented? Jewish heritage, in its general and highly localized meanings, is an industry in Israel. It is also an arena for political contestation. Dalal's work must be understood in the context of competing interests and differing values placed during the first decades of Israel's existence on the heritage of Jewish ethnic groups (e.g., Iraqi Jews versus Polish Jews). Other questions and expectations arise outside Israel where even those performers who were not explicitly dedicated to the presentation of heritage, can be inadvertently pulled into this arena when they perform at Jewish music festivals.[34] Questions of authority also arise in relation to hybrid creations, where criticism for insufficient knowledge of constituent elements is common.

Hybridity lies at the heart of this book, located in the members of the group with their multiple, compound identities, in individual and group playing styles, compositions, performance programs, and recordings, and in audiences. In keeping with the critique voiced by Staring and his co-authors, who state that in the field of cultural studies "Bob Marley has definitely succeeded Che GueVara [sic]" (1997: 13), I do not rush to greet such hybridity as a sign of subaltern resistance. The subjects of this study have not achieved Marley's iconic status; many of them are not downtrodden and oppressed. Hybridity, in this instance, has other causes and uses. We have already seen that Bustan Abraham made bold claims for the creation of a new, unique form of music, which would speak to "both Eastern and Western audiences." To do so they drew on musical practices that they associated with "East" and "West" to create new combinations. But none of these musicians seems to want to tout the fact of hybridity itself because it bears the mark of a bastard, of rootlessness, of artificiality. Musicians seek authenticity by establishing their credentials with regard to the various musical resources they use and by claiming an organic synthesis of those resources. Sources are recurrent concerns for musicians, their listeners, and those who write about them. How authoritative is the musicians' knowledge of those sources and how unique is their access to them? What is special about the particular mix of sources? On the answers to such questions depend judgments of authenticity and representation. Thus, for

34. Barbara Kirshenblatt-Gimblett's account of competing ideas about Israeliness and Jewishness with regard to the representation of heritage at various American exhibitions (1998: 70–72) shows the nature of the problem, although she makes no mention of music.

instance, performers and promoters find it useful to stress the ethnic origins of band members who are Middle Eastern in descent. To note that someone has played jazz with international stars lends another sort of credibility. Having both types of authority present in the same band, perhaps in the same person, heightens the authenticity quotient of the band.

If, as Line Grenier points out on the basis of rock criticism (1989: 137–38), authenticity is associated with otherness—an association whose exclusivity I am not willing to grant—then the foregrounding of difference in an ensemble stands to enhance its authenticity. Those bands that include Jews and Arabs or "Westerners" and "Easterners" (however defined) sport such mutually constitutive otherness (keeping in mind that these two oppositions are not parallel at all; many Jews identify as Eastern, for instance). In this situation certain pedigrees are more valuable than others. To cite an extreme contrast, Yair Dalal makes much of his Iraqi roots in his self-presentation, choice of repertoire, publicity, and lectures; but association with the ultra-religious is not an asset in secular Israeli society. Dalal told me that his frequent collaborator Eyal Sela resisted promoting his own competence in klezmer music, despite being one of the finest exponents of klezmer in Israel today, particularly outside the walls of the ultraorthodox community. Dalal saw the need to represent his heritage in the face of imminent loss; Sela apparently did not at that time.[35] This is not reducible to a contrast in personality or motivation. The objective circumstances differ, with Iraqi and Iraqi Jewish music finding far less currency in contemporary Israeli society. Perhaps not unrelated to this, these musics are also more exotic for the general Israeli public and pique the interest in the exotic, the ancient, and the Middle Eastern. At this time, in this place, a performer's identity as "Eastern" adds value and cultural capital, enabling identification for those listeners who are themselves of Middle Eastern descent and a sense of authentically exotic rootedness for those who are not. This requires consideration of questions of otherness, exoticism, and orientalism, which clearly are pertinent here.

Identity has received so much attention in recent ethnomusicological studies that it has pushed aside many other equally valid issues. In this study, I have tried to maintain balance in this regard. Sociologist Motti Regev and ethnomusicologist Edwin Seroussi have said much of what needed to be said about music and identity in Israel. Following Pierre Bourdieu, they have theorized the concept of Israeliness in terms of several competing positions within the field of national culture that contest Israeliness through popular music (2004). They provide several insights relevant to the present study. In particular, some of the songs that I will discuss are *shirei erets yisrael* ("songs of the land of Israel") one of the three

---

35. I base this on Dalal's account when I interviewed him in 1998. Five years later, Sela released *Call of the Mountain*, an album that featured a particular repertoire of klezmer music, updated with elements of electronic dance music.

repertoires central to their book. However, most of the music analyzed here is not part of their study because they chose to focus on the major popular musicians and allude to ones such as the members of Bustan Abraham only in passing. This is not merely a matter of lesser popularity: the particular scene in which Bustan Abraham played a central role does not have a clear link to a specific social group and hence to an identity that is easily labeled, either by the state or by individuals such as musicians, promoters, listeners, and scholars.[36] Audiences at Bustan Abraham concerts I have attended in Israel have been heterogeneous in age, class, gender, and ethnicity, judging by appearances, speech, and modes of interaction with one another and with the performers. Furthermore, the audience for this music includes not only inter- and transnational Jewish communities, but also a nonethnically defined community of people who are interested in Middle Eastern-based music—I am thinking of the clientele at summer camps devoted to Middle Eastern, or more broadly, ethnic music and dance[37]—and an overlapping community of peace activists and sympathizers. The music and musicians may well symbolize aspects of a desired identity for some, pointing to social transformations that could enable peaceful coexistence. This is very nearly the diametric opposite of the transformative processes analyzed by George Bisharat in his work on Palestinian refugees (1997). We shall return to this point at the end of the book.

If this music is not, first and foremost, an expression of group identity, then we must turn our attention to the particularities of individual performers. As a counterweight to the body of work on popular music that delineates the tentacles of multinational corporations and the careers of stars, it is important that we pay close attention to the exercise of individual agency by those who struggle at the margins of the international world music scene. This is particularly important for a study of music that borders uneasily on the popular.[38]

Individual agency must be scrutinized in relation to the social and cultural institutions and the political and economic realities of Israel, the Palestinian territories, and more global frameworks. I follow Erlmann here, who stated that ethnographies should examine the choices performers make "in moving about the spaces between the system and its multiple environments" (1996a: 474). By tracing individual musicians' career trajectories— of interest in their own right—we can also learn something about general conditions. It is important and necessary to understand their actions and the formation of their individual capabilities and proclivities as musicians against the various group affiliations and identities with which they grapple, even as we remain aware of the danger of making an individual stand for a particular group.

36. Dardashti appears to concur on this point though she states it differently (2001: 120).
37. Lausevic 2007 is relevant here.
38. See Guilbault 2000 for an articulation of this challenge.

So we return to individuals and groups, to questions of affiliation and identity. Erlmann, too, cites Straw's work, using it to reflect on transcultural sounds as a global phenomenon and to examine "the production of social differences through the 'building of audiences around particular coalitions of musical form'" (1996a: 470, citing Straw 1991: 384). In my research, however, I argue that it is the production of social unity out of difference that is the musicians' goal. The mission statement of Bustan Abraham makes this claim explicitly, and it is not hard to find corroborating evidence from other sources for the imagining of a community in a non-nationalist sense, a space in which Jews and Arabs come together to partake in music rather than to fight. This brings us, once again, to questions of identity, but this time, identity as constituted by the experiences that the subject undergoes rather than by circumstances of birth.

The subject matter of this book has garnered little attention in scholarly publications on music in the Middle East, perhaps because it is a very recent phenomenon involving a relatively small number of musicians.[39] But this belies the significance of what these people have accomplished. This scene is indicative of a much broader phenomenon, a shift in the cultural balance and orientation of a sizable portion of the Israeli public that has been characterized by Shohat and Stam as a "seismological shift: the decolonization of Eurocentric power structures and epistemologies" (2003: 9). The lack of scholarly interest in this musical scene is also due, I believe, to the "in-betweenness" of this music. I already noted the lack of a concrete group identity for the producers and consumers of this music. Nor does it fit the art/popular/folk divisions or the ethnic categories that have structured Israeli academic research and publication in musicology and ethnomusicology thus far.[40]

The timeliness of this study can hardly be in doubt as the Israeli-Palestinian conflict continues to occupy a central position on the world

39. Dardashti 2001, comparing the discourses of *musika mizrahit* and Israeli ethnic music, is the closest to my study in subject matter. I discovered it after I had completed almost all of my research and conceived most of the book.

40. A vast literature covers musical practices that are related in one way or another to the subject of this book, including: studies of transplanted European art music and the interaction with a new, eastern Mediterranean context (Bohlmann 1989 and Hirshberg 1995); studies of popular music, such as *shirei eretz yisrael*, rock, and *musika mizrahit*, the hybrid popular music from marginalized North African and Middle Eastern immigrant communities that broke into the mainstream in the 1980s (Regev 1995 and 1996, Horowitz 1997 and 2002, Halper, Seroussi, and Squires-Kidron 1989); and a varied body of literature on Jewish religious and folk practices by authors such as A.Z. Idelssohn, Edith Gerson-Kiwi, Amnon Shiloah, Avraham Amzaleg, and Edwin Seroussi that has been less directly relevant to this book. Among the far more numerous publications on mainstream Arab musical practices, publications by A. J. Racy (1976, 1977, 1981, 1983, 1986, 1988, 2003) have been particularly useful as have Scott Marcus's writings on *maqam* (1989a and b, 1992, 1993, 2002) and publications on Palestinian village music (Sbait 1989 and 2002, Yaqub 2002, Regev 1993, Bar Yosef 1990, Poché 2001, and Cohen and Katz 2006).

stage and extremist positions continue to attract the spotlight. As scholars increasingly trumpet the deterritorialization of cultural difference due to the mass migrations and transnational culture flows that mark the post-colonial world (Gupta and Ferguson 1997a: 3), it is vital to examine both the reterritorialization of cultural difference and attempts to bridge that difference on contested ground.

2

Arab Musicians in Israel and the West Bank

"The audience is a donkey."
"I am a merchant."

With these two pithy statements, Jamal Saʻid, a popular Palestinian drummer, summed up his experience playing for weddings and other celebrations in the West Bank and Israel when we spoke in Jerusalem in the early 1990s.[1] He derided the public for its lack of taste but put himself at its service, ready to play requests. This ambiguous relationship—a stance of aesthetic superiority juxtaposed with pragmatic subservience—says much about the occupation of musician among Arabs in Israel and the West Bank in recent decades. Music flourishes as an essential element of celebration, but quality languishes under the tyranny of the lowest common denominator. Or so, with remarkable consistency, said all the musicians whose careers I followed over nearly two decades. Most have withdrawn completely from this mainstream; those who continue to participate do so for the sizable income or to fulfill social obligations. But this mainstream is not the only show in town. Frustrated musicians seek out or create other opportunities. In order to appreciate fully the choices they have made, we need to understand the situation from which they emerged, the circumstances that led them to experiment with new combinations of music and musicians. A pair of vignettes will serve as a point of departure.

An Evening at the Hakawati
September 1987, East Jerusalem
A concert sponsored by a charitable association for the blind drew a full house of men and boys to the Hakawati Theater, a few blocks north of the Old City walls.[2] I seemed to be the only non-Arab present.

---

1. Jamal and I conversed in Hebrew, a language he knows imperfectly but far better than I know Arabic.
2. The Hakawati is a center for Arab cultural performance, presenting political plays and children's theater as well as music (see Slyomovics 1991). Jamal Saʻid performed there frequently as an actor as well as a musician.

The program featured a series of three singers, the last of whom was clearly the "draw" of the evening, eliciting enthusiastic audience response. Bassam Bishara related directly to the audience, speaking briefly before most songs and urging people to sing along in several. Musically, he commanded the evening firmly, his voice riding high above the sound of his *buzuq* (long-necked, fretted lute) and the rest of the ensemble. Jamal Sa'id was one of the musicians who accompanied him on hand drums, violin, *'ud*, synthesizer, and electric bass guitar.

The crowd responded noisily to everything the musicians did, clapping along whenever possible. A few members of the audience, mainly boys, danced at the foot of the stage. While the concert was clearly aimed at listeners rather than dancers, the catchy, melodically straightforward songs of Marcel Khalife seemed to dovetail with the audience's expectations. The content of the songs also met with their approval: Khalife is an extremely popular Lebanese composer, singer, and instrumentalist, whose passionate songs about Lebanon gave hope to many Lebanese during their civil war. He has also taken up the plight of the Palestinians in his highly political songs. Other songs, written by Lebanese singer-songwriter Ziad Rahbani and the Rahbani brothers (Ziad's father and uncle), also spoke of economic hardship and the difficulty of life today, as did a song by the Egyptian songwriter Sheikh Imam, famed for his songs attacking both the Egyptian government and Israel. They resonated with the audience on the eve of the first *intifada*, the Palestinian uprising that broke out a mere two months later, radically affecting the lives of everyone there.

A Concert Sponsored by the Workshop for Non-Western Music
April 1987, West Jerusalem

A few months before the Hakawati fundraiser, several of the same musicians had participated in a concert at the prestigious Jerusalem Music Center. In a semicircle, they faced a small audience of university students, faculty, and a few curious others. Musicians and listeners alike were seated on folding chairs, belying the opulence of the wood-paneled room that serves multiple functions, housing master classes by internationally renowned performers of European art music such as Janos Starker and Isaac Stern, as well as high-caliber chamber concerts, recording sessions, and workshops for teachers and school children. This concert was a departure from the usual fare at this venue, presented as part of the Workshop for Non-Western Music that I directed. The Workshop served music students from the Israeli universities, many of whom were in the audience that night and had already studied with some of these same musicians in our classes.

The concert was a self-conscious presentation of *turath*—music dating from the nineteenth to the mid-twentieth centuries that is commonly labeled classical, Arab, and art music. Two medleys featured Bassam Bishara as a singer (without his *buzuq*), accompanied on violin, 'ud, nay (end-blown flute), *darbukkah* and frame drum.[3] Each medley featured songs in the venerated *muwashshah* form preceded by solo instrumental and vocal improvisations (*taqasim* and *layali*, respectively). Before each medley the musicians performed instrumental compositions associated with the major icons of twentieth-century Arab music—Muhammad 'Abd al-Wahhab (ca. 1901–1991) and Umm Kulthum (1904–1975)—and the talented young violinist Taiseer Elias played a lengthy improvisation.

The atmosphere was that of a classical concert mixed with a lecture, as ethnomusicologist Avi Amzaleg introduced each piece with didactic remarks. The audience consisted almost entirely of Israeli Jews who were largely ignorant of the world of Middle Eastern art music. They had come to learn and enjoy, greeting each piece with politely enthusiastic applause as it ended but utter silence while the musicians sang and played, in stark contrast to the vocal reactions that performers expect of a knowledgeable audience (see Racy 2002). This left the musicians feeling isolated and somewhat ill at ease.

Concerts versus Party Music

It is a matter of minutes to drive between the Hakawati and the Music Center, but the two are worlds apart, one situated in Arab East Jerusalem, the other in Jewish West Jerusalem, in the historically important Mishkenot Shaananim, the first Jewish settlement outside the walls of the Old City.[4] Established under the aegis of world-renowned violinist Isaac Stern, the Music Center is the jewel in the crown of European art music in Jerusalem. It is beautifully but inconspicuously situated in humble old stone buildings that look out across the valley to Mount Zion and the Old City, with the bulk of the space dug into the rock. The financial support it garners, the international caliber of the guest musicians, and the audiences that it attracts could hardly differ more from what we find at the Hakawati, a somewhat shabby theater that struggles to get by despite its importance to the local Arab community.

The musicians who performed at both the Jerusalem Music Center and the Hakawati—the singer, Bassam Bishara, and the two drummers, Jamal Sa'id and Walid 'Id'is—did not undergo a radical political transformation during the few months between these two performances. They were serving different constituencies and needs. Presentation of Arab art music in a prestigious setting in West Jerusalem, albeit for an unprepared audience, boosted their standing as musicians and offered them a small measure of

3. The drummer alternated among several types of frame drum.
4. These stone buildings were built by the wealthy English Jew Moses Montefiore in the mid-nineteenth century in an effort to alleviate the poverty of Jews in the Old City by giving them cleaner, less crowded living spaces and a windmill as a means of livelihood.

recognition in Israeli society. The mixture of classics, popular hits, and highly political statements that they served up in East Jerusalem enabled them to connect with fellow Palestinians on other levels. It is a measure of their versatility that they were willing and able to handle such different contexts, repertoires, and audiences.

Both concerts were unusual, a welcome relief from the spate of wedding gigs where these same musicians would play current hits late into the night, answering audience demands on the spot, but rarely in the spotlight. Here they received undivided attention, playing a rehearsed program of their own choosing. At the Music Center they were able to include older, more "classical" songs in literary language, the sort of material that the dominant elements in the audiences at weddings and other celebrations had become less and less willing to hear. At the Hakawati the lighter popular songs, which expressed a shared aspiration for freedom from Israeli rule, were also more meaningful than the latest hits.

The *haflah* (pl. *haflat*),[5] a celebration featuring music and food, is the most common performance context for Arab musicians in Israel and the West Bank. It generates substantial income (paid in cash) and is also the common training ground for all these musicians. Even the most elitist get their start in such performances, which have offered a form of economic self-empowerment,[6] an attractive alternative to the low-paying construction jobs that are the common employment for other young Palestinians. This is also the type of employment that most musicians I know come to hate, quitting as soon as they have other sources of income. But this was not always the case. Musicians speak readily of the changes that altered the character of the *haflah* in the last decades of the twentieth century.

The minimal instrumentation for a *haflah* is a variant of the standard Arab *takht*:[7] singer, *'ud*, violin, and drum, usually the goblet-shaped *darbukkah*. In a really small band, the *'ud* player may double as the singer. If more musicians are available, there may be a second drummer (playing one of several types of frame drum) and a second violin.[8] The drummers often double as a chorus. *Nay* or *qanun* (plucked zither), typical of ensembles in Egypt and other Arab countries, have been less common due to a lack of instruments and competent players of these two instruments. For instance, Jamal Sa'id noted that there had been only two good *nay* players in the Jerusalem area in his experience. One spent much of his time in the

5. Generally sponsored by an individual or family to celebrate some occasion, these take place in a house, in a tent erected outside the house, or—in recent years—in community halls, restaurants, hotels, and other semi-public places. Ali Jihad Racy, writing primarily about Egypt and Lebanon, uses the term differently to denote public performances in general (2003: 58–66).

6. Cf. Oliver Wang's findings on Filipino American DJs (2004).

7. See Racy 1988 for a history and analysis of this small ensemble.

8. According to Taiseer Elias, in the late 1980s and early 1990s, the second drum was likely to be a large, relatively deep-pitched frame drum (*tar*) as a result of Egyptian influence.

U.S., while the other had moved to Jordan where he played on television.[9] In some areas, particularly those most influenced by Lebanese and Syrian music, the *buzuq* favored by Bassam Bishara may be found instead of or in addition to the *'ud*.

This basic instrumentation, which used to vary only slightly, has changed in significant ways in recent years. In the early 1970s, electric guitar and electric bass began to be used by some musicians, though the frets limit the use of these instruments to pieces or sections of pieces that require no quarter tones. During the same period, some musicians started adding a trap set consisting at least of bass drum, snare, and a few cymbals. More recently, synthesizers have come into vogue, spreading greatly in the late 1980s and early 1990s. These are usually manufactured specifically for the Middle Eastern market, with settings for the various scales that use quarter tones, imitations of the timbre of standard Arab instruments, and a drum machine programmed for Arab music.[10] With this armament at his fingertips, an enterprising musician can actually get work as a one- or two-man band, cornering a significant part of the market. Over the years, I heard disparaging comments from various musicians about this development. Jamal Sa'id complained to me in 1992 that there were dozens of bands starting up. A couple of kids would pool their resources to buy a synthesizer and drum set, sometimes adding a violin or *'ud* to the band, and undercutting experienced musicians by charging less. They could get away with it, said Jamal, because the audience did not care about quality, they just wanted enough noise coming out of the speakers. A local singer whom he sometimes accompanied was making a fortune from the rental of twenty PA systems through his electronics shop.[11]

The synthesizer is also used in bands with other instruments due to its ability to substitute for traditional instruments, to add rhythmic punch, and to provide chords for those popular songs that require them. Taiseer Elias explained both the ascendancy of the synthesizer and the lack of interest in *nay* and *qanun* in the following portion of a conversation we had in 1998:

> The scarcity of *nay* and *qanun* players stems from . . . the difficulty of the instruments and the lack of teachers . . . There's an archetype of the guy with . . . tie and lapels, grease on the hair, a slick, good-looking guy with girls around him. He learns all the Franco-Arabe material

9. June 30, 1991. The instruments themselves were hard to buy even after trade relations were established with Egypt. One Israeli Arab musician actually asked me to obtain Egyptian instruments for him from an American source! The situation has begun to change in the past few years with the emergence of several fine young Arab and Jewish players.

10. See Rasmussen 1996 for discussion of the synthesizer in Arab American music. Some recent models have more refined microtonal possibilities to differentiate *maqam*s but I believe that they were not yet in use in the early 1990s.

11. September 22, 1992.

[contemporary popular songs, see below]. The organ/synthesizer has become the leader of the group today, with a lot of volume . . . Everyone goes to [the synthesizer] because it's the easiest to play. My nephew, for instance, began to fool around by himself. [He was] self-taught and after a year and a half—and he plays really nicely—he fit into bands. Everyone does that. You start to be, as it were, a musician, a star, earn money. Why bother with violin and tuning and a bow? Or *qanun?*

The *qanun* is particularly important to imitate since it is emblematic of the Egyptian ensembles that everyone hears through mass media, but is usually lacking from live bands. The synthesizer player can also evoke rural musical traditions with synthesized imitations of the various double reed and single reed instruments typical of village music. When played in bands, the synthesizer's drum capabilities are not usually exploited since there are already several drummers in the band.

Some of the pressure to update the ensemble comes from patrons. In the late 1980s, Jamal Sa'id and Walid 'Id'is told me how various people, when inviting them to perform at a *haflah,* insisted that they bring a trap set because they associated this Western percussion battery with contemporary popular music. A few years later, musicians in the Galilee verified this independently, telling me that they could not be hired without electric bass, guitar, and drums.[12] Jamal and Walid would oblige when they had no choice, setting up the drums and cymbals so that all the guests could see them, but Walid would play them only sporadically if at all.

The repertoire for *haflat* consists mainly of songs, with a few instrumental pieces and solo improvisations played mainly as introductions or interludes. The songs are drawn from a variety of sources, representing the different "colors" (*lawn*) of Egyptian, Lebanese, Syrian, and Jordanian music.[13] As they play styles and genres associated with various parts of the Arab world, the performers attempt to gauge audience reaction to suit the pieces to their tastes. George Sama'an (who sings and plays 'ud, violin, and *buzuq*) says that he and his partner, the drummer Salem Darwish, do not go in with a set program but adapt to the audience, judging by location and ethnicity even when playing for school children.[14] What the renowned Syrian singer Sabah Fakhri said to Jihad Racy—that the *mutrib* (singer) must be a psychologist who can read his audience (2003: 64)—holds true here, too, but in a broader sense, applying to instrumentalists as well. Although he is a drummer, Jamal Sa'id, sees himself as a merchant who strives to find the right wares to sell to each customer and takes pride in his ability to identify the different factions or taste communities within the audience. He does not hesitate to tell the other musicians what he thinks the audience wants.

12. Michael Maroun and Husam Hayik, Dec. 17, 1993.
13. Cf. the aesthetic Racy reported for Cairo in the 1970s (1981).
14. Jan. 1, 1999.

The First *Intifada*

At the end of 1987, Palestinians in the West Bank and Gaza began an uprising against Israeli occupation. Continuing for several years, it involved strikes, violent confrontations with the Israeli army, and attacks on Jewish civilians and Palestinians suspected of collaboration. While there was sympathy for this *intifada* among Israeli Arabs, overt resistance was limited to Palestinians in the occupied territories. The leadership maintained anonymity while exercising wide-ranging control over the Palestinian population through leaflets, word of mouth, and radio broadcasts. One edict decreed that this was to be a time of national mourning; therefore celebrations were to be cancelled or postponed. The ban was widely observed, shutting down musicians' careers. It was also enforced through violence and threats of violence: I heard of a Palestinian musician in Jerusalem who was invited to perform at a *haflah* and directed to go to a certain address in the Old City. He was beaten and threatened with worse retribution if he continued to perform. This was a trap, a warning to other musicians. The musician who related this complained bitterly to me that the leaders of the *intifada* were demanding that musicians give up their livelihood without offering any other way of feeding their families, whereas Palestinian shopkeepers and workers were only being asked to go on strike on certain days but could continue to earn a living the rest of the time.[15]

In these dire circumstances some musicians turned to other occupations. The synthesizer player whom I heard at the Hakawati on the eve of the *intifada* became a devout Muslim and gave up music altogether, earning enough from work at an electronics plant. Walid 'Id'is, one of the drummers at that same concert, continued to play whenever he could find an opportunity, despite the fact that he too became a far more devout Muslim in reaction to the *intifada*'s difficulties (including the imprisonment of his daughter). Some who had played occasionally on Israeli Radio's Arabic broadcasts found that they ran too great a risk to continue doing so, but Jamal Sa'id continued to act on Israeli TV, counting on his fame and connections to protect him from violence.

Other musicians found ways of circumventing the ban, crossing into Israel proper to play for Israeli Arabs. One band that I knew kept its instruments in the trunk of a car parked outside the Old City walls so that they would not be spotted carrying instruments from their houses. Evading detection was not their only challenge. They had to compete in a market that was already saturated with Israeli Arab musicians so the work that they were able to obtain in Israel rarely made up for what they had lost in the West Bank. One Jerusalem musician told me in 1991, three years into the *intifada*, that he had started turning down offers to play weddings because

---

15. I have not named sources so as not to endanger particular individuals. Palestinians have killed many fellow Palestinians on suspicion of collaboration, without trial.

he felt too bad, coming home from the lively atmosphere of Tel Aviv to the besieged feeling of the Old City.

While Israeli Arabs did not participate as actively in the first *intifada* as did Palestinians in the Occupied Territories, the effects were felt widely. Musical performances became increasingly politicized, particularly in the heavily Muslim "Triangle" situated southeast of Haifa and bordering on the West Bank. A Christian Arab musician told me that he found playing *haflat* there increasingly intolerable. The audience called for anti-Israel political songs that would get the musicians arrested by the police if they were caught or beaten by the audience if they refused to play.

This was the period when I began research into the life of Arab music and musicians in the West Bank and Israel. The circumstances were not particularly conducive to the project due to a lack of performances, but I elicited examples of repertoire and performance practice typical of a *haflah* in recording sessions organized with the help of Jamal Sa'id. In 1991, with the *intifada* at its height, we gathered behind closed blinds in Beit Hanina, an Arab suburb of Jerusalem. The host was a prosperous small businessman, who sold recordings, instruments, and electronic gear, but also performed on occasion as a singer. Ahmed Abu Ghannam, one of the two others selected by Jamal, had been the leading musician in Jerusalem in earlier years. He had studied in Cairo in the 1940s and, according to Jamal, was said to be the first to play *'ud* really well in Jerusalem. He had taught in a Jordanian music school before the Six Day War, led a small orchestra at one of the hotels for many years, and had had many of his songs played on Israel radio after that war. Now in his sixties or seventies, he was having a hard time finding work due to the *intifada*. The fourth member of the group, Ghidian al-Qaimari, was another long-time musical companion of Jamal's who had also been involved in the Hakawati concert described earlier. He played music in hotels and at parties to supplement his income as an English teacher. With these steady sources of income the *intifada* did not affect him as it did Abu Ghannam and Jamal.

Two years later, we tried again. By 1993 the *intifada* was in its last stages, Israel had been negotiating with the Palestinians for some time and the Oslo Accord was imminent. Musical performances were less risky and celebrations in the Jerusalem area once again included music, though business was not booming.[16] In addition to Ghidian, Jamal invited Hatem al-Afghani, a fine violinist and *'ud* player, and Walid 'Id'is, his regular partner who had drummed and sung with him at the Hakawati and Jerusalem Music Center concerts (see figure 2.1).[17] We gathered at Ghidian's house in Abu Dis, a small village on the southeast edge of Jerusalem, but drove to

16. Jamal Sa'id, Sept. 22, 1992.
17. This session almost did not take place because Jamal's oldest son had been arrested on suspicion of throwing rocks at Israeli soldiers outside the Damascus Gate—a case of being in the wrong place at the wrong time according to Jamal. He was released after a few hours of frantic maneuvering, but it took Jamal a couple of hours to return to his usual joking manner.

Figure 2.1. Jamal Saʻid, Ghidian al-Qaimari, and Walid ʻIdʻis outside Walid's house in At-Tur, Jerusalem, after recording session in Ramallah (photo by Ben Brinner)

Ramallah to the studio where Hatem worked as a recording engineer because he had left his violin there. This meant using my American passport to pass Israeli army checkpoints while putting a checkered head cloth, emblematic of the *intifada,* on the dashboard of the Israeli rental car to ward off Palestinian stone throwers. The recording studio was brand new and up-to-date, located on the top floor of a large building that contained a cassette factory, an investment by brothers who had made money in the U.S. and brought it back to the West Bank.

We managed to record quite a few songs, illustrating the typical tour-of-the-Middle East approach that Jamal and friends might take at a *haflah:* an Egyptian piece, a Lebanese one, then something Jordanian. Two young musicians who had a recording date with Hatem arrived and listened. When Jamal and the others discovered that one of them was a competent singer and the son of a well-known *zajjal* (village poet/singer) from a village in Northern Israel, they invited him to perform what they termed "Palestinian folklore." Though they had never met the singer before, the four musicians managed to accompany him in a medley of traditional pieces that included numerous stops and starts, alternation between metered playing and free rhythm, and choral refrains that they were required to sing while playing their instruments. This was not their usual fare, but it was familiar, a part of their heritage. Inviting the singer's friend to add his synthesizer they then performed "'Ala Dal'una," a widely known song type involving extensive improvisation of lyrics or choice from numerous existing verses.[18] On another occasion, Jamal Sa'id stressed that this song varies greatly from one locale to the next, even from Beit Hanina to Ramallah, just a few miles apart. Although all Palestinians probably know this song, it is strongly associated with village culture and the *dabke* dance. Jamal said, "you can play it in the city but the audience will not get as excited."[19] To give the song the right flavor, the synthesizer player chose to imitate the *mijwiz*, a double-pipe, single-reed instrument typically played in villages. Again the musicians had no trouble performing despite the lack of prior rehearsal. After the recording session, Ghidian asked me for a copy of the tape so that he could write down the singer's improvised lyrics because he was about to travel to Germany to perform for a Palestinian students' association and wanted to provide them with some "authentic Palestinian folklore," as he put it.

These examples reveal numerous characteristics of Palestinian musical life. There are differences both major and minor in the musical practices of village and town dwellers. Regional variation in repertoire and performance practice is pervasive even over short distances. The musical competence of musicians such as Jamal and his companions encompasses some of these differences, but questions of cultural roots and authenticity arise with regard to who sings and what he sings. "Folklore" is indelibly associated with villagers and a vital resource for the construction of Palestinian national culture. Ghidian's request for the lyrics also points to the transnational network that connects Palestinian constituencies in various parts of the world via musical performers. Leaving some of these issues for later chapters, I turn next to sketching sociomusical differences.

Villagers and Nomads

The music performed at the Hakawati, the Jerusalem Music Center, and my recording sessions is typical of Arab musical life in cities, towns, and some of the more urbanized villages in Israel and the West Bank. A different musical life prevails in many villages and holds a place in the memory of most Palestinians as their "original" culture. Ghidian (who resides in a village on the outskirts of Jerusalem, but comes from an educated urban family) explained that it is also considered very "country" (implying unsophisticated) due to the singers' pronunciation.[20] In the villages of northern Israel, these musical traditions are very closely related to those of Lebanon, sharing genres, instruments, and performance practice.

18. See Cohen and Katz 2006, pp. 386-87 and track 16 on their CD.
19. Dec. 21, 1994.
20. Dec. 27, 1993.

Much of the improvised sung poetry central to village celebrations is the domain of specialists who often work in pairs to perform a duel of wits before the assembled male celebrants.[21] But this is also communal music making. Many genres have refrains sung by anyone who wants to participate. Line dances are performed to some of them and dancers' stomping provides the main accompaniment for some genres.

Instruments played in the villages have traditionally been restricted to a short, wide-bored flute, various reed instruments, and the goblet drum (*durbakki* or *darbukkah*) that is prevalent throughout the Middle East. The *'ud* and violin have entered many villages within living memory[22] and some villages are so cut off from the musical mainstream that they have yet to see and hear these instruments live—as I was told in 1995 by two musicians from Hebron who had recently played in such a village, and found that their *'ud* elicited great interest from the villagers.[23] The *qanun* and *nay* are even less frequently encountered in the villages.[24]

Bedouin, who live principally in the southern part of Israel, but also in parts of the Jordan valley and the Galilee, have yet another type of musical life. Much of this is shared with Bedouin in the Sinai Peninsula and Jordan, as the borders remain somewhat porous for those who are still nomadic. Much of the music centers around sung poetry accompanied on the *rababa* (spike fiddle). There is some overlap with Palestinian village music, such as the "'Ala Dal'una" song type noted above.

With the settling of most Bedouin into permanent homes (coaxed or forced there by the government in Israel and neighboring countries), the urbanization of more and more villages, and increasing access to mass media, these sociomusical differences are not as clear-cut as they were a generation ago. Nonetheless, they form part of the conceptual map according to which musicians categorize and understand playing styles, instruments, and songs. Sometimes they are linked to deep-seated feelings about cultural roots. The figure of the Bedouin, for instance, has strong appeal, not only for Lawrence of Arabia, but for some urban Arabs and Israelis, too, standing in contrast to all things modern as a symbol of traditional strength, honor, and hospitality.

21. Several scholars have researched this music, including Dirgham Sbait (1989, 2002), Amatzia Bar-Yosef (1990), Dalia Cohen and Ruth Katz (2006), and Nadia Yaqub (2002). Note that Yaqub had to record from a rooftop overlooking the performance area as such performances are usually restricted to males (personal communication). Women's distinctive singing has hardly been researched.

22. Nassim Dakwar said that Simon Shaheen's father Hikmet Shaheen was the first to bring the *'ud* to Tarshiha (July 16, 1999). Elias Jubran claims to have been the first in Rame (Rakha 1999). Both villages are in the Galilee.

23. Jamal Sa'id and friends, Jan. 3, 1995.

24. In an interview, Omar Keinani told me that only the very richest villagers might engage a group of musicians with a *qanun* (July 1, 1997).

Listening with the Feet

The drive to be modern—to keep up with changing fashion and "make a splash"—has altered the *haflah* significantly since the 1960s. Young people with tastes formed through extensive exposure to mass media in an increasingly connected world have become the major cultural force, gender segregation has lessened in some areas, and the number and type of occasions celebrated with a *haflah* have increased. Taiseer Elias discussed some of these changes with me in 1991 based on his experience as a performer in various bands at numerous *haflat* throughout the Galilee and occasionally in other areas of Israel as well. He had witnessed a rise in the number of celebrations due to an increase in types of occasions celebrated, with *haflat* held not only for weddings, but also to celebrate circumcisions, a local soccer team's advance in league standing, and even less important occasions. This created greater demand for musicians answered by growth in the number of musical ensembles. He saw increasing gender integration, even among Muslims, and attributed some of the changes in repertoire to the differing tastes of men and women that now needed to be considered. He also noted increasing commercialization as celebrations moved from private homes with home-cooked food to catered events in rented halls, causing both the host and the guests to calculate expenses. The host feels more compelled to give a good show, marked by lots of "noise" and dancing, while the guests, who traditionally hand the host an envelope with money as a contribution to the event, calibrate their contribution according to the estimated cost of the meal.

In addition to these economic changes, musicians mention audience behavior, repertoire, and technology as aspects that have changed greatly. The relationship between musician and audience has changed as people have become far more forthright and less polite in communicating their desires. Omar Keinani, an Israeli Arab from the Galilee who has lived in the Jerusalem area for many years said:

> In Jerusalem it's very hard. Suddenly you have someone [from the audience] shouting at you "I want this and that"—he's drunk. Suddenly you feel that you're a slave to people, they shout at you. They show off, they want to project their weakness on you because there are girls [watching] on the side . . . They use drugs actually. They don't have any respect for the band. (Jan. 7, 1997)

Omar's day job as a social worker in East Jerusalem dealing with Arab youth and problems such as drugs is evident here both in his assessment of the underlying problem and in his psychological analysis of the processes at work (we were sitting in his office). But other musicians also reported threatening behavior experienced at gigs as a recent development.

The audience is split along age lines in a way that it never was before, there is an overriding expectation of danceable music, and members of the audience have taken to making strong demands rather than polite requests.

This has fundamentally altered the whole experience. Jamal Saʿid described the division of the audience in a conversation in late 1994:

> The audience around here is difficult because it is mixed. There are three age groups. The young (about 10–20 years old) like strong rhythms. They listen with their feet, not with their ears. The middle group (20-40) likes music that is between strong and *tarab*.[25] The older group (over 40) won't listen to the music that the young like. They want *tarab*—the classics—and they also take from the music of the middle group. It is rare to have an audience with all three groups [present and listening at the same time].

He articulated his policy for handling this difficult situation:

> First you play for the young to tire them out, then you play to the middle and at the end give *tarab*. This is a *planned* progression, like pushing (driving) something smoothly along a path [he made a long pushing motion]. Sometimes things go wrong—the young come back in and want more. Then you have to start building the drive all over again. There is often a war between two audience groups pulling in opposite directions. Musicians are caught between the hammer and the anvil. If the musicians play for the younger crowd the older ones blame the musicians rather than their own children's taste. (Dec. 21, 1994)

Jamal also noted that older people sometimes have the younger crowd's music played and even dance to it just to please their children. Warming to the topic he explained, "This division of the audience is relatively new, just the last ten years. It came like a disease, like AIDS or cancer. No one knows who brought it, but we know where it came from—the West." To my comment that the West has influenced Arab music far longer than this recent change, Jamal countered that earlier musicians such as ʿAbd al-Wahhab and ʿAbdel Halim Hafez modified the Western instruments that they utilized or limited their use to sections that had no quarter tones. Now Western "soft music" is adopted whole, with very few modifications: "Egypt kills all of us. Every day there are twenty new singers, all playing the same rhythm." The pervasiveness of one drum pattern in contemporary Egyptian music is corroborated by Scott Marcus (2007: 69).

Jamal elaborated on his disparaging assessment that the people "listen with their feet" a few days after the conversation cited above:[26] "People here have gotten used to something strong. They want to hear the drums

---

25. See Racy 2003 for a comprehensive discussion of *tarab*, a term that denotes both a state of ecstasy and the music that induces that state.

26. Jan. 3, 1995. Omar Keinani echoed this assessment a few years later. The same criticism was voiced fifteen years earlier and half a world away by a Lebanese musician speaking with Racy in Los Angeles (2003: 39).

loud. They don't want to hear the good, natural sounds." He imitated a loud, repeated electronic sound as an illustration. What has been lost is the opportunity to play the longer instrumental and vocal pieces that musicians find more meaningful and that their audiences used to appreciate. Delicate nuances, too, have fallen by the wayside.

This trend among audiences to demand music for dancing rather than for listening, noted by every musician who spoke with me, has been a source of great frustration, particularly for instrumentalists who feel pushed into the background, to serve as a mere engine for the dancers and backdrop to the singer's flamboyant display. The most poignant proof of this shift that I witnessed was a videotape of a *haflah* that Jamal Sa'id showed me. An older man from the audience had come to the microphone to honor the host by singing, but the song was not in a duple meter, unlike all the current popular music. While the musicians had no trouble playing along, the audience's discomfort was obvious as the video camera panned across them. Half-hearted attempts at dancing quickly died out as people stood uncomfortably until the singer had finished.

From his perspective as director of Arab music programming for the Israel Broadcasting Authority (IBA), Taiseer Elias's assessment of current listener preferences was similar to Jamal's. The pieces requested at *haflat* in recent years have shifted from a stable repertoire—based on pieces associated with Egyptian and Lebanese stars such as 'Abd al-Wahhab, Wadi' es-Safi, and Fairuz—to a rapidly changing list of current hits, both Franco-Arabe (see below) and Western, that spread through recordings and broadcast media.[27] He and his staff were inundated with CDs of new popular music sent by musicians and distributors and with requests for this type of material phoned in by listeners.[28] To counter this he also programmed "classic" singers such as Umm Kulthum, Muhammad 'Abd al-Wahhab, Sabakh Fakhri, Wadi' es-Safi, and Fairuz on a regular basis and wrote, produced, and broadcast numerous educational programs devoted to analysis of recordings by artists whom he values highly.

Israel's political borders are permeable when it comes to broadcasts and recordings. In addition to Israel's Arabic-language radio and television broadcasts, listeners receive numerous stations from neighboring Arab countries. Legitimate recordings from the Arab world are imported mainly through a Greek company, but piracy is rampant. Even Israeli radio gets in on the act, taping new Lebanese songs from broadcasts by pirate radio stations in Lebanon and then rebroadcasting them.[29] Some of the older, "classical" repertoire is also available through these channels, just as it is on Israel radio. But this repertoire is relatively fixed and occupies a very small portion of overall broadcast bandwidth compared with the flood of pop songs.

27. When we spoke about this a few years earlier, Taiseer insisted that there was very little local creativity, most material coming from abroad (June 21, 1991).
28. June 28, 1998.
29. Taiseer Elias, June 28, 1995.

Musicians subsume much of the new repertoire of popular songs under the rubric Franco-Arabe, a term that has various meanings related to blending of French (representing a broader European palette) and Arab (North African or Middle Eastern) music.[30] As Jamal and his friends use it, the term seems to denote a style of music pioneered in Lebanon that combines elements of recent European popular music—including synthesizers, harmony, and bass lines—with Arabic lyrics and characteristic Middle Eastern melodic and rhythmic idioms. The ready availability of these songs, along with the latest hits from Egypt, Jordan, Syria, Iraq, and the Gulf states has contributed to the accelerated repertoire turnover.[31]

Cassettes and compact discs serve different purposes for consumers and musicians. Consumers buy them in order to hear their favorites or satisfy their curiosity about new singers. Musicians tend to view them quite differently, as a means to keep up with the market. Ghidian al-Qaimari told me that he was constantly buying cassettes and asking audience members what the latest songs were in order to satisfy audience requests. Given the low prices and the prevalence of piracy, musicians made their own recordings, not as a means of earning income directly, but as publicity—sonic business cards. In 1993, when I asked Jamal whether he had recordings for sale, he made it clear that it would be beneath his dignity to put out a cassette because it was so cheap and easy to do.

Technological change has not been limited to the spread of cheap recordings and the adoption of electric guitars and synthesizers.[32] Jamal and other musicians were critical of the heavily rhythmic sound of drum machines (different in quality from the loud and aggressive sound that Jamal and other drummers produce on a *darbukkah*), the repetitive musical structure, the lack of opportunity for instrumental improvisation, and the over-amplified sound that has made events much louder. According to Bassam Bishara, primitive amplification was introduced in the years 1967–1970. More sophisticated equipment was imported in the following years, but "nobody knew how to use it." By the late 1980s, when we spoke about this, he had hired his own sound engineer and sent him to a course in order to know the equipment and do the job right. With this amplification and the advent of cordless microphones in the early 1990s the singer was "freed" from the band, becoming a star who moved out into the crowd, leaving the instrumentalists behind, both physically and in status. This increased role differentiation within the ensemble as most singers became front men and did not play instruments.[33] With his microphone the singer

30. The term applies to contemporary Lebanese music, but also to popular music of the 1930s and 1940s from Tunisia, for instance, such as songs by the Algerian Jewish composer Maurice el Medioni.

31. The Internet has probably become a factor in this, but it was not yet a significant part of these musicians' lives when I conducted my research.

32. According to Taiseer (June 22, 1991), the electric guitars were a passing fad, but the synthesizers have proven their staying power.

33. The smallest bands are still fronted by singers who accompany themselves, usually on *'ud*. Taiseer started on *'ud* rather than violin because his father

has the power to call attention to an instrumentalist or to demean him if he thinks he's grabbing too much attention.[34] He also earns far more than the instrumentalists, often taking half the pay, and dividing the rest among them. Taiseer attributed this, in part, to the model of Jewish bands and audiences, recounting performances for Jewish audiences who shower money on performers and tell the singer that he should take half. Omar Keinani noted a change in musicians' attitudes, a drive to earn money that overrode all other interests and led to new tensions between musicians over payment.

There is little incentive for an instrumentalist to organize a gig, according to Taiseer, since it is the singer who will profit most. An outstanding musician might receive a bit more pay (above the $100 that was standard in 1991), although it was still little in comparison to the singer's pay (as much as $1,000).[35] There is thus more competition within the band, starting with increased volume on each of the amplified instruments—a war initiated by the synthesizer players according to Taiseer—and continuing with displays of ornamentation and speed. Taiseer noted further that the singer would get the credit for a good performance, while the band would be blamed for a bad one. This alienation within the band—together with the public's taste for a repertoire of songs marked by rapid turnover and danceable rhythms that leave little, if any, room for instrumental finesse—has caused many experienced musicians to turn elsewhere for employment and musical satisfaction.

Most of these changes are not limited to Israel. Anne Rasmussen's research among Arab Americans points to numerous parallels, such as the prevalence of *haflat* over other performance contexts and the dominance of dancing over listening. Rasmussen implies that this is an Arab American phenomenon that recent immigrants from the Middle East have failed to alter, but these immigrants may well reinforce it since the same change in taste has occurred not only in Israel but also in other parts of the Middle East, as Racy has documented.[36] The following excerpt from my fieldwork illustrates many of these changes.

Shefa'amr, Western Galilee
December 17, 1994
    Ten days before I recorded Jamal and friends in Ramallah, I traveled north at the invitation of Taiseer Elias to observe a rehearsal in his hometown of Shefa'amr. Although this town lies a few miles east of

---

encouraged him to sing as well as play, which is difficult to do when playing the violin.

34. Taiseer Elias, June 22, 1991.

35. Jamal Sa'id was reporting considerably higher sums for instrumentalists at that time. This may have been a difference between the Jerusalem area where he played and the Galilee where Taiseer usually performed.

36. See Racy 2003, p. 58, for example, and Rasmussen 1989, especially p. 17. The dynamic of this interaction between diaspora and homeland requires further research.

Haifa, Israel's major port city, in some ways it resembles an overgrown village.

I found ten young men crammed into the stark, whitewashed bedroom of a house. From the mixer on a table in the porch a tangle of cables snaked through an open window to the microphones, pickups, and amplifiers in the bedroom. A crucifix over the bed was the only decor in the singer's crowded bedroom. Husam Hayik had assembled this band for a New Year's Eve party sponsored by the local Christian Arab community. Like many of the other musicians present, he is a competent performer of Arab art music, but on this occasion he selected repertoire that the public preferred, recent Franco-Arabe hits from Lebanon.

For several hours the musicians labored to recreate the arrangements of several currently popular songs by Milhem Barakat and other Lebanese composers. They combined traditional hand drumming with electric trap set, adding harmony on electric guitar and synthesizer supported by electric bass guitar, and melodic parts on electric violin and 'ud. Husam worked out such arrangements for pay, filling a niche in the local music industry by arranging Lebanese, Syrian, and other new material for local singers and creating a complete score on synthesizers that include the sounds of all Middle Eastern instruments. Singers would take this backing and add their vocals to make a cassette.[37]

Eventually two of the drummers left the rehearsal to play a gig. Almost as soon as they were gone the others began to complain about Muslims. As they were all modern young Israeli Arabs, dressed in contemporary clothes, speaking Arabic peppered with Hebrew amongst them, the religious affiliations had not been obvious to me. They explained that the two drummers were Muslims, the 'ud player—still present—was a Druze, and the rest belonged to the Greek Orthodox Church.[38] The complaints did not stop there, moving on to musical frustrations. Like Jamal Sa'id, several of them characterized the Arab public as "donkeys" drawn to the cheapest popular music. To satisfy the audience and sponsors musicians had to perform "Franco-Arabe" repertoire and include electric guitar, bass guitar, and drum in their band. When I pressed one of them he admitted that they did slip pieces that they liked into the program, too, but clearly this was not a particularly satisfying artistic outlet. It is a relatively quick means of making money and those musicians who belonged to the church that sponsored the celebration were fulfilling a social obligation to their community and presumably gaining some appreciation in return. The others were simply making money.

37. Dec. 23, 1993, Taiseer Elias, who was Husam's 'ud teacher.
38. Christian and Druze Arabs do not necessarily live in harmony either. George Sama'an told me in the late 1990s that he was working to alleviate frictions between them in Rame, his hometown in the Galilee.

Several of these musicians played in a local orchestra dedicated to Arab art music, a relatively recent development. Although the orchestra performed their preferred music they complained that the conductor was incompetent, a political appointee who enjoyed the patronage of the Israeli ministry of culture. As evidence of this, they recounted how he had ignored their suggestion to add a bass player until he went to a conference in Cairo and saw that other orchestras had a bass. Now they had Russian Jewish immigrant players, who were technically proficient but had no feel for the music. This anecdote reveals some of the peculiarities and recent changes in Arab music in Israel.

A number of seemingly independent but roughly synchronous changes reduced the peripherality of Palestinian musicians by the mid-1990s. Following the signing of the Oslo Accords in 1993, it became easier for ensembles and individual musicians to travel to Egypt and Jordan (but not to other Arab countries) where they performed and met other musicians. Obtaining musical instruments and recordings from Arab countries also became easier. Although musicians and audiences had stayed in touch with neighboring countries through radio and TV broadcasts, connections improved considerably with the easing of travel restrictions, the spread of the Internet, and the proliferation of private radio and television stations. At the same time, Israeli Arab musicians trained in European classical music were making more connections with Jewish musicians, and Jewish players, primarily bassists, began to find employment in larger Arab ensembles.

Differences and Distinctions

In this fragmented sociocultural landscape, religion is one of the dimensions along which musicians differentiate among themselves and their audiences. Christian, Muslim, and Druze musicians perform together, but differences are not necessarily ignored as I learned at the rehearsal in Shefa'amr. Jamal, who is a Muslim, once remarked to me that he was certain that all the singers who were able to perform both Western-style popular music and the traditional Arab music and its pop offshoots were Christians, attributing this to their church background where he thought they would have learned some form of Western music.[39] As an example, he cited Bassam Bishara who led a band in the 1970s and 1980s that played both Western-influenced Arab pop and more traditional Arab music.

Musicians also have a strong sense of territoriality, linked not only to features of given geographical areas, but also to the social and cultural life in those areas. Shefa'amr, for instance, lies northeast of Haifa in the west-

39. Jan. 3, 1995. A Christian Arab would likely have taken this distinction further, being more alert to the deep divisions within the Christian community among the various sects.

ern Galilee, which Kanaaneh characterizes as a large "dimension of space that is powerfully present in the minds and social interactions of people. It is a practice of location that I deploy along with many other Palestinians. The Galilee is an important locale for . . . the formation and re-creation of identities" (2002: 10). More specifically, this sense of territoriality is also linked to musical tastes, practices, repertoires, and styles. Musicians develop a keen sense of regional difference as they mingle with musicians from other parts of Israel and the Palestinian Territories. As noted earlier, Jamal claimed that regional variation in the performance of the widely known song "'Ala Dal'una" could be measured from one village to the next, even in the urbanized area of Ramallah. Differences between that area on the West Bank and the Galilee should be much larger. Martin Stokes has analyzed somewhat analogous situations among Turkish and Irish musicians (1994), but I would note a couple of crucial differences: Israel and the Palestinian Territories are far smaller than either Ireland or Turkey, yet a highly localized sense of place and regional difference is common; and there is far less institutional reification of such differences than in Turkey or Ireland. Of course, as musicians have become more mobile, distances have collapsed, too. At the Shefa'amr rehearsal, for instance, all the musicians came from the Galilee, with the exception of the backup singer and the 'ud player, who came from nearby Druze villages on the Carmel, the hills southeast of Haifa. Yet, most of them have worked—and some have studied—in other parts of the country.

Not more than half an hour south of Shefa'amr is the Triangle, a densely inhabited, predominantly Muslim area, which has a musical life of its own. Taiseer Elias and others from his area often played there and knew that they need to cater to local tastes. As Martin Stokes has written of Turkish musicians, "the skill [I would substitute competence] of the good regional musician involves an ability to manipulate these quite distinct representations of region in a variety of distinct performance contexts" (1994: 105). Taiseer characterized the *haflat* in the Triangle in socioeconomic terms that affected the performers' experience: parties just for men, who sit and talk without refreshments; when they drank and smoked hashish they would "participate" more. Since there was no outlay for hall rental and catering, there was also no psychoeconomic pressure on the host, as there was elsewhere, to sponsor an extravagant performance, according to Taiseer. The audience preferred Arab pop, but if they wanted serious music then it had to be Egyptian—pieces associated with Umm Kulthum, 'Abdel Mutalib, and 'Abd al-Wahhab—rather than Lebanese music such as the songs of Wadi' es-Safi, which are favorites in the North, just a few miles away. Taiseer achieved a reputation in the Triangle and was sometimes asked to play *taqasim*, instrumental improvisations, that were longer than he was ever allowed to play in the Galilee.[40] Another Christian Arab musician said that it was not just that the Triangle is all Muslim while the

40. June 23, 1991.

Galilee has many Christians, there was an important political difference, too: "Hawatmeh's people are from the Galilee, the Fatah is the triangle."[41] He cited this as proof that geography shapes people, giving them different tastes.

Other areas that musicians frequently name in mapping out musical regions include the West Bank north of Jerusalem, the Hebron area (south of Jerusalem), and Gaza. While the Jerusalem area has its own musical life, in which local musicians such as Jamal, Walid, and Ghidian have figured centrally, it also draws musicians such as Omar al-Keinani, Bassam Bishara, and Taiseer Elias from the Galilee because of the Hebrew University and the Jerusalem Academy of Music and Dance. Musicians also used to circulate in and out of the West Bank and Gaza before Israeli military closures in response to suicide bombers made that difficult or impossible. When Jamal began to work as a professional musician in the late 1970s, he would travel from Jerusalem to play at the belly dance clubs in Gaza. This type of establishment is not common, if it exists at all, in other Palestinian areas. Years later, Jamal brought this knowledge of belly dance to his work with Arabeska, a Jerusalem-based troupe of Jewish belly dancers who have transferred the genre into a radically different social framework.

Musicians further categorize their audiences according to ties to the music of particular Arab countries. Residents of the Galilee, for instance, are generally assumed to have a greater affinity for Lebanese than for Egyptian or Jordanian culture due to their geographic proximity. This is connected not only to historic family ties and the greater availability of Lebanese radio and TV, but also to an assumed inborn nature. George Sama'an, who lives very near the Lebanese border, told me that he loves Lebanese music more than Syrian and feels less connection to Egypt. To describe its foreignness, he said that when he visited Egypt he felt that he was in Africa.[42] Taiseer noted that before the Lebanese civil war broke out in 1975, Lebanon was the primary influence for musicians in the Galilee and only the most prominent Egyptian musicians were known.[43] When the war adversely affected Lebanese musical life, Cairo rose in influence.

With all these potential affiliations to neighboring Arab countries and the resulting taste communities, what has struck me repeatedly is the peripheral position of these musicians within the Arab world. They are located as close to the center as anyone, yet constrained by travel restrictions imposed by Israeli and Arab governments, and marginalized politically and culturally, in contrast to the penetration of "Oriental" Israeli popular music (*musika mizrahit*) into Arab markets from the late 1980s onward.[44]

41. George Sama'an (Jan. 1, 1999) was referring to two militant Palestinian organizations: Nayef Hawatmeh is the leader of the Democratic Front for the Liberation of Palestine, a rival of Fatah organization.
42. Jan. 1, 1999. Geographically this is correct, but "African" indicates completely foreign music.
43. June 21, 1991.
44. See chapter 3, and Swedenburg 2000.

Other axes of difference important in defining the geocultural makeup of Palestinian musical life include the contrast between rural and urbanized areas noted above. The latter term indicates not only urban areas but also villages that are usually more or less absorbed into the life of urban areas due to their proximity to cities. Ghidian al-Qaimari's village of Abu Dis is one such area. The village/urban contrast manifests musically in differences of instrumentation and in the maintenance of a repertoire of traditional songs and dances in villages in contrast to the rapid turnover of popular music in urbanized areas. Another division of great practical importance is citizenship, which is directly tied to individual circumstances of birth and residence. The situations, opportunities, and restrictions of Israeli Arab citizens, Arab residents of Jerusalem, and those in the West Bank and Gaza all differ radically from one another as I will discuss below.

Career Trajectories

How does an aspiring musician make his way in the world that I have just described? And how has that career trajectory changed over the past generation? Although they came from differing socioeconomic backgrounds in terms of geography, religion, and level of education, among other things, the musicians introduced here have much in common. They all started by playing for weddings and other celebrations. A good portion of their training was autodidactic, attaining basic competence through contact with music and musicians without the benefit of formal instruction. At most they had a few lessons from older musicians, often relatives.

Taiseer's early experience is not atypical, although his professional career has been highly exceptional. His older brother had "seven lessons" from someone in Acre (a town north of Haifa that has a mixed Arab and Jewish population) and he later gave Taiseer "seven lessons." Taiseer started performing at age 12, learning much of the practical knowledge that he needed on the job. He then turned to Haifa, the nearest city, to a Jewish teacher of Western violin for technique. He feels that he started Western classical violin too late to master the amount of repertoire expected of a professional soloist in that type of music. But he applied that knowledge to the performance of Arab music, not only to his violin playing, but to the 'ud as well.[45] The mixture of osmosis and guidance through the family network extended to the next generation when Taiseer taught his brother's son Western violin. He said that he did not teach him Arab violin because he "gets that on his own."

Nassim Dakwar, who played 'ud in the Jerusalem Music Center concert mentioned at the beginning of this chapter, also comes from an Arab town in the Galilee and followed a very similar path. Like Taiseer, he sought technical instruction in Western art music to formalize his musical

---

45. June 22, 1991.

knowledge and augment his largely informal education in Arab music. In the absence of a school for Arab music, both Taiseer and Nassim progressed from private teachers to studying Western music at an academy. As Israeli citizens, educated in Israeli schools (primarily in Arabic), they gained high school diplomas and were able to enter the Rubin Academy (now the Jerusalem Academy of Music and Dance) where, in addition to technical knowledge, they absorbed teaching methodology and distinctly European sociocultural attitudes and expectations concerning music.[46] These included ideas about music's relative autonomy, the dignified presentation of high art in acoustically optimal concert halls that require no electronic amplification (as opposed to the over-amplified *haflat* of the Arab sector that take place in various settings not ideal for music while people eat, talk, and dance), the elevation of talented, highly trained instrumentalists to equal status with singers (who reign supreme in the world of Arab music), and a repertoire-centered approach to music, one that values the work and its composer at least as highly as it does the performer. Taiseer Elias continued on to graduate studies in ethnomusicology at the Hebrew University where he was taking classes at the time of the performances described at the beginning of this chapter.[47] Both Taiseer and Nassim progressed in their playing and gradually found more satisfying opportunities than *haflat*. The next stages of their careers will be discussed in depth in later chapters.

Bassam Bishara, from northern Israel's Galilee like Taiseer and Nassim, had studied at the Hebrew University's musicology department a decade before Taiseer. He pursued the path of popular music in the Arab market and when I last saw him in 1988 he had just returned from recording studios in London where he had produced a cassette of original compositions on which he played all the instruments except *nay*. He hoped to distribute this to radio stations in Arab countries and had gone abroad to record not only to circumvent the Arab boycott on goods produced in Israel but also to avail himself of the best technology. He complained to me about the difficulty of finding musicians to participate in serious concerts and the lack of suitable venues for such concerts. Shortly thereafter, this multifaceted musician moved to the U.S. and dropped out of the musical world that is the concern of this book.[48]

In many of his performances, including the concert at the Hakawati, which opened this chapter, Bishara was accompanied by Jamal Sa'id and

46. Racy points to their contemporary, Simon Shaheen, as an example of the increasingly common bimusicality of Arab musicians trained in both Arab and European music (2003: 30). Note that Arab conservatories such as those in Cairo and Beirut have "Eastern" and "Western" music programs side by side.

47. He was my student in ethnomusicology seminars and in Javanese gamelan.

48. His friends and former musical companions in Jerusalem would hear from him occasionally when he returned home for a visit, but I was unable to get his perspective on the musical developments that took place in Israel after his departure or ascertain whether he left for political or economic reasons.

Walid 'Id'is, who supported his singing not only with their energetic drumming but also as a male chorus responding to his solo verses and undergirding his vocal improvisations. These two played together in other bands as well, performing at weddings and clubs or cafes, some of them at the very bottom of the social rung. Jamal had left school after seventh grade, while Walid had gone further with his education, taking the initiative to attend an intensive Hebrew language program so that he could get jobs in hotels or other parts of the tourist industry. With their relative lack of education and their "in-between" citizenship—residents of East Jerusalem who enjoyed some of the rights of Israeli citizens, but were schooled in and subject to Jordanian-controlled institutions—they were unable to follow the paths taken by Taiseer, Nassim, and Bassam.

Jamal had a few lessons from an older musician whom he regarded very highly, but picked up most of his knowledge on his own. Despite his lack of formal education, Jamal became a widely recognized figure in the Arab community and beyond, due to his frequent appearances in the theater and on television, usually as a slapstick clown. This led to appearances at weddings, where he could make far more money as a comedian than as a musician. He has told me on various occasions that he considers himself an actor by profession whose musical skills that bring in money "just came to him."

Jamal and Walid were a pair until a heart attack left Walid completely incapacitated. Walid was clearly subordinate to Jamal, the straight man for his jokes and the one who played the basic drum patterns on which Jamal elaborated. Usually there is a clear status and age hierarchy in such pairs. Taiseer noted that each *darbukkah* player takes a younger musician under his wing to play frame drum, the two then form a unit within the ensemble and if the main drummer leaves the band his frame drummer goes with him.[49] But Walid and Jamal were close in age and best friends.

One thing that has changed since these musicians were teenagers, first learning their craft, is the makeup of bands. Whereas they were inducted into bands with older musicians who trained them, either directly or indirectly, Taiseer has pointed to "kid bands" as a phenomenon that began in the 1990s. Teenagers began to form their own bands, learn the current songs from a friend or recording, and start to perform within a few months[50] (a pattern common to the sociomusical networks of rock and pop bands around the world). This has supplanted intergenerational transmission of musical knowledge. Mitigating this is the increase in opportunities for formal instruction in Arab music during the same period.

With the exception of Bassam Bishara and Walid 'Id'is, these musicians have gone on to teach in institutions that did not exist when they began their careers. Taiseer Elias is the founding director of the program in Arab music (titled the Department for Oriental Music) at the Jerusalem Academy of Music and Dance where both he and Nassim Dakwar teach Arab and

49. June 23, 1991.
50. June 21, 1991.

Jewish students.[51] Students focus on 'ud, violin, and *maqam* theory and take courses in Western music already offered by the Academy. When he started the program, Taiseer faced the challenge of finding qualified teachers since there was no tradition of formal pedagogy in Arab music in Israel and the Palestinian Territories. He also had to accommodate the disparate levels of experience of Arab and Jewish students, the former often coming to the program with years of performance behind them and a lifetime of listening, while the latter are often devoting their attention to this music for the first time.

Jamal Sa'id took a teaching position in a rival program, The Center for Classical Oriental Music and Dance. Founded at almost the same time as the Jerusalem Academy's program this institution had the support of Yehoram Gaon, a major Jewish star of Israeli popular music in the 1960s and 1970s, and was one manifestation of the rising power of Israeli Jews from Arab countries.[52] The school has three goals: "to preserve Oriental cultural traditions; to foster cultural pluralism in Israel; to create a bridge for peace with the Arab world."[53] With a varied staff that draws on recent Jewish immigrants from the Central Asian republics as well as local Jews and Arabs, this program has offered instruction in a number of instruments and styles. Jamal taught Arab drumming there for several years, mainly to Jewish students, until health problems forced him to stop.

Several other programs of instruction began during the late 1990s, including the school for Arab classical music in East Jerusalem run by Palestinian protest singer and instrumentalist Mustafa Kurd. Several of the younger Arab musicians whom Jamal later brought into Alei Hazayit studied there. But autodidactic learning is still prevalent and musicians' knowledge is still shaped by lack of widespread formal training.[54]

A. J. Racy has proposed that a general model can serve to describe the education of most musicians in the Arab world (2003: 18–31). This model includes five stages:

1. talent appears, usually in childhood;
2. musical obsession, accompanied by struggle against family and cultural barriers;
3. family and societal recognition of budding talent;
4. training of some sort; and
5. the undertaking of a performance career.

51. This program began in fall 1996 (Taiseer Elias, June 1998) and is far more professional in its approach than an older program at an Arab teachers college.

52. See chapter 3.

53. Filing by the Kagan Educational Foundation on the Web site "Giving Wisely: The Internet Directory of Israeli Nonprofit and Philanthropic Organizations" www.givingWisely.org.il/cgi-bin/xGWexpandKF.pl?language=E&amuta =103. Accessed Feb. 21, 2003.

54. Taiseer Elias, June 1998.

While the model does not fully conform to the biographies I elicited, each musician mentioned several of these stages. Jamal was discouraged in his musical pursuits by his father, an underwear peddler, and discouraged his eldest son, Raed, when he began to play drum on his own. When Raed was twelve, Jamal reported to me that he kept "stealing" Jamal's drum to go practice. But after Raed had proven himself, Jamal took great pride in his accomplishments, bragging that Raed's technique was better than his own. As far as I could ascertain there was no direct instruction, but the availability of drums and the aural model of Jamal's drumming were catalysts for Raed, who worked on his own and with friends to achieve a high level of technique.

The musical education of George Sama'an, who is a bit older than most of the musicians mentioned thus far, most closely parallels Racy's model. At age eleven, George found a violin in a closet, hidden from him so he wouldn't play. It had a broken bow, which he fixed with pipe, and plastic strings that he wetted with water, not knowing any better. After learning the tune from a radio program that broadcast greetings and song requests, he showed what he had learned to Elias Jubran, a prominent musician in his Galilee town, Rame.[55] Jubran agreed to teach him, but when George's family found out he was beaten. Jubran took him in his car to his family and said "this boy's a musician, not a doctor or lawyer. I've got an extra room, I'll teach him." When he heard George sing, Jubran said he had to learn 'ud so that he could accompany himself. To earn money to buy an 'ud, George picked and pressed olives from his family's trees for a month. Later, he went to the conservatory in Haifa and studied European classical violin from Kagan, the same teacher who taught Taiseer Elias and Nassim Dakwar. He reported that he spent six months just working on holding the instrument and bow.

The contrasting experiences of a father and son will round out this brief survey. Ahmed Abu Ghannam, who played in my 1991 recording session, was born to a fairly well-to-do Jerusalem family, and was sent to Cairo in 1944 by his father to study Islam at Al Azhar University, the premier institution there. However, Abu Ghannam told me that he was attracted by music instead and spent four years learning to play in Cairo. He later taught in various schools in the Jerusalem area and exerted considerable influence on other musicians, including Jamal, who started his career as a drummer in his band. Years later, Jamal called on Abu Ghannam's son Fu'ad to play in Alei Hazayit. Fu'ad did not need to go abroad to Cairo, but was able to study at Mustafa Kurd's school in East Jerusalem. He gained a more orderly, formalized music education than his father, evident both in his 'ud playing and his knowledge of Arab music theory.

In addition to the increase in educational opportunities, the possibilities for performance became more numerous in the 1990s. Taiseer Elias summed these up:

55. This is the father of Khaled and Kamilya Jubran mentioned in chapter 1.

In reality there are better opportunities today than when I started, for instance. You remember when I studied at the university [in the 1980s]. Then I really didn't have opportunities. Today it is much, much easier because the model has been created and you can follow it. There are more opportunities. There is more awareness and openness to this from the Jewish society, more media. It's easier to arrive [i.e., make it]. For instance, I get a lot of invitations today. But because I'm busy with this job I refer a lot to Michael, to Husam Hayik, to others so they too have become known in Jewish society. It rolls on . . . Also today there are many pirate stations and that gives more opportunities to musicians to play, to be interviewed, to express themselves. There is TV, channel 2, cable . . . Once, if you invited a musician to play on TV he would dream about it for a week. Now it doesn't interest him. Because if you don't [invite him] then he has ten others who will. (June 28, 1998)

And yet, there is still considerable frustration because the Arab community gives only occasional support to the music that these musicians value most and the Jewish sector does not provide sufficient ongoing frameworks for musicians to maintain a professional career playing only Arab art music.[56] In response to my question about the Arab community Taiseer continued:

There are concerts every now and then. Let's take the Tarshiha ensemble [founded and directed by Nassim Dakwar]. It plays a concert once every year or two. They fill a hall with six hundred people with a lot of public relations and they drag people from their village in five buses. But if they wanted to do it once every six months or every two . . .

BB: They wouldn't have an audience?

Taiseer: No. It's a seasonal thing. Every group's like that. Now and then, community centers,[57] other centers invite groups. There's the Arab Culture Month for instance—it started as a week and then developed into a month. There they organize all kinds of performances of music and theater in community centers in various Arab villages. They invite bands. There aren't concert halls or productions like in the Jewish sector. You get invited by someone who is organizing something so it's not a dedicated audience coming [especially to hear you or the music] . . . The situation is not brilliant, but by comparison to the 80s, for instance, or the early 90s, that period when we lived here in Jerusalem—I hardly had any opportunities. I'm really proud of that. I paved a long, difficult road. Today they enjoy that and it's a lot easier for them. It's a positive thing.

56. See Ben Ze'ev 2004 for a recent expression of this frustration.
57. A *matnas* is a "Center for Culture, Youth and Sport" found in most communities in Israel.

Like Nassim, Taiseer also founded an orchestra devoted to Arab art music but it did not last long, for lack of funding. Nassim's performs only on an occasional basis, as Taiseer noted, and consists mainly of amateurs. Nonetheless, they have used these ensembles to raise consciousness in the Arab community and beyond. Nassim's ensemble performed three years in a row in Cairo at a major annual festival. Taiseer's ensemble, in particular, has served as a stepping stone for younger musicians, a place to gather, become known to more experienced musicians, and enter a network that facilitates careers, as Taiseer noted above when he talked about referring gigs to Michael and Husam, his former students (and participants in the Shefa'amr rehearsal described earlier).

Taiseer and a few others also benefited from exposure to the academic community. The key figure here is music professor Dalia Cohen,[58] who was the driving force behind the establishment of the Workshop for Non-Western Music (in which Taiseer and Jamal first taught Jewish students Arab music) and the Department of Oriental Music at the Academy. By bringing in Taiseer, Nassim, Jamal, and a few other musicians to perform at university functions, Cohen gave these musicians and their music greater exposure to an elite audience.

A strikingly different career path, not taken by any of the musicians discussed thus far is the explicitly political route. Musicians most often mentioned Kamilya Jubran to me in connection with this path. Daughter of Elias Jubran, the prominent musician, instrument builder, and teacher who adopted George Sama'an, she was the vocalist and an instrumentalist in Sabreen, a politically oriented Palestinian band active in the area of Jerusalem and Ramallah from 1980.[59] Most musicians who mentioned Kamilya Jubran praised her singing but disparaged the music that she chose to perform. George, for instance, was opposed to topical protest songs as too connected to a particular time and place and therefore not artistic.[60] He also criticized Amal Murkus, the other female Palestinian singer prominent in Israel in the 1990s, who mixes explicit statements about the plight of the Palestinian people with less overtly political music. By collaborating with some of the bigger names in Israeli rock (see chapter 8), she achieved greater exposure than Kamilya Jubran.

With the exception of these two prominent women, the field of publicly performed Palestinian Arab music has been a man's world.[61] Despite the prominence in the Arab world of stars like Umm Kulthum, Fairuz, Warda,

58. See chapter 8.
59. See www.kamilyajubran.com/life81.html for Kamilya's account of the history of this group and of her own career.
60. July, 1999. He has strong beliefs regarding spirituality and the powers and proper uses of music. He was not opposed to protest songs of a more universal nature and taught me one that is a veiled protest against class differences in Arab society.
61. This has changed in recent years with the arrival of Lubna Salame and a few other singers. The repertoire of songs performed by and for women in the house, at celebrations, is not a commercial, public music.

and Laila Murad (all singers), there are still very few professional female musicians in Israel and the Occupied Territories. Musicians whom I asked about this cited a strong social stigma in local Arab society. Despite the increasing modernization and liberation of many Palestinian women, they claimed that no respectable family would want their daughter, sister, wife, or mother staying out all night and traveling with a male band to perform in front of a crowd of men. It is perhaps not coincidental that the first two women to have the strength and determination to fight this perception turned to political songs.

Political songs that were repressed by Israeli authorities before the first *intifada* had become extremely popular by the end of the *intifada*. In late 1992, Jamal reported that they were being sung at all the *haflat*, after everyone learned them from broadcasts by Syrian radio stations aimed at the Occupied Territories. He said that the authorities' attitude seemed to be that as long as the Palestinians didn't throw stones, they could sing what they want all night long. But he critiqued the songs from a musical standpoint, characterizing them as melodically simple, with most melodies "stolen" from existing songs. In his opinion, they were not nearly as well put together as the songs by Marcel Khalife that he and his friends had performed at the Hakawati on the eve of the *intifada*.[62]

A subtler, but no less political, use of music by Palestinian nationalists is the presentation of Palestinian folk music and dance. Village traditions become a resource for the legitimation of the Palestinian nation. Recent efforts to document these traditions are motivated by a need to distinguish Palestinian culture from that of neighboring countries, some of which—Lebanon in particular—have very similar traditions.[63] This overlap is evident in a CD of *'ud* and voice recorded by Ghidian al-Qaimari (who asked me for a tape so he could reproduce "authentic Palestinian folklore") on one of his trips to Germany. Titled *Sounds of the Orient*, it contains nine tracks, eight of which are classified as "folklore;" of those, two are marked as Palestinian, the others being attributed to the larger geopolitical area of *bilad al-sham* that includes Syria, Palestine/Israel, Lebanon, and parts of Jordan. Such actions bear out Sant Cassia's observation that tradition "needs to be identified, packaged, and made the subject of discretion and taste" and his further observation that such packaged tradition "has acquired a special role in migrant communities as a means to manufacture an imagined utopian community through 'the retention of tradition as identity'" (2000: 291). The appropriation of Palestinian folk songs by Israeli Jewish musicians such as Shlomo Bar, Yair Dalal, and Eyal Sela,[64] is evidence that these efforts to claim Palestinian folk music as a political tool have only partially succeeded.

62. Sept. 22, 1992.
63. See, for instance, *Traditional Music and Songs from Palestine* (Shammout and Boss 1997), which has been reviewed by Issa Boulos (2002), and *Zaghareed* released by el-Funoun.
64. All three perform "'Ala Dal'una," for instance.

This is not a complete picture of Palestinian musical life. For the sake of narrative simplicity I have focused on Arab music performed primarily for Arabs by Arabs and saved an account of the growing number of interactions between Arab and Jewish musicians for later chapters. It is important to keep in mind that all of this is happening within Israel or in areas under its control. In the next chapter, I outline some primary characteristics of other types of musical life in Israel before returning to these Arab musicians and their music for a comparison.

3

Israeli Musical Life

The courtyard of the Hebrew Union College in West Jerusalem fills with a mix of Israeli adults and rowdy Colorado teenagers on a summer trip to Israel. Rows of plastic armchairs face a temporary stage flanked by speaker towers and banks of colored stage lights. Shortly after 10:00 P.M. the band finally mounts the stage, one of the youngest musicians supporting the oldest, Samson Khamkar.[1] Shlomo Bar, the leader of Habreira Hativ'it, enters last and sits on a high stool in front of and higher than the arc of musicians on chairs. He holds a *darbukkah* between his knees, rather than resting it on his thigh, and plays it like a conga. Two young, Israeli-born musicians play acoustic guitar and a truncated, amplified double bass. A young Indian man plays various drums, a Persian plays *santur* (hammered dulcimer), and Khamkar, also from India, plays violin. I wait in vain for him to pick up the *sitar* that he used to play.

Bar tells the audience in Hebrew how happy he is to perform in Jerusalem. He is always excited to perform in this place toward which the Jewish people have turned for such a long time. "There is lots of dew in Jerusalem. They say that dew is Torah so there is lots of Torah." He then declaims the first song's title. After vocalizing in unison with the melodic instruments, he begins to sing original lyrics, a mystic prayer that asks to be able to love "in the language of rising pitches," the language of the elements.[2] Bar raises his arms high for dramatic drum strokes that cue frequent lighting changes. There are exciting musical moments in the song, sudden tempo changes in the driving 6/8 meter, a *santur* solo, and shifts in rhythmic emphasis. Bar sings without restraint, drumming all the while. As they do at many points during the evening, the audience members clap along, but are often thrown off by rhythmic complexities. At one point, Bar

1. His last name is transliterated in various ways on the band's albums.
2. This is my translation and paraphrase of "Erom veerya anochi" (stark naked am I).

interacts with the audience, engaging them in a call and response vocal exchange that gradually expands a small melodic kernel into a song.

When Bar calls out "Shedemati" audience members who know this old Israeli song applaud. Over a soft, rhythmically indeterminate accompaniment, Bar begins to play an end-blown plastic flute answered by Khamkar on pennywhistle. Then Bar picks up a drum and dances with his upper body. Many rise to dance in the aisles. He begins to sing in Arabic, a few lines from "Balla Tsoubou Hal Kahwa," a song about Bedouin honoring guests with coffee, then switches to "'Ala Dal'una," the Palestinian/Bedouin song perhaps most familiar to Israeli Jews.[3] Later he slows the tempo, Khamkar switches to violin, and they finally begin "Shedemati." This pastoral song was written in poetic language[4] in the early twentieth century when most Zionist immigrants were farmers and the first modern Hebrew songs celebrated this return to the land. Bar makes a powerful statement by linking such songs in a medley, combining the symbolism of the land and two ancient peoples long associated with it: Jews and Bedouin Arabs.

Bar turns to socio-political critique, calling for national unity when he introduces a song about the chaos of time before time. He recites, "On the waters, the first wind blows" evoking the opening lines of Genesis, then, "Let there be light" as the stage lights go up. The ensuing musical depiction of chaos features strongly contrasting moods and outbursts connected to the light show.

Bar is not yet through with his philosophical teachings. He announces "Libbi," which he wrote after visiting Morocco, the land of his birth, in 1995. Its pentatonic is a "scale of innocence" (*sulam shel tmimut*) that "all kids sing." Here he returns to that stage of innocence and sings in vocables that are a pre-language (*kdam safa*), using the sounds of Moroccan Arabic, which are, indeed, the sounds of his earliest memories.

Honoring an audience request, Bar begins "Shir Lashalom" (Song of Peace), an early hit for this band. Inspired by Anglo-American rock and the musical *Hair*, in particular, it was composed in 1969 (music by Yair Rosenblum and lyrics by Yitzhak Rothblit) and first performed and recorded by an army entertainment troupe.[5] Popular in various renditions, the song carries layers of meaning for most Israelis and was indelibly impressed on public memory when Yitzhak Rabin was assassinated just after singing it at a mass rally in Tel Aviv in 1995. The Left has adopted it to evoke the memory of Rabin as peacemaker and when the Israeli Postal Service issued a commemorative stamp, the lyrics of the chorus were printed on the first-day cover in Hebrew, Arabic, and English.

Bar follows the end of each chorus ("sing a song of peace with a great shout") by shouting "aywa" (yes) in Arabic, a simple yet powerful linguistic choice to underline the message of the song. Continuing the peace theme,

3. See chapter 2. Jamal Sa'id's band Alei Hazayit performed "Balla Tsoubou Hal Kahwa," too; see chapter 9.
4. Yedidya Admon set Yitzhak Shenhar's lyrics to music.
5. Nachal Troupe [1970?]. Regev and Seroussi recount the controversy the song engendered within the army and the cultural establishment (2004: 106–07).

he announces that the final song is "from the Golden Age," the medieval period of Muslim rule in Spain when Muslims, Jews, and Christians are said to have lived in harmony. Audience members who recognize the reference to one of the band's biggest hits shout "Dror Yikra," an arrangement of a traditional Yemenite setting of a poem written by the tenth-century Jewish poet Dunash Ben Labrat. This hymn about freedom is shared by Jewish communities everywhere, but sung to various melodies. Bar uses a Yemenite tune that is widely known, giving it a new twist by opening with a slow, but wild, vocalization. Khamkar stands for his solo, sawing wildly with his bow. To enthusiastic audience response he plays rapid triple subdivisions, then quadruple ones, following an Indian practice of successively smaller subdivisions of the beat. Menashe Sasson plays a slow *santur* melody over the drums. Shlomo Bar improvises a vocal solo before building to a rhythmic climax with the other drummer that leads back to a final rendition of the song. The ecstatic crowd will not let them leave. Bar holds up a finger, says "last one" in Hebrew, then turns to the American kids in the audience and says in English, "Remember the smiles here, maybe you'll come back because this is your land, this isn't Colorado."

Bar conveyed many messages about Israel and music in this concert. With his opening words, he set a tone of ethnic and religious pride as well as spirituality. He is not orthodox in the usual sense of the word, but there is a sizeable religious component in his work, including Hassidic songs.[6] There is also a Zionist angle, most explicit in his words to the American youth at the end of his concert, but also evident in his choice of material. After the performance he lectured me at length on ideas from Jewish mysticism, relating them to rhythm and pitch. According to his bassist, Naor Carmi, Bar often spoke about such matters with band members.[7] Bar told me that he believes that music can be used for good or for evil and characterized himself as one who can help others to approach the truth, not by teaching but by showing the way.[8]

Early in his career Bar made his mark in the sociopolitical sphere with songs celebrating Jewish life in Morocco, a theme that had been conspicuously absent from public culture in Israel, despite the fact that Moroccans and their descendants made up the single largest Jewish group after those of Polish descent. His songs expressed ethnic pride congruent with the campaign for recognition and representation headed by the Israeli Black Panthers, a movement that drew inspiration from the American Black Panthers as it fought discrimination against Jews of North African and Middle Eastern origin. More recently, he has turned to fighting for original Israeli/ Jewish music, as he calls it, and against Western mass-mediated culture and the Israeli media establishment. "We need to have our own music, not this TV trash," he said to me. Many of the musicians under consideration

6. He has recorded a song by Rabbi Shlomo Carlebach whose Jewish spirit he told me he admires (June 24, 1998).
7. June 29, 1998.
8. June 24, 1998.

in this book would agree with these sentiments, if not with all of Bar's statements or musical choices. Nearly all are aware of his pioneering work.

When Shlomo Bar and Habreira Hativ'it broke into Israeli musical life in the mid-1970s, no specific market or niche awaited their music. Over the next decade and more the band gained recognition and some popularity but was not successfully followed by other like-minded musicians. Conditions were not yet right in terms of attitudes toward Middle Eastern music or the availability and interest of musicians. In the late 1980s, other musicians, including two founding members of Habreira Hativ'it who formed other ensembles, began to work in a similar vein and by the 1990s enough people were participating to constitute the scene that is the subject of this book.[9] While I do not intend to crown Bar and his band as the sole progenitors of a new musical style, it is widely acknowledged that they pioneered a path and served as an inspiration to others. They demonstrated possibilities for presenting a mix of "East" and "West" (highly problematic but widely invoked categories, see chapter 9) with solo instrumental improvisations, catchy melodies, and driving rhythms, that was not packaged in the pop song formats then common in Israel, the compositions of contemporary Israeli art music, or the various types of Middle Eastern music consumed by Palestinians and Mizrahi Jews.

This chapter surveys musical life in Israel in the late twentieth century to highlight Jewish musicians' motivations to explore new directions that incorporated elements of Middle Eastern music, often in collaboration with Arab musicians. Thus, it complements the previous chapter's depiction of the changing conditions of music making among Palestinians that caused dissatisfaction among musicians and led some to explore other options. I begin with the main divisions that characterize Israeli society and musical practices, then discuss connections to the outside world and earlier musical interactions between Jews and Arabs, concluding with a comparison of the conditions of Jewish and Arab musicians within Israel and the Palestinian territories around 1990.

Social and Musical Differences

Deep sociocultural, religious, and political rifts divide Israeli society.[10] A struggle over legitimacy and power between those of European and those of North African and Middle Eastern descent is waged in various cultural fields. Another deep divide separates the orthodox religious from the secular. A third splits the nation along political lines between the Left, who seek compromise and coexistence with the Arabs, and the Right, who do not see such accommodation as a realistic possibility, preferring a strong

9. The formation of this scene is the subject of chapter 8.
10. In a compact mosaic of music clips and interviews, the documentary *Israel Rocks!* (Abrahami and Netz 2000) represents these divisions and some of the ways that musicians express them.

Israel that dictates relations with Arabs. None of these divisions is a strict dichotomy: There are many who either do not care about the culture wars or seek a middle ground; large numbers of traditionally observant Jews find that neither the ultraorthodox nor the militantly secular speak for them, and the majority of Israelis appear to occupy political middle ground. I have simplified the nature of the arguments, particularly regarding political divisions,[11] but not the fact of deep, irreconcilable differences between those at the extremes, who often wield disproportionate power.

Israelis may take diametrically opposed views as to how to solve a given problem, but at times of crisis a deep-seated feeling of national unity often emerges. National solidarity also finds expression in the shared rejection of external criticism of Israeli policies, whether it be from Europeans such as the French (viewed, with some justification, as inherently anti-Semitic) or American Jews, who are thought to have forfeited the right to criticize because they choose to live in the comfort of the materialistic U.S. rather than make personal sacrifices to realize national goals in Israel. National solidarity manifests in the world of online music where some Israelis will pass up the opportunity to download files of Israeli bands from file sharing services like Kazaa while freely participating in the pirating of other music.[12] Even as morality fails, a sense of nationalism prevails. As in every other facet of Israeli life, different views exist regarding solidarity: some see it as a constant while others see the spirit of national unity seriously eroding over time. Supporting the latter view is the rise in the number of young Israelis seeking to evade military service either through conscientious objection or through psychiatric disqualification.

In words and song, Bar attempts to bridge these divides. He offers a Jewish spirituality rather than orthodoxy dictating how one lives. He preaches for unity and attempts to create a new Jewish Israeli music culture that will belong to the people, connect them with their heritage, and express their reality as a renewed nation. His wide-ranging tastes are noteworthy in this regard. Putting together elements from Moroccan, Ashkenazi, Israeli, and Bedouin musical traditions in one program, sometimes in one piece, he strives for inclusion, and is able to do so thanks to the multiple musical competences of his musicians, which are among the original band's most striking assets. Bar, who came from Morocco as a child in the 1950s and became involved in Afro-Cuban drumming as a young man, joined forces in 1977 with Samson Khamkar, a mature musician with thirty years' professional experience in India, newly immigrated to Israel; Miguel Herstein, an American-born musician fluent in flamenco guitar and various American banjo and guitar styles; and an Israeli-born double bass player, Yisrael Borochov. Despite numerous personnel changes over the years, such variety has remained.

11. I omit, for instance, the division between capitalists and the adherents of the socialist labor ethos that once dominated Israeli life.
12. I owe this information to my son Omri Brinner.

Similar attempts at musical inclusiveness have increased in frequency in a growing variety of venues in recent years. Some musicians devote their careers to such efforts, while others dabble. The musicians who are the subject of this book are deeply committed to musical dialogue across sociocultural divides. They address the rift between Jews and Arabs that is largely untouched by Shlomo Bar. While he professes and appears to practice an encompassing attitude toward Jews and the music they bring from their respective diasporic homes, Arabs and Arab music are largely absent from his music, the appropriation of a Bedouin song or two notwithstanding.

Deriving from the complex demographics of Israel and feeding back into it is an equally complex array of musicians, musical styles, institutions, and taste communities. One could say that it is like the situation in many other countries in the postcolonial, globalized, and extensively transnational world, only more so. The complexity is heightened by Israel's relatively short history and by the enormous influx of immigrants from many other parts of the world layered on top of a long history of conquest by foreign powers. Mapping the cultural terrain is a daunting prospect and must be less comprehensive than the previous chapter's sketch of Arab musical life. In the previous chapter I endeavored to give a sense of Arab musical life in Israel and the territories under its control. Here I shall note only those aspects of musical life in the Jewish state that are necessary background to the coming chapters. Others have published far more comprehensive studies.[13]

As in many post-colonies, Israeli law and government institutions bear the traces of past colonial regimes. The Ottoman Turkish empire and, to a greater extent, the British Mandate governments left behind far more than mere traces. This is evident in the hodgepodge of laws, offices, and buildings in which power resides, where older elements coexist with newer ones imported from Jewish religious law, Euro-American liberalism, socialism, and so on. The educational system and the cultural apparatus, too, bear the marks of external formative influences.

Israel's cultural map includes diverse musical fields that cluster around different centers. Distinctions are commonly made according to the perceived "seriousness" or popular orientation of the composers and performers, musicians' innovativeness or adherence to tradition, and the religious and or ethnic affiliation of the performers and audience. For our purposes this diversity is important in terms of musicians' and audiences' backgrounds (both their habitus and dispositions, to use Bourdieu's terms) and as a set of competing and intersecting fields of cultural production in relation to which musicians position themselves and their product. The musi-

13. In addition to Regev and Seroussi 2004, see Seroussi 2002a and Hirshberg 2002 for overviews and see Hirshberg 1995 for a detailed history. Erik Cohen and Amnon Shiloah categorized aspects of the musical life of Jewish immigrants from the Middle East (Shiloah and Cohen 1983; Cohen and Shiloah 1985).

cians under discussion here have emerged from various musical fields, bringing with them the experiences, standards of evaluation, and other expectations gained there. To be heard they seek to create new niches in the market or to fit into existing ones. The most prominent types of music have been Israeli folk song, Western art music, and popular music, both foreign and Israeli (recognizing that folk, art, and popular are problematic terms, open to multiple interpretations).

The dominant type of music for Jews from the days of Zionist settlement in Palestine through the first two decades of Israel's statehood was a large repertoire of songs generally known today as *shirei erets yisrael* (songs of the land of Israel).[14] Composed mainly from the 1920s through the 1950s, this invented tradition of folk songs known to all was performed at group sing-alongs in farming collectives, on school outings, in community centers, and other gatherings. The songs covered a range of subject matter but tended to express a connection to the land and to a pastoral life. Some songs were about specific places, others told tales of heroism or loss. "Shedemati," which Bar sang, exemplifies early attempts by European-born musicians to create an "Oriental" style reflective of their new surroundings. These songs were a powerful tool in the building of political movements and national solidarity, effects that were reinforced by the social nature of group communal singing in unison. Many songs were also embodied through dance, another "folk tradition" invented on the basis of elements taken from sources as diverse as Eastern European, Yemenite, and Palestinian dances.

Shirei erets yisrael have receded in prominence since the 1960s but are very much a part of the collective national memory and resurface in various guises. The ever-popular Chava Alberstein has been singing them for decades to audiences in Israel and abroad. Group singing enjoys periodic resurgences. Many songs have been reworked over the years, most prominently in a highly successful multialbum series in the 1970s performed in rock-tinged arrangements by Arik Einstein, the star of Israeli popular music. These songs are important for the present discussion both because they were the dominant repertoire against which Middle Eastern Jews reacted and because Alei Hazayit, the subject of the next chapter, arranged some of these songs in an Arab style, a revolutionary gesture at least as transgressive as Einstein's electrified performances two decades earlier.

Western art music is firmly established in Israel, growing rapidly from the early seeds planted by immigrants from Central Europe fleeing the Nazis in the 1930s.[15] Ensembles of all sorts perform in numerous concert series in a wide variety of venues throughout the country. The music is widely available, through numerous concerts and a government radio station that for decades was dedicated solely to this music.[16] The immigration

14. See Regev and Seroussi (2004) for a comprehensive discussion of the history, meaning, and impact of this music.
15. See Bohlmann 1989.
16. Due to budget cuts broadcasts have been cut drastically.

of thousands of highly trained musicians to Israel from the former Soviet Union has glutted the market with teachers and performers. There are chamber ensembles and orchestras everywhere one turns. Many of the best Israeli musicians go from the conservatories or academies of Jerusalem and Tel Aviv to Juilliard and other premier institutions in the West. Israeli musicians tour widely and a few are international stars.

Until the very last years of the twentieth century, the major public performing organizations—symphonies, choirs, presenters, and so on—were relentlessly Eurocentric. The Israeli component in their output was limited to works that stemmed from European art music traditions, sometimes drawing on generic Jewish or Middle Eastern material. But from the 1930s to the present, musicians with training in Western art music have composed a steady trickle of works that include *'ud, darbukkah* or some other emblem of Middle Eastern music.[17]

The consumption of Western art music, whether in concerts or through recordings and broadcasts, is a badge of cultural refinement and elite status, as it is elsewhere. Its appeal, aside from aesthetic pleasure, lies in its trappings and attitudes: the well-appointed concert hall; dignity and respect for the performer, the composer, the work, and the occasion; good careers for the best performers; and significant exposure in the media through broadcast, recordings, and printed reviews. No less important are the well-established schools for training with rigorous, time-tested curricula for developing technical competence. This package of privileges appeals to performers of other types of music, some of whom have benefited from the rigors of classical training but have chosen not to pursue a career in classical music.[18] On the other hand, the formality and fixity of the music and its performance contexts have driven some classically trained musicians to explore new musical options, such as those discussed in this book, in search of greater creative freedom and opportunity for individual expression.

The popular music industry dominates the musical landscape through broadcasts, commercial recordings, and coverage in print media. Popular music styles from many parts of the world have had a huge impact, either directly or mediated through translation into Hebrew by Israeli singers. The influence of reggae, for instance, is satirized in songs by two leading composer/performers. Matti Caspi's "Reggae Ivri" is a masterpiece of playful reference to musical style and of Hebrew wordplay centered on the sound of the word *reggae*.[19] Ehud Banai's "Yiddishe Rastaman" is no less witty, combining stereotypical reggae rhythms and textures with pseudo-

17. See Hirshberg 2002: 1028–31 for examples.
18. This includes figures as diverse as Shem Tov Levy, Taiseer Elias, and Shlomo Gronich.
19. The title "Reggae Ivri" is a pun: literally meaning Hebrew Reggae, it plays on the Hebrew word *rega*, which means instant or moment, hence a Hebrew moment, which plays on the somewhat pompous "Minute of Hebrew" (*rega shel ivrit*), a short program on Israeli radio that instructs listeners on correct Hebrew grammar and usage.

Hassidic vocalizing, while cataloguing the exotic experiences young Israelis seek out in the wide world, usually after their military service. Most popular music is not so ironically self-aware, but it is no less influenced by foreign styles ranging from English and American rock, punk, and hip-hop, to Euro-pop (whether French, Italian, or Greek), and various Latin American musics. Musicians face the public expectation that they will make something specifically Israeli of such influences, as Regev and Seroussi have shown (2004).

Shirei erets yisrael, Western art music, and popular music in Israel have strong links to the establishment and to cultural norms. The government supports not only portions of the classical music world, but also various aspects of popular music, particularly through song festivals. Israel participates in the hotly contested Eurovision contest, for instance, holding a nationally televised Pre-Eurovision contest of Israeli entries and then fielding the winning candidate in the international contest, which is followed by millions throughout Europe. The state also supports music through the military and, in the past, the schools. Music programs in the schools were overwhelmingly oriented toward European art music and its popular offshoots, with school choirs and instruction in recorder playing, shaped according to European aesthetics (Hirshberg 2002). In addition to extensive broadcasting of popular music on Army radio, each branch of the military has entertainment troupes, which attract some of the best young musicians. These troupes serve as a crucial springboard to a professional career after military service, affording not only stage experience, but also a network of connections that dominates the popular music industry.[20] Since most Israeli Arabs do not serve in the military, this avenue of access to the entertainment world is closed to them.

Proponents of other types of music performed and consumed in Israel have had to struggle for recognition alongside *shirei erets yisrael* and Western-oriented mainstream pop and art musics. I will discuss only musical practices most pertinent to the topic of this book: jazz, the type of Israeli popular music most commonly known as *musika mizrahit*, and mainstream Arab music.

Jazz of various sorts, from Dixieland through bebop to avant-garde enjoys relatively high status although it is not as well supported as Western art music. American and European jazz musicians have included Israel on their tours over the years, with Eilat's Red Sea Jazz Festival as the most prominent venue. The local scene has been enriched by immigrants who learned to play in the U.S., Russia, and France and professionalized by the Rimon School for Jazz and Contemporary Music, an offshoot of the Berklee School in Boston.[21] The Jerusalem Academy of Music and Dance has had a jazz department longer than it has had one for Arab music. But

20. This effect may have lessened considerably in recent years, but was very strong for decades, from the 1950s until at least the 1980s.
21. See www.rsojazz.co.il for information about Rimon.

the market for such music remains very small, insufficient for a full professional career.[22] Some Israeli jazz musicians have found success abroad, the most prominent being Avishai Cohen who has played with Chick Corea. Others have added training in jazz to their tool kit while working in other styles. Several musicians have enriched the collaborations that are the subject of this book with the virtuosity and particular approaches to improvisation and interaction they gained from playing jazz.

In the struggle for attention and market share, *musika mizrahit* (literally, Eastern or Oriental music) has been the most successful. Based first on songs from Arab countries, Turkey, Iran, and Greece that were translated into Hebrew or given new Hebrew texts, this grassroots popular music also includes numerous original compositions. Creation of a pan-ethnic audience of "Oriental" Jews was integral to the development of *musika mizrahit* in some of Israel's poorest neighborhoods. Broadcasters and record companies neglected this music until well into the 1980s, ignoring the thriving street market for cheaply produced cassettes, which gave rise to the appellation *musikat kassetot* (cassette music), an early term for *musika mizrahit*.

Terminology has been one of the areas in which supporters of this music have contested its status. Edwin Seroussi's analysis (2002c) is worth quoting in this regard:

> Two major social themes related to *musika mizrahit* are its discrimination by the Israeli media establishment and its aspirations to become a representation of authentic Israeliness, not just of *mizrahi* Israeliness. . . . The new Mediterranean identity of *musika mizrahit* seems to emerge from this feeling of discrimination. One can best understand this transformation from "Oriental" to "Mediterranean" by analyzing the public airing of the "narrative of discrimination" that developed among *mizrahi* composers, performers and producers. For example, discrimination became the theme of a relentless campaign by Avihu Medina, one of the most influential composers of this style (wrote over 400 songs) and one of its performers too.

Medina and others level charges of Eurocentric cultural hegemony and dominance of Ashkenazi Jews against a range of institutions and arenas, including the IBA (Israel Broadcasting Authority), government ministries, and the recording industry. In scholarship, it has become a commonplace to celebrate *musika mizrahit* as an expression of resistance to the cultural elite.[23] The music is taken to be the voice of the people, particularly the

---

22. Gelfond 2004, while not scholarly, is a good account of the obstacles encountered by Israeli jazz musicians.

23. Publications by Jeff Halper, Edwin Seroussi, and Pamela Squires-Kidron (1989), Peter Manuel 1990, and Amy Horowitz (1994, 1999, 2002) develop this point.

majority of Israeli Jews who trace their ancestry to North Africa and the Middle East.

But is this differential in government support simply due to European Jews' attitudes toward "Eastern" Jews? The complexity of the situation is usually ignored in both popular and scholarly discourse. In the 1940s and 1950s, new immigrants from Europe were also under considerable pressure to shed their diasporic identities and reject parts of their culture, whether it was their native Yiddish or the music of Wagner and Strauss. Still, they also found much that was familiar in the dominant culture of Israel and did not face the discrimination that confronted Jews from Arab countries.

The portrayal of Israeli culture and society as dominated by Ashkenazi Jews of European origin is too simplistic. The hegemony of European cultural and social forms is linked to but not the same as Ashkenazi domination. For instance, some Jews of Sephardic or Mizrahi origin are ardent supporters of aspects of European culture, dating back to the days when they or their parents lived in European colonies in North Africa and the Middle East. Likewise, numerous Israelis of European descent do not identify with Europe in cultural matters. Furthermore, the high degree of intermarriage in Israel among Jews of different ethnic groups has produced a substantial portion of the population that is not exclusively Ashkenazi, Sephardi, or Mizrahi by birth, identification, or enculturation. Despite the undeniably strong influence of Euro-American ideas and material goods, contemporary life in Israel is highly mixed both culturally and socially.

Musika mizrahit's academic champions do not question the aesthetic value of this hybrid pop form, which tends to feature sentimental lyrics sung with pathos and relatively simple, but frequent and unvaried ornamentation to an accompaniment that is dominated by synthesizers.[24] The musicians interviewed for this book, many of whom have deep knowledge of Middle Eastern music, detest *musika mizrahit,* viewing it as a low-quality imitation of the finesse and beauty of Middle Eastern music performed by untrained musicians. Their opposition to this music was an important factor in their efforts to create a new kind of music and a niche in the Israeli market that would be seen as distinct from *musika mizrahit.* A second, largely powerless cultural hierarchy is at work here alongside the Eurocentric one that is usually demonized.

Arab mainstream musical practice has been treated somewhat similarly to *musika mizrahit,* encountering establishment indifference or worse. In addition to Palestinian Arabs, there were significant numbers of Jewish performers and listeners in the flood of immigrants that arrived from Arab countries after the founding of the state of Israel. The only substantial institutional support they found for their music was at the Israel Broadcast Authority, which formed an orchestra to broadcast mainstream Arab music, i.e., a repertoire and set of associated performance conventions well known,

24. See Horowitz 2002 for a concise history.

if somewhat varied, from Cairo to Damascus and Baghdad. This orchestra comprised some of the best musicians from Egypt, Lebanon, Syria, and a particularly large contingent from Iraq, where Jewish instrumentalists had dominated the art music world of the radio and the palace.[25] As Cohen and Shiloah have noted, immigrant musicians from Morocco, Algeria, and Tunisia were not admitted because their competence rarely included the mainstream practice that was dominated by Egypt (1985: 207).[26]

Prior to the 1990s, younger Israeli Jews showed little inclination to pursue training in mainstream Arab music. Lack of instruction was doubtless one of the causes and this was linked to negative attitudes toward Arab culture in the Israeli cultural establishment. Jews who had participated as performers and listeners in the musical practices of Muslim countries not only found little support for their music after immigrating to Israel, but they also encountered outright hostility toward cultural expressions associated with the Arab enemy, as well as pressures to assimilate to the new Zionist culture. Thus, Arab music remained foreign or marginal for decades to the interests of many Israeli Jews, particularly those of European ancestry, despite its ready availability on radio and television (including broadcasts from neighboring countries). The title of Regev's article "Present Absentee: Arab Music in Israeli Culture" (1995) summarizes the situation well.

The rise of *musika mizrahit* brought "Easternness" to the fore. Dating the change is difficult because gradual shifts in public opinion and personal tastes were as important as explicit events. While some see this as a new trend around 1990 (Robinson et al. 1991: 68), Perelson has argued that the political shift of 1977—the rise to power of the right-wing Likud party based largely on the votes of non-Ashkenazi Jews whose cultural roots were in the Arab world—"opened the door for Arabic writers, singers and performers, whose cultural and aesthetic norms are similar to those of Oriental Jews" (1998: 127). This was the year that Bar founded Habreira Hativ'it.[27] As Jews of Middle Eastern and North African background have gained ground in Israel's so-called culture war,[28] they have attained certain objectives. The status and availability of both Arab music and *musika mizrahit* have changed dramatically in recent years. It could be argued that *musika mizrahit* is well on its way to becoming one of the dominant sounds in Israeli music. Arab music, which was presented to the Israeli public very sporadically, has also become more widely accepted, with more

25. See Warkov 1986.
26. See Nettl and Shiloah 1978 for a pessimistic, but realistic account of Persian music in Israel and Warkov 1986 for an account of the Iraqi Jewish community.
27. Barry Davis even chose to lead an article about the band with this historic confluence (Davis 1999).
28. As in other areas of Israeli life, social and cultural activists have looked to the U.S. for precedents, adopting terms such as culture war and multiculturalism to describe a situation that only partially resembles that in the U.S.

frequent concerts, including a considerable number in which Jews and Arabs perform side by side, festivals that feature Arab music, and instructional programs such as *Amanut La'am* (Art for the People), which sponsors performances of dance, music, and theater all over Israel, usually in schools and particularly in the smaller communities. During the first *intifada*, for instance, Jamal Sa'id found temporary employment playing for Jewish kindergartens first at the Jerusalem Music Center, then throughout Jerusalem. George Sama'an told me that he and his partner Salem Darwish were well paid by Amanut La'am because they could play for both Jews and Arabs.

As the tenor of the public debate over "Oriental" music changes and Israelis are exposed to more non-Western music, an implicit boundary between highbrow "art" music and lowbrow "popular" music is being crossed more frequently. For instance, the Ra'anana Symphonette commissioned an orchestral work from Avihu Medina, one of the leading arrangers and composers of *musika mizrahit* (mentioned by Seroussi above). Medina, who had never attended a classical concert, worked with an arranger and a computer to "see how the trivial, popular material would sound in a concert environment." The orchestra's general manager, identified in the same article as a great fan of the "trivial" and the "popular," attempted to justify this experiment to classical listeners with the words "Don't forget, Brahms composed works based on folk songs" and called for the erasure of cultural divisions in Israel (Davis 2001e). Both the gap between musical worlds and the attitudes that form and are formed by those worlds are evident here. The Medina experiment smacks more of ethnic tokenism than of a change that will reach a new audience or convince an old one to broaden its listening habits.

An event that is likely to have lasting impact and is indicative of recent cultural shifts is the annual "Mediterranean Musical Dialogue" initiated by ethnomusicologist Edwin Seroussi. Musicians gather to talk, listen, and play in master classes and workshops. Seroussi pointed to the social-cultural import of these meetings:

> The gathering is part of a much larger process. The fact that institutions like Mishkenot Sha'ananim [The Jerusalem Music Center] and AZIT [Association for Israeli Mediterranean Music, founded by Avihu Medina, the aggrieved composer of *musika mizrahit*, who was commissioned by the Ra'anana Symphonette Orchestra] are behind the event says a lot. They represent opposite ends of the Israeli cultural spectrum. Ten years ago there would not have been a chance of them cooperating. (Davis 2002b)

These events are closed to the general public, but the musicians—including several key figures in this book—are likely to disseminate what they learn through their performances. This workshop was established on the heels of a spate of institutional activity that began in the mid-1990s when one institution after another began to supply the growing demand for knowledge of Middle Eastern musical traditions. In addition to those mentioned in chapter 2, a program was established at Bar Ilan University in 1992[29] and the Rimon School of Jazz and Contemporary Music began to offer a world music performance course. In a short time a sea change had occurred and even young musicians who had grown up outside traditional networks of transmission could obtain instruction in Middle Eastern music.

Redressing the slighting of Middle Eastern culture is not always straightforward and the benefits do not necessarily accrue to those most in need. Government support for the Israeli Andalusian Orchestra is a tangible attainment, brought about by political pressure to devote resources to the heritage of Moroccan and Algerian Jews that would begin to redress earlier wrongs. Ironically, many of the members of this orchestra are immigrants from the former Soviet Union because the founding director, Avi Amzaleg, himself an immigrant from Morocco, chose to augment the traditional North African instrumentation with European orchestral instruments.[30] Thus, while North African cultural heritage is put in the spotlight, it is dressed in a half-European outfit and many of the musicians who benefit from employment in the orchestra have no personal link to North Africa. The orchestra's size and instrumentation demonstrate the persistence of European models.

When peace with the Palestinians and neighboring Arab countries appeared to be the wave of the future in the early 1990s, animosity or indifference toward Arab culture were replaced by a desire to get to know Arab neighbors better, at least for some Israeli Jews. The increased prominence and acceptance of *musika mizrahit* probably paved the way for greater acceptance of Arab music, too. These two trends converged when Zehava Ben, one of the stars of *musika mizrahit,* undertook to sing some of the songs most closely associated with Umm Kulthum, the most famous Arab singer of the twentieth century. Ben performed to the accompaniment of an orchestra of Israeli Arabs, even appearing at the Opera House in Cairo—a triumph of cultural diplomacy and a tremendous display of nerve.

Despite setbacks related to the second *intifada,* the Israeli public at the beginning of the twenty-first century has far more opportunities than ever before to hear music from all over the Middle East, North Africa, and Central Asia. Jerusalem's annual Oud Days Festival, involving both Arab and Jewish performers of Middle Eastern music, did not stop with the second *intifada* and similar events continue to take place in Haifa and Tel Aviv. The new political situation has also enabled Israelis to travel more extensively in the Middle East and Asia, increasing their exposure to and interest in non-European cultural expressions.

29. Central Asian immigrant musicians had begun to teach there as early as 1989.
30. Amzaleg is a Western-trained composer who earned a doctorate in ethnomusicology for research on Moroccan Jewish singing.

The Politics of Labeling

Musical labels often constitute areas of contestation where different positions and agendas are played out, as noted in Seroussi's analysis of *musika mizrahit*.[31] Individuals position themselves and their music in relation to specific situations, defined by time, people, circumstances, and may switch between terms to situate things best. In the preceding pages I have used terms such as art, classical, popular, or folk in commonly accepted ways in order to facilitate communication, while ignoring certain problems such as the denotative overlap between "Middle Eastern," "Arab," and "Oriental," or the status implied by "art" and "classical" relative to "popular," "ethnic" and "folk." When I first met Taiseer Elias in 1986, he was irritated that I was using the broader term Middle Eastern rather than Arab with regard to the music he played. He was aware of the Turkish contribution to this musical practice but, given the attitudes that he and other Arabs encountered in general Israeli society, the use of Middle Eastern could be construed as an erasure of his identity as an Arab while implying disregard for Arab culture.

While some see both Eurocentrism and denial of Arab ownership in the label "Middle Eastern music," others find "Arab music" exclusionary as it ignores the essential contributions of Turks, Greeks, Armenians, and Jews, to name other ethnic groups that partake of and contribute to this area of musical practice.[32] Muslim Arab cultural hegemony masks ethnic, religious, and political diversity in many parts of the Middle East, just as it diverts attention from circum-Mediterranean similarities and connections. Such connections may serve as tools when convenient for particular actors on either the cultural or the political stage. The "Golden Age" of Muslim rule in medieval Spain is a case in point, invoked by Shlomo Bar and by many others. The message may be one of peaceful coexistence between Muslims, Jews, and Christians (ignoring the subordinate position of Jews and Christians under Islamic law) or a reference to a perceived pinnacle of Jewish or Arab or Muslim cultural creativity, depending on the circumstances, the speaker, and the audience.

The application of modifying labels such as art, classical, popular, and folk leads us to consider certain types of Arab music as equivalent to certain types of European music and not to others. As cognitive categories they lead to analogies that, upon closer examination, are problematic because social, cultural, and political meanings depend on time, place, people, and

---

31. See Guilbault 1997b for a key work on this issue.

32. A third option, adopted by several institutions in Israel, is to use the no less problematic rubric "Oriental Music." Note that Taiseer later founded the Orchestra of Classical Arab Music, but recorded an album titled *Oriental Art Music* and founded the Department of Oriental Music at the Jerusalem Academy. He said that the department title was chosen to allow for expansion to include Asian musical practices (Apr. 26, 2008).

musical "worlds." For instance, the art/popular and art/folk boundaries differ considerably in European and Arab music for a given period and have also changed over time. Yet a simple equation is implicit in the typology of the music of "Oriental" Jews in Israel proposed by Eric Cohen and Amnon Shiloah. They define "ethnic fine" music as "artistic fusion by ethnic artists of elements of their own tradition with elements from other styles (Oriental or Western), resulting in the production of innovative musical works intended for an external audience" and contrasting this with "fine" (by which they clearly mean art music), which denotes the "artistic use of ethnic musical elements, such as folk melodies as thematic material for the production of essentially Western musical composition" (1985: 201). This distinction clearly rests on the standards of twentieth-century Western art music. Cohen and Shiloah categorize Shlomo Bar as an exponent of "ethnic fine" music because he turns toward a broad public, rather than speaking only to those who share his cultural background and because he incorporates a broad array of sources. Note the hierarchy implicit in the contrast constructed by the authors. By refining their resources, "ethnic" musicians may approach but can never attain the level of Western art music. When Cohen and Shiloah state that Bar seeks to "elevate his art so as to equalise its status with that of Western 'serious' music" (209) they imply that ethnic music is of lesser complexity or aesthetic worth than "serious" music.

This sociocultural hierarchy is a widely held belief, shared even by some of the participants in the scene to be discussed here. Some covet European classical music's position of eminence and benefits that accrue for its practitioners and audience. Amzaleg's shaping of the Israeli Andalusian Orchestra in a symphonic mold is a prominent instance of the power that this model exerts. It conveys the message that to legitimize one's music as refined and dignified one must emulate the model of the symphony orchestra. Avihu Medina stood to increase his legitimacy as a composer through the commission mentioned earlier, even though he was not the one who actually orchestrated his composition.

The dividing line between "art music" and "ethnic fine" may have seemed considerably clearer when Cohen and Shiloah wrote their article than it is now. For instance, institutional support was available for composers and performers in the former category, but not in the latter. Those who wished to participate in the latter arena had to find or create an audience and venues, and engage in far more self-promotion. To some extent this is still true, though that difference is lessening and the collaborations that straddled these two categories increased in the last decades of the twentieth century. Composers such as Menahem Wiesenberg, Tsipi Fleischer, and Avi Amzaleg (writing for ensembles other than his Israeli Andalusian Orchestra), have involved Middle Eastern instruments and instrumentalists in central roles, organically integrated within the ensemble. Taiseer Elias and Yair Dalal, among others, perform such works and cannot fail to compare the whole network of relations surrounding the conception and production of "art music" to their own endeavors as composers and band members.

Where does the music that is produced by the subjects of this book figure in the overall world of music in Israel? The answer is complicated by the lack of stylistic homogeneity. I have chosen these subjects because in some fundamental ways they address the same problem, not because they discover similar solutions. Despite this diversity music critics have referred to them most frequently as the ethnic music scene and their recordings would all be found under the odd label "Israeli ethnic music" in music stores in Israel.[33] The term makes some sense in relation to the neighboring bin, "ethnic music," in which the store places discs that would usually be classified as world music or international music by stores in the U.S. and online. By this logic Israeli ethnic music is world music produced in Israel. But in answer to the question "can the increasingly popular 'world music' tag be attached to the kind of ethnic music to be played and discussed at [Seroussi's Mediterranean Musical Dialogue workshop]?" Barry Davis reported, "many performers of ethnic music strenuously reject all attempts to place their work at that end of the market" (2000b). There appears to be a desire to maintain aesthetic distance from world music, reminiscent of performers' attitude toward *musika mizrahit*. Israeli ethnic music is problematic as a label for at least two other reasons: It focuses on the geopolitical locus of activity, but ignores Palestinian Arab participation; and "ethnic" distinguishes the music from "art" and implies that its power derives from traditional roots and peoples as opposed to contemporary innovation, bringing us back to the dichotomy delineated by Cohen and Shiloah.

Israel and the World

No matter what the label, this music has definitely taken root in Israel, as Davis notes in an article about the fourth annual "Hearing the World" festival in Tel Aviv. He quotes festival organizer Dubi Lentz, whom he dubs "Israel's Mr. World Music," on the recent increased receptivity to such music:

> I think we are naturally more open to influences here. We come from 80 countries and everyone brings their darbouka or clarinet from home. As much as we try to think of ourselves as Europeans, we are still part of the Levant and we absorb the local culture. Once, Israelis were ashamed of their roots and tried to escape to the world of rock and pop. Today, even [major stars in the Israeli pop/rock scene] are getting back to their cultural source." (Davis 2001b)

Several important points emerge from this statement: Israelis' fraught relationship with their diasporic heritages; the immensely varied musical resources that Jews have brought with them from various parts of the world;

33. In the American stores that carry this music it is filed under "Israel" in the "World Music" or "International" section.

and changing musical values that have shifted mainstream musicians' efforts from adapting foreign musical trends to creating music that incorporates more "local" influences. Lentz naturalizes Israeli ethnic music, asserting its legitimacy—even centrality—in Israeli culture. The implicit assumption that Israelis start from a position of Europeanness should not go unremarked. It is to Europe and North America that Israeli musicians tend to look for markets. "Israeli ethnic music" has become an integral part of the international "world music" scene, presented at prestigious festivals such as WOMAD (World of Music Arts and Dance) and its offshoots, played on world music radio shows in Europe and North America, and spread across the Internet via discussion groups and commercial Web sites that sell recordings.

Counterbalancing the geophysical centrality of Israel within the Middle East is its sociocultural isolation. Located amidst hundreds of millions of Muslims in numerous Arab states, most of which are many times larger and more populous, Israel is irreducibly different from its neighbors. For Palestinian Arabs and Jews from Arab countries there are, of course, many potential connections to the neighbors, but for Israelis of European descent the differences could hardly be more striking. Mainstream Israeli culture is out of step with the "neighborhood," as Lentz noted above. Leaving home almost invariably entails a huge change in perspective, whether one is traveling to Arab countries, Europe, the U.S., or the many other parts of the world that Israelis have visited in increasing numbers since the 1980s. This sense of crossing borders derives not only from the difficulty of leaving Israel by land, but also from Israel's political confrontations with Europe over Israeli-Arab relations and from a long history of economic deprivation and official regulation of travel. After finishing military service, many young Israelis leave for extended periods of travel, primarily in Asia (especially Nepal, India, and Thailand) and Latin America. The connection with India has been important in Israeli musical life and will surface in later chapters.

Israelis' relationship with the United States is particularly complex. The economic giant is Israel's main source of mass culture as well as political, economic, and social models in recent years. But it is also held up as a negative example. Widespread yearning for the riches and relative peace that America has to offer is counterbalanced with a disdain for a perceived lack of moral fiber and maturity on the part of American youth. Some of these attitudes date back to Israel's socialist past and the forced frugality of Israeli life until the 1970s. Some of it is a reflection on America's cultural exports or a reaction to U.S. government dictates tied to its economic largesse. The tremendous worldwide influence of the American music industry affects musical life in Israel in numerous ways.[34]

On the cultural front, Israel has fought off insularity since its establishment. Continual efforts have been made by the Israeli government to

34. For instance, American and multinational recording companies have had Israeli subsidiaries for decades.

be accepted as part or partner of Europe to offset isolation by Arab neighbors. Israel plays soccer in a European league, has various commercial ties with Europe, and so on.[35] Israel has been a regular part of the classical music tour circuit for renowned musicians, except in times of war or heightened terrorism. As early as 1936–37, Arturo Toscanini conducted the musicians who would later form the Palestine Symphony Orchestra (today the Israel Philharmonic) and Leonard Bernstein's appearances in Israel in the 1950s were another highlight of a trend that continues to the present. The Jerusalem Music Center, mentioned in the previous chapter, is a regular stop on the international circuit for world-class musicians who conduct master classes there. Israeli musicians have likewise toured extensively abroad. Peace with Egypt and Jordan reduced Israelis' isolation somewhat as did improved relations with Turkey, but such relaxation of boycotts and other isolating measures are highly sensitive to shifting political moods. Israelis flock to neighboring countries but are not welcome there and find little if any reciprocal visit from Arab neighbors.[36]

As far as the commercial viability and dreams of Israeli performers are concerned, Israel is peripheral to a Euro-American industry comprising recording companies, concert venues, festivals, and corporate sponsors operating at a level several orders of magnitude larger than the Israeli market. Israeli popular musicians—including figures as prominent as Shalom Hanoch, Shlomo Gronich, and David Broza—have tried to move from the periphery to the center by moving to cities such as New York or London for a year or two.[37] To date, the late Ofra Haza has had the greatest success internationally (though Noa approaches her fame in Europe).

Foreign markets appeal to Israeli musicians because their local field of cultural production is so small and densely populated. In such a social space, with relatively few media channels (until very recently), it is easy for popular culture to achieve saturation through mass media and patterns of constant interpersonal association. Most like-minded musicians—and many who are not at all similar in their tastes—have performed together. This is why a network approach (discussed in chapter 8) is so appropriate for understanding this musical scene. But it also means that most musicians must tour abroad to survive because local performances opportunities are

35. Israel is partially integrated into the European market, but also has strong ties to America (through loans, grants, and imports). It also has connections with various African and Asian countries and, apparently, a fairly strong black or gray market economy that reaches into neighboring Arab countries.

36. See Stein 1998.

37. In 1970, at the peak of his success, Shalom Hanoch left for England. In an interview for *Sof Onat Hatapuzim*, a television documentary on Israeli rock, he said that he thought he would become a millionaire by the age of twenty-seven. But he had a hard time writing in English and found he could not work with pop writers. He released an album of songs in English that flopped and finally returned to Israel after a few years. In the same program late 1970s "happenings" in Israel are characterized as "echoes of Woodstock" (Yoav Kutner, 1998, episode 10)—delayed by ten years!

simply insufficient. The problem is particularly acute for those involved in the music that is the subject of this book. They depend on tours abroad for their survival (see chapter 12) because the demand for their music at home is too small. Even popular musicians feel that they are in a tight spot.

The messages Israelis get about their relationship to the larger world are decidedly mixed. Some sense of cultural validation flows from that massive "outside," but there is also a strong sense of self-worth, a feeling shared by the individual musicians and bands discussed here: They have something of great and unique value to offer the outside world. In a newspaper interview, one young Israeli musician complained that most Israelis

> want to feel like we are in America, but if music is made in Israel in English they won't buy it because "it must not be good enough." On one hand, they preach nationalism, on the other hand they want things that were made in the USA. If people thought that Rockfour [an Israeli rock group that performs and records in English] came from San Francisco, they would be all the rage, but since they come from Israel, not as many people buy them. It is total hypocrisy. (Lemor 2001)

Most Israelis will not follow all the dictates of this larger world, but neither can they ignore it, however much they might want to at times. They need it, economically and culturally. So we find Israelis attempting to be citizens of the world, players on the international scene, and to be worldly on the Israeli stage.

Cosmopolitan attitudes are central to Israeli life for various reasons. Israelis in general are intensely First World in aspiration; the desire to equal the best in American and European educational and cultural institutions is deep-seated and feeds an intense interest in those areas. Israeli musical cosmopolitanism strives for elite sophistication. Salwa El-Shawan Castelo-Branco has noted that for "cosmopolites in Egypt, European 'art' music was an important cultural resource, and a symbol of social ascension and power" (2002: 610). Though she is referring to the late nineteenth and early twentieth centuries, the same was true in Israel several generations later. An appreciation of European art music signified cultural refinement and belonging to the larger world dominated by European cultural values. But to underscore Turino's point that cosmopolitanism is always localized (2000: 8), we have only to turn to the music of renowned Egyptian composer Muhammad 'Abd al-Wahhab. Greatly influenced by European classical music, he produced some of the best known, most widely performed works of Arab music in the twentieth century. To Arab listeners they are sophisticated and grand, Arab yet enriched with European musical sophistication. To listeners whose first frame of reference is the European music that influenced 'Abd al-Wahhab, his borrowings are likely to sound embarrassingly close to kitsch. Taiseer Elias, torn between two musical worlds that he valued highly and knew intimately, articulated this contradiction when we first met in the 1980s during his student days.

Multilingualism is a frequent, though not essential, feature of cosmopolitanism. Most Israelis know at least two languages; many know three, four, or more. This multilingualism extends into song. Some musicians record songs in English hoping to break into a larger, international market.[38] Others pepper their songs with words from a variety of languages. For instance, the refrain of "Karim Abdul Zamar," by the popular band Mashina, is a multilingual tour de force. The title is a pun on the name of Kareem Abdul-Jabbar, the famous basketball player, replacing the last name with the Hebrew word for singer. Both the song and album reference Genesis's *Shock the Monkey*.[39] The mixture of Hebrew with English, Arabic, French, and German reflects the linguistic competence of the lower class, young Israeli men who used to hang out on the streets of Israel's cities accosting young women in any language they could. As such it highlights the presence of foreigners, another factor reinforcing the cosmopolitan in Israel.

A substantial flow of tourists from most parts of the world has had a substantial impact on Israeli life except in times of war or intensified terrorist activity. The first and second *intifadas* reduced tourism, but increased the number of long-term foreign residents as Israel began to replace Palestinian laborers from the occupied territories with laborers from places as different as Eastern Europe, Southeast Asia, and Africa in order to reduce the threat of suicide bombings by Palestinian workers.[40] Of course, these laborers—many of whom are illegal aliens, having entered on tourist visas and overstayed their visas—interact with Israelis quite differently than do tourists or the foreign volunteers who have lived and worked on Israeli *kibbutzim* for lengthy periods since the 1960s. But they, too, contribute to the ongoing presence of many languages in everyday use.

Cosmopolitanism is enhanced by first-hand experience of other countries and foreign cultures. In recent years, nearly every Israeli seems to have traveled abroad and quite a few people do so frequently, despite the country's depressed economy. But cosmopolitanism is more deeply rooted than that. It can be traced back to the foreign roots of much of the population, who are immigrants or children of immigrants and whose consciousness therefore straddles international boundaries. It can also be traced to the transnational existence of many Jews over centuries, who moved from one country to another, either by choice or out of necessity, and maintained

38. See Lemor 2001 for commentary on this history. She cites young Israeli rock musicians who speak of being treated as traitors by the media for singing in English. One charges Israelis and their government with hypocrisy for wanting to be like America but not supporting locally produced music in English.

39. The chorus is preceded by the words "Mock de shonkey" (it took some perceptive fans of the band Genesis among my students to point this out to me) and the album cover is a photo of clothed chimpanzees.

40. Many of these people are quite poor. They have formed their own communities, particularly in south Tel Aviv, which has a sizeable international population.

links with far-flung family and communities. It has roots, too, in the doubleness of Jewish life in exile, always maintaining at least one language and set of relations in an internal community life and other languages and relations with the external Christian or Muslim majority. This doubleness is evident not only in the polylingualism of most Jews in Europe, North Africa, and the Middle East, but also in a polymusical environment. Hybridity has been a common feature of the social and cultural life of Jews wherever they have lived in the world, maintaining their own ways of life but always subject to and influenced by the dominant cultural and social regimes of the non-Jewish majority. This is evident in hybrid forms of expression in linguistic—Yiddish, Ladino, and Judaeo-Arabic are quintessential hybrid languages—and musical domains, as well as in other areas of life.

What this has meant for Israel is a rich set of cultural resources, drawn from many parts of the world, the fruit of the Diaspora. The social phenomenon of the ingathering of Jews from most of Europe, Asia, North Africa, and the Americas has brought together a tremendously varied pool of musicians into a very small country. This provides the multiple competences that enable Shlomo Bar's work, for instance, as well as the phenomenon of "ethnic fusion" under investigation in this book. But it took many years for Israeli musicians to imagine the viability of such hybrid work and for the Israeli public to be ready to support it.[41]

This long path to acceptance has much to do with Israel's fraught relationship with its foreign roots. Many Israelis' attitude toward Diaspora culture is ambivalent at best, for this rich panoply of cultural resource has also been a source of shame. In Zionist ideology, the Diaspora represented the weak, oppressed Jew. The new, strong Israeli was not only to supplant this image, but to supplant the culture linked with it as well. Immigrant culture was suppressed, replaced, or transformed. Dances and music of various groups were "developed" in order to create a new culture that Israel could present to itself and to the world, as Barbara Kirshenblatt-Gimblett has noted.[42] For instance, Jerusalem's long-running folk dance troupe Tsabarim[43] included highly stylized Eastern European Hassidic dances alongside Yemenite and Moroccan ones (all accompanied by the same band of musicians). It seemed to say to tourists visiting Jerusalem "we are all this and more."

While the Arab world has long had important cosmopolitan clusters in major cities—Cairo and Beirut in particular—Israel probably is more cosmopolitan and less tradition-bound than other Middle Eastern or Eu-

41. The immigration of Jewish musicians from Central Asian republics of the former Soviet Union may be a factor in this growing openness to hybridization of various resources.
42. She does not discuss the music that accompanies these dances (1998: 70–72).
43. My daughter Maya danced in this troupe, whose name refers to native Israelis. Its long run ended when the second *intifada* destroyed the tourist economy.

ropean countries, both as a country and as a collective of individual practitioners. This pervasive cosmopolitanism developed because this is a society built, more or less, from scratch, and because a significant portion of the population subscribes to "objects, ideas, and cultural positions that are widely diffused throughout the world, yet specific only to certain portions of the population" (Turino 2000: 8). As Turino notes, cosmopolitanism is always shaped locally but is connected via "cosmopolitan loops" to other distant sites through media, contact, and other types of exchange. Israeli cosmopolitanism may be best understood as having two faces: one turned toward Europe and the Americas, the other toward the rest of the Middle East. The two loops may overlap in one person, particularly those who were raised in the large cities of the Middle East and North Africa and were oriented toward the colonial powers and cultures of France and England.

Cosmopolitan attitudes are evident in various facets of musical practice, including repertoire items, instruments, and playing styles. The enormous variety of musical styles practiced in Israel is indicative of a high degree of cosmopolitanism and is not simply a result of the ingathering of immigrants noted above. A significant portion of the performers are not "native" to the traditions they perform, but have chosen them from a highly varied menu of options available to those who partake of the cosmopolitan ethos of international exchange. Thus, alongside European art music, Israeli pop, various types of jazz, Arab music, and so on, we can find Celtic music, for example, played principally but not only by "Anglo-Saxon" immigrants—those who have come from English-speaking countries (though their own parents or grandparents are likely to have emigrated from Eastern Europe)—and Afro-Cuban music, in which Shlomo Bar got his start before returning to his personal roots and creating the ethnic mix that he has made famous. Emmanuel Mann, French-born bass player in Habreira Hativ'it and Bustan Abraham, told me in 1998 that he was involved in a Celtic/Irish project with an Israeli Jew of Turkish descent who played Uilleann pipes and Irish flute. They were working on a standard Irish repertoire of jigs and reels, but wanted to give it a Middle Eastern twist and hoped to tour Europe.[44]

Cosmopolitan attitudes often manifest in a desire to stay abreast of the latest developments abroad. The incorporation of the drum set and, more recently, the synthesizer into Palestinian Arab bands is indicative of this. By adopting and adapting these items of musical culture, Palestinian musicians are attempting to keep up with the leading edge of the Arab music industry, connecting with similarly minded musicians and audiences elsewhere in the Arab world, but also deploying symbols of contemporary popular music in the world as a whole. The adoption of the double bass and cello, dating back to the early years of the twentieth century and still spreading in parts of the Middle East, is an older example of an attempt to display cosmopolitan sophistication. So, it could be argued, is the entire Franco-Arabe style with its adaptations of elements of European popular

44. Aug. 13, 1997.

music. It was clear from comments of musicians whom I interviewed in the 1980s[45] that having this music at your party was a sign of cosmopolitanism for Arab music consumers in Israel. Similar phenomena are evident in the Jewish sector: Israeli musicians rushed to emulate and adapt not only mainstream rock and pop, but the more esoteric progressive rock. In other words, the move toward participation in a cosmopolitan musical world is shaped not only by individual musicians, but also by consumer expectations.

Arabs and Jews: Intersecting Musical Trajectories

I have discussed Arab and Jewish musicians in relative isolation thus far because these two groups have often moved in separate, self-sufficient musical worlds. Yet there have also been numerous instances of interaction between Jewish and Arab performers and audiences. A brief summary of these[46] will serve as background to the recent self-conscious collaborations in which Jews and Arabs have come together to pool their resources and create new music, in contrast to earlier situations where musicians were absorbed into one existing musical world or another.

Jews have served as musicians in many parts of the Arab world for generations, performing both for a general Muslim audience (sometimes with Muslim musicians) and within their own religious community, often playing much of the same repertoire. This is the reason that so many musicians competent in mainstream Arab music arrived in Israel during the first years of the State. It also meant that these immigrants shared a common musical "language" with Palestinian Arabs, in addition to the fact that they all spoke Arabic.

A symbiosis developed in Israel between Jewish audiences from Arab countries, particularly Iraq, and musical groups that included both Jews and Palestinian Arabs. Because this interaction occurred mainly at private parties, it had no direct public impact, but it was a formative experience for young Arab musicians, such as Taiseer Elias, Nassim Dakwar, and Jamal Sa'id, who had the opportunity to learn some of the Iraqi repertoire and to perform the most sophisticated musical repertoire of the Arab world for appreciative connoisseurs who listened rather than demanding dance numbers like local Arab audiences. This symbiosis overlapped with connections formed at the government radio station where the orchestra that performed Arab music added more Palestinian Arab musicians as its original Jewish members aged and retired.[47] Conversely, Iraqi Jewish *qanun*

45. These included Bassam Bishara, Walid 'Id'is, and Jamal Sa'id.
46. See also Shiloah and Cohen 1983.
47. According to Taiseer Elias, who became director of Arab music broadcasting after the orchestra had been disbanded, but had performed frequently with members of the orchestra before then, there were two regular Arab members of the orchestra and freelancers were brought in principally as drummers or to strengthen the violin section (interview, June 28, 1998).

players used to be much in demand among Arab ensembles because of a lack of Arabs who could play the instrument. Ethnic and religious identities were not an issue in these situations as a common interest in mainstream Arab music was the focus. This differs from the reliance, in recent years, of large Arab ensembles on Jewish bass and cello players, who have had to learn a new musical idiom.

Interaction between Jews and Arabs in popular music usually involved one group providing the performers and the other the audience. In the 1970s, Israeli Arabs hired Jewish bands to play Euro-American pop at those *haflat* where the hosts wished to be fashionable. The Jewish bands would play in alternation—not in collaboration—with Arab bands playing Arab music. They were supplanted in the 1980s by the spread of the Franco-Arabe style and by Arab bands that played both contemporary, Western-oriented pop and Arab music. Jamal Sa'id explained:

> There are bands that work with both kinds of music. For instance, there are bands that half of their musicians play Western music and [the others] Eastern music. And you'll see that in the band itself one plays lead guitar and bass guitar [Jamal actually used the English terms "lead" and "bass"], and there's a singer who sings Western and in [the other] half of the band you'll see *'ud*, violin, *darbukkah* . . . and he sings Eastern. . . . they want to eat up the market from door to door . . . [the hosts] want two kinds [of music] and [instead of] bringing two bands they bring one band that has both kinds in it . . . it's cheaper. (Jan. 3, 1995)

Jamal noted that Bassam Bishara had led such a band (with an English name, the Silvertones).

A few Israeli Arabs have made a career performing for a larger segment of the Jewish public. Samir Shukri performs songs with Hebrew lyrics, often translated or paraphrased from Arabic. A string of collaborations between Jewish and Arab singers started in the 1980s, often aimed at children (Perelson 1998). These were revolutionary in their Hebrew/Arabic and Jews/Arabs juxtapositions, but did not lead to long-term working relations, unlike the endeavors discussed in this book.

As isolated from the world as they were in the 1960s and 1970s, some Israeli Jews acted as agents of change for Arab communities within Israel, which were even more isolated. It was through these intermediaries that many of the technologies and styles of American and European origin were imported to Arab musicians and audiences according to the accounts I elicited from several Arab musicians in the 1980s while asking about their early experiences of music. With increased access to broadcast media, recordings, travel, and the Internet, differential and mediated access is far less evident today.

Some mixing also occurred through musical instruction. Some Arab students learned *'ud* from Jewish immigrants from Iraq and other Arab countries and others learned European art music from Jewish teachers. A reciprocal trend, Jewish students learning Arab music from Arab teachers, began in the mid-1980s when the Workshop for Non-Western Music, which I directed at the Jerusalem Music Center, brought in Jamal Saʿid and Taiseer Elias to teach Arab music to students from the Hebrew University, Bar Ilan, and Tel Aviv University.[48] Such interactions became more common with the opening of the formal programs in Arab music instruction described earlier.

Around 1990, when the main story of this book begins, the musical situations of Arabs and Jews in Israel contrasted in several ways. Arab musical life was marked by a great deal of musical activity for specific social occasions and little, if any, regular concert life or institutional support for music. Furthermore, there was a relative lack of local stars dominating the market. It was constituted of musically distinct regional scenes characterized by differences of repertoire and minor details of performance practice. This, too, contrasted with the more geographically homogenous world of Israeli Jews. Where thousands of immigrant Jewish musicians enriched Israeli musical life with their professional competence in many different traditions, the Palestinians suffered a depletion of musicians, as some fled to other countries after the creation of Israel in 1948 and others have left subsequently for various reasons, including lack of support for their music. Building up a sufficient supply of professional musicians has been a gradual process that accelerated greatly in the 1980s and found new instructional support in the mid-1990s as noted above.[49]

During the period surveyed here, performance has tended to be more lucrative for Israeli Arabs than for most Jewish musicians, at least relative to the standards of their community. Hosts at *haflat* pay well and musicians also can earn a lot in tips. On the other hand, recordings have not been a significant source of income for Arab musicians due to their low cost and the pervasiveness of piracy. Recordings made by Israeli companies are sold at much higher prices.[50] Making a high-quality recording is an expensive proposition, which probably explains why Jewish musicians operating in the larger Israeli market prize recordings as marks of achievement rather than disdain them as utilitarian calling cards.

Compared to Palestinian musicians, who often follow fairly similar paths in their musical education, there has been far more variety among Jewish Israeli musicians. This derives from fewer societal constraints on musicians' options and desires and a greater variety of musical opportunities available in the aggregate, if not for each individual. Some of the Jewish musicians who will figure in this book are autodidacts. Some have gone through the entire gamut of training in the classical music establishment.

48. We also hired two Iraqi Jewish musicians as teachers.
49. Elias Jubran's complaints, made to Egypt's *Al-Ahram* newspaper about the situation of Arab music in Israel (Rakha 1999), were no longer true by the time he made them.
50. I do not know whether this translates into significant income for musicians, but composers do receive royalties for airplay from ACUM, which is roughly the Israeli equivalent to BMI or ASCAP.

Still others have studied jazz informally or in a variety of frameworks that have existed in Israel over the past three decades.[51] Most musicians are conversant with the harmonic and melodic language of Western popular music and commonly have some knowledge of several other types of music. No less important an explanation for the greater variety of training among Jewish musicians is the fact that many studied in other countries before coming to Israel. Many musicians emigrating from the former Soviet Union benefited from that country's state-supported professional training. In Israel, training in European art music has been more readily available to Jewish children than to Arab children, both in practical ways (e.g., located in their own community) and in social and cultural openness. As a result Jewish musicians tend to have started formal instruction at a much earlier age.[52]

Over the years I encountered repeated expressions of frustration from Arab musicians. Some are specific to the Arab music scene, but some are relative to other music going on in Israel, their impact sharpened by that comparison. As we saw in chapter 2, the rapid turnover in repertoire called for at *haflat* has been a prime concern. In recent years, the main challenge for musicians has been to keep up with the latest hits so that they can play audience requests. Arab musicians also complained about the lack of appropriate venues and concert opportunities other than the pervasive *haflat*. Rather than the regularly scheduled series of European art music performances in dedicated venues, concerts in Arab communities tended to be held in community centers and other multipurpose buildings for charity events[53] (like the Hakawati concert for the blind) or to mark special occasions, such as New Year's Eve. Despite plentiful opportunities to play, they do not have the chance to really develop their ideas in public. The singer controls the band, regulating even the instrumentalists' right to solo and rarely allowing them sufficient time to modulate from one *maqam* to another, which is one of the hallmarks of artistry in Arab improvisation.[54] The audience at a *haflah* is demanding, even threatening, and often does not appreciate the musicians. Jamal, like several other musicians, complained bitterly about this, saying that he spends his time looking at his watch or falling asleep while he drums. The only appreciative audience, he said in 1992, consisted of the Iraqi or Moroccan Jews who would occasionally invite him down to Tel Aviv to play.

Discussing the lack of audience, venues, and opportunities for new artistic Arab music in Israel, Nassim Dakwar said,

> If you give someone a good melody, where will he take it? It won't go anywhere. It won't be recorded on disc and it won't get out. It won't

51. Formal instruction in jazz began in the early 1970s as far as I know but there may have been some earlier offerings.
52. See Ben Ze'ev 2004, for example.
53. Note that Rasmussen found a similar situation in the Arab American community that she researched (1989: 15).
54. Taiseer Elias, 1991.

reach Arab countries. There's no marketing. It will simply get lost. If I were in a different place, a different country, I would give the songs. I would know whether those songs would go. And there would be an artistic project with which I could appear. (July 16, 1999)

At issue here are the status of the artist—the respect accorded or implied—and the status of the music. Four years later, Nassim had become music director for singer Amal Murkus and had added his own instrumental compositions to her program (see chapter 8).

In *Making Music in the Arab World*, Ali Jihad Racy reported a similar dissatisfaction with the current status of music. Musicians live in two worlds: "professional reality marked by what may be perceived as artistic expediency, and an ideal or imaged world of music making . . . lived somewhat vicariously through memorable past experiences" (2003: 39). The Arab musicians with whom I have worked all point back to a time when they were able to play music that they valued for people who sat and listened rather than commanding dance tunes. They say little about more distant cultural memories, perhaps because they are mainly of rural origin, not so closely linked to the long history of the *tarab* culture that Racy portrays in the Arab urban centers. They differ from Racy's subjects in a more significant way, central to this book. Rather than suffer an unsatisfying reality and dream of an idealized past, they have endeavored to create a new musical present that will lead them into the future, not simply as bearers of a long tradition, but as initiators of a new musical language and repertoire that engage with other ways of making music.

I did not find a similar systemic frustration among Israeli Jewish musicians. Most were unaffected professionally by the *intifada* and did not perform in contexts that were as vulnerable to audience demands. Reasons to seek out collaborations and new forms of musical expression appeared to be more individualized, owing in part to the greater variety of backgrounds and options sketched above. It was a sense of challenge and excitement that was shared by the Jewish and Arab musicians involved in projects to be analyzed in coming chapters.

In this chapter and the previous one, I have attempted to delineate musicians' differential "room to maneuver."[55] The limits for Palestinian Arabs differ depending on whether they are Israeli citizens, residents of East Jerusalem, or residents of the West Bank. And these spaces differ from those available to Israeli Jews, who do not enjoy uniform opportunities either. By space I refer not only to physical space, although the system of roadblocks and permits affecting Palestinians, as well as the very real threats of attack on Jews in Palestinian areas, clearly articulate significant

55. De Certeau points to the different types of "room to maneuver" available to consumers depending on their situation as well as to the different "engagements" that the "system of products effects within the consumer grid" (1984: xvii). Both observations are pertinent to the present study, despite the fact that I am concerned more with small-scale producers than with the consumers of mass production and marketing.

differences in that regard. Differences in socio-cultural constraints and possibilities are at least as significant, including areas such as linguistic abilities and education, both general and musical. For professional musicians, the network of employment possibilities is tied to these factors and is also in itself an area of major difference (see chapter 8). Although the training ground of Arab weddings, available to virtually any Palestinian musician, is much reviled on artistic grounds, it clearly plays a formative role for all of them. No Israeli Jewish musician in this study ever went through this initiation into a repertoire consisting of village, popular, and art music and their associated performance practices.

These are but a few instances of the numerous intersecting distinctions, constraints, and opportunities to consider. It is crucial to understand that, in this instance at least, differential possibilities are not a simple matter of degrees of privilege or freedom. The situation is far more complex and we ignore its nuances at our peril. This book is an extended attempt to delineate and shed light on this convoluted socio-cultural terrain.

The ethnic music scene is not the first occasion that elements of Middle Eastern music have been combined with elements drawn from other types of music, either in Israel or elsewhere.[56] But earlier mixes differed qualitatively and quantitatively. Here we find an unprecedented mixing of performers enabled by several important political and sociological changes. It is difficult to say whether they would have sufficed in and of themselves since the phenomenon coincides with the tremendous surge in distribution of world musics and the growth of World Beat and other globalized fusions. Part II centers on three clusters of musicians who traveled different paths into and through this emerging field of musical production.

---

56. Shiloah and Cohen (1983) discuss instances of Israeli Jews from Arab countries combining their music with aspects of Western music. See also Flam 1986 and Fleisher 1997.

PART II

Musicians, Bands, Networks

4

Alei Hazayit

In 1991, the third year of the first Palestinian uprising, the band Alei Hazayit was formed in Jerusalem by two strong-willed individuals who differed in gender, class, ethnicity, religion, and linguistic and musical competence, yet found the basis for a deep personal connection (see figure 4.1). Their band merged very different musical strands, taking well-known songs in Hebrew and Arabic, but giving them a new flavor, a new color, and in so doing, representing the possibility for peaceful and fruitful collaboration between Jews and Arabs, Israelis and Palestinians.

Shoham Einav, born in one of the oldest neighborhoods of West Jerusalem a few years before the State of Israel, first turned from her career as a head nurse in Israel's premier hospital to professional singing in her forties. After half a lifetime singing in the home and among friends she took a few lessons from a voice teacher and began to give public performances of *shirei erets yisrael* and Ladino ballads. She added a few Arabic songs as an "act of faith" that peace could be achieved through mutual understanding. She took her first tour abroad to Spain in 1989 and undertook several more in the ensuing years, taking two or three accompanists.

As early as 1990, Shoham began to be dissatisfied with the musicians who accompanied her on guitar, bass, drums, flute, or piano (the instrumentation varied). Concluding that she needed a different kind of accompaniment—something unique, more Middle Eastern—to spice up her performances, Shoham decided to try singing to the accompaniment of Arab drumming in preparation for two 1990 performances in Italy. One was an event devoted to the composer Isaac Albeniz while the second, the Conference of Italians of African Descent, brought together Jews, Muslims, and Christians, mostly of Libyan heritage.

Through a mutual acquaintance at the television station, Shoham contacted Jamal Sa'id, whom we met in previous chapters. Jamal had tired of the wedding gigs that were the staple of his musical career. In any case, the ban on music and celebrations during the *intifada* had almost completely

Figure 4.1   Shoham Einav and Jamal Saʻid (photo by Ben Brinner)

squelched that career and put a damper on his work as an actor, too. He was no longer performing in plays at the Hakawati Theater in East Jerusalem or getting roles in television commercials aimed at the Arab public. Jamal had plenty of contact with Israeli Jews before meeting Shoham. He was acting in the pioneering Israeli television show *Neighbors*, about Jews and Arabs living in the same apartment building, but that was coming to an end. Together with two other Arab musicians, he had participated in a government-sponsored tour to Europe, sharing the program with Jewish musicians in alternation, but not collaborating musically. Shoham's invitation to work together was, in a way, the logical next step in extricating himself from the doldrums of local Arab music life.

After meeting Jamal, Shoham continued to perform occasionally with her old accompanists. Although he was unable to accompany her when she gave a couple of concerts in Egypt at the invitation of an Israeli government agency, Jamal helped her develop an Arabic paraphrase of some of her Ladino songs that she recited at these concerts. When she performed in Cairo in 1992, she told me she was so well received that some people traveled to Alexandria when she tried to appear there in 1993. Egyptian authorities intimidated the performers and audience, eventually shutting down that concert.

The collaboration between Shoham and Jamal was not easy, tested by periods of tension and practical obstacles, many of them arising from the political and military mess that impinges on the lives of Jews and Arabs.

That they managed to overcome these obstacles testifies to the strength of the connection that they felt and to their mutual respect.

The first challenge was to bridge their vastly different backgrounds. Married to a leading cardiologist, Shoham lived in one of the posher neighborhoods of Jerusalem. Her children were grown and had their own families. An intuitive singer with no formal musical knowledge, she grew up in a Sephardic household where her father sang and played violin, performing Jewish religious tunes on the Sabbath. Shoham characterized the tunes as a mixture of East and West, noting that her father loved the songs of American Rabbi Shlomo Carlebach. She had no training in Arab music prior to her work with Jamal, but was open to hearing many kinds of music.

Jamal, nearly twenty years Shoham's junior, lived with his wife and six children in a two-room stone house, crammed among other small houses in the Muslim Quarter of the Old City. With many years of experience performing Arab music in diverse settings, he told me on numerous occasions that he was not particularly interested in other kinds of music. Nonetheless, he became deeply involved in the material that Shoham brought to their collaboration.

Shoham and Jamal's forty-five-minute presentation in Italy was so well received that it led to an invitation for a return engagement at a conference of Libyan Jews to be sponsored by Qaddafi in Libya itself. Shoham also gained a devoted fan, Camilia Sadat, peace activist and daughter of the Egyptian President Anwar Sadat who was assassinated for making peace with Israel. As the Libyan hosts expected a full performance, Shoham and Jamal put together a band. Among his many contacts in the Arab musical circles in the Jerusalem area, Jamal found four who were willing to work on the creation of a mixed Arab-Israeli musical repertoire: Walid 'Id'is (frame drums), Ghidian al-Qaimari ('ud), and Omar Keinani (violin), all members of the band that accompanied Bassam Bishara in the Hakawati theater concert described in chapter 2. Jamal added a synthesizer player, to "strengthen" the sound, and later a *nay* player. They began to rehearse, working out a mixed program of songs in Hebrew and Arabic (see figure 4.2).

The massacre of Muslims by a Jewish fanatic in Hebron on February 25, 1994 led to cancellation of the trip to Libya, which would have been the first appearance there by a group from Israel. The band began to find other opportunities to perform, many of them politically charged in one way or another. One of the more important was the 1994 West Bank ceremony described at the beginning of chapter 1, in which the musicians felt that their mixture of Arab and Israeli music established a middle ground with which both sides could identify. In July 1995, Alei Hazayit was the first Israeli group to perform in Jordan after King Hussein came to terms with Israel in the wake of the Oslo Accords. Once again, the audience consisted chiefly of officials, mixed with Jordanian and Israeli business people. When President Bill Clinton visited Gaza in December 1998, the group was asked to play there, but the engagement was cancelled at the last moment. This would have been their first performance sponsored by an official Palestinian

Figure 4.2   Shoham Einav and Alei Hazayit in an early formation:
Ibrahim (synthesizer), Jamal Sa'id (*darbukkah*), Walid 'Id'is (*mazhar*),
Omar Keinani (violin) (photo courtesy of Shoham Einav)

entity. They played a concert for UNESCO in Ramallah, and another in
Jerusalem sponsored by a broad assortment of organizations,[1] but most of
their non-commercial performances were sponsored by Israeli agencies,
including concerts at the President's House, the Knesset (parliament), and
in David's Citadel in the Old City. In addition to these high profile occasions, Alei Hazayit also performed at concerts aimed at the general Israeli
public and less often for Palestinians. Unlike the other musicians discussed
in this book, they performed too rarely to become well known, despite
some airplay on radio and television and the use of one of their recordings
by a leading folk dance troupe.[2]

In 1998, Jamal and Shoham led the group to their most ambitious engagement yet, the 17th Festival of Asian Arts in Hong Kong (see figure
4.3).[3] Earlier Israeli representatives at this festival included: the Inbal Dance

1. This was the Concert in Honor of Children of the Millennium, sponsored
by Israeli and European organizations.
2. This renewed a connection that had been important in the early years of
Israeli/Hebrew song; cf. Regev and Seroussi 2004: 54–55.
3. I recommended them when the festival director asked my advice, but I
had no further influence. He also auditioned other groups on a trip to Israel.

Figure 4.3   Shoham Einav and Alei Hazayit in a later formation (photo courtesy of Shoham Einav)

Theatre (1988), which specializes in reworking traditional dances, particularly Yemenite Jewish dance; Habreira Hativ'it (1990), discussed in chapter 3; Bustan Abraham (1992), with its two subsets, White Bird and the Arab Classical Music Trio (later named Ziryab); the East-West Ensemble (1994); and Yair Dalal with his Al-Ol Ensemble (1996). Alei Hazayit had clearly been slotted into a category that could best be described as "world/ ethnic music band from Israel." They also appeared frequently as "poster children" for peace and coexistence. The press release for a "Concert for Peace, Frieden, Schalom, Salam" in Basel, in 2002, announced under the headline "Rhythmen für den Frieden!" (rhythms for peace), that the Olive Leaves Band displays universality and a great commitment to peace, performing a repertoire that expresses humanity, tolerance and peace.[4] Despite their nonpolitical repertoire, these musicians were inevitably perceived through a political lens.

The Hebron massacre was just one of many instances of political violence that plagued the band. Whenever the Israeli-Palestinian conflict heated up, invitations to Arab countries, such as Libya and Morocco, were cancelled because Alei Hazayit was associated with Israel. Because of their implicit message of peaceful coexistence and their explicit mix of Hebrew and Arabic, they found that they were not always welcome in Israel either where some promoters apparently were afraid to present performances by the band after bloody terrorist attacks. In spring 1996, for instance, three

4. See www.openhearts.ch/german/events/020106Basel.html.

of their performances were cancelled after a deadly bombing on Dizengoff Street in the heart of Tel Aviv. Shoham felt that she was a *persona non grata* for a few months and that the Arab musicians were, too, in their own communities.[5] Performing alone as a guest on someone else's show, Shoham had people shout out "not in Arabic" when she sang in that language. After each heightening of tensions, the members of the band had to regroup and to reaffirm, implicitly, their commitment to their common goals, despite the canceled performances.

Other factors that threatened to undermine the musicians' commitment included infrequent paying performances, hard work at frequent rehearsals, and—at times—the possible dangers involved in belonging to such an ensemble. As typical participants in Palestinian musical life, the Arab members of the band were accustomed to receiving a handsome sum in cash at the end of a *haflah*. They were also used to performing with little, if any, rehearsal because frequent performances afforded them sufficient "practice" to maintain their competence. By contrast, Alei Hazayit required extensive rehearsal because some of the material was new to them and the arrangements departed from the conventions they knew. Several musicians left the band or were asked to leave because of their reluctance to commit to regular rehearsals. A few returned when their circumstances changed or when they understood that they were missing something valuable.

The risks associated with participating in this endeavor were clearest in 1998–99. Shoham was unable to accept invitations for performances that could in any way be construed as related to the yearlong celebration of fifty years of Israeli independence because the Arab members of the band feared retaliation from other Palestinians if they performed. Ghidian al-Qaimari did not consider this possibility when he traveled to Paris at the invitation of Sara Alexander, a self-exiled Israeli Jew, for a concert involving Israeli and Palestinian singers. "She's a leftist," Ghidian told me, "so it was fine with me." Indeed, Alexander touts herself as a pioneering activist for Middle East peace.[6] But Ghidian did not know that the concert was also to be billed as part of the celebrations of Israel's 50th anniversary. Only after arriving in Paris, did Ghidian cancel when he received a letter from the Palestinian Authority in Ramallah forbidding him to participate in the concert. He was denounced in Arabic newspapers in Jerusalem. These same papers published the fact of his cancellation, too, Ghidian said,

5. Jan. 10, 1997.
6. Her Web site states: "In 1967, Sara Alexander left Israel . . . Quickly she got involved into peace building between Israelis & their neighbors, proclaiming the rights of the Palestinian people to get a national home too. Fearing not the price to pay for her career, as soon as the early 70's, Sara Alexander started touring around with a leitmotiv: mutual recognition and understanding. This wholehearted involvement makes her one of the very first Israeli peace activists." (sara.alexander.free.fr/professional.html, accessed Nov. 13, 2002; archived at http://web.archive.org/web/20021004095207/sara.alexander.free.fr/peace.html).

but people did not read about that and months later he was still encountering hostility.[7]

One of the dividing lines between Palestinians and Arab citizens of Israel is the level of personal danger and hence the risk involved in collaborating with Israeli Jews in musical performances. To date, the worst consequence for an Israeli Arab might be damage to his reputation among certain segments of the Arab community. He has no concrete reason to fear physical harm and I am not aware of the Palestinian Authority issuing orders to Israeli Arabs concerning musical performances. Not so for Palestinians in the territories, as Ghidian's experience with Sara Alexander proves. There were also difficulties crossing borders. Ghidian was unable to go with the group to perform in Jordan in 1995, because the Jordanians refused him entry on the basis of his having "used an enemy port" when he flew out of Israel's Ben Gurion airport on earlier trips (as had other members of the band!) and when the group was poised to perform in Gaza in early 1997, Shoham said that the Arab musicians were nervous about being seen there as political collaborators, i.e., traitors.[8]

Motivations

In the face of such obstacles, what drew musicians to this endeavor and kept most of them there? Jamal told me that it provided an opportunity for him to play cleanly and delicately in contrast to the over-amplified, aggressively competitive atmosphere at a *haflah*. It also was clear that the opportunity to shape an act, including repertoire, arrangements, and the singer's presentation, attracted him. I received the most explicit analysis of motivations from the violinist, Omar Keinani.[9] After complaining at length about the current situation in Arab music in Jerusalem, he said that when Jamal suggested this collaboration he thought it might be a refuge from the "boring atmosphere, this mess, that's not music, it's a factory," referring to *haflat*. Noting Alei Hazayit's problems with personnel stability, he said that this kind of commitment was not suitable for everyone. He had rejected a more stringent commitment ten years earlier when playing with the political Palestinian band Sabreen:

> I began to play with them in '82 and didn't continue for personal reasons. One was that they asked me not to perform elsewhere. They're not against weddings but the manager said that they want to preserve

7. July 3, 1998. Around the same time he dropped out of an Israeli-Palestinian group that was trying to rent a house for activities of Jewish and Palestinian youth. He attributed such problems to the stalled peace process.

8. Jan. 2, 1997. The Gaza trip was postponed repeatedly because of delays in signing the Hebron Accord between Israel and the Palestinian Authority. In the end the trip did not take place.

9. The following comments were made during an interview on Jan. 7, 1997.

their own special style—"we're Sabreen. We need to work hard [literally 'break our heads']." That was a certain policy that I admire.

But at that point, Omar needed to earn money to feed his family while the members of Sabreen had other sources of income. Furthermore, he did not want to limit his playing to Sabreen's style. He wanted to play the music of Syrian and Lebanese greats Sabakh Fakhri, Wadi' es-Safi, and Fairuz, too. When Jamal invited him to form a group with Shoham some ten years later, circumstances had changed. Omar had earned his MA and obtained a steady job as a social worker. He had become disillusioned with *haflah* bands, describing the Palestinian musical marketplace after the first *intifada* as a world in which "you had to fight with your fingernails" over money. He no longer enjoyed performing because the music had been cheapened by insistent dance rhythms and the playing was not on a level that he considered professional.

Clearly, Alei Hazayit filled a void for Omar. The idea of accompanying a new singer—and a female one, too, which was a rarity in the Palestinian arena—appealed to him, as did the possibility of really focusing on the musicality of performance. There was also a certain element of nostalgia. He was back with his old partners, Jamal, Walid, and Ghidian and saw it as a chance to "do some beautiful things, maybe . . . reconstruct some of the music we used to play." The difference in political status between Omar, who is an Israeli citizen and the others, who are not, had put a great stress on their relationship during the first *intifada*. Omar said that they had drifted apart:

> For them I was an Israeli. [They said or thought] "He's over there with his citizenship and we're here suffering from the *intifada*." Maybe it was my fault that I didn't contact them. I worked really hard during that period, coming home late . . . occasionally, we would talk on the phone but it wasn't like it used to be.

Working together with Shoham gave them the opportunity to renew their friendship and their musical partnership.

A further distinction in citizenship status differentiated Jamal from Ghidian. As a resident of Jerusalem's Old City, Jamal is accorded many of the rights of Israeli citizens as part of the state's attempt to extend and normalize Israeli control over all of Jerusalem. Ghidian, who lives in Abu Dis, a few minutes southeast of the Old City, is subject to military closures and required to obtain and renew permits in order to move around, particularly at times of heightened violence. This difference enabled Jamal (and Omar) to be far more available for rehearsals and performances than was possible for Ghidian or several other Palestinian members of the band who lived in the West Bank. This was a constant organizational concern for Shoham and Jamal.

These musicians were also motivated by the opportunity to shape every detail of a piece. Omar emphasized this, saying that he had urged Shoham not to perform at all until they had everything just right. But he under-stood that she had to accept some performances in order to keep the other musicians involved, to bring in at least symbolic payment. In fact, Shoham sometimes paid out of her own pocket in order to maintain the band.

Shoham and Omar were the constant members of Alei Hazayit as it fluctuated over the years. Tensions during the Hong Kong trip led to Jamal's departure from the group. He returned after a couple of years, replaced in the interim by one of his Jewish students. The 'ud position originally held by Ghidian was filled on several occasions by Fu'ad Abu Ghannam when Ghidian traveled abroad. Rajay Ayad, the *nay* player, joined the group late and left when political pressures became too uncomfort-able—he lived in Bethlehem on the West Bank—only to return a few years later. During his absence the group made their first recordings and Jamal brought in two older, more experienced musicians to play *nay* and *'ud*. They did not stay in the band due to personality conflicts. After the tragic loss of Walid, Jamal was forced to seek a replacement for his longtime drumming partner. At first he introduced a much younger drummer who, like Fu'ad, had studied Arab music formally at Mustafa Kurd's school. For the Hong Kong trip he brought Ahmad Jabber, more for his ability to sing with Jamal as the male chorus supporting Shoham, than for his very lim-ited abilities as a drummer. The synthesizer player, Ibrahim, was let go after he stood up the band at a concert, preferring to honor a conflicting commitment to another band.

After Ibrahim's departure Jamal felt that some other instrument was needed to give some support in the low register. Through the recording studio engineer he found Jean Claude Jones, head of the jazz department at the Jerusalem Academy of Music and Dance, who added tracks to the band's first recording and went on to rehearse and perform with them for a while, but left over the question of commitment. Another Jewish Israeli bassist, Shlomo Moyal, was brought in for the group's appearance at the 1998 Festival of Asian Arts in Hong Kong. He continued to perform with them after that, but also failed to demonstrate sufficient commitment be-cause he played in several other groups, including Yemei Habeynatayim, an Israeli ethnic music band. This turnover was hardly surprising given the pressures on the group and its lack of commercial success. It changed the overall character of the group far less than one might expect.

Repertoire

The band's character derived from the strong lead personalities, the close personal connections among core members, and the repertoire they chose. Shoham and Jamal sought to balance their program by alternating Hebrew and Arabic texts from one song to the next and sometimes even within one song. Aside from one or two songs by Shoham, they chose songs from three types of Israeli and Arab sources. Shoham taught the band *shirei erets yisrael* (see chapter 3 and 🔊 audio tracks 1, 2, and 3) and also introduced

Ladino songs in Hebrew translation (rather than singing them in Ladino as she had in her earlier performances). Most of these, such as "The Drunkard's Song,"[10] are familiar to older Israeli Jews but Arab band members did not know them. The third category of repertoire consisted of songs in Arabic suggested by Jamal. Most of these were relatively light in nature: "Til'it Ya Mahla Nurha" and "Zuruni," composed in the early twentieth century by the famed Egyptian Sayyid Darwish, and more recent songs, such as "Wihyat 'Inayya" by the preeminent Syrian singer Sabah Fakhri. Shoham wanted to perform "heavier" songs from the classical Arabic repertoire, but Jamal, as her teacher, limited her to the well-known *muwashshah*[11] "Lamma Bada Yatathanna." In addition to these songs, the musicians also played standard Arab repertoire as instrumental introductions and interludes.

The band connected with Jewish and Arab constituencies through songs that were familiar to one group or the other, but they also innovated by performing arrangements that differed from the mainstream and other currents in Israeli and Palestinian musical life. Unlike the textual balance between Arabic and Hebrew, the initial frame of reference for musical interpretation was comprised of the conventions of Arab musical performance practice. This is normal for Arab songs, of course, but refreshingly new for the Hebrew songs that they arranged. It can also be seen as a radical undermining of the communal Zionist ethos, the "Israeliness" developed precisely through these "Songs of the land of Israel."[12] On the other hand, the "Arabness" of the ensemble was disrupted by the non-Arab bassists and by some of Shoham's vocal touches that were atypical for Arab singing.

Shoham and Jamal insisted on the uniqueness of their music and did not hasten to acknowledge models or forerunners in our conversations. Each was vociferously critical of current pop music, whether in Hebrew or Arabic. But when they spoke of other musicians, their tastes ran in strikingly different directions. Shoham considered Rita, an Israeli star of Iranian birth, to be a good singer, but did not like her material. She also named Chava Alberstein, one of the mainstays of Israeli and Yiddish folk music, and David Da'or, a countertenor who has become a pop sensation.[13] These are singers who perform in a soft, lyrical style. Jamal, on the other hand, most admires what he terms "heavy" Arab voices, pointing to Umm

10. "Shir Hashikor" is translated from the Ladino "La Vida Do."
11. This is a poetic form that dates back to medieval Spain but most *muwashshahat* sung today were probably composed in the nineteenth and early twentieth centuries.
12. Shamma Boyarin brought this to my attention when I played Alei Hazayit's recording of "Sheharhoret." Seroussi has traced the history of this Hebrew reworking of a Ladino song, "Morenica a mi llaman," which probably originated in Saloniki (2002b). The song has been a staple of Habreira Hativ'it's repertoire since the 1970s, in an arrangement that differs greatly from Alei Hazayit's.
13. Jan. 3, 1995.

Kulthum and 'Abdel Mutallib, while disparaging Fairuz and other singers whose sound is smooth rather than gutsy.

Emotional Appeal—Love and Peace

Differing in almost every respect, including their taste in singers, Jamal and Shoham found ways to collaborate based on a shared belief in the emotional power of music and the central role of the human voice in unleashing that power. Shoham recounted her strongest experience of this power at a memorial ceremony where she sang on behalf of bereaved mothers and put everyone in a state of shock with the power of her improvised song. She said that she took something from within herself and sang her anger against God. The mother who had asked her to sing completely lost her senses for a while. Shoham also related how she used to test the power of her voice on her sister's babies, trying to affect their emotional state.

Jamal's most powerful experiences are of a different nature and bring us to a forum for Jewish and Arab coexistence that is seldom discussed—the criminal underworld. Based on several years of performing at a Jerusalem pub frequented by Jewish and Arab pimps, prostitutes, and the like, Jamal claimed that criminals are the listeners most deeply moved by music. He said they have hardened themselves to the world, but their hearts are open to the musician who knows how to steal inside: "You're the only one stronger than them because you get inside and play on the strings inside them. You don't knock on the door—you enter their heart like a thief and steal it. They respect no one but musicians because musicians are the only ones who can still make them cry." Because of this Jamal would give them more "art" than he would present in a big concert.[14]

Shoham and Jamal both regard the human voice as the primary vehicle for achieving the desired emotional effect. Shoham not only sings texts with great expressivity and dramatic gesture, but often croons in a voice that ranges from rhapsodic to mournful to enchanting. She uses her striking features to good effect and dances with her arms and torso as she sings. Jamal's poetic declamations, delivered with dramatic—some might say melodramatic—flair, augment the effect. As a comedian he, too, is a master of broad gestures. As a musician his principal goal is to present the song in as colorful and strongly affective a manner as possible.

Jamal repeatedly stressed to me the importance of imagination, of envisioning the right mood when arranging and performing a song. When he listens to the great singers, he says he can describe the exact picture they evoke. To communicate in this manner, the singer must believe in what he or she is singing, he said, supporting this assertion with creative etymology by linking the Hebrew words for belief (*emunah*) and art (*omanut*).[15]

14. Dec. 21, 1994.
15. Dec. 20, 1994.

Jamal's concern was to evoke moods and places with his "colorful" arrangements. While we listened to one of his arrangements, Jamal asked me "where are you now?" Caught unaware, I did not know what he meant. To him the band's sound at that moment evoked Saudi Arabia and the Gulf States. Jamal used the word *tseva* (meaning color in Hebrew) on many occasions to refer to different national styles, a direct translation of the word *lawn* (color), which is used in Arabic to denote musical style.[16] He extended the metaphor, conceiving of his arrangements and performances as painting pictures with sound. Shoham took up this usage and spoke of Jamal as a great painter. She said that she wanted each song to be a different color, aggressive in one song, very soft in another.

While the initiative to seek Arab drumming was Shoham's, the choice of musicians and instruments was largely shaped by Jamal's artistic tastes and his personal connections. It was Shoham's great luck, she told me many times, that Jamal is far more than a drummer. As an experienced actor with a rich creative vision and a dramatic sense developed through years of acting in Palestinian and Israeli productions, he took a theatrical approach to the interpretation and arrangement of songs. Shoham especially liked Jamal's idea to use props, such as a scarf, a cane, or other accessories, to heighten the effect of certain songs.[17] The unabashedly dramatic arrangements and staging were intended to achieve the primary goal that they shared with each other: to touch the hearts of their audience. Choosing songs that were well known to a large portion of their audience enhanced such communication.

These songs evoked themes, such as hope, peace, love, and nostalgia. Omar summed up their repertoire as

> songs of hope. Love songs, [about] a simpler life . . . a simplicity that we need. Today everything is so complicated, modern life. [In the song "Til'it Ya Mahla Nurha"] you are reminded of the young girl who wakes in the morning and looks at the sun. Those are the days that we long for. It's already nostalgia for us. And we can find them through this nostalgia, we reconstruct them, we sing them and play them . . . You're in modern society, everything's not straightforward, everything's according to laws, forms, computer, waiting for the computer, to send the material, to wait for the material . . . it's all complicated. Suddenly, according to this song, you're walking in the field with a water jar on the shoulder and you're singing love songs.[18]

The image of contemporary life that Omar presents may be shaped by the bureaucratic particularities of his job as a social worker, but his outlook is not atypical.[19]

16. See Racy 1981.
17. Jan. 3, 1995.
18. Jan. 7, 1997.
19. The Israeli government and public services are highly bureaucratized.

Shoham explained that Alei Hazayit expresses its message of peaceful coexistence through songs of love rather than through overtly political texts.

We speak about interpersonal relations; we speak about love of a man for a woman, of a woman for a man. We speak about things that are beautiful. The very fact that we are together and singing them it's fraternity, it's being together. In my opinion that is the greatest message of peace. [It's] not necessarily to wave it [like a flag].[20]

She noted that one of their Arabic songs, "Jib Li Salam," includes the word *salam* (peace) in its title and text, although its literal meaning in this context is to bring regards. An Israeli government publication mistranslated the song title as "Bring me Peace" when it reported on Alei Hazayit's performance in Jordan.[21] Shoham herself played on ambiguity in her spoken Hebrew introduction to this song, ending with "they say that the dove is the messenger of peace."[22] She felt that their message was clear: "From all that we are doing together it is evident," she said, adding that, "the essence of our love songs is fraternity."[23] She believed strongly that peace must be created from the bottom up, through personal interaction and connections, not through elite events, such as their concert in Jordan that was attended by business executives.[24]

When the band performed at the Festival of Asian Arts, a Hong Kong reviewer received the message clearly:

People might fight each other, but we all have the same concerns underneath: everyone wants to love and be happy. The message— understated in this non-political performance—is a fine musical argument for peace. (Finlay 1998)

Given the severity of Palestinian violence toward other Palestinians who are suspected of collaborating with Israel, this is probably as explicit as the Arab members of Alei Hazayit could dare to be. The love songs find their way into people's hearts because they deal with experiences and feelings that are nearly universal. The partnership of Jewish and Arab performers impresses itself upon the audience as an example of a productive relationship, a glimpse of a possible future of coexistence, while the complexities of such relationships and the obstacles that stand in their way temporarily recede from view.

20. Jan. 3, 1995.
21. On www.mfa.gov.il/mfa/go.asp?MFAH0a580, Web site of the Israeli Ministry of Foreign Affairs, in 1995.
22. This is my translation from a recording that Shoham gave me of a concert at her house.
23. Jan. 3, 1995.
24. Jan. 2, 1997.

5

Bustan Abraham

Formed in 1991, the same year as Alei Hazayit, Bustan Abraham also brought together Jewish and Arab musicians but differed greatly in constitution and focus. It was the brainchild of Avshalom Farjun, a concert promoter and self-taught musician who gathered some of the best young musicians in Israel to perform instrumental music. The band built up a repertoire centered on original compositions utilizing a broad and variegated stylistic palette. The members of the group brought a wealth of experience from a variety of musical practices, including not only Arab and Western art musics, but also flamenco, jazz, blues, and other American vernacular instrumental styles, as well as Turkish and Persian music. They learned from one another and built on this broad foundation of multiple competences.

During the 1980s, Farjun had pursued his interest in "Eastern" music—by which he meant traditional music from Turkey, Persia, and India—as an impresario bringing foreign musicians to perform in Israel. He approached me in this capacity to arrange appearances at the Hebrew University for Japanese and Indian musicians whom he brought to Israel. One of the latter was Krishnamurti Sridhar, a *sarod* player. In addition to Sridhar's main concert with a *tabla* player at the 1987 Israel Festival, Farjun produced a late night jam session with three local "ethnic" musicians.[1] According to reports from my students, the audience was enthralled by the musical dialogue and the group and solo improvisations that lasted until morning. Two of the participating musicians, Taiseer Elias and Miguel Herstein, enjoyed their collaboration so much that they formed a duo called White Bird.

Taiseer, who has already appeared in earlier chapters, brought to White Bird his *'ud* and violin along with his training in Arab and Western art

---

1. I use this term here as most Israelis would: to indicate musicians playing music that is perceived to be rooted in a tradition other than Western art or popular music.

musics. Miguel Herstein, a founding member of Habreira Hativ'it, brought guitar and banjo, on which he played flamenco and various vernacular American musical styles. Their repertoire consisted of arrangements, improvisations, and a few original compositions. The duo enjoyed some success and began to tour abroad, promoting their music and spreading a message of peaceful coexistence between Arabs and Jews, just as the first *intifada* was beginning. Miguel recalled, "It was like a statement. We really believed [in peaceful coexistence] and we wanted to play in schools, to show kids—Arab kids, Jewish kids—peace can work."[2] Inside the cover of their one commercial cassette, they stated: "It is our sincere hope that through these concerts we can help build a bridge of understanding that will bring us all closer to peace." This is one of the earliest such statements by a musical group of the message of peaceful collaboration that was to be picked up by other bands in the 1990s.

Four years after the seminal "ethnic" jam session, Farjun realized his dream of forming an "ethnic super group." In consultation with Taiseer, he brought together instrumentalists interested in mixing diverse musical styles to create new instrumental compositions. Though he did not set out to form a representative mix of Jews and Arabs, the group included both.

Through intensive rehearsals that took the form of extended jam sessions, the musicians began to discover ways to play together. Looking back a decade later, Miguel Herstein described the formation of the ensemble for me:

> And we're all banging away, you know, trying to figure out what . . . after a few rehearsals like this I think a couple of them decided okay we don't want to do this. And it distilled down to, I think, nine. And then we started working and we started recording. . . . I think the first piece that we ever recorded came out of that . . . and then we kept rehearsing all the time to build a repertoire and get tight. (Jan. 6, 2002)

Other members of the group told me these sessions began as a tug of war, each musician attempting to pull the others into his own style. Over a period of weeks they began to listen to one another, stopped pulling so hard, and started finding meeting points between their various positions, gradually developing a sense of how they might work together as a unit.

The work process did not suit everyone, causing considerable turnover in the first few weeks. Miguel recalled that,

> We were working like four days a week. Rehearsals, you know, six, seven hours, four days a week, people coming from all over the country. So it was hard and there was no income from it. So [a top Arab drummer] left after a while. He said, "You know, my wife is giving me a hard time and I'm not earning any money and I've got to feed my family. . . . Even if we do make it so how much am I going to make? I

2. Jan. 6, 2002.

make more playing at weddings. That's what I want to do." And then [another Arab drummer] dropped out for the same reasons basically. (Jan. 6, 2002)

Within a relatively short time, a group of eight musicians emerged from these intensive jam sessions. Avshalom played the Turkish *kanun* (plucked zither similar to the Arab *qanun*).[3] Taiseer settled on playing *'ud* rather than violin in this ensemble, leaving that part to his friend Nassim Dakwar (also equally adept at *'ud* and violin). Others included Miguel on guitar and banjo, Amir Milstein on flute, and Yehuda Siliki, who had immigrated to Israel from Turkey, on *baglama-saz* (Turkish long-necked lute). They tried several drummers[4] before they found Zohar Fresco, who was very young at that time and just shifting from playing drum set in rock style to *darbukkah* and other Middle Eastern hand percussion. A few weeks after Fresco joined, Emmanuel Mann was brought in to replace a double bass player whose style other members thought too jazz-oriented.[5]

Avshalom and Taiseer formed this group by drawing on networks of musicians who had worked together or were otherwise acquainted. Avshalom invited musicians from among his friends and the bands that he had promoted. By then he knew many of the Jewish musicians active in ethnic music in Israel. Taiseer provided access to a network of Arab musicians, although only Nassim stayed with the band. Prior associations linked the band members: Taiseer had extensive experience playing with both Miguel and Nassim, while Miguel and Emmanuel had both been members of Habreira Hativ'it (though at different times), and Avshalom had produced concerts by that group. Emmanuel and Zohar abandoned a band they had just formed to join Bustan Abraham.

Bustan Abraham remained almost unchanged over the next ten years, except for the departures of Yehuda Siliki after the first album and Emmanuel Mann after the fourth (see figure 5.1). Both left because the band was not earning enough to provide a steady source of income. Siliki was not replaced, probably because there were enough other plucked string instruments (*qanun*, *'ud*, and guitar or banjo) covering the same registers.[6] But when Mann moved to New York in search of better performance opportunities, the lack of a bass instrument had to be remedied. Naor Carmi, who had replaced Mann in Habreira Hativ'it years earlier, almost immediately replaced him in Bustan Abraham. The membership was otherwise so stable that when Miguel Herstein was forced to take a leave for medical reasons, his name was still announced at concerts and he went right back

3. Hereafter I will follow Avshalom's use of the Arabic name.
4. One was Avi Agababa who went on to work extensively with other musicians pursuing similar musical goals, such as the East-West Ensemble, Darma, and various projects with Yair Dalal. See chapters 7 and 8.
5. Amir Milstein, who was the most jazz-oriented band member, said that he really liked the first player, too (Jan. 15, 1997).
6. He did appear on one track of their second album as a guest singer rather than an integral member of the band.

Figure 5.1 Bustan Abraham, from left to right: Amir Milstein, Avshalom Farjun, Nassim Dakwar, Taiseer Elias, Zohar Fresco, Emmanuel Mann, Miguel Herstein (photo courtesy of Avshalom Farjun, Nada Productions)

into the band when he recovered. And when the drummer Zohar Fresco was temporarily unable to tour due to other commitments, it was clear that his replacement was only temporary.

Nada Productions: Recordings, Promotion, Sub-Ensembles

Bustan Abraham issued recordings at a steady pace of one CD every two years or so. The eponymous *Bustan Abraham* appeared in 1992, less than a year after the band formed. The second album, *Pictures Through the Painted Window,* included one song, performed by three guest artists in Hebrew, Arabic, and Spanish. The inclusion of guests expanded on the next two albums. *Abadai,* released in 1996, showcased the band's collaboration with Greek music specialist Ross Daly and two of his band members, whom Avshalom Farjun had brought over for the Israel Festival. The album was a full collaboration involving several pieces by Daly, in addition to compositions by members of Bustan, and the guests played on every track. The following year, this formula was modified for *Fanar.* Most of the compositions were by members of Bustan and each guest artist performed only one or two tracks. The stature of some of those guest artists was particularly high. World-renowned Indian musicians Hariprasad Chaurasia and Zakir

Hussain were showcased in a composition by Taiseer Elias, while Israeli-American pop star Noa (Achinoam Nini) sang a song of her choice. There were no guests on the final album *Hamsa*, released in 2000, the tenth year of the band's existence. That same year, Avshalom Farjun also released *Ashra: The First Decade Collection*, a compilation of Bustan Abraham's "best temperamental [expressive?] and upbeat compositions."

Bustan Abraham's recordings all appeared under the imprint of Avshalom Farjun's company Nada Productions.[7] Through this company Farjun has conducted several interconnected business endeavors—band management, concert promotion, impresario for foreign musicians, and record production—earning the characterization "the Israeli musician who introduced world music to this land."[8] In addition to the guests on Bustan Abraham's albums, Farjun promoted other foreign musicians, such as the Turkish American musician Omar Farouk Tekbilek and his band, with whom Bustan Abraham performed but did not record.

Farjun managed Bustan Abraham's concerts and tours as well as those of two ancillary bands—White Bird (the Herstein-Elias duo) and Ziryab Trio—that were subsets of the main band. The Ziryab Trio was named for a legendary musician who fled from Baghdad to Muslim Spain in the ninth century and is credited with founding the Andalusian musical tradition.[9] It consisted of the two Arab members of the group, Taiseer and Nassim, with Zohar on *riqq* (Arab tambourine) playing Arab and Turkish art music. For some pieces Emmanuel Mann (and later Naor Carmi) added a simplified version of the melody or a contrapuntal line on fretless bass guitar or double bass. The members of Bustan Abraham who played instruments that are harder to adapt to Arab music (flute, guitar, banjo) or who lacked the knowledge to render such pieces idiomatically were not included. This subgroup is significant as evidence of Farjun's entrepreneurial sense, the demands of the world market for such music, and the economic realities of international touring. With the possibility of offering foreign concert promoters a package that included not only the seven-man Bustan Abraham, but also the more intimate and less costly Ziryab Trio and White Bird duo, Farjun sought to maximize potential bookings (see figure 5.2). So we find, for instance, both White Bird and Bustan Abraham on the roster of the 11th Jewish Culture Festival (Festiwal Kultury Zydowskiej) in Poland in 1991 (Ziryab was not yet formed at that time); all three groups appeared at the 1992 Festival of Asia in Hong Kong; and the 1998 Festival of Jewish Music in London featured concerts by Ziryab and Bustan Abraham.[10]

Anchored by Bustan Abraham's recordings, the Nada series includes various allied projects such as *Oriental Art Music* by the Ziryab Trio, *Tucan*

7. It was renamed Nada Records and Productions by the time *Hamsa* was issued in 2000.
8. Aijzenstadt 2000.
9. Shiloah has called him a culture hero (1995: 74).
10. See www.jewishfestival.pl/festiwal.html. The London festival was sponsored by the Jewish Music Institute (JMI) at the School for Oriental and African Studies.

Figure 5.2   Nada business cards for Bustan Abraham and its sub-ensembles White Bird and Ziryab

by Amir Milstein's Tucan Trio, and a CD devoted to noted Iraqi Jewish *qanun* player Avraham Salman, who had appeared with Bustan Abraham in concert. Another recording in this series, particularly noteworthy for the subject at hand, is *Arabandi,* a live recording of a concert featuring Krishnamurti Sridhar in a return engagement with Taiseer Elias and two other musicians that is reminiscent of the 1987 jam session that laid the foundation for Bustan Abraham.[11]

The band's record sales were never as high as expected, but Farjun told me in a 2003 interview that they had remained surprisingly steady for all the albums over the years. Sales had averaged around 25,000 units per album, not bad for the Israeli market, but hardly significant on the world market.[12] The band's true impact was greater than these sales figures would indicate. One piece was included in the widely sold *Planet Soup* anthology of world music, for instance, and they performed widely throughout Europe and North America, including the leading world music festival WOMAD in England and Canada. Internet searches I conducted every few years showed that some of their pieces received repeat airplay on stations in various countries.

Farjun was frustrated in his attempts to improve distribution outside Israel. Neither the deal he signed with the Belgian company Crammed, which markets the CramWorld recording label (ZapMama is one of its better known bands), nor a deal with a second-tier American company pro-

11. See chapters 8 and 9.
12. June 23, 2003. In the Israeli recording industry, sales of 20,000 units qualifies an album as gold, a status frequently achieved by local recordings according to Regev and Seroussi (2004: 40).

duced the hoped-for surge in sales. Outside Israel a large portion of the band's album sales were generated at concerts rather than through distributors.[13] Regev and Seroussi note the bifurcation of the Israeli recording industry into "three major local companies that produced approximately 70 percent of Israeli music and between them represented the six major international record companies; and a second sector consisting of various smaller companies, which produced specific styles of Israeli music" (2004: 40–41). Nada clearly belongs to the latter group.

Concerts, Festivals, Repertoire

Judging by newspaper reviews, repeat invitations, the musicians' accounts, and my own observations, the band's performances were well received inside Israel and abroad, gaining a loyal fan base in Israel and considerable recognition outside. In addition to individual concerts, they often performed at festivals. The nature of the festival varied considerably. Sometimes the band fit the theme of a festival closely; at other times the connection was tenuous. Their earliest foreign appearance was as the sole Israeli act at the 1992 Festival of Asia in Hong Kong (where Alei Hazayit later performed). At a world music festival in Hamburg, part of Welt-Kultur-Sommer '93 (World Culture Summer 1993), Bustan Abraham performed in a lineup with Kurds, Algerians, and Turks. At the 1994 Festival d'Elx in Spain, which had a medieval theme, Bustan Abraham appeared as an "intercultural" group alongside ensembles billed as Sephardic and Muslim.[14] When they toured Europe in the summer of 1995, they performed in England at WOMAD and the Royal Festival Hall in London. The WOMAD program, as is usual for this premiere world music festival, was highly eclectic: On the open air stage Bustan Abraham was preceded by the Tanzanian Afro-Pop band Hukwe Zawose and followed by the Tongan sisters Vika and Linda Bull. The day before, the same stage had hosted Pow Wow Drummers, the Master Musicians of Jajouka, a Laotian troupe, and the Hungarian singer Marta Sebestyen with her band. On Sunday night a Ceilidh with Shooglenifty, a "progressive Celtic band from Scotland," preceded the Ziryab Trio's midnight performance.[15]

Earlier that year, Bustan Abraham had already visited London to play the Royal Albert Hall in an event titled "Towards Humanity: Music to Celebrate the Middle East," a fundraiser for charities in Egypt, Israel, and other Middle Eastern countries that included musicians from England and several Arab countries. That same summer they performed in Marseille, at the "Festival Marseille Méditerranée." This was a celebration of the

13. June 23, 2003.
14. See See http://web.archive.org/web/20030916202839/http:// www.festival medieval.com/en/festival/historia/?id=3 for an official description of the festival's content.
15. WOMAD Festival 1995.

Mediterranean basin so the program booklet appended to each group's name its country of origin—Corsica, Sicily, Israel, Tunisia, Italy, Egypt, Syria, Turkey, Morocco, Sardinia, Albania, Greece/Macedonia, and Lebanon —proving that most Mediterranean countries were represented.

December 1995 found Bustan Abraham in Europe again, this time participating in a festival titled l'Art de la Paix (the art of peace) in Brussels. Here Bustan Abraham and the Ziryab Trio performed alongside Simon Shaheen, the New York-based Israeli jazz-fusion band Esta, and a group of Palestinian music students in a festival of Israeli and Palestinian culture that also included theater and paintings. The program book opened with statements by the Israeli and Palestinian Ministers of Culture, Shulamit Aloni and Yasser Abed Rabbo. In some senses Bustan could be perceived as an embodiment of the conceptual divide around which this event was constructed. It is indicative of the complexities of Israeli/Palestinian politics, allegiances, and identities that Simon Shaheen and the two Arab members of Bustan Abraham (Taiseer and Nassim) performed on opposite sides of the divide. All three are from Arab towns in the Galilee and each followed nearly the same professional path, studying with Shaheen's father, then at a Western music conservatory in Haifa, followed by the Academy in Jerusalem. Their ways parted when Shaheen left for the U.S., where he has established himself as the most visible Palestinian musician, suppressing any mention of his former Israeli citizenship and education; Taiseer rose to high positions within Israeli cultural institutions and Nassim also achieved prominence in Israel, though less visibly tied to the establishment.

Bustan Abraham also performed at various Jewish music festivals. For example, in 1998 they played a Jewish music festival in Holland, where both White Bird and Bustan Abraham appeared in a weeklong series that also featured Duo Kol Tof (voice and drum duo) from Israel, and several klezmer bands. From these diverse examples, it is clear that the band had broad appeal and its image was malleable enough that promoters could fit it into programs with themes as varied as Jewish, Israeli/Palestinian, Mediterranean, Asian, and world music.

Despite the favorable reception at concerts, the frequency and extent of these tours was subject to many pressures, some of them common in the music business and some uniquely linked to Middle Eastern politics. The band toured as frequently as Avshalom could obtain bookings and extract commitments from the musicians, which became more difficult as individual musicians built reputations and became involved in other projects. However, the tension was apparent as early as 1994 when the group first reached California. At that time Taiseer told me that he and Avshalom had opposite expectations in this regard.[16] Taiseer continued to be one of the most difficult to take on tour because of his numerous professional commit-

16. Avshalom wanted to reach a larger audience through more frequent tours. Taiseer did not relish frequent trips abroad, because of familial reasons and his many professional obligations,

ments. He was considered irreplaceable, unlike Zohar, for whom Avshalom was forced to find substitute drummers when he was on tour with pop singer Noa.

Since all members of Bustan were Israeli citizens, travel was much simpler to arrange than it was for Shoham's Palestinian partners. But the band was not immune to shifts in the political situation, even if they did not suffer as many cancellations as Alei Hazayit did. When Benjamin Netanyahu became prime minister in 1996 and scuttled any hopes of progress toward further agreements between Israel and the Palestinians, Bustan Abraham suddenly found itself much less popular with festival organizers and other promoters in Europe. The situation later improved, but with the onset of the second *intifada* in late 2000, Israel's economy slid downward. By spring 2003, Bustan was forced to disband due to internal creative tensions and to lack of sufficient income, one of many victims of the difficult times that afflicted Israel's music industry.

For all his connections and business acumen, Avshalom found it hard to secure enough engagements to support the high costs of sending seven musicians, their sound engineer, and all their gear on tour. In early 1997, he decided to experiment with a run in a small Tel Aviv club. I happened to be present at the rehearsal where he announced this plan, which met with mixed responses from other members of the group. Taiseer replied, only half in jest, that they should leave him out and there would be more space for others on the small stage because he was not interested in playing at a club. By contrast, Amir told me after the concert that it was a great success and he would like to do more club dates as this would enable Bustan to tour more easily and profitably. If they had a week between large concerts in Paris and Belgium, for example, they could do two or three evenings at one of the many world music clubs in Amsterdam.[17]

Vastly different assumptions and expectations regarding suitable audiences, venues, and occasions are evident. Avshalom and Amir sought larger audiences, more numerous engagements, and greater profit. They were not deterred by preconceptions of a club setting as relatively undignified. Taiseer was not averse to gaining greater audiences and earning more money, but was more concerned with the respect accorded the musicians and their music. He linked this to the status of the venue, preferring formal concerts in "dignified" places (*mekomot mekhubadim*, he said in Hebrew) to the livelier and perhaps more chaotic atmosphere of a club. A similar divergence of opinion arose at the same rehearsal with regard to the type of pieces the band should play. Avshalom wanted the band to develop more light, crowd-pleasing pieces because booking agents found the group too serious. Several members of the group were firmly opposed. Zohar was particularly vocal on this matter, saying that he could play crowd-pleasing music elsewhere but Bustan was special. Ironically, it was at that very rehearsal that Taiseer, who was equally loath to "cheapen"

17. Jan. 15, 1997.

their music, introduced his composition "Sireen," one of the catchiest and "lightest" pieces in the group's repertoire.[18] Several years later, the issue was still alive. In an interview, Nassim told me that Bustan wants to play "interesting pieces, not dance pieces, not light music" (June 1999).

This debate was a manifestation of the fundamental problem facing the band. Marketing their music proved no less difficult than the decidedly non-trivial challenge of inventing a new type of music. It required identifying, attracting, and retaining an audience where none existed before. This challenge is hardly unique to Bustan, but the band's dedication to instrumental music was an added handicap, at least in the Israeli market, where purely instrumental music is harder to sell and receives little airplay. Early in their career, when they played the Arad Festival in July 1992, Israeli music critic Avi Efrati predicted some of the difficulties the band was likely to encounter. Comparing them to Habreira Hativ'it and the East-West Ensemble, the only other bands playing such "ethnic fusion" in Israel at the time—comparisons that the band members came to detest—he said that they were less communicative than the former and less commercial than the latter, so their chances of success were not high. He reported that only a few dozen had listened among the tens of thousands attending the festival, but noted his pleasure in this intricate music in a festival that was otherwise full of rock 'n' roll. Taking a dig at the Israeli music industry and audiences he wrote

> In other countries such ensembles can cover their costs and even earn a bit. In Israel that won't be possible so it seems that the fate of the members of Bustan will be to wander from one festival to the next in Europe and the US. They certainly have something to sell abroad. . . . Perhaps when additional high quality ensembles that play such music arise in Israel the delegitimization in the media will be removed. Lately signs of rock activity such as one sees in normal nations are appearing here, and the attitude toward jazz is improving a bit, too. Now it's the turn of locally produced "world music." The ensemble "Bustan" definitely can be the flagship of that process. (Efrati 1992, my translation)

Efrati's prescience was remarkable. Although Bustan did build an audience at home, it was indeed forced to tour extensively. It became well known in Israel, but received relatively little airplay and concerts in Israel were infrequent. There was considerable rejoicing in the press, for instance, when they gave a concert in Tel Aviv in 1998 after a year's hiatus. One critic wrote that the band had proved that their audience was loyal (Harel 1998).

Building on his prior experience promoting performers from various parts of Asia, Avshalom sensed not only what he would like to play, but also what type of music might appeal to an Israeli audience. He experimented with different types of festivals and performance venues. He pushed the

18. "Sireen," discussed in chapter 9, is named for Taiseer's daughter.

group into inserting vocal tracks on two of their albums and he attempted a crossover strategy, featuring well-known guest artists who had established audiences. However, these experiments appeared to have relatively little impact on album sales, according to several members of the band.

In contrast to Alei Hazayit, Bustan Abraham mainly played original compositions. From the first album onward they favored compositions of considerable length and stylistic variety such as "Jazz Kar-Kurd" (🔊 audio track 6). Unlike Yair Dalal (see chapter 7), the members of Bustan were not concerned with preserving and presenting heritage in the framework of this particular band. When asked whether they drew on the established forms of Arab art music for their composition, for instance, Taiseer Elias responded vehemently that they were not playing Arab music.[19] They began to build a distinctive repertoire at their first meeting when Avshalom Farjun pulled out a sketch for "Canaan," a piece he and Yehuda Siliki had been composing. For variety, some recordings and concerts also included arrangements of traditional pieces and compositions drawn from the standard repertoire of nineteenth- and twentieth-century Arab and Turkish art music, despite Taiseer's denial. Examples included Arab tunes, such as "Ah Ya Zeyn" and "Igrig," as well as Turkish and Azeri melodies. The widely known, short and simple melody of "Ah Ya Zeyn," for instance, was a useful contrast to the more complex and demanding pieces that band members tended to compose. It provided a vehicle for virtuoso performance while giving the audience an easily identifiable tune as a frame of reference. Some pieces—such as the *muwashshah* "Lamma Bada" (the same classical Arab song that Jamal Saʻid "allowed" Shoham to sing)—were given straightforward arrangements, but "Abadai" (on the album of the same name) went well beyond its source, "Nikriz Sirto" by the renowned Turkish musician Tanburi Jemil Bey (1873–1916).

Goals

In its first release, *Bustan Abraham* (1992), the band declared its mission in a bold statement that makes strong claims for the originality of this music and its superiority over other attempts at synthesis due to the care taken to integrate and balance different forms of musical expression.

> Many attempts have been made by musicians to create a synthesis between Eastern and Western cultures. Generally the result of these projects is that only one of these cultures dominates while the other is merely used for ornamentation. Bustan Abraham is attempting to face this challenge and has succeeded in pioneering a unique form of instrumental music which combines elements of both Eastern and Western forms without sacrificing the musical integrity of either.

19. Nov. 16, 1994, at a U.C. Berkeley presentation.

After explaining the band's name and origin, the notes list the instruments and styles that they assembled to "create original music on an international level." Escalating the claim to originality, the notes assert that "the combination of these instruments has never before been presented on the concert stage" and ends by stating that "Bustan Abraham aspires to become a landmark in the creation of a new musical form which speaks to both Eastern and Western audiences and to pave the way for other joint creative efforts between Arabs and Jews."[20] Beginning with a list of musical resources, they culminate in a fundamental geo-cultural assumption: There are two discrete musical worlds, Eastern and Western. Members of Alei Hazayit also invoked this binary opposition, though their musical referents for "East" and "West" were rather different from Bustan's. A rival band went so far as to call itself The East-West Ensemble. Because conceptions of the world that place Israel at the juncture of two opposing constructs pervade Israeli thought, constantly surfacing with regard to music and many other facets of life, they will be discussed at length in chapters 9 and 12.

Bustan hoped to bring the Israeli musical scene, so peripheral to the economics and hit parades of the international music industry, to the center of the world stage by presenting an example for the world and for Jews and Arabs, in particular. From here it is but a small step to the biblical prophet Isaiah's statement that Israel be an exemplary "light unto the nations" (Isaiah 42:6), a goal burned into the nation's psyche by Israel's first prime minister David Ben-Gurion (Keren 2000: 342). But the hyperbole common to liner notes should not blind us to the genuine intentions that are expressed here. The members of this band invested a great deal of time, thought, and energy into exploring ways to make music together that would derive inspiration from, but not be limited by, the various types of music that they already knew.

When I interviewed Miguel Herstein ten years after this statement first appeared on *Bustan Abraham*, he objected strongly to the use of "fusion" or "hybrid" to label the band's music because he saw their accomplishment as nothing less than the creation of a new musical language that promised to continue to develop in the future. He pointed to the continuing technical development of his younger colleagues as evidence of the success of this mission. Fusion, in his eyes, was a more apt description for experiments such as John McLaughlin's Shakti, a late 1970s venture pairing the jazz guitarist with a group of Indian musicians that included Zakir Hussein many years before Zakir performed with Bustan Abraham. In Miguel's eyes that experiment did not yield a new synthesis, no matter how exciting and inspirational he and other musicians might have found it at the time. Avshalom Farjun has expressed similar sentiments regarding the long-term trajectory of this music: "As long as there is no genuine musical tradition in Israel we must invent one. There are many . . . Yemenite music, Russian music, Rumanian and Moroccan . . . it will certainly take 100 or 200 years

20. The liner notes also include a Hebrew version of this statement, discussed below.

before a definite style emerges from all that. We are only an attempt to bring that all together."[21]

A more explicit critique of fusion is offered in the Hebrew notes to Bustan Abraham's first album, which makes a similar claim with a few significant differences. Here is my translation of the beginning:

> Despite the existence in Israel and in the world of bands that combine Western and Eastern music, it is difficult to find ones that attempt and succeed to create original instrumental music that is the product of genuine, deep-rooted, authentic synthesis of these cultures. Often the Eastern music is merely an exotic ornament to the Western music or, on the other hand, an attempt to give Western harmony and character to well-known Eastern music.

Various members of the group have enlarged on this critique in our discussions of other bands. Most often they criticize other musicians for not having a deep enough grounding in the musical traditions from which they draw and for failing to integrate them well. The steadfastness with which Avshalom, at least, held to the program laid out at the beginning of the band's career was evident in his remarks at the last Bustan Abraham concert I attended in 2000. Between pieces he spoke to the audience of the band's music being the "essence of the Israeli experience." It is a "mixture of cultures, origins, religions" and "Eastern, Western and worldwide influences."

The liner notes to the second CD (*Pictures through a Painted Window*, 1994) developed the goals of the group in another direction. Having demonstrated their ability to create new musical means of expression, they went on to tout egalitarian creativity:

> The desire to create a new standard of originality in Israeli music, as well as world music in general, brought the members of the group, musicians and composers of the highest order, both Jewish and Arab, to devote the best of their time and talents to this joint creation. All are partners in the composing and arranging.

All the evidence I gathered supported this claim. The band's emphasis on originality of expression manifested in the high proportion of original compositions in their repertoire and in the impressive variety of compositional devices deployed by members of the group over the course of their five CDs. Five years after the band formed, Taiseer and I discussed their process of composing and arranging as a group. He said, "Occasionally we get frustrated . . . but usually we find a solution together and the more we progress—I don't know if professionally, but in terms of time—it becomes more difficult because we don't want to repeat ourselves and don't want to compromise and that creates difficulties" (Jan. 13, 1997). These liner notes

21. Meyer 2000a, my translation.

also imply an evolutionary trajectory heading toward a distinctive Israeli music that is expressive of the local mix of cultures. Band members had quite different ideas about what the exact nature of that mix should be (see chapter 9), but the lack of a unitary "sound" or formula may well have been one of their strengths. Even as they integrated their ideas and resources into a synthesis that many judged highly successful, they maintained considerable variety.

In our conversations over the years, Taiseer repeatedly contrasted Bustan Abraham to his collaborations with Israeli composer and pianist Menahem Wiesenberg, which were firmly situated in the established institutions and practices of contemporary art music, with their associated respectability. He struggled to locate Bustan Abraham's music between that of professional composers such as Wiesenberg, on the one hand, and what he characterized as "horrible, commercial music," on the other.

> We know a certain type of solution . . . we don't have any problem to find it but some of the [members of the band] have become more sophisticated as it were and have worked with others. When we started Bustan it was more spontaneous, more on the emotional, personal level . . . there was a fun atmosphere, we didn't have any plans. . . . Now Zohar has advanced a lot, works with very professional people, the same for me, for Amir. And solutions that worked for us six years ago no longer work as successful musical solutions. It's a problem. . . . We don't want to make concert music, complex and sophisticated of the type that Menahem Wiesenberg, for instance, writes for me because we're not that kind of band and we can't do it. But on the other hand we don't want to make terrible music. So in my opinion the way we started out was correct: to do something good, sophisticated but that remains more in the area of folk/popular music [*musika amamit* does not imply commercial pop], that speaks to people more. . . . And then we shouldn't look for sophisticated, complex solutions because that doesn't suit us, that's not what we are. (Jan. 13, 1997)

This points back to the band's dispute over appropriate repertoire and venues (and belies the considerable complexity of some of Taiseer's compositions). If one has been inculcated, as Taiseer has through his education at the music Academy and the university, with the values of European art music and its attendant norms of performance and respect for performers and composers, then light catchy pieces, played in a night club may well seem repugnant.

Taiseer Elias was not alone in struggling to define the place of this music among the various types of available music, to locate it on a "map" of world music. The difficulty of defining the band's style beset critics and promoters who must capture style in words, either to attract an audience or to communicate their aesthetic judgment to readers. An overly complicated headlline in *Der Aufbau* is typical, the editors resorting to a title and a bipartite subtitle in their effort to capture the complexity:

Wanderer zwischen Orient und Okzident
Jazz, Ethno, Reggae: Die israelische Gruppe Bustan Abraham[22]

The reviewer sets the stage with the hallowed East/West binary and the plot thickens as he strews it with stylistic appellations of varying imprecision. "Reggae" may evoke fairly consistent images to most North American and European readers (though I find no connection to the band's music) while "jazz" probably indexes a broader spectrum of playing styles, but it is difficult to begin to imagine the limits of what "ethno" might mean for someone unfamiliar with the band. Interviewing members of Bustan Abraham, the same reporter writes, "Without denying its sources, an independent musical form has arisen which can only very imprecisely be described with the term Ethnopop. Drum machines and synthesizers do not occur [in this music]. The core remains under the control of acoustic instruments."[23] The reporter was struggling with placement on a folk-art continuum—that much is evident from the "pop" that he popped in—but the statement that no drum machines and synthesizers were used qualifies that assessment. We learn more about the reporter's expectations than we do about the actual music. The challenge of describing and positioning the band's highly varied array of musical practices is discussed further in chapter 9.

Musicians' Motivations: "Bustan Is Our Home"

Speaking with me in 1999, at a time when the band was not particularly active and each member was deeply involved in other ventures, Nassim could still say "No matter how busy we are Bustan is our top priority because our home is in this ensemble. We don't work for anyone. We don't belong to anyone. Everyone feels that this is *his* project." He elaborated on the democratic process that made this possible, "And I say this in all honesty: In Bustan there are very good musicians, with the correct view of things. And everyone who says a sentence we weigh what he has said and analyze it. And we play it and listen and decide whether it's right or not, appropriate or not. There are enough ideas, and very good ideas."[24] This process involved disagreements, of course, sometimes expressed with great conviction. After the argument over repertoire and venue that I witnessed in 1997, one member of the group told me he thought that they needed to disband for a while, perhaps six months, until they missed one another, so that they could recapture the early excitement of discovery.

The band's high standards and its seriousness of purpose were as important as their joint ownership of the music. The sense that this was a group of equals, who derived great artistic satisfaction from participation

22. "Travelers [or Wayfarers] between Orient and Occident/Jazz, Ethno, Reggae: The Israeli group Bustan Abraham" (Meyer 2000b, my translation).
23. Meyer 2000a, my translation.
24. July 1999.

in Bustan, was very strong in many conversations I had with individual members of the group. In addition to the appeal of the democratic model, musicians also saw Bustan as a place to retreat from the commercial music world. Miguel called it a haven, a place where they could get together to make the music they wanted without considering commercial pressures. He did note that it was not a completely detached utopia. They were realistic, to varying degrees, regarding the mix of light and serious music necessary to draw an audience.[25]

In the end the group did break up, not without some bitterness. Accounts were a bit hazy, even though I collected them less than half a year later. The deteriorating economic situation at home hurt. A few months before the second *intifada*, Nassim noted that local municipalities in Israel were no longer putting on festivals, thus depriving the band of one of their main venues in Israel.[26] Things got worse once the *intifada* was underway, as touring opportunities abroad disappeared in a de facto European boycott of musicians from Israel, whether Jews or Arabs. As each musician became busier with alternative engagements, scheduling rehearsals became more problematic. There were also artistic differences, strongly divergent opinions over which way the group should proceed. The old East/West dichotomy surfaced again when I discussed the demise of the band with Amir and Avshalom, each blaming it on members pulling in opposite directions. Nassim left first, feeling that the band had reached the end of the road. Amir, Zohar, and Taiseer regrouped without the others, adding a jazz pianist to form a quartet under the name Bustan Abraham, but this did not last long. Plans for a reunion tour in 2007 fell through due to scheduling conflicts, but the very fact that all were willing to discuss a reunion shows that the rift had started to heal.

Coexistence

To conclude this chapter, I return to the final sentence of the band's mission statement: "Bustan Abraham aspires to . . . pave the way for other joint creative efforts between Arabs and Jews." Speaking with band members and reading interviews published over the years, I found that opinions diverged regarding the importance of promoting peaceful existence. Miguel noted that while this was the intended message of White Bird, his duo with Taiseer, in the case of Bustan Abraham it was forced upon them by reporters.[27] When I asked Taiseer about the motivations for founding Bustan, he contrasted the band with certain other groups that had arisen (in his opinion) principally to promote joint efforts by Jews and Arabs:

> We in Bustan, for instance, started the group not for political reasons. We started it because . . . by chance I met Avshalom and we wanted to

25. Jan. 6, 2002.
26. May 2000.
27. Jan. 6, 2002.

do something together and he telephoned Paco de Lucia and so on . . . and then we wanted to start a band and it was by chance that there was this combination [of people] . . . at first, I was alone, the only Arab. I played violin and 'ud and then I saw that we needed both violin and 'ud all the time so we brought Nassim. And that's why the division is unequal, two Arabs and five Jews. We're not going to do that kitsch [of mixing Jews and Arabs just for political purposes]. So it's great that there are [groups that combine Middle Eastern and Western music] but you know sometimes they start because Jews and Arabs say let's make a group and sometimes that's at the expense of the quality . . . when Bustan started there were hardly any other groups like it. There was just Habreira Hativ'it and East-West, neither of which had Arabs. That wasn't Jewish/Arab fusion but a group of Jews playing music from various Eastern cultures. (June 26, 1998)

It was clearly important to Taiseer to prioritize artistic motivations over sociopolitical ones, without denying the latter. Amir told me, several years earlier, that political messages were peripheral to their work, complaining that reporters often focused on those issues rather than talking about the music, which was the musicians' primary interest. The band found such interviews very frustrating,[28] a fact noted by *Der Aufbau*'s reporter: "It is tiresome to get the members of the group to comment on politics. To questions about the peace process one hears 'I am no politician' from the founder of the group" (Meyer 2000).

Yet the fact remained that the band exemplified peaceful coexistence and artistic collaboration between Jews and Arabs. When it suited them they exploited interest in that message to their benefit. In return for crucial financial backing received from a New York foundation for the recording of the first album and subsequent U.S. tour, the band added Abraham to its name and included the following statement in the liner notes:

The Abraham Fund, a not-for-profit organization registered in the United States, Canada and Israel, encourages Jewish and Arab citizens of Israel to live and work together with mutual respect and harmony. The Fund supports, rewards and publicizes individuals and institutions that foster coexistence and reconciliation between Israeli Jews and Israeli Arabs. It is the only institution focusing exclusively, singularly, and broadly on the enhancement of Jewish-Arab coexistence in Israel.

The band's original name, Bustan (orchard), is common to Hebrew and Arabic with slight differences in pronunciation. The addition of Abraham,[29] forefather of Jews and Arabs, was congruent with the group's goals.

28. Jan. 15, 1997.
29. Like *bustan*, this name exists in both languages: Avraham in Hebrew and Ibrahim in Arabic.

Whatever their intentions, the very fact that Israeli Jews and Arabs formed a cohesive ensemble and presented themselves as such on stages in Israel and abroad exemplified for audiences the fruitfulness of collaboration and the possibility of removing or, at least, lowering barriers.[30] That barriers disappeared within the group is evident in Taiseer's response when I asked about the band's statements regarding the blending of Arabs and Jews:

> Arabs and Jews? I only remember it when people ask us. Personally I don't think about it at all. When I'm performing or rehearsing I don't think about who is with me. I'm not trying to slough it off or apologize. They're my friends, really. I see myself there as very dominantly at home. I don't think that anyone in the group now thinks, "Taiseer's an Arab" or "Zohar's a Jew." I think of him as an amazing drummer who I love as a person. I know how to get along with him better than X in the group because X is a little crazier, but it has nothing to do with Jews and Arabs. (Jan. 13, 1997)

Other members of the band corroborated this in our conversations and interviews. On stage, without saying a word, the members of Bustan Abraham embodied the principles on which the hope of future peaceful coexistence must rest.

30. This idea is developed in chapter 12.

6

Two Bands, Two Interactive Musical Networks

Musical ensembles are richly entwined, multifaceted networks in which interaction of various sorts flows among the members. From explicit decision making to nuanced adjustments, myriad aspects of performance depend upon and emerge from such interaction. Competition and cooperation may coexist, power may shift among musicians, be distributed more or less equally, or be grasped by a central figure. When one considers the numerous musical and not-so-musical domains in which such relationships are formed and altered, the possibilities appear endless. They are played out in musical and verbal discourse, as well as in body language, ranging from large gestures and demonstrative stances to the subtlest facial expressions (or lack thereof). But one need not trace every thread of this multifaceted complexity to gain insight into the workings of such networks. In this chapter, Alei Hazayit and Bustan Abraham (hereafter AH and BA), serve as contrasting instances of small networks that formed and functioned within a particular set of circumstances. But first, three caveats regarding omniscience, representativeness, and balance.

To document completely the microdynamics of these two bands, their members and their interactions over a period of twelve years would be a gargantuan task, demanding omnipresence and omniscience, positions that are unattainable. Given the potential, even the likelihood, of intensely personal interaction among members of an ensemble, it would also run the risk of degenerating into voyeurism and begging the question as to what generalized knowledge could be gleaned from an analysis that is too particularized and intimate. But much can be learned without peeling back all the layers. While recognizing the individuality of the particular musicians and bands, it is possible to observe dynamics and structures that are more widely applicable in the larger musical network within which BA and AH both came to work (see chapter 8); as Erlmann reminds us: "systems exist only in connection with and through the singular" (1996b: 44).

Each band was a unique entity with a distinctive character, yet from a macroscopic viewpoint they represented different positions within a single field of cultural production and consumption that draws on local musical resources, and more geographically and culturally distant ones, to synthesize new means of musical expression. Aspects of Middle Eastern musical practices were fundamental to their music, although they did not make the same use of those resources. These bands contrasted in stylistic palette and in the levels and types of musical competence. They differed, too, in the structure of their networks, in their musical and social interaction, though not as radically as one might expect given the deep contrast in individual backgrounds between the two bands. Finally, they had different aims and expectations regarding interaction with their audiences.

Taken together, these bands present a pair of contrasting possibilities for collaborations involving musicians coming from disparate social and musical backgrounds in the convoluted intersections of various Israeli and Palestinian worlds (recall from chapter 1 that this is not a simple binary opposition). We need not assume that either band represents an extreme on some hypothetical continuum in order to gain insight into the effect of the numerous variables on the interaction within each band.

Some parts of the following analysis will not be as balanced as I would have liked because the circumstances under which I observed interaction differed considerably for AH and BA. I was present at only one BA rehearsal, albeit a particularly important one marked by heated discussion of the core values of the band, but I attended the band's concerts over the course of most of their career and interviewed every member. By contrast, I attended quite a few rehearsals of AH, but was never able to see a live performance due to their sporadic appearances and the fact that many, perhaps most, of their performances in Israel were not for the general public. They did, however, provide me with recordings of concerts. Interviews and conversations with members of AH were also crucial to the formulation of the following analysis, but I did not interview every member in depth.

Relatively large audiences at BA concerts enabled me to blend in with the audience (though scribbling notes in the dark usually elicited comments from my neighbors). In AH rehearsals, I never had "fly on the wall" status. Although I tried to minimize distraction, some musicians found my note taking funny while others sometimes tried to enlist my support in disputes over arrangements, appealing to me as "Doctor Ben," a musician and professor of music.

The comparative analysis begins with a discussion of musical competence, then shifts to interaction and how this derives from and affects the band members' musical competences. The approach taken here is an extension of the analytical frameworks developed in *Knowing Music, Making Music* (Brinner 1995), in which I demonstrated that musical interaction is deeply dependent upon and entwined with musical competence. Not only do musicians' knowledge and abilities enable them to interact in performance, assessments of their playing partners' competences also affect how musicians interact. It is through interaction, in turn, that competence may be increased. In the second half of the chapter, I discuss other dimensions of interaction among the musicians, concluding with a consideration of stability and change in these two small networks.

Differing Competences

The term *competence*, which can be understood in several ways when applied to music and musicians, is used here to denote the knowledge and skills involved in performing a particular type of music. It includes active and passive knowledge, gained intuitively and, perhaps, through explicit instruction. Competence extends beyond the mechanics of singing or playing an instrument to comprise all the knowledge required to perform appropriately for a given type of music and context. Thus competence is *not* a measure of a musician's talent, as in the judgment "he's competent but not particularly talented," nor is it intended to connote mediocrity as implied in the judgment "merely competent."[1]

Musicians who participate in a given musical practice generally share a core competence, but this core is subject to variation over time and space, and usually is supplemented by more specialized knowledge. This can generate numerous overlapping competences, often differentiated with regard to particular instruments (or singing) and repertoires. For instance, within common Arab musical practice, a drummer's competence differs from a violinist's in many respects, not just in playing technique, yet they share core knowledge. Furthermore, the competence required of a musician playing at a *haflah* is quite different from that acquired in formal study of Arab art music.

AH and BA differed greatly in matters of musical competence. Jamal assembled a typical Arab *takht* that would look and sound familiar in many Middle Eastern countries, without any unique Palestinian markers, such as folkloric instruments. He had performed with these musicians before in various configurations and their competences overlapped extensively as far as performance style and repertoire were concerned. They were professional within the expectations and possibilities current in Israel and the West Bank at the urban *haflat* that formed their realm of experience and employment possibilities. That is, they were fully competent to perform a mix of popular and light classical music and were familiar with a large selection of Egyptian, Lebanese, Syrian, and Jordanian music absorbed from radio, television, and audiocassettes, but not through formal training. Most of them knew all the common *maqamat* (modes) but not the rarer ones. With one minor exception they lacked training in Western music and rarely performed the *turath*, the Arab classical repertoire of vocal *muwashshahat* and instrumental *sama'iyat* and related genres, or the more modern works of the mid-twentieth century, although they were well acquainted with the

1. See Brinner 1995 for extensive discussion of many aspects of competence and interaction.

modern works and respected the classical ones. Their competences diverged with respect to the particularities of a given instrument: The *'ud* and violin players knew their own instruments, the drummers knew theirs and also could sing as a unison male chorus to offset or support Shoham's voice. Shoham's competence was entirely different, derived almost entirely by osmosis without formal guidance. She spoke some Arabic and had sung a few Arabic songs. Her Hebrew songs were taken from the stock known to all older Israelis (and many younger ones), while her Ladino songs were learned from family.[2]

The Arab members of BA, on the other hand, had mastered the *turath* and did not value the songs typically played at *haflat* or stay current with the latest hits. They had also trained in European art music in the same conservatory system in which some of their Jewish partners studied. This affected not only their technical expertise on violin and *'ud,* but also their aesthetic sensibilities. Treasuring the late nineteenth- and early twentieth-century instrumental works of the *turath* and creating an orchestra to perform such pieces, as Taiseer and Nassim each has done, may not have been a direct response to classical European training, but it was fully congruent with the values embodied in that training. It was also compatible with the high value placed on instrumental compositions in BA's repertoire. But most important,this training gave Taiseer and Nassim a substantial competence in common with Amir, who took a leading role in deliberations over the band's arrangements. They literally spoke the same language.

The Arab members of AH, by contrast, did not have such common ground with their singer. Instead they initiated her into elements of their music and applied their knowledge of Arab music to arrangements of the Jewish repertoire that she brought to the ensemble. Compared with Shoham, the Jewish members of BA had a more sophisticated understanding of Arab and Western musical systems, particularly on a technical level.

It is significant then, that more explicit training in Arab music occurred in the collaborative work of AH than in BA. With occasional input from his companions, Jamal taught Shoham and the Jewish bass players aspects of Arab music needed for a given piece, well aware that he was conveying only partial competence. I found it striking that the non-Arab members of BA did not go further in the study of Arab music than what they learned by osmosis. On the other hand, they showed far greater motivation to invent or reshape musical competence as part of their mission to create a new musical "language" without a priori standards of competence. The instrumentalists in AH did not focus their attention on expanding their abilities.

Musical competence comprises more domains than repertoire, theory, and technique. Socially situated knowledge of what to play for whom and when is as crucial to the success of a *haflah* musician as improvisational skill or command of repertoire or technique. Of all the musicians in AH and BA, Jamal probably had the most highly developed sense of adapting

2. Her mother was a native speaker of Ladino.

to an audience. At the tense performance for Israeli and Palestinian officials recounted in chapter 1, it was he who changed the order of the pieces on the spot to work the audience into the right mood and he took similar control in other concerts.

Since BA's prominence derived mainly from the diversity and strength of individual musicians' training and experience, it is worth giving a brief account of each member's training and strengths.[3] As we have just seen, the two Arab members of BA, Taiseer Elias and Nassim Dakwar, came to the group with deep knowledge of Arab art music in addition to extensive knowledge of European art music gained through years of training at Israeli conservatories and academies. Taiseer also had begun to learn about American vernacular musics through his association with Miguel Herstein in White Bird.

Avshalom Farjun, an Israeli Jew whose family has lived in Israel for ten generations, has a degree in Arabic language and literature. This, along with his interests in Turkish, Persian, and Indian music, put him closer in orientation and aesthetic sensibilities to Taiseer and Nassim than to some of the other members of the group; but lacking formal training and the ability to read notation, he could not match their theoretical knowledge. On the other hand, he exceeded them in his experience with and openness to other types of music and became quite fluent on his instrument, holding his own in the ensemble and contributing greatly to the overall texture. Avshalom's fellow musicians were not as uniformly superior to him in competence as one might think based on his self-deprecating statement to the *Aufbau* reporter:

> Everyone in the group is an academically trained musician except for me. I am genuinely ignorant. I never studied music. I discovered the Qanun, the oriental zither, only ten years ago. I simply took it and began to improvise on it. I don't busy myself with theory and I can't read notes. The others are music teachers, they play with great orchestras, they are true musicians. (Meyer 2000a, my translation)

Musical illiteracy was probably the most obvious difference, necessitating the recording of pieces so that Avshalom could learn them by ear, while the others could immediately start to work on a notated sketch of a new piece. Some found a further difference significant: They all played in other bands while Avshalom's outside work was as a producer and manager.

Zohar Fresco, whose parents immigrated to Israel from Turkey, had learned to play drum set in the idioms of rock and other internationally widespread popular musics. Shortly before joining BA, he had begun to switch to Middle Eastern hand drums, learning by taping and participating in private sessions that consisted primarily of old Iraqi Jewish musicians. He continued to learn about Arab music through his association with Taiseer and Nassim, who both regard his abilities highly.

3. Yehuda Seliki, who participated only in the first CD, is omitted here.

The other three BA members had somewhat more tenuous connections to Middle Eastern musical practices offset by extensive expertise in vernacular musics of Europe and the Americas. Amir Milstein, a native Israeli who spent some of his childhood in South America, trained at the music academy, like Taiseer and Nassim. In addition to European art music, he has delved into jazz and Brazilian music, composed for modern dance, and played in a flamenco band. His flute technique is virtuosic, enriched by timbres of flutter tonguing and singing while playing. He cites Rahsaan Roland Kirk as an influence in that regard. In the late 1990s he formed a trio, Tucan, to perform Brazilian music and original compositions inspired by that music.

Miguel Herstein, a native of Colorado, studied flamenco guitar since childhood, but also played blues and other American vernacular styles. He is also fluent in bluegrass and old-time banjo playing. The eldest of the band, he had the longest track record in experimenting with combining musical styles. Before joining BA, he engaged with Middle Eastern musical practices through his membership in Habreira Hativ'it and his collaboration with Taiseer in White Bird, but his interest in Middle Eastern music dates back to his youth in the U.S. when he sought out Middle Eastern recordings and tried to adapt aspects of 'ud playing style for the guitar.[4]

Emmanuel Mann grew up in Paris, son of American and French parents. He played electric bass guitar in jazz and funk bands in Paris before immigrating. In Israel he joined Habreira Hativ'it where, like Miguel (who had preceded him in that band), he encountered a mixture of North African, Indian, and Middle Eastern Jewish music. He also collaborated with a Persian musician and listened extensively to various types of Middle Eastern music, but had no formal training in any of them.

Naor Carmi, who replaced Emmanuel, is younger than the others and, as one of the first graduates of the Arab music program developed by Taiseer at the Jerusalem Academy, represents a different generation musically. Like Emmanuel, whom he also replaced in Habreira Hativ'it, he experienced a range of North African and Middle Eastern musics through playing in that band, but he also performed in groups devoted solely to the performance of Arab music.[5] His contribution to the band differed from Emmanuel's due to this and to the fact that he played amplified double bass rather than electric bass guitar. Naor attributes his affinity for Arab music to hearing it frequently in the markets of Acre[6] as he was growing up in one of the few cities in Israel that has a mixed Jewish and Arab population. He played euphonium, then trombone, switching to electric bass guitar before serving in the army, where he played in army entertainment bands. Only at age twenty-three did he take up double bass, drawn to it by his desire to play jazz. He has since diversified further, playing the Turkish

4. E-mail, June 2004.
5. This included an ensemble led by Khaled Jubran (see chapter 1).
6. This ancient port is named Akka in Arabic and Acco in Hebrew.

yayli tanbur, a bowed, long-necked lute, and performing bass with leading Israeli jazz musicians (see chapter 8).

Polymusicality such as Naor's was featured in the band's publicity materials and picked up by promoters and critics, becoming a central component of the band's image and sense of self.[7] When Taiseer played an extremely rapid bass passage on the *'ud* in rehearsal, one of the others said that he was a frustrated bass player and Taiseer countered that he was a frustrated flamenco player. It was this kind of cross-pollination and emulation that fueled much of the band's creativity. Taiseer cited as influences not only the other members of the group but also the many outstanding musicians he had met through the group and particularly through Farjun's production of concerts. He built improvisations on models that he learned from these associations (see chapter 10). While I discussed this feature of the band most with Taiseer, who said that he really enjoyed this kind of work because it broadened his horizons, the others expressed similar views. With the multiple competences mastered by these musicians came an understanding of musical differences that was a powerful tool for interaction and for the invention of new ways of making music, a point that Avshalom and others stressed in press interviews.[8]

Musical Interaction

A band that works together for years develops a rich history that lends depth to the slightest of actions or silences, even as it may mitigate the apparent violence of a confrontational statement or action. That members of the band allow themselves to challenge one another vigorously must be understood on the background of long association. Likewise, an apparent failure to respond and a seemingly uncued response may both be products of this sedimented delta of creative flow. The linked images of sedimentation and flow provide an apt metaphor for the group dynamic of a web of relationships that follows a certain path at any given moment but shifts as the silt of previous interactions blocks some possibilities, while the stronger currents carve a main channel. And like a clogged channel in a delta or small lake formed when a bow in the river is cut off, certain ideas—and even musicians—may be left behind and cut off as the network of a band evolves. Something like this occurred at the end of BA's career.

A key difference between AH and BA with regard to interaction stems from the fact that AH drew its musical resources from a relatively focused pool based almost exclusively on normative local Arab and Israeli styles and repertoires, while members of BA exploited a highly eclectic and

7. Writers sometimes overstate these competences. Regev, for example, writes that Taiseer and Nassim were equally at home in Arabic, Western, and jazz, but this was not true for jazz (1993: 42).
8. E.g., see Meyer 2000a.

cosmopolitan palette. As BA used more varied resources and collaborated with a range of guest artists, the band had more models of interactive networks, structures, and systems from which to choose and a greater variety of motivations to drive that interaction. Since I have discussed these concepts at length in *Knowing Music, Making Music* (1995), I will define them briefly here before elaborating on this comparison.

The *interactive network* of an ensemble comprises the roles that musicians assume, their relationships with one another, and the domains in which they operate. Certain musicians might lead or otherwise play in the foreground, for example, while others provide support of various sorts, perhaps filling foundational roles by marking musical time or playing a drone.

Interactive structure refers to the ways in which composers, arrangers, and performers organize the simultaneous relationships of the different musical strands at any given moment and the sequence of music in the course of a piece. Using this term to subsume the more common terms *texture* and *form* emphasizes that these structures are created or recreated through the joint efforts of the musicians involved and that simultaneous and consecutive relationships are not necessarily independent aspects of performance.[9]

Interactive system refers to the means by which musicians communicate with one another in performance. A communicative code of cues and responses may range from explicit and codified to largely intuitive and ad hoc.

Interactive motivation denotes the reasons musicians respond to (or ignore) one another and choose to compete or collaborate in performance.[10] Assessing motivation entails consideration of the values that either support or suppress being prominent or blending into the overall sound, taking a long solo or playing just enough to set the mood or respond to another member of the band. Aspects of interactive network and structure, such as the confluence of particular performers, conventions of musical form and ensemble roles, as well as the dictates or possibilities of a particular composition, allow varying scope for agency and the playing out of interactive motivations.

The singer-centered interactive network of AH differentiated it fundamentally from BA: While every AH arrangement was constructed in terms of the band's interaction with Shoham, BA compositions varied greatly in the deployment of forces and the relative prominence of parts. The bands' interactive networks also differed with regard to drumming: Zohar Fresco was the sole drummer in BA, but AH had two drummers who worked as a unit. Most of the other interactive musical roles and relationships in AH were also direct continuations of the interactive network of a *takht* that these musicians had learned in the world of wedding *haflat*. While the pair of drummers worked together to provide a metrical foundation and

9. See Brinner 1995: 191–200.
10. This is more specific than the motivations to perform discussed in chapters 4 and 5.

rhythmic drive based on conventional Arab drum patterns and elaboration, the violin, 'ud and nay players rendered the melody in ways idiomatic to their instruments within the frame of reference of mainstream Arab musical practice, paraphrasing the singer and filling in "spaces" between her phrases.

Some of the arrangements, particularly of those Hebrew songs that had a harmonic progression, called for some extension of the musicians' habitual practices. The arpeggiated chords that introduce "Erev Shel Shoshanim" (⬤ audio track 1) and serve as underpinning to the song "Yad Anuga" exemplify this. AH augmented the network when they added double bass. Jean-Claude Jones was more than adequate for the job in terms of technique, but he was not accustomed to playing in an Arab band. As is common when bass is added to an Arab music ensemble, Jamal tried to have Jean-Claude double the basic drum part, but Jean-Claude was used to a different interplay between bass and drums from his experience playing jazz and sometimes added basslines derived from that. He also extended his role by bowing the bass for certain passages.

The core interactive structures for AH were the textures typical of Arab music and the strophic song structures typical of their repertoire. Extending these beyond the norms of their *haflah*-based competence in various ways necessitated rehearsals in which they meticulously scripted their performances. They set the overall program order and wrote on large index cards the order of verses, choruses, instrumental solos, and interludes for each song. To guide the ensemble, Jamal used the same cues that I had observed when he was performing mainstream Arab music, but the extensive rehearsal and scripting of performances greatly reduced the need for cues. For the Arab members of the group, this was a stark contrast to performance at a *haflah*, where a shared interactive system allowed them to successfully perform pieces selected on the spot in response to audience requests or their perceptions of audience proclivities. The extent of scripting was a point of conflict between the two leading Arab members of the ensemble. Where Omar wanted to adhere to the script at every level of the performance, Jamal wished to limit scripting to the individual pieces, not to the overall flow of the event. In our conversations over many years, Jamal continually emphasized the need for flexibility to adapt to the mood of the audience, saying that he could "smell" the audience.

BA's performances also were very well rehearsed, but as they incorporated lengthy solos in almost every piece and these solos could change from one performance to the next, they needed to develop musical cues specific to each piece to augment the various looks, nods, and other body language with which they communicated. Speaking with Emmanuel and Zohar, I tried to ascertain the extent to which members of BA had systematized their communications. When I probed for particular cues and for ambiguities and misunderstandings, Emmanuel insisted, "We don't have misunderstandings. Taiseer's cues are very clear. They come at certain points and we know what is about to happen. It's usually where he's playing the main part so naturally he cues. Miguel sometimes makes a gesture with his body to cue a crescendo—sometimes we see it, sometimes we don't." He added that their tightly coordinated ensemble depended on "a mutual feeling, even though we all come from different backgrounds." When I asked whether they had solidified this understanding in an initial period of discovery, Zohar answered, "we're always discovering new things. That's what's fun. You keep on discovering more and more things. We didn't talk about it to begin with." Zohar also insisted that they understood one another from the beginning and never misinterpreted cues. He explained, "I always look at [others'] hands. And others watch my hands. It's like dance, you bring your hand to something and everyone tries to go with it." But he also noted that body language differed greatly depending on the musician. When accompanying Nassim, Zohar had to be attuned to the most subtle change: "For instance, if he starts a solo and we're pressing him a bit—it has happened several times—he looks at me just a little and I immediately understand because he usually doesn't [look at Zohar] . . . it's a matter of individual character, it's not just body language . . . so I understand him, but if I were playing with him for the first time I wouldn't know what he wanted." BA's ensembles were indeed characterized by impressively well-coordinated interaction based on extensive mutual discovery.

An important aspect of the diverse musical competences that BA members brought to the band was their experience with a variety of interactive networks that differed with regard to roles, systems of communication, sound structures, and so on. This did not dictate the workings of the new band; it simply offered a range of models from which to adopt and adapt. The band took little for granted, examining and reworking the roles conventionally associated with their instruments in other ensembles. Developing orchestration specific to each piece was a crucial part of the group work process. Since multisectional pieces were the norm for this band and they also had a tendency to vary repetitions within sections, their arrangements were complex and not the product of conventionalized playing processes. While the composition of captivating melodies with interesting rhythms remained at the forefront of the group's efforts, many of their pieces also involved counterpoint and harmony, which they also worked out in detail, rather than relying on formulaic application of conventionalized procedures.

This approach manifested in rhythmic foundation and elaboration, too. Zohar augmented frame and goblet drums with a wide array of instruments. He also went well beyond conventional Middle Eastern drum patterns, inventing new ones and making timbral contributions unrelated to those patterns. Thus he distinguished himself and the band from the majority of so-called ethnic bands in Israel, which tend to rely on conventional drum patterns to set a groove and provide markers of Arab or Middle Eastern musical identity. Zohar worked most closely with the bassist (either Emmanuel or Naor).

Taiseer, playing 'ud, assumed a driving role in the "engine room," often in the company of Miguel, who played guitar chords or an energetic banjo pattern to help move things along. In their duo White Bird, Taiseer and

Miguel had already worked out ways to enhance each other's playing rather than interfere, but in BA the challenge increased. The overlap between bass guitar and the low register of the 'ud, guitar, and qanun was a problem even for the recording engineer, said Taiseer. They tried to solve it through orchestration, by assigning instruments to different registers or finding a musical line for the bass or the 'ud. They sought ways to open up spaces in the texture, but also to fill in spaces that opened up.

I discussed this issue most extensively with Taiseer, who reported that there had been intense group debate over the extent to which any player should dominate. He developed a style specific to performance in BA, playing to be heard, to be present, even when he was not the soloist. He said that he saw this as a matter of investing energy, not ego, with the potential to make a relatively small band sound like a large orchestra. He had developed his highly percussive 'ud style to sound different and to play every note as if it were a solo. He might, in principle, be playing unison with at least four others in many of the pieces but he did not want to just double another player. He tried not to "get stuck" in either the high or low register—a claim that is borne out in many tracks by his rapid moves between registers.

The precision of BA's ensemble playing provided a foil for individual instruments, whether inserted in brief pauses or long "windows" that opened for extensive solos (e.g., "Tini Mini Hanem," 🔊 audio track 8).[11] The musicians found various ways to provide support for the soloist or subtle commentary on what he was playing. In this case they did tend toward a model that they crafted from elements of Middle Eastern practice, combined with the rhythm section developed in American jazz and popular music. The drum-bass dyad was central to creating and maintaining a groove for most solos (e.g., "Dub Dulab," 🔊 audio track 20). Even here they displayed considerable variety. The bassist might maintain a steady pattern either without the drummer or while the drummer took great liberties and vice versa. Other instrumentalists took on the bass role in some pieces. While one musician played a lengthy improvisation over this foundation, others might contribute sporadically or more continuously.

BA's interaction in performance was highly egalitarian. Every member of the ensemble was capable of improvising a solo and did so in particular works, but unlike many small ensembles that incorporate considerable improvisation, BA was not bound to a model in which each member took a turn in every piece. Pieces were generally composed and arranged to feature one or two soloists. Certain works, such as "Fanar" (🔊 audio track 11) and "Seven Eleven" were conceived as showcases for guest artists. This represented yet another form of variety for the band and extended a practice whereby the composer of a given piece was not necessarily the main soloist in that piece. Taiseer, Amir, and Nassim might have played more frequent and longer solos, but the overall sense was one of equality and

11. See the book's Web site for audio examples. "Solo" here refers to relative prominence, not to sounding alone. See chapter 10 for extensive discussion of BA's improvisation in relation to their compositions.

open, free exchange, each member of the band having as much input as he desired.

There are few precise analogies in AH's work because of the centrality of song and singer. Performances sometimes included a violin, *'ud,* or *nay* solo as an introduction or an interlude, usually involving improvisation typical of the traditional Arab *taqasim,* which explores the characteristics of a given *maqam.* The time constraints of the song meant that these solos were never long enough to allow for extensive exploration or modulation to other *maqam*s. The use of instrumental improvisation as a mood-setting background to declamation by Shoham or Jamal also limited the scope of solo instrumental improvisation while altering the division of labor within the network (🔊 audio track 1, beginning at 2:54, or track 3, beginning at 5:18).

Despite some intense discussions in rehearsal, AH was not as egalitarian as BA, which debated nearly every decision fully. Shoham and Jamal clearly carried more weight than the others in AH. Each member of BA contributed compositions to the repertoire and felt free to critique others' compositions. Most of the early pieces were altered substantially through collective recomposition and arrangement. Although he was the band's founder, the only domain in which Avshalom Farjun had a greater role than the other members was in bookings and other practical arrangements. Even there members of the band could override his decisions. A single member who had a schedule conflict or some other opposition to performance could derail plans. One could dub this ethos of interaction a "fierce" democracy. Even after the disintegration of the band, individual members maintained sharply differing stances on choice of live tracks for a "posthumous" release that Avshalom Farjun was promoting. They wanted to retain veto power over selections and the entire project.

BA's mutual responsiveness, developed during the intensive rehearsals of their formative period, was striking. Individual band members told me independently that they knew what the others were thinking because of the time they had spent together. This extended from music into speech. After the rehearsal in which I witnessed heated debate over the band's direction with regard to performance venues and "light" versus "heavy" composition, Amir told me that a lot was left unsaid because they knew what the others were going to say.

Around and Beyond the Music

Speech is usually an important counterpart to musical communication in the life of a musical ensemble. The transitions between these two types of discourse can be particularly telling as indicators of communicative preferences, weaknesses, or failures. Communication in AH rehearsals was marked by aggressive overriding of turn taking and inclusive use of language, as well as failures that engendered transitions between modes of discourse.[12] The polyglot nature of AH involved considerable crosstalk, misunderstandings, and translation. Some members of the group spoke Arabic and Hebrew, others Arabic and English. Most had rudimentary knowledge of the third language but no language was equally comfortable for everyone and no one was fluent in all three. Due to this lack of a single common language, deliberations in rehearsals were often prolonged as musicians translated for one another.[13] Overlapping conversations and frequent shifts from one language to another, sometimes in mid-sentence, led to comic situations when one member of the group would turn to another in the wrong language—usually one of the Arabs speaking Hebrew or English to another Arab who did not understand that language.

Such levity enhanced the camaraderie of the group. Shoham furthered this at certain moments by stressing the gutturals in Hebrew—distinguishing the letters *het* from *khaf* and *'ayin* from *alef*—to sound more like Arabic or the Hebrew of Arabic speakers. This code switching appeared to be a gesture of solidarity[14] somewhat akin to a white American altering accent, intonation, and vocabulary to fit in with black musicians. It is also a hip thing for younger Israeli Jews to do among themselves, but for those Israeli Jews who grew up in homes where Arabic was spoken, it is not an affectation. While Shoham was born in Israel, her father grew up in Iraq and was a native speaker of Arabic, so for her this gesture was not as forced as it might be for some Israelis. Yet neither was it completely "natural," as she deployed it selectively. I did not note any negative response from Arab members of the band. If anything, it may have strengthened connections.

The band's high level of cohesion was evident in the fact that they did not use language as an exclusionary device nearly as much one might expect given the distribution of linguistic competences. On the contrary, people were constantly translating for one another so that everyone understood nearly everything. This strengthened certain bonds: Ghidian, for instance, was dependent on Walid or Omar, both fluent in Hebrew, to translate Shoham's remarks in that language, while Ghidian could return the favor when he and Shoham conversed in English. On the other hand, conversation was often disrupted by overlapping and by outright interruption. The norms of Israeli social interaction favor aggressive conversational interaction with frequent interruptions. Jamal generally held his own in the competition with Shoham for airspace. Musicians who were relatively soft-spoken had fewer chances to enter the fray.

12. Verbal communication in this band is worthy of extensive sociolinguistic analysis. Here I point only to salient features that directly affected the group's music making.

13. Complicating matters further was the addition of bassist Jean-Claude Jones, a native speaker of French who also knew Hebrew and English, but not Arabic.

14. See Wardhaugh on metaphorical code switching (1986: 103) and Tannen 1984.

Some verbal communication failures were attributable to linguistic and musical shortcomings. Jamal's command of Hebrew was far from complete. Unlike Omar and Walid, he lacked formal schooling in Hebrew although he had spoken it with Israelis for years. Sometimes he was at a loss for words as he tried to explain his ideas to Shoham or debate hers. Such failures often caused a shift from verbal to musical discourse. Moves in the opposite direction were caused by lack of a common musical competence: Shoham was sometimes at a loss for words not because of linguistic limitations, but because she had not acquired musical terminology through formal training. Her comments were sometimes poetic or expressive, but not specific enough to communicate her wishes.

A lack of terminology might also be circumvented by reference to prototypes: Shoham did not know the names of the drum patterns, but if she was thinking of a certain rhythmic feel that she wanted she would refer to a song that they had already performed with that type of drumming. This was only possible, of course, once the group had built up a common stock of experience, a shared competence and language of interaction. Shoham was aware of this, telling me "we're building our own language" after they had worked together for a few years.[15] The relatively high frequency of such transitions can be attributed to the performers' disparate backgrounds, which also necessitated considerable effort devoted to constructing common plans and mutual understanding.

There was no parallel to this Tower of Babel effect within BA because everyone was fluent in Hebrew and tended to have musical knowledge that was broader, more varied, and less intuitive, including music-theoretical tools to communicate intentions and discuss options. This was linked to a greater openness to things outside their personal realms of experience. BA spent far more time together, at least in the early years, working out musical communication and mapping out common ground. The fact that they performed original repertoire almost exclusively may also have contributed to the flow of communication. Rather than dealing with the juxtaposition and balancing of well-defined musical repertoires and "languages," they were striving to integrate elements drawn from a broad array of resources. While BA was more heterogeneous in musical expertise, AH encompassed greater social difference. This was apparent in the band's interaction, which was shaped by various social differences, including economic standing, citizenship, age, and gender, in addition to the differing types and degrees of musical and linguistic competence already noted.[16]

The presence of a singer usually indicates a fundamental difference in group organization compared to instrumental ensembles. In particular, bands formed by a singer tend to be dominated by that person. Habreira Hativ'it, formed and dominated by the charismatic singer/drummer Shlomo Bar, is the prototype within this cultural field and many Arab bands oper-

15. Jan. 3, 1995.
16. Since I observed AH rehearsals, rather than BA's, I continue to emphasize AH in this discussion.

ate in a similar manner. By comparison, AH operated in a less hierarchical manner than one might expect. Monetary decisions and organizational aspects of promotion remained in the hands of Shoham. Most other musical decisions evolved from group discussion in which Jamal and Omar played prominent roles, largely due to their greater competence in Arab music.

Jamal's prominence in the band's discussions can also be attributed to his position as the co-founder of the band, the one to whom everyone else owed their participation. Over the years, the personnel of AH underwent many changes as Jamal brought in new musicians, either to supply a sound that the ensemble had lacked or to replace someone who had left. These replacements rarely became integrated into the social fabric of the ensemble to the same degree as the initial band members, who had been a tight-knit group in the 1980s. Jamal drew on two categories of local Palestinian musicians for replacements. Older, more experienced musicians were brought in to record the demo, but were not retained for reasons that I was never able to fully clarify. "They're real mafia" was the most Jamal or Shoham would say and, given Jamal's earlier experience playing music in a club that catered to the Arab and Jewish underworld this could be taken literally. That they were somewhat older than Jamal might also have made them more difficult for him to "manage." Musicians in the second category lasted longer in the group. These were younger, less-experienced players, whom Jamal took under his wing, almost as apprentices.[17]

This patronage of younger, less-experienced players opened up gaps in age and competence in the ensemble, creating a two-tiered network in which the lead parts and main performance decisions were taken by the older musicians and the younger ones did what they were told. This was clearest when Jamal brought in eighteen-year-old Mahmud to replace Walid, who was in his forties when he was incapacitated. Their interaction contrasted starkly with the long-time partnership with Walid. By comparison, the members of BA were closer in age and socioeconomic background. The age spread between the oldest and youngest member was considerable, but not nearly as marked as in AH. The level of education was by no means uniform, but again less diverse than in AH. It was the greater musical differences that enriched BA, but ultimately tore it apart in an artistic tug of war.

The cross-generational interplay in AH had particular significance. Jamal started to work as a teenage drummer in a band led by the late Ahmed Abu Ghannam, whose son Fuad he later brought into AH. And it was in that earlier band that Jamal had learned to establish his credentials musically and to offset his youth and lower status as a drummer. It is worth lingering on this for a moment because Jamal used the same mechanism to reestablish his dominance at an AH rehearsal as I had seen him use against the elder Abu Ghannam in a recording session years earlier. By playing a

17. These included Rajay on *nay*, Mahmud on drum, and Fu'ad on *'ud*.

forceful cross-rhythm during a drum solo, he managed to disorient the other musicians so that they missed their cue to reenter. This undermined their authority and served notice that Jamal would not take others' leadership for granted.

Gender was as clear an axis of differentiation as anything between these bands. The image presented by all-male BA differed from AH's image, which foregrounded a female singer (see figures 4.2 and 5.1). There is no shortage of female singers in Israeli popular music, but relatively few have appeared in the Israeli "ethnic music" scene, where female instrumentalists are rarer still. In local Arab music they were virtually unknown in the early 1990s (see chapter 2).

It would be a mistake to consider gender in isolation when examining the network of relationships operative in AH. Had Shoham not been older than her male accompanists the dynamic would almost certainly have differed greatly. As it was, there was considerable playful teasing at some rehearsals. On one occasion the musicians joked with her, saying "if only you had a daughter" by way of implying another sort of involvement (and knowing full well that she had two grown sons).

Shoham's higher socioeconomic position and her network of connections to individuals in the upper echelons of Israeli government were at least as important as her gender in shaping the dynamic of the group. Her readiness to utilize connections in the health system, police, and military to advocate on behalf of individual band members strengthened her bonds with the musicians. The results—ranging from permits from the military government to faster access to medical care—probably were worth far more than the pay earned in concerts. The importance of amassing and utilizing social capital in the form of links with well-placed individuals is hardly unique to Israel. Known by the Russian word *protektsiya*, it was especially prevalent in the tightly knit social world of Israel in the early days of the state, but remains a common way to get things done, as evident in the scandals enveloping the government in the first decade of the twenty-first century.

Beyond these practical, nonmusical links, the band displayed considerable affective and musical interdependence. Shoham found the accompaniment that she had sought, enabling her to offer her audience an unusual combination of materials and people. The veteran instrumentalists of the group were able to continue their long association with one another while creating something new and escaping the humdrum music and increasingly competitive and unpleasant wedding band scene. Jamal attributed the younger players' commitment to the opportunity that they had to work with him, a well-established musician. Judging by their responsiveness to Jamal in rehearsals, this was not an overly self-serving assessment. Shoham and Jamal's musical connection was strongest, reaching back to their successful duo performance in Italy that led to forming the larger group. Over the years they performed as a duo again on several occasions and even in the larger ensemble Shoham continued to focus on Jamal's drumming as the motivation and framework for her singing. "I live from his rhythm," she said and set great store by his ability to find the right feel or groove for a given song and by his theatrical sense of arrangement.

A playful dynamic among all members of the band marked almost every rehearsal I attended over the years. Most members of the band contributed to this atmosphere, however the undisputed source was Jamal. He was well known to Palestinians and Israelis as a comic actor (see chapter 2) and used this fame and comic ability more than once to resolve potentially unpleasant encounters with military patrols on his way in and out of the Old City. In the rehearsals of AH he used humor to smooth over disagreements and to motivate the others. His jokes were particularly effective at generating solidarity among the band members and stood in stark contrast to the seriousness of Omar, who often opposed Jamal in matters of interpretation. But there were rough spots when humor did not serve. For one extended period Jamal left the band altogether. Even though he returned after this, the long-standing ties with Ghidian and Omar in the end loosened as the three drifted into different endeavors and social circles, due at least in part to personal rivalries and misunderstandings, as well as to Jamal's poor health. But the main reason for the hiatus in the band's activities (ongoing as of this writing) was the death of Shoham's husband.

BA was held together by musical interest and by economic incentives, not by social interdependence. The members were genuinely excited to compose and perform together until near the end of the band's life. This joy was apparent on stage where they expressed overt approval for one another's solos with smiles and verbal responses. They did not become wealthy from playing in the band, but they were paid well and were able to take numerous trips abroad. Exchanges of social capital were not an important factor. No one depended on another member of the band for favors or connections. Yet various members of the band pointed out to me how close they were to one another. This may have changed over time as they grew older and several of those who had not had families got married and had children, but they remained in touch even when the band was breaking up.

BA had a more stable membership than AH. It may be hard to prove that seven was an optimal number of musicians, but it is difficult to imagine that the band could have remained as egalitarian had there been many more musicians involved. In that light the band's initial period could be seen as a search not only for a musical language and methods of intra-group communication, but also a process of optimizing the network size. Thereafter, substitutes were required only occasionally and those substitutes entered a mature band. This required that they begin by emulating the role taken by the person they replaced. Since Naor Carmi permanently replaced Emmanuel Mann, he was able to establish his own personality and contribute a piece to BA's final album. He acclimated quickly to the band not only because of his experience, training, and excellent musicianship, but also because he already knew Emmanuel Mann's bass parts well from listening to BA's recordings and he had studied with Taiseer and Nassim at the Jerusalem Academy. By contrast, Noam Chen, who substituted for Zohar on percussion when Fresco was unavailable, had to fill that spot without becoming an equal member of the band.

Veit Erlmann has observed that the world music industry and individual musicians are mutually constitutive (1996b: 307). I suggest that the degree of mutuality varies greatly and that a major indicator of the extent of an individual musician's influence on the world music industry is the number and type of links the musician has within that industry, i.e., the network of connections to international institutions and "players." BA far outpaced AH in this area (see chapter 8), but I know of no musician in Israel better connected to the "world music" network than Yair Dalal, who truly appears to have a mutually constitutive relationship with the world music industry. Therefore, the next chapter introduces Dalal's highly varied constellation of musical projects to open up further dimensions of contrast and give a more richly textured sense of this field of musical activity.

7

Yair Dalal

$\mathcal{Y}$air Dalal occupies an intermediate position in the constellation of musical possibilities that encompasses Alei Hazayit and Bustan Abraham. With an international reputation for performing music that is both "ethnic" and Israeli, he draws on a greater variety of musical resources than the former, but fewer than the latter. Like Bustan Abraham, he favors instrumental music, but songs also have an important place in his recordings and performances. The three most important areas in which the inclusion of Yair complicates and extends our view of this field of cultural production are his social and cultural activism, his choice and presentation of musical sources, and the unusually diverse array of musicians with whom he has worked. As an activist he has advocated for peace between Israelis and Palestinians, as well as for recognition of Iraqi Jews and their musical heritage. His repertoire choices include religious songs, with their attendant implications of spirituality, and desert musical tropes and practices alongside items of Middle Eastern art music. Perhaps most striking is his success in joining and bridging professional networks.

Career Overview

Born in 1955 to Iraqi Jewish parents who had immigrated to Israel the year before, Yair experienced a mix of musical influences.[1] He studied violin at the Givatayim Conservatory from the age of eight to eighteen. As a teenager he turned away from his parents' music, showing greater interest in the Beatles and other Anglo-American rock, only picking up the *'ud* in his early twenties. But the Indian film music that his neighbors heard also made an impression.[2] After military service he earned a teaching certificate and

1. His resume is available at www.yairdalal.com/index1.html.
2. Interview, June 1998.

149

Figure 7.1   Yair Dalal (photo courtesy of Yair Dalal)

spent time in the desert, both in Israel and in Sinai, rode a camel (while playing violin, he says), and associated with Bedouin. He also became a member of Kibbutz Samar in the very southern tip of Israel's Arava desert, where he taught music in the local high school. He played in various bands that broke up before they made much headway, an experience that he found deeply frustrating. One of these bands, named after the biblical desert kingdom Midian, recorded a cassette, but by the time I met Yair that was lost. During the first Gulf War, Yair composed a piece for Midian that included violin glissandi in imitation of the Scud missiles that Iraq was raining down on central Israel. Around this time he reconnected with his Iraqi musical heritage by participating with Zohar Fresco in weekly sessions with old Jewish musicians who had come from Arab countries in the 1950s.

Not until 1993, at the age of thirty-eight,did Yair commit to a full-time career as a performer.[3] But he did so with tremendous energy and productivity. Between 1995 and 2002 he put out seven albums under his name and appeared on a rather astonishing variety of recordings initiated by others (see below). He was prolific as a composer, too, with at least thirty-four original compositions recorded during the same period.[4]

3. Note that this occurred at the end of the first *intifada,* two years after the founding of Bustan Abraham and Alei Hazayit.
4. Seven of these are group efforts, leaving twenty-seven for which he takes sole credit.

These are material traces of the numerous performances, tours, festivals, and collaborations that form a major component of Yair's professional life. He has also filled his time with teaching and promoting older Jewish music and musicians from Iraq and other parts of the Middle East and North Africa. In addition, he has worked in various ways to promote peaceful coexistence between Jews and Arabs.

Riding the Peace Train

Activism is central to Yair's public persona. Like Alei Hazayit and Bustan Abraham, he has performed at events sponsored by organizations working for peace in the Middle East, as well as under the aegis of Israeli consulates and embassies, but Yair has gone further than either band. Where members of Bustan Abraham were ambiguous about the political dimension of their collaboration, resenting the attention taken away from their music, and Palestinian members of Alei Hazayit were wary of explicit ties to the Israeli government, Yair openly advertises his activist stance. In reviews and publicity he is consistently characterized as a peace activist. He gives performances titled "Concert for Peace,"[5] issued a CD titled *Inshallah Shalom* (2005),[6] and has toured with Palestinian musicians and performed with other Arabs.

Yair made a big splash as a musician and peace advocate early in his career with two concerts in Norway in 1994. He played for the ceremony awarding the Nobel Peace Prize to Yitzhak Rabin, Shimon Peres, and Yasser Arafat in December, a few months after the concert mentioned at the beginning of this book. That event in September, marking the first anniversary of the signing of the Oslo Accord between Israel and the PLO, took on diplomatic significance when Yasser Arafat and Shimon Peres signed a further agreement backstage during the intermission. A Finnish singer, Arja Saijonmaa, originated the concept of the concert, including the idea of featuring children's choirs. She approached Yair, who enlisted Ilan Mochiach, a veteran Israeli arranger, to create an orchestral realization of a song that was a joint effort.[7] The resulting extravaganza involved three children's choirs (Palestinian, Israeli, and Norwegian), a solo singer, three guitars, bass, and drums, in addition to Yair (on violin and *'ud*) and the Oslo Philharmonic Orchestra led by Zubin Mehta who, according to Yair, called him "out of the blue" and volunteered to conduct the piece.

5. For example, the Concert for Peace at UCLA with Persian musician Houman Pourmehdi (March 20, 2001) benefited the Open Tent Middle East Coalition's international conference "The Israeli/Palestinian Crisis: New Conversations for a Pluralist Future."

6. The title is a clever combination: *Inshallah* means God willing in Arabic and *shalom* means peace in Hebrew.

7. Amnon Abutbul and Dalal translated Arabic lyrics by Fathi Kasem into Hebrew. Dalal took Abutbul's melody and created the piece around it.

The concert and the efforts that went into it are the subject of a documentary film by Yvonne Kahan, Yair's Norwegian-born first wife (Kahan 1995). These efforts included managing a multifaceted collaboration with singers and instrumentalists from Israel, the Occupied Territories, Norway, Finland, and the U.S. Yvonne Kahan even enlisted the aid of the Norwegian embassy when Israeli bureaucracy threatened to squelch the Oslo concert through delays in granting travel documents to the Palestinian children's choir. This extended the crucial mediating role of Norway from the Oslo peace talks into the realm of musical production. Yair has worn this concert, the result of serendipity and his ability to seize the moment, as a badge of honor ever since.

The work had great symbolic value and was effusively welcomed by the audience, as is readily apparent from the documentary and the live recording that ends Yair's first CD. The melodramatic orchestration, bearing the mark of the arranger's experience in Israel's commercial pop world, is far removed from the mood of Yair's other work. But the impact of the song has been considerable and Yair continues to perform it in more intimate arrangements. Ten years after the Oslo concert, he told me that on several occasions since the onset of the second Palestinian *intifada,* the film about the concert has melted the hostility of Palestinians he has encountered in Europe.

The collaboration also inspired George Sama'an, introduced in chapter 2, who undertook a cross-border project in 1999, toward the end of Israel's occupation of southern Lebanon. He brought children from southern Lebanon to meet and make music with children from northern Israel on a regular basis. At the time, an Israeli-Syrian peace agreement looked possible and Sama'an told me he hoped to have the Lebanese and Israeli children in his program singing at the celebration of such a deal, just as Yair had done in Oslo. His hopes were dashed when negotiations between Israel and Syria fell apart and Israel's unilateral withdrawal from southern Lebanon cut off contact with children there.

Yair has toured with Palestinian musicians, originally teaming up with Jowad al Tamimi and Saed Sweiti from Jericho. This collaboration, which included recording *Music Channel* with a Norwegian rock band, was a victim of the second *intifada,* which made communication and travel between Jericho and Israel too difficult and dangerous. The closing "bonus" track of their album, an arrangement of the Beatles' "We Can Work It Out," is now a sad reminder of the optimism that was widespread at the time it was recorded.[8] Eventually Yair found other musical partners from Bethlehem (which is just across the Green Line, the border marking Israel's pre-1967 borders), but even this collaboration was complicated by military closures in the West Bank.

Yair continues to advocate for peace, coexistence, and mutual understanding based on a common heritage and the lack of any viable alterna-

8. The album appeared in 1995, prior to Yitzhak Rabin's assassination and a general worsening in Palestinian-Israeli relations.

tive. When he curated the 2001 Oud Festival in Jerusalem, he told music critic Barry Davis: "Oud music, and music in general, is a bonding factor. . . . This touches on the very heart of our shared culture. This is the music which Jews and Arabs grew up on together" (Davis 2000c). Davis also noted Yair's hope that the festival would "provide some relief from the pervading *intifada*-induced tension and help to accentuate the regional common denominator." When I heard him sing "Zaman el Salaam" solo, in 2004 in San Francisco, he introduced it by saying that it was written at a time of great hope and stressed the need for hope now that the situation is much worse "because peace is the most important thing."[9] Such sentiments are popular with his audiences, but they are also sincere.

Cultural Advocacy

Yair's activism extends to other arenas, seeking to increase awareness and respect—through concerts, lectures, and teaching—for people and musical practices ignored or denigrated by mainstream Israeli society. His work with his Bedouin neighbors of the Azazme clan falls in this category, as do his more extensive and varied efforts on behalf of mainstream Iraqi, Jewish Iraqi, and other *Mizrahi* traditional musics. Like the members of Alei Hazayit and Bustan Abraham, Yair is highly critical of the Israeli popular music known as *musika mizrahit* or Mediterranean music. He is interested in maintaining, continuing, and promoting music that he considers to be more deeply rooted in Middle Eastern traditions. These efforts and attitudes constitute a mission of cultural stewardship and advocacy.

Like Jews in many other parts of the world, Iraqi Jews participated in mainstream secular musical life. It has been argued that they did so to an unusual extent in Iraq, with Jewish musicians serving as the primary instrumentalists of Iraqi art music prior to the mass emigration of the 1950s.[10] Iraqi Jews also had their own music, related to but distinct from mainstream Iraqi music and the music of other Jewish communities. Iraqi art music was likewise related to but distinct from the mainstream of Middle Eastern music centered in Egypt. Yet Iraqi Jewish musicians were fluent in most, perhaps all, of these practices. Against this background, Yair's advocacy of a variety of musical repertoires—pieces as different as Salim al-Nur's instrumental "Sama'i Wachi al-Naharein," the Aramaic Jewish hymn "Ya Ribon Alam," and the Iraqi folk song "Ya Aziz al Rouh"—makes sense.[11]

Yair has been centrally involved in the publication of archival recordings of Middle Eastern Jewish musicians who are either very old or no

9. June 15, 2004.
10. See Warkov 1986.
11. These are recorded on Dalal 1996, 2000, and 2002. Salim an-Nur was an Iraqi Jewish composer and performer who had a long career in Israel after leaving Iraq.

longer alive. He compiled a disk of selections by Filfel Gourgy (d. 1983), an Iraqi Jewish singer and composer who immigrated to Israel in 1950, and has worked on at least one other such compilation by a singer of Egyptian origin (which has yet to appear due to copyright problems). These and other projects are a joint effort with the Magda label.[12] In his own performances and recordings, Yair reclaims and promotes the works of Iraqi Jewish composers, such as the brothers Daud and Sallach el-Quweiti,[13] whom he characterizes as in danger of erasure from collective memory and cultural history in Israel and the Arab world. He has also featured older Iraqi musicians on his recordings. These efforts resemble and go beyond Avshalom Farjun's promotion of *qanun* master Avraham Salman through performances and recordings (Salman 1997, Ziryab Trio 1996) that included members of Bustan Abraham.

Why do these musicians and their music need an advocate? By the time Yair undertook this mission, Israel Radio's Arab orchestra had been disbanded and the musicians had retired into relative oblivion. Iraqi Jewish music and musicians were in danger of disappearing from public view and memory. Only a few younger musicians had made an effort to study and continue the musical practices these musicians had mastered and brought with them to Israel. Yair is not the only exception to this generalization—Avi Agababa, Asaf Zamir, and Yinon Muallem are also continuing the music of their cultural forebears—but he is by far the most vocal and is active on the most fronts. A notice on his Web site encapsulates these efforts:[14]

THE BABYLONIAN HERITAGE
As one of the last representatives of the vanishing Judeo Arabic music (the music of the Iraqi Jews in Iraq and Israel), Yair Dalal invest[s] much of his time in promoting special projects to keep this legacy alive . . .
NEW HOMAGE "Sallah & Daoud El Kuweiti"
A unique evening in the memory of the Kuweti brothers. The concert include[s] the music of Sallah and Daoud El Kuweti—two of the most well known musicians and composers of Iraq in the first half of the 20th century. A musical encounter between two generations: Imman-Suzanne Sharabani, Yousef Shem Tov and Elias Sasha—famous musicians who were part of the Bagdadi [*sic*] music scene until their emigration to Israel, and Yair Dalal, Avi Agababa & Assaf Zamir—the second generation of Iraqi emigrates [*sic*] who continue the tradition of Judeo Arabic music.

Such efforts are featured in *Baghdad Bandstand* (Halfon 2002), a documentary about a reunion concert that Yair helped to organize for the elderly

12. See chapters 8 and 11.
13. The transliteration of their names varies on Yair's recordings.
14. www.yairdalal.com/index1.html, accessed July 17, 2004.

musicians who had immigrated in the 1950s and in which he and his peers, Agababa and Zamir, participated.

Yair's advocacy of heritage also includes an array of educational programs aimed at bringing various traditional musics to a wider audience. He became involved in the work of Kehilot Sharot (Singing Communities), an organization devoted to the dissemination of sung liturgical poems from North Africa and the Middle East. He offers workshops with titles such as "Israel and Judeo Arabic Music—A Bridge to Babylon," "Multicultural Music in Israel," "Oud and Oriental Violin," and "Music as an Agent for Social Change" that reflect the same interests that motivate his other endeavors. Yair has also taught in frameworks as different as the Middle East Music Camp in Mendocino, California, and the School of Ethnic Music at Bar Ilan University in Israel. He has even started his own school, Almaya, on the waterfront of Jaffa, teaching long weekly group sessions.

In his work with Bedouin musicians from the Azazme clan, Yair was driven by aesthetic affinity, rather than shared biological descent or cultural identity. This collaboration enabled him to realize his sense of connection to the desert to the fullest and it brought the Azazme musicians an outside audience that they had not yet reached. In this respect they benefited from Yair's prominence in Israel and abroad. The connections extend beyond the album and the concerts with the full Azazme Tarab ensemble. Yair has toured abroad with one member of that group, Heleil al-Awiwi, and in other contexts he performs and teaches Bedouin songs taken from that collaboration.

Yair capitalizes on his "Eastern" heritage in ways that Zohar Fresco and Shoham, to take examples from Bustan Abraham and Alei Hazayit, do not. This is not limited to perpetuating the past. His settings of poems by Roni Someck, of Iraqi descent like Yair, brings this heritage into the present by reflecting the lived experience of Israelis like himself.[15]

Yair's heritage serves as a means of legitimization. He presents himself as an advocate of Judeo-Arab culture, wearing this identity with pride and referring to it as the basis for claims to brotherhood with Palestinians and other Arabs. This stance establishes authority from which flows authenticity. He also asserts authenticity through his connection to the desert and the iconic people of the desert, the Bedouin. The international world music trade fair WOMEX described Yair in its 2001 Showcase (which features one band or artist per country): "Dalal has preferred to remain as authentic as possible. Therefore also the choice of recording the CD [*Azazme*] in the tent. Bedouin music and culture is slowly eliminated and this is an attempt to preserve at least a small repertoire of Bedouin music from the Negev" (WOMEX 2001). This text, probably derived from Yair's own publicity materials, positions him well with regard to one of the primary yardsticks of desirability in the world music market.

15. These poems are "Rabin," " Solo Arak," and "Rice Paradise."

Yair's control over his image and representation extends to the video, the Internet, his stage presence and his choice of musical material. Three documentaries about Dalal's projects demonstrate that he is unusually media-savvy. Only Tomalak 2006 is ostensibly about Yair, but he also features centrally in Kahan 1995 and Halfon 2002. His Web site is unusually copious in its offerings, including photos and video clips of performances, extensive information for promoters, a discography, and press clippings among its fifteen sections.

Yair tends to appear in a loose white robe or long jacket, sometimes topped by cloth draped over his shoulders like a prayer shawl. With this constructed assemblage he evokes aspects of his heritage that many Israelis of similar age repressed in the face of the hegemony of Western norms of dress and a general Israeli tendency to view traditional Middle Eastern manners of dress as "backward" and associated with the Arab enemy. This is precisely the clash of cultural values and ethnicities that played a major role in the rise of the ethnic music scene in Israel. The assemblage is likely to be read as Middle Eastern and exotic by European and North American audiences. It also can index a certain non-Orthodox spirituality. Yair exudes a quiet charisma, quite different from the rather wild stage persona of Shlomo Bar, founder of Habreira Hativ'it. While acknowledging Bar as a pioneer who demonstrated the possibilities of generating new music from ethnic roots, Yair has not emulated the more extroverted aspects of Bar's act.

Like Bar (but unlike the members of Bustan Abraham), Yair has turned for some of his material to songs of a religious nature. Yair is not demonstratively religious in an orthodox sense—he does not wear a skullcap, for instance, lives a secular life in other ways as well, and has not turned to the Jewish mysticism that motivates Shlomo Bar. Espousing parts of his religious heritage while maintaining a secular lifestyle is congruent with the practices of a large portion of the Israeli public, particularly those of Middle Eastern and North African descent. His choices and his approach probably resonate with other segments of his audience, too.

With his penchant for unadorned singing, extensive repetition, and gradual layering and intensification, Yair creates a powerful impression in songs such as "Ya Ribon Alam" and "Adon Haslichot" (⊙ audio track 4). His arrangements differ markedly from the way most other Israeli musicians have arranged similar songs. When Yair engages in fusion in his arrangement of "Adon Haslichot," he creates a meditative mood, unlike the rock and jazz-tinged arrangements of "Dror Yikra" by Israeli jazz-fusion band Esta or an Israeli army entertainment troupe.[16]

An apparent simplicity pervades much of Yair's music and is important to his image. When asked at a San Francisco concert about the style

16. I refer here to *Mediterranean Crossroads* and *From Israel With Love*, respectively. The version of "Dror Yikra" recorded by Habreira Hativ'it on *Origins* is much closer to Dalal's sound world.

of music he plays, Yair explained that there are basically two types of Arab music: of the tents and of the city.[17] "I'm more of the tents," he said. "The city people play so fast." He played his signature piece "Al Ol" (⊙ audio track 5) and ended the concert by inviting the audience to sing "Ya Hbayeb," a short, traditional Bedouin song, over and over again, creating a hypnotic effect. When Yair plays Bedouin material—with the whole Tarab ensemble on *Azazme*, with a single Bedouin musician Heleil al-Awiwi, or alone—he enters a highly restricted, but intensely expressive world miles removed from the urban *maqam* tradition of Taiseer Elias and Nassim Dakwar or the more popular Arab music favored by Jamal Sa'id and his band mates in Alei Hazayit.

Yet Yair draws on those two musical practices, too. His musical persona is not strictly one thing or another. Besides touching points along this Middle Eastern spectrum, Yair also turns to aspects of European and North American musics. Like the other musicians discussed in this book, he takes an opposition between East and West as a basic frame of reference. Running through his discography for an American audience, for instance, he characterized *Silan* as "East and West," differentiating it from other efforts that he perceives as restricted to Eastern styles.[18]

Like Shoham and Jamal, Yair believes profoundly in the emotional, transformative power of music. Over the years he has told me numerous anecdotes about moving people to tears. This is clearly a benchmark of the efficacy of his music. The sheer diversity of people he reports bringing to tears—ranging from students in his Jaffa workshop who end nearly every session in tears, to Iraqis nostalgic for the "true" Iraqi music, to a Lebanese musician whose deep personal associations are aroused by Yair's singing—is another indication of his perception of the power of his music. Yair's music is also transformative in that it is intended to overcome the fears and ignorance that have driven Jews and Arabs apart. This desire to bring people together, to bridge divides, finds expression in pan-Middle Eastern and Mediterranean aspects of his work, such as his associations with musicians trained in Turkey, Iran, Iraq, and even India, as well as his choice of geographic themes for compositions and albums (see chapter 11).

A Network of Connections

With partners ranging from the Azazme Bedouin to Jordi Savall, a leading proponent of European early music, Yair Dalal stands out as a collaborator and connector. His array of partnerships contrasts with Bustan Abraham and Alei Hazayit, small networks that were more stable and closed. In the period from 1994 to 2002, Yair recorded with no fewer than thirty-nine

17. Clarion music store, June 14, 2004.
18. June 14, 2004. See chapter 11 for discussion of the East-West topos.

Figure 7.2 Yair Dalal's musical partners. Key to album titles: 1 = *Al Ol*, 1995*; 2 = *Hijaz*, 1995; 3 = *Music Channel*, 1995*; 4 = *Samar*, 1996; 5 = *Silan*, 1997; 6 = *Perfume Road*, 1998; 7 = *Azazme*, 1998; 8 = *Darma*, 1999; 9 = *Shacharut*, 2000; 10 = *Asmar*, 2002. * indicates that some musicians who participated are not named individually in the table.

Recording # (See Key):	1	2	3	4	5	6	7	8	9	10
Avi Agababa	X					X	X	X	X	X
Heleil al-Awiwi							X		X	
Jowad al-Tamimi	X		X							
Haim Ankri										X
Ilan Ben Ami								X		
Sharon Ben Zadok								X		
Avi Cohen	X									
Shai Dayan	X									
Albert Elias	X									X
Ariel Eliav (Elayev)										X
Eyal Faran	X				X	X		X		
Zohar Fresco		X		X						
Coby Hagoel	X									
Gustavo Herzog	X									
Erez Mounk										X
Yinon Mualem								X		
Maureen Nehedar										X
Eylon Nuphar					X					
Nurit Ofer	X				X	X				
Yosi Ron		X						X		
Herzl Sagi	X									X
Eyal Sela	X	X	X		X	X		X		
Izhar Shabi	X									
Youssef Yaakub Shem Tov				X			X			X
Shoushan										X
Asaf Sirkis		X								
Yaron Sofer	X									
Saed Sweiti	X		X							
Noam Topelberg		X						X		
Tal Yaniv								X		
Amos Yifrach	X									
Assaf Zamir							X		X	X
Yoav Zohar	X									
Tarab ensemble*							X			

different Israeli and Palestinian musicians on eight albums produced in Israel (see figure 7.2).[19] A few of these musicians, such as Avi Agababa and

19. An asterisk indicates that the recording also included musicians who are not otherwise part of the ethnic music scene in Israel and are therefore not represented in the chart. Names are spelled as on the CDs. The Tarab ensemble

Eyal Sela, are regular partners. Between 1994 and 2002 Agababa and Dalal appeared on at least six albums together while Sela appeared on at least eight albums with Dalal. They toured in various configurations.[20]

Yair's first solo album, *Al Ol*, was a hodgepodge of ensembles and styles. In addition to three children's choirs and the Oslo Philharmonic (for the aforementioned "Zaman es-Salam"), eighteen individual musicians are credited, including one of the old Iraqi Jewish musicians so influential in Yair's training, as well as two Palestinian musicians and some younger Israeli Jews, including his long-time collaborators Agababa and Sela. His second album, *Samar* (1996), differed greatly, consisting almost exclusively of solo *'ud*. He then formed a group that he called Al Ol, touring with them and recording *Silan* (1997) and *The Perfume Road* (1998), both colored by the musical training several band members had received in India. In 1999, Yair took a different turn, recording *Azazme* with the Tarab Ensemble (drawn from the Azazme Bedouin), Avi Agababa, and Asaf Zamir. One member of the Tarab ensemble also appeared on *Shacharut* (2000) together with Agababa and Zamir. Yair slowed his pace a bit, taking two years to produce *Asmar* (2002) in which he once again employed a rather large number of musicians in various combinations.

During this period, Yair also appeared on other projects, including Eyal Sela's *Hijaz* (1995) and *Darma* (1999). Outside the Israeli ethnic music scene (or on its periphery) Yair participated in several other recordings. He was centrally involved in two collaborations in which he shared equal billing: *Music Channel*, a collaboration sponsored by the Norwegian Broadcasting Corporation and the Norwegian Foreign Ministry, involved two Palestinians (Sweiti and al-Tamimi) and one other Israeli (Sela), as well as a Norwegian progressive rock quartet; and *Sheshbesh* (1998), which brought Yair together with three Israeli orchestral musicians to perform contemporary "art music" scores but also one of Yair's own compositions. Yair also recorded and toured with Jordi Savall, who became interested in reconstructing old Sephardic music from Spain and working with improvisers (*Diasporá Sefardí*, 1999). Yair has had guest spots on other musicians' projects as well: Oliver Shanti's *Seven Time Seven* (1998) incorporates recordings of Yair, Eyal Sela, and two Israeli Arab musicians (Amal Murkus and Nizar Zreik) on separate tracks while Sheldon Sands' *Dead Sea Strolls* (2002), recorded in Colorado, includes not only Yair and Sela but several members of the Israeli ethnic band Sheva. Yair also contributed to the CD *One* by Yuval Ron and Omar Faruk Tekbilek (2003).

Yair appears to seek variety through diverse musical partners. Aside from a few key relationships, such as ongoing partnerships with Sela and Agababa, figure 7.2 shows considerable turnover. His band Al Ol

---

consists of Mohammad Abu Agag, Abu Youssef Gerbia, Aouad Shalibi, Attiya Shalibi, Farhan Shalibi, Shadi Shalpi, as well as Heleil al-Awiwi (who is listed separately in the table because he appears on an additional album).

20. These connections are discussed in greater detail in chapter 8.

encapsulates such variety, with several members trained in Hindustani music, while Eyal Sela brings Turkish, klezmer, and various other Balkan pieces and practices to the mix. More recently, however, Yair has turned toward homogeneity, working with Avi Agababa and Asaf Zamir, both Israelis of Iraqi Jewish parentage, a fact conveyed in the liner notes to *Shacharut* (Dalal 2000).

There are also interesting connections to be found among musicians within this assortment. Asaf Zamir, for instance, was Avi Agababa's student; they are characterized in the liner notes to *Shacharut* (Dalal 2000) as an "almost indivisible unit," performing and teaching together. This replicates the traditional pattern of Arab ensembles, noted in chapter 2, in which the lead drummer brings a student or disciple to play support patterns. A number of the musicians are members of two overlapping bands, Al Ol under Yair's leadership and Darma led by Sela. Note, too, that Zohar Fresco appears on two of Yair's albums, renewing contact that predated Bustan Abraham.

Not all of Yair's collaborations are apparent from figure 7.2, which represents only commercial recordings. He has performed at one Israeli festival with Shlomo Bar and at another with Israeli rocker Alon Olearchik. Prior to the latter festival he told a reporter:

> My music isn't quite the kind of stuff that brings in large crowds. So I thought of Alon, with his raspy vocals—neither of us is a great singer, we rely more on the feeling we impart. The idea is to take his songs more towards the East, and for Alon to connect with my material, like the music from *Al Ol* [Dalal 1995]. But I'm not looking to make compromises, rather to take the essence of his music and of my music. (Davis 2001c)

In this passage Yair reveals both aesthetic and pragmatic motivations for his many interactions.

Yair has displayed considerable business acumen in the charting of his career path. He told me that he decided to be billed as "Yair Dalal and Al Ol," rather than submerging himself in the band, due to his experience assembling several earlier groups that fell apart after a short time, effectively shelving the use of the band name and losing any name recognition he might have accrued.[21] By keeping his name separate he is free to form several bands and undertake various endeavors without losing continuity and recognition. This successful marketing strategy suits his multifaceted array of performance formats. Much of the credit for this strategy and for the polished, widely dispersed publicizing of Yair's endeavors is due to his wife at that time, Yvonne Kahan, who continued to manage Yair's career for nearly a decade after helping him with the successful "Zaman el-Salaam" performance in Oslo. She attended world music festivals and trade shows to network with promoters and other world music agents. Like Farjun,

21. June 21, 1998.

Yair and Yvonne understood the workings of the world music industry well. They took a modular packaging approach—similar to Farjun's packaging of Bustan Abraham with its subsets White Bird and Ziryab (see chapter 5)—but developed it further, offering a spectrum of "products" to fit nearly every budget and programmatic need.

The publicity efforts paid off. In late 2002, Yair was one of four nominees in the Middle East category for BBC Radio 3's World Music award. Although Yair and the other two male instrumentalists (Kayhan Kalhor and Omar Faruk Tekbilek) lost to Samira Said, a Moroccan pop singer resident in Egypt, this nomination is perhaps the best indicator of Yair's success in establishing himself in the world music market.[22] In Web searches conducted annually from 2002 to 2004, I found far more references to Yair Dalal (growing from more than 1,200 to more than 2,700) than to Bustan Abraham (growing from 400 to 1,200).[23]

The extensive recognition is due to Yair's frequent performances abroad and intensive networking, but also to his versatility and his modular marketing plan. He can perform with his band Al Ol, with a Bedouin musician or ensemble, in a trio with two Israeli Jewish drummers, or solo on violin and 'ud. He can play explicitly Jewish repertoire, new pieces that are a fusion of "ethnic" musics, or a program laced with Arab art music. Conducting a workshop one day at a university, he may be found lecturing the next at a synagogue on topics ranging from the music of the Iraqi Jewish community to collaboration for peace. When he tours as a sideman with Jordi Savall, he enters yet another musical world. Yair's multifarious activities and connections are a fine subject for network analysis, topic of the next chapter.

22. Badley 2003 (published on the BBC Web site) attributes the selection of Said to the fact that she is the only one of the nominees to be widely played on the radio in the Middle East. See also Lobeck 2003 for ruminations on the meaning of world music in relation to this award.

23. Alei Hazayit barely surfaced in these searches. By 2008 a Google search for Yair Dalal yielded 33,100 hits while one for Bustan Abraham yielded 17,300 —not bad considering the band had been defunct for five years.

8

A Larger Network—The Ethnic Music Scene in Israel

Beyond the interactive network of a single ensemble, explored in chapter 6, professional musicians are always enmeshed in larger sets of relationships as they join, create, and reshape networks relevant to their musical work. At all stages of their careers they navigate the links that bind them to others with related interests and needs in order, for instance, to find employment and partners for performances. Reputations, musical ideas, fads, and other intangibles flow along the same links, which extend to nonmusicians who act as producers, managers, critics, listeners, performers in other media, and so on. The network concept can usefully be extended further to include institutions such as schools, events such as festivals, venues such as particular clubs or concert halls, and artifacts such as recordings.

Networks have been analyzed from different perspectives in a broad array of disciplines, ranging from sociology through epidemiology to computer science.[1] Sociologists, for instance, have formalized network theory through quantification, mathematical representations, and computational approaches that have generated copious publications.[2] In the study of musical practices, however, networks have yet to be theorized. They are sometimes mentioned in passing in writing about popular music, for instance, yet little attention has been paid to their structure and dynamics or how they intersect, change over time, and affect musical knowledge, values, and production.[3]

1. Barabasi surveys this variety (2002). Monge and Contractor (2003) is one of several recent works that take stock of social network analysis.
2. The bibliography of Degenne and Forsé 1999, a primer on such approaches, includes nearly 300 articles and books in English and French.
3. Thompson 2002, on London studio musicians, is a rare exception. Despite its title, "The Music-Network" (Koskoff 1982) concerns cognitive maps, i.e., networks of concepts not of people. In a bid to update subcultural theory, Stahl

In this chapter, I explore three related perspectives: networks, scenes, and art worlds. Scene and art world (a concept developed by sociologist Howard Becker) offer ways of conceptualizing the whole "package" of people, organizations, and places involved in the production and consumption of music. Network theory encompasses these and offers more detailed ways of thinking about relationships and roles. Mapping relationships enables us to examine the topography of professional musical life and its change over time. It offers a framework for talking about individual agency in relation to larger forces and structures by moving from a middle level toward both the micro and the macro. We can trace the formation of institutions, the emergence and reinforcement of a network, and individual trajectories while highlighting the key roles played by hubs, gatekeepers, and other types of mediators.

I offer this chapter as a demonstration of the utility of central concepts from network theory. This is a qualitative, rather than quantitative, analysis of the growth of "ethnic music" in Israel from a few groups of like-minded musicians to a scene that has gained professional and critical recognition and undergone significant institutionalization and growth. Network diagrams help to visualize this field of action while concepts such as centrality, prominence, and prestige aid in specifying the differing positions and connections of Yair Dalal, Bustan Abraham, and Alei Hazayit. Beginning with a presentation of select network theory concepts, this chapter proceeds to analyses of Yair Dalal's web of connections, the larger ethnic music scene, and its intersections with other musical networks in Israel. I then suggest that the dynamic network of institutions, venues, and market situations that grew up around the musicians in the scene is an emergent art world, and conclude by analyzing aspects of network dynamics within this art world.

The value for ethnomusicologists of this particular configuration of network theory lies in its aim for comprehensiveness in understanding the layout and dynamics of a complex social and cultural nexus. It enables us to think about this phenomenon both as self-contained and as engaged in numerous ways with the "outside," and it suggests an array of questions to identify and assess the numerous types of connections that link people, institutions, things, and concepts.

––––––––––

uses the term *network* loosely and almost interchangeably with a string of related terms such as *affiliation, alliance,* and *circuit* (e.g., 1999: 24). Martin 2006 surveys three case studies in popular music to demonstrate the applicability of Becker's art world (see my discussion below). Eliot Bates, whose dissertation I directed, has made a significant contribution in network analysis of Turkish recording studios (2008).

Some Basic Concepts of Network Theory

Network Structure

A network comprises a set of *nodes* and the *links* (or ties) that connect them. The number and type of nodes, the number and type of links that connect them, and the network's structure, i.e., the configuration of those nodes and links, enable and constrain interaction among nodes and the action of the network as a whole. The term *structure* is used here in a flexible sense to denote a set of mutually constitutive relationships that has the potential to change at any time, rather than a rigid, a priori organization.

Each of the small networks diagrammed in figure 8.1 has six nodes but differs in the distribution of links, and thus in the possibilities for interaction among the nodes. Those in figure 8.2 also vary in size. One can show particular characteristics of a network in such two-dimensional representations, but it is impossible to capture all aspects of a network, especially the more dynamic ones, such as shifts in network membership, or relative rigidity or flexibility, i.e., the network's change or potential for change over time. Family trees and organizational charts, for example, show hierarchies of descent and command, respectively, but tell us nothing about the love, hate, knowledge, rivalry, or other exchanges taking place within a family or business over time.

Figure 8.1 shows that small differences in the configuration of the nodes and links can substantially alter the possibilities for interaction within a network.[4] In the first configuration, a ring network, each node (represented by a small circle) is connected via links (represented by lines) to two others and through them to every other node. By contrast, configuration 2 is far more *centralized:* Node A is directly linked to every other node and is more highly connected than the other nodes, which have one link apiece and must communicate through A. Yet the maximum "distance" traveled between two nodes is never more than two links, less than the maximum of three in the first configuration. Such a highly centralized network can also be represented as a star.

The third configuration is a variant of the first, but lacks a link between B and C. Communication between them must therefore pass through each of the other nodes.[5] Moreover, B and C are relatively distant from each other, separated by five links. (Arranging the nodes in a straight line might represent this network even better but would obscure the similarity to configuration 1.) This distance is reduced to three links in configuration 4 by increasing the number of links. Although there is still no direct link

---

4. The positions of the circles are arbitrary for the moment.
5. For the sake of clarity and consistency I discuss the structural characteristics of these configurations in terms of the facilitation (or inhibition) of interaction, each link or path of links representing some form of communication or interaction between the connected nodes. Such an understanding suits communications theory well; however, links may also represent other types of connections.

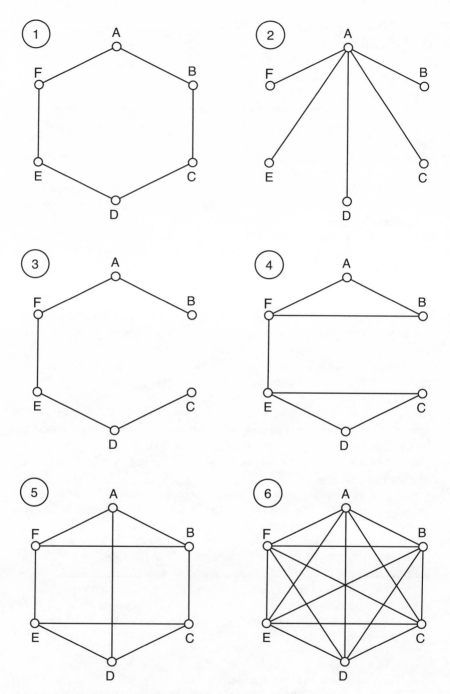

Figure 8.1   Basic six-node network configurations

between B and C, each of these nodes connects to two others, enabling them to interact via F and E, bypassing A and D. In comparison with the configuration 3, nodes A and D have lost some of their control over interaction even though they have not lost any links. This network has two subnetworks, ABF and CDE, that are maximally connected (i.e., each node is linked to the other two within its triad). Called *clusters*, they are connected via the link between F and E, which are *cut points* because they have the potential to cut one portion of a network off from another and therefore may control interaction between the two subnetworks. Nodes F and E are also slightly more connected than the other nodes, having three links apiece rather than two. Still greater connectivity is evident in configuration 5. The addition of links A-D and B-C preclude any node from having exclusive control over the interaction between any other pair. In other words, there are no cut points. This is also true for configuration 6, representing a maximally connected network in which each of the six nodes is linked to each of the others and there are no obvious subnetworks.

Several fundamental network variables are apparent in the configurations of figure 8.1: (a) the number of links per network, ranging from a minimum of five in configuration 3 to a maximum of fifteen in configuration 6; (b) the number of links per node, ranging from one to five; and (c) the shortest distance between any pair of nodes, ranging from one in configuration 6 to five in configuration 3. These variables concern the degree to which each person, group, or institution is connected to other nodes in the network, the overall connectivity of the network, and the number of links and intermediaries through which any two members of the network must communicate. Applied to musical networks they can visually represent the ability of people to work together, the probability that they will share musical knowledge and interests, and the relative importance of particular members of the network as intermediaries.

Nodes, Homogeneity, and Heterogeneity

The number of nodes is a crucial variable. As one moves to larger networks, with nodes and links numbering in the hundreds, thousands, or more, the number of possible configurations quickly becomes enormous. Yet the structural properties noted in figure 8.1 are operative at much larger scales and can be analyzed in terms of the same concepts. Configurations 1 and 2 in figure 8.2 are clearly variants of the same type of network, although the highly connected node in configuration 2 has many more links than the analogous node in configuration 1. Likewise, configurations 3 and 4 represent differences of scale rather than inherent organizational differences. Configuration 4 is considerably more complex than 3, but it also consists of a pair of maximally connected subnetworks joined by a single link. In each instance, the nodes at either end of this link are cut points that can control the flow between the subnetworks.

These simple representations suggest that the structure of a network affects possibilities of interaction within the network; however, they differentiate neither the nodes nor the links except by their position within a

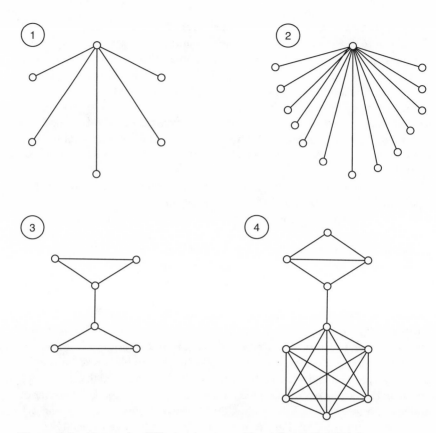

Figure 8.2   Networks differing in size and configuration

given configuration. Any network involving human beings is never completely homogenous, due to each person's individuality and other distinctions deriving from the network's structure and interactions internal and external to the network. Heterogeneity in a musical network may manifest in aspects as different as stylistic specialization, instrumental competence, age, gender, or ethnic background.

In music-stylistic terms, the bands of Jewish and Arab musicians who are the focus of this book are far from homogenous. They constitute a subset of the larger network of the field of "ethnic music" in Israel and also have links to several other networks. This field is more heterogeneous than many others in Israel because it has attracted musicians who began—and often continue—their careers in other networks. Within the ethnic music field, Arab musicians form a relatively homogeneous group in terms of cultural habitus, including types of musical competence and performance experience, if not education and socioeconomic status. They differ greatly in those respects from their Jewish partners in bands such as Alei Hazayit and Bustan Abraham.

Judgments of relative homogeneity or heterogeneity depend on analytical perspective. A musicians' union, for instance, is a network of people who share a common occupation and therefore differ from the members of a teachers' or plumbers' union. Yet beneath the occupational identity of musician and apparent homogeneity we can expect to find considerable variation in ability, experience, and professional specialization.[6] This sort of role differentiation is fundamental to the structure of the typical "ethnic" band in Israel: all drummers occupy an equivalent position within the ensemble (though clearly they differ in areas such as talent, style, and experience), which differs from the position of 'ud players. Everyone expects them to make different types of contributions to the ensemble. Engineers and managers occupy other types of position in the larger ethnic music network. Any audio engineer is expected to provide certain services in amplification and/or recording, while a band's manager generally takes responsibility for much of its nonmusical interaction with the outside world —booking concerts and tours, disseminating publicity, and so on. Replacing one engineer with another or one manager with another does not, in itself, change the structure of the network, though a good engineer may improve the band's sound and a more efficient manager may increase the volume and speed of the flow of information, engagements, fame, and money.

These are manifestations of *class equivalence* that are reflected ethnolinguistically in the categorical rubrics I have just used—drummer, 'ud player, engineer, and manager.[7] These rubrics say something about a person's possibilities in terms of individual agency and relations with others in the network. People may transgress the boundaries of a class, of course: Avshalom Farjun has worked as a manager, an impresario, a record producer, and a professional musician. And some of these classes are more restrictive or tightly delimited than others. Among performers of Arab music, dual competence in violin and 'ud is common, just as Miguel Herstein's dual competence on guitar and banjo is not uncommon within the context of American vernacular musics. In the ethnic music scene it is now common to find guitar players who double on other plucked lutes, such as banjo, 'ud, and various other lute-type instruments from Turkey, Iran, and India. They take advantage of the portability of technical skills (such as the motor patterns and conceptual models of left-hand fingering and right-hand plucking) from one instrument type to another due to the similar physical properties of these instruments.

Class equivalences affect how people relate to members of other classes. In terms of network theory, *structural equivalence* implies that all members of class A relate in the same way to any member of class B. Class

6. In the following examples most of the nodes are people, but network theory applies equally to nodes of many other sorts, as different as airports and Internet routers.

7. There is no inherent relationship to social class, although in a given social context distinctions between different types of nodes in a network may correspond to differences of social class.

equivalences lead us to expect that musicians in a band will depend on their manager for certain types of information, services, and directives, while managers will relate somewhat predictably to the musicians they manage. Such equivalences underlie Eliot Bates' analysis of patterns of interaction among engineers, arrangers, and studio musicians in Istanbul recording studios (2008). This is not to deny the infinite shades of individual relations that emerge from a particular group's "chemistry" (or lack thereof), but to recognize the structures and expectations that tend to channel the course of such relations.

The small interactive networks of Alei Hazayit and Bustan Abraham analyzed in chapter 6 were clusters within the larger network of ethnic music. This means that in this larger context they constituted maximally connected subnetworks in which every member related directly to everyone else in the band. The nodes in this comprehensive network included everyone involved in the production of recordings and live performances: booking agents, recording company personnel, and institutions such as record labels, festivals, arts organizations, and other producers and sponsors—in other words, heterogeneous actors belonging to various professional classes who differ fundamentally in personal interests, motivations, and professional competences, as well as positions and roles within the network.

Links, Directionality, and Hierarchy

The links in a network may differ just as the nodes that they connect may be heterogeneous. Among the more commonly analyzed link variables are *strength*, *directionality*, and *relationship type*. An ethnographically informed analysis of networks of humans must assume the dynamic nature of links and resist rigid typologies. Even as we classify and characterize links with descriptive terms, we must be alert to the possibility that these links may be in flux and should be evaluated within the context of particular networks rather than in the abstract.[8]

In a classic study of job seeking that aimed to bridge the gap between macro and micro levels of social analysis, Granovetter found that the strongest links are not always the most useful, and drew attention to this with the seemingly paradoxical title "The Strength of Weak Ties." Noting that the stronger the ties between two people the more likely their circles of close friends will overlap, he hypothesized that weak ties (or links) greatly extend one's information-gathering network by connecting to people beyond one's immediate friendship network. Defining the strength of a link between two people in terms of duration, intensity, intimacy, and exchange of services, he demonstrated the utility of weak links when he discovered that people tend to find jobs not through their closest friends but through more casual acquaintances (1973).[9] Reaching beyond one's immediate

8. See Emirbayer 1997 for an extensive argument for this view in sociology.
9. Subsequent research showed that this effect is not even across all categories of employment, being most pronounced among lower-skilled workers. See Degenne and Forsé 1999: 112.

circle, in which people are likely to share a lot of the same information, one connects more broadly, potentially accessing more information and gaining more contacts.

While Granovetter's chief concern was the flow of information, weak ties may be important in other ways, too, extending, for instance to social obligations or links to cultural practices beyond an individual's immediate circle. And Granovetter's chief finding has direct relevance for explaining the formation of musical ensembles. Shoham Einav found Jamal Sa'id through weak ties, referred through a chain of casual acquaintances who knew of Jamal through his work on Israeli television, rather than through the musicians with whom Shoham had been performing up to that time. The intermediaries had no further hand in the band's career, but it could be argued that they played a seminal role by connecting two people who moved in such different circles that they were otherwise unlikely to connect. On the other hand, Jamal then drew on his closest connections for core members of the ensemble until he asked Jean-Claude Jones, whom he found through weak ties, to add a bass part to Alei Hazayit's demo. When musicians play as guests on an album their links to the project are generally weaker than the links among the regular band members, although their contributions may be key to the final product. Jean-Claude transitioned from this marginal role to being a member of Alei Hazayit, but the transition ultimately failed because he did not fulfill the group's expectations in terms of commitment to the rehearsal process.

Individual nodes may be *multiplexed*, meaning that they are linked to each other in several ways and involved in several types of exchange. An analysis that would do justice to the complexity of human relations must therefore distinguish links according to the domain within which they operate, such as musical performance, training, economic relations, and various types of social affiliation and interaction. The musical links that will be cited most frequently here include those between members of a band, teacher and student, student (or teacher) and school, composer or arranger and performer, and bandleader and other musicians. Economic relations include the links connecting musicians to managers, producers, record companies, booking agents, and the paying public. Other types of sociocultural affiliations include kinship and shared ethnicity or enculturation. As I noted above, the Arab members of Alei Hazayit shared—with one another and with the Arab members of Bustan Abraham—a habitus characterized by deep enculturation in the values and practices of modern Arab music despite the fact that they came from different social circles. Different types of links need not be congruent. Economic links among musicians may be at odds or interfere with musical links, for instance, when there are disputes over fees.

Links also vary in *directionality*. A tendency for flow in one direction, even to the complete exclusion of flow in the other, produces a directed relationship. Interaction between musicians and their audiences consists of several directed links. Members of the public pay to hear musicians perform (a directed economic link) and give their approbation for a good performance (a directed social link), while musical sound is expected to flow in the opposite direction. To take another example, explicit instruction flows from teacher to pupil, however much teachers may learn from their students, while the students pay their teachers money and (usually) respect. The flow of ideas, music, publicity, and money along the link between a band and a record company is also asymmetrical because each entity has something different to offer the other. On the other hand, Emmanuel and Zohar described a relationship within Bustan Abraham that was characterized by a high degree of mutuality (see chapter 6). While they occupied different positions in the network, fulfilling roles associated with bass or percussion, they enjoyed a bidirectional flow of mutual musical support and stimulation. In each of these examples the actors are multiplexed, i.e., joined by several types of links.

The direction of flow along links affects the character of that network. A directed network, such as the organizational structure of a business, has well-defined paths to channel interaction: Orders come in, are processed, and goods are sent out in accordance with the directed links built into the network's structure. A bandleader who employs other musicians controls employment opportunities, the flow of money, and hence many of the operating decisions. But musicians often work in more than one band, so the leader may have considerably less control than the head of a business might wield over full-time employees. Furthermore, it is not a given that musical directives also emanate from this leader. Even in a relatively clear-cut hierarchy where directives flow from the leader to the members of the band, other types of musical (and social) exchanges may flow in the reverse direction. Shoham Einav led the band she founded in nonmusical matters, but communication was far less directed for musical decisions. Mapping the flow between members of a musical ensemble can be exceedingly complex.

Hierarchy often involves more than the directed links within a network, particularly differences of rank or status (particular types of heterogeneity in the classes of nodes in the network). Some of the diagrams in figures 8.1 and 8.2 could represent hierarchies where the vertical positions of items represent relative rank, yet they contain some ambiguity. Does node A in configuration 2 of figure 8.1 represent a shopkeeper who interacts independently with each of his customers, a boss who requires that all communication between subordinates pass through her, the receptionist at a dysfunctional firm in which no one is on speaking terms with anyone but her, or the guard at the center of Foucault's panopticon, gazing at each of his isolated prisoners? Alternatively, is it a major train station at the hub of a network of minor stations that connect to one another only via rails laid to and from this central station? The relative status of center and periphery varies with each of these scenarios.

Centrality, Prominence, and Prestige

The property of *centrality* expresses the degree to which certain nodes have more connections than others. In a network with high centrality a few nodes have far more connections than the rest. They are commonly known as *hubs*. In the global network of airports, for instance, international hubs have far more links than any of the thousands of regional and local airports. The ratio of hubs to other nodes can vary from a star network—in which all nodes connect to one hub—to a hubless circle network that has even connectivity from one node to the next. Most social networks fall somewhere between these extremes.

Centrality can also be used to describe an individual's position relative to others. Avshalom Farjun is a hub in the ethnic music network. In his multiple roles as impresario, producer, agent, manager, and musician he interacts with hundreds of people, institutions, festivals, and projects in Israel and abroad. Yair Dalal is another hub whose connections overlap with Farjun's in various ways. Shoham Einav, on the other hand, is not a major hub in any musical network, as she does not have many links in the network of ethnic music outside her own band. Neither does Jamal Sa'id, but his centrality in another network—Arab musicians in the Jerusalem area—enabled him to draw on a large resource pool to keep Alei Hazayit staffed. He has since moved on to organizing this larger network by forming an organization to promote Arab arts in the Jerusalem area, an endeavor facilitated by his position as a hub.

Sociologists have devoted extensive attention to theorizing and quantifying the nature of *prominence* within a network. In an oft-cited (prominent) article, Knoke and Burt write "an actor is prominent within a social system to the extent that his relations make him particularly visible relative to other actors in the system" (1983: 195). If we go beyond a simple tally of links (equating more links with greater prominence) to consider the strength and direction of connections, as well as the relative position of each node within the network, the analysis becomes considerably more interesting and closer to life. Being "well connected" refers to the prominence of the people, organizations, and institutions with which one is linked. Note that this does not necessarily correlate with centrality. A node that is connected to prominent nodes is likely to be more prominent than one with a similar number of connections to peripheral or poorly connected nodes, an observation encapsulated in the cliché "it's not what you know but who you know."

Prestige, a quality of particular importance in musical networks elaborates on the concept of centrality. Whereas centrality is based on the quantity of a node's links, prestige accrues to a node that is the object of numerous asymmetrical relations, of attention from others that is not necessarily reciprocated (Knoke and Burt 1983).[10] A prestigious university, for instance, has asymmetrical links to numerous colleges of lesser prestige from which it draws students and to which some of its graduates go to teach.

The concepts of prestige, prominence, and centrality clarify important aspects of the relationship between Taiseer Elias and Avshalom Farjun.

---

10. Note that a node's prestige and number of links do not necessarily equate: Think of the person at the front desk of a school or other organization who interacts with many people but is not high in prestige.

Taiseer's prominence in the Arab music and ethnic music networks is due to his performance abilities; his leadership positions in mainstream cultural institutions also bring high visibility. Avshalom is also well known as a musician, but cannot match Taiseer's prestige as a virtuoso. But he has also amassed an unusually high number of links due to his long professional experience in intermediary roles. This gives Avshalom what sociologists call *betweenness centrality*.[11] Both men benefited from their association in Bustan Abraham. It can be argued that Avshalom owes a good deal of his prominence in ethnic music to his association with Taiseer, who benefited, in turn, from Avshalom's betweenness centrality. As Taiseer's prestige grew through acclaim in the press and recognition by fellow musicians, audiences, and cultural institutions he derived less benefit from Farjun's centrality and his increasing commitments led to greater conflict with Avshalom over performance priorities (see chapter 5).

Intermediaries

Intermediaries such as Avshalom fall into several large categories. Those who mediate between the musicians and their audiences by providing and controlling performance opportunities include managers, promoters, booking agents, club owners, festival directors and other staff members of venues that sponsor and produce performances. Another category of mediators consists of producers and audio engineers, who exert extensive control over the actual sounds reaching the audience, whether through the amplification at a live performance or the tracking and mixing of recordings.[12] People in these network positions are likely to listen with a different "ear" than performers or audience members, because evaluating financial risk and profit is key to their jobs. Proposing a reorientation of the sociological study of music, Antoine Hennion asserted that "no one operates within a more realistic network" in the production of popular music than producers and engineers because they are the first audience, representing the general public and re-presenting the music to that wider audience (1989: 402).

Perhaps one of the most telling differences between the ethnic music scene in Israel and the mainstream popular music world studied by Hennion lies in the degree of mediation between musicians and consumers. The subjects of this book enjoyed a greater immediacy of exchange because in their fledgling subfield there was relatively little mediation by record company producers and A&R people. On the other hand, these same musicians

11. See Degenne and Forsé 1999, chapter 6, for a tripartite typology of centrality: *degree centrality* refers to a node with an above average number of links; *closeness centrality* refers to the nodes that are closest to all other nodes in the network, i.e., whose access is least mediated; and *betweenness centrality* refers to a node being located on an unusually high number of paths connecting other nodes in the network.

12. As their financial stake in the success of recording or performance varies greatly, I will not attempt to generalize that aspect. See Bates 2008 for a detailed case study of such issues in Istanbul recording studios.

operated without the fan literature and extensive press coverage that can provide concrete feedback beyond the simple assessments of record sales and applause or apathy in the performance venue.

Two further categories of intermediaries can be subsumed under the rubric of image-makers, differing with regard to the nature of their link to the musicians. Those who provide costumes, publicity materials, and the cover art and inserts for recordings have an interest in enhancing the attractiveness of the product, considerable influence on its presentation, and little or no say regarding the sound of the music. The second group, consisting of music critics whose assessments may influence the musicians and their reception and public image, are generally assumed to have no overt financial interest in the success or failure of a particular musician or band.

Intermediaries who bridge the gaps between networks are *articulators*. They manage musicians' connections to networks such as the festival circuit of the international world music scene and state institutions within Israel in the areas of entertainment, education, cultural sponsorship, and citizenship. Some have the potential for powerful action to the extent that they control, even monopolize, the flow between musicians and others. The people who select music for radio programs, recording companies, and festivals wield considerable power as gatekeepers. That is, they are positioned at a cut point in or between networks, with control over which music to broadcast, record, or present on stage. The gatekeepers of radio and television in Israel did not give Bustan Abraham and Yair Dalal much airplay. The intermediaries working on their behalf, Avshalom Farjun and Yvonne Kahan, respectively, were more successful working connections for them at festivals. Each developed and maintained numerous links to others in intermediary positions. Yvonne, for instance, made a point of attending world music marketing events such as WOMEX (World Music Expo) for this purpose and succeeded in getting a coveted showcase spot for Yair in 2001.[13] Bureaucrats involved in policing borders are gatekeepers in another network and are often less amenable to persuasion by musicians' representatives than booking agents are. Yvonne used her connections at the Norwegian embassy to pressure the Israeli Interior Ministry to grant travel documents for the Palestinian children traveling to the 1994 peace concert in Oslo. Restrictions on movement of West Bank Palestinians had a major impact on relations within Alei Hazayit, creating a link of dependency between certain members of the band and Shoham, who served as an intermediary, using her personal social links to officials who could facilitate permits.[14] But her connections were not sufficiently strong

---

13. See www.mondomix.org/womexshowcases2001/artistes/yairdalal.html, archived at http://web.archive.org/web/20041107162915/http://www.mondomix.org/womexshowcases2001/artistes/yairdalal.html.

14. This was a connection that Omar Keinani, as an Israeli citizen, did not need (see chapter 4). Recall that Shoham also provided privileged links to the health care system.

to override security service objections to granting entry to Israel for a Palestinian musician resident in Jordan whom Jamal wished to introduce to Alei Hazayit. In each case, government officials who grant travel documents or review them play gatekeeping roles that can make or break a concert, festival, and, by extension, a career.

Network Analyses

Yair Dalal's Network

Yair's career exemplifies the challenges and rewards of analyzing a network of professional musicians. The diagrams included here represent the many types of relationships he has formed as a performer, bandleader, composer, educator, and sociopolitical advocate. They are intentionally selective in order to highlight certain relationships pertinent to a particular analytical point. Links to recordings are privileged over participation in concerts⌊For instance, Yair Dalal has appeared in concert with well-known musicians, such as Shlomo Bar, Alon Olearchik, and David Broza, but they have not recorded together so those links are omitted from the diagram. I obtained most of the information from Yair Dalal, the members of Alei Hazayit, and the members of Bustan Abraham.⌋The rest is derived from CD credits, concerts that I attended, and conversations with others knowledgeable about this scene. The different arrow types (explained in figure 8.3) do not do full justice to each person's contribution or involvement in a project or band. Finally, the format of each diagram is just one of many possibilities; the more complex diagrams could have been laid out in many other ways. Given all of these limitations, one should assume that the actual links are more numerous and the networks more complex than represented here. Due to the lack of a temporal axis, time may seem to be collapsed into an undifferentiated present or the sum total of an individual's links. Neither of these impressions is correct: Some of the relationships shown are simultaneous, some overlap in time, and some are sequential.

A significant portion of Yair's professional network during the period 1995–2003 is depicted in figure 8.4. For legibility I have omitted some CDs, some links, and many of the individual members of the five ensembles indicated by octagons.[15] Yair actually performed with more musicians during this period, but those shown suffice to give a good idea of the multifaceted approach he has taken in his career. CDs are indicated by circles containing the year of issue below the title. Each band is represented by a single node, a method called *punctualization* that emulates everyday discursive practice. Rather than naming every individual involved, one often speaks of a band, a company, a school, or the record industry, reducing a complex network of people to a single entity because "punctualized resources offer

15. For instance, Avi Agababa and Asaf Zamir played on *Azazme* and Avi also played on *Al Ol.*

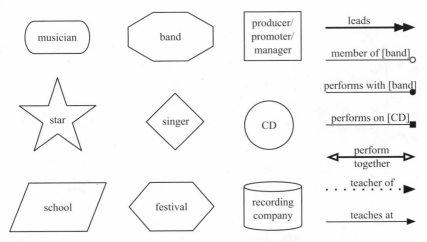

Figure 8.3 Key to symbols used in network diagrams. Arrowheads and relative thickness of lines represent the directionality and quality of links.

a way of drawing quickly on the networks of the social without having to deal with endless complexity" (Law 1992: 385).[16]

Yair has recorded and performed with his band Al Ol, a relatively stable cluster in which every member is directly linked to every other member, and with looser, ad hoc clusters of musicians on tours and albums such as *Asmar, Azazme,* and *Shacharut.* Links within these clusters can be relatively temporary or they may be strengthened when, for instance, the same musicians are involved both in a recording and in the tour to promote that recording. Thanks to multitrack recording practices the musicians connected to *Asmar* need not have formed any direct links with every other musician on that CD, although they are listed in one oval to save space. The CD *Asmar* itself may be viewed as a hub of sorts, with a high degree of centrality within the subnetwork of musicians involved in its production.

Thick lines with hollow arrowheads indicate long-term associations extending beyond a single album. These dyads have a strong bidirectional flow. Yair has performed frequently with Agababa, for instance, on tours and on numerous CDs. Yair has other long-term connections, featuring older Iraqi Jewish musicians Albert Elias and Yosef Shem Tov on other CDs and playing with them on many occasions.

The connections between Yair and Eyal Sela are particularly noteworthy from a network perspective. Each has played in the other's band (Sela's Darma and Yair's Al Ol). These two bands overlap further: Eyal Faran is a member of both and Avi Agababa has recorded at least one album with

16. I owe the term and reference to Eliot Bates, who has argued in his study of interaction in Istanbul recording studios (2008) that entire groups or institutions can legitimately be represented thus because they are often viewed as single entities by those who interact with them.

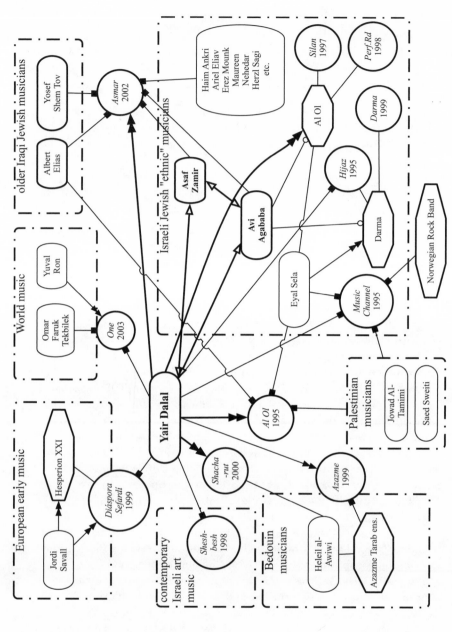

Figure 8.4   Partial diagram of Yair Dalal's network of musical partners

each band. Yet the bands have distinctive repertoires and sounds. Sela and Yair have performed in other combinations on various other occasions, including the collaboration with two Palestinians (Jowad al Tamimi and Saed Sweiti) and four Norwegians that resulted in *Music Channel*.[17]

Despite its incomplete representation of Yair's network of connections, figure 8.4 gives a strong sense of the multifaceted network of connections in which Yair is a major hub. It also makes apparent that Yair has developed connections to several discrete networks. Represented in the diagram by large rectangles with broken lines, these include: European early music performers led by Jordi Savall; world music as exemplified by his work on *One* with two U.S.-based musicians, Israeli Yuval Ron and Turk Omar Faruk Tekbilek; contemporary Israeli classical/art music (*Sheshbesh*); older immigrant musicians from Arab countries, represented here by two Iraqi Jewish musicians; and musicians from the Azazme Bedouin clan. The other musicians are a subset of the Israeli ethnic music scene, which will be more fully represented in figure 8.6.

Yair's work with the Tarab ensemble of musicians from the Azazme Bedouin clan is a route to the exotic, a means of engaging with the desert through the emblematic desert people.[18] But rather than lump Yair together with First World popular music stars, such as Paul Simon and Peter Gabriel, who have foregrounded the exotic by recording once or twice with Third World musicians, it is best to view this in the context of Yair's other work. The Azazme project was by no means Yair's only means of engagement with these themes. Proclamations of love for the desert run throughout his work. As a child of the Middle East and as an Israeli who has chosen to spend significant periods of his adult life in the desert, Yair is far less a tourist than stars of the rock world who descend briefly upon musicians and studios in South Africa, Brazil, or other "exotic" locales to make a recording before flying off to the next engagement, album, theme, and interest.[19] Yair's collaboration with the Azazme ensemble is, at least in some respects, more lateral than North-South or East-West.[20] Traditional Bedouin songs constitute most of the material on the CD and Yair's hand is relatively light in the arrangements of these pieces. There is still a power imbalance, however, as it is Yair who has the access to Israeli and international performance and recording opportunities. Thus he serves as an intermediary between the Tarab ensemble and a mass audience via the recording industry and concert opportunities.

17. Also missing from the diagram are other packages involving performance with Palestinian musicians that have constituted an important branch of Dalal's multipronged musical marketing campaign, but have yet to result in a CD.

18. This is discussed in chapter 11.

19. See Meintjes 1990, Taylor 1997, and Feld 2000, among others. Dalal is not the only Israeli Jew to play with Bedouin (see Amos Ifrah's biography on the Adama Music label Web site, http://web.archive.org/web/20041208153105/http://www.adama-music.co.il/html/frameset.html), but he is probably the most prominent.

20. See Guilbault 2001.

Multiple affiliations such as those evident in figure 8.4 may strain a network due to conflicts over goals, understandings, and commitments. Yair has managed to achieve and protect his prominence in the marketplace while working with multiple clusters of musicians, not only through his musicianship but also by maintaining a distinctive identity and a high profile. He has become adept at promoting his brand, one might say. Recall that he has billed his performances and albums as "Yair Dalal and Al Ol" after learning from his earlier experiences with clusters (i.e., bands) that dissolved too soon and left him to start building name recognition anew.[21]

Among Yair's numerous short-term collaborations not shown in the diagram are guest spots on recordings and concerts in which promoters bring Yair into "dialogue" with other musicians. For instance, the Jewish Music Festival in Berkeley staged a joint concert for Yair and renowned Nubian musician Hamza El Din in 2001. The two performed together again the following year in New York, bolstered by Yair's band Al Ol, demonstrating that world music matchmakers can sometimes produce the conditions for a "chemistry" that lasts beyond a single collaboration.[22] I have also seen Yair invite local musicians to join him for a piece or two to enhance a concert when he tours solo.

Yair is often the chief instigator of a project, the one with the most contacts in Israel and abroad. He may well exercise a greater variety and number of links than anyone else in the ethnic music scene in Israel. Despite this he has not taken on the managerial role that Avshalom Farjun did for Bustan Abraham, leaving such work to his production company Najema. But he has taken on several other roles within his network of associates, shown in figure 8.5, that are no less important to his professional career than the links in figure 8.4 and affect the nature of those links, often endowing Yair with considerable power. In this diagram entire institutions are punctualized as single nodes.

As a teacher Yair has connected with many musicians and would-be musicians. He taught a performance course at Bar Ilan University for several years.[23] He has also taught repeatedly at the Rimon School of Contemporary Music during the school year and at the Middle East camp in Mendocino, California, during the summers. On tour he often conducts workshops at universities, a smart business move that augments income and exposure. While performing in San Francisco in 1998, for instance, he gave workshops at four universities in the area. This provides Yair with opportunities to make additional contacts and build a larger audience for his concerts and recordings. It is also a good way to spread Judeo-Arab and

21. See chapter 7.
22. Dalal maintained a personal connection with Hamza el Din until the latter's death. Such encounters raise musical challenges and issues of representation that are beyond the scope of this book.
23. He left because he felt the students did not take it seriously enough and the Central Asian faculty did not know Middle Eastern music (p.c., September 2003).

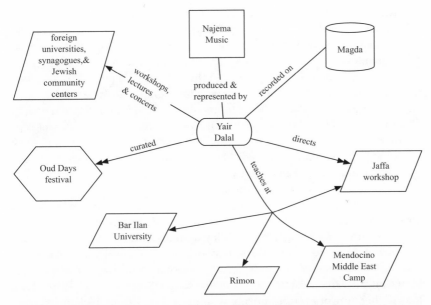

Figure 8.5   Yair Dalal's teaching, recording, and performing connections

Bedouin songs to a growing, widely dispersed network. He serves and builds a transnational community by connecting Jews with parts of the Jewish musical heritage that they may not know. Many value this highly. Each time he has taught Jewish songs at the Mendocino camp many Jews have identified themselves to him, seeking to strengthen a link through ethnic or religious affinity.

By establishing his own school Almaya, on the waterfront in Jaffa, Yair has taken greater control over his teaching. This school serves as an important gathering place, a hub for a nascent network of people interested in Middle Eastern music. For a few it is also a stepping-stone to higher-level training at the Jerusalem Academy in Taiseer Elias's program. Yair draws a socially diverse array of students, but as of July 2007 he had no regular Arab students, just occasional visitors despite the fact that Jaffa has a mixed population of Arabs and Jews.[24]

Yair is prominent on the roster of Magda Records, one of the leading labels for ethnic music in Israel, which advertises his concerts on their Web site. He has a production agency, Najema Music, running his own extensive Web site (www.yairdalal.com) on which he offers booking agents a full range of options, ranging from solo performances through duos and trios to larger ensembles featuring various styles and repertoires. This flexible packaging enables him to satisfy a wide variety of audiences and venues.

24. As this book was going to press he wrote to tell me he had opened a school in the Galilee with both Jewish and Arab students.

Although Yair's activities are varied, ranging from early music performance with Savall to lectures on Babylonian Jewish music, the ethnic music scene is his main field of activity. Curating "Oud Days," the annual Jerusalem festival celebrating the *'ud* and its music, is another example of Yair's multifaceted prominence within this field. On an international level, his high connectivity is evident in the 2006 *Rough Guide to the Music of Israel.* By helping to shape the contents of this compilation CD in a widely distributed world music series, Yair and Yvonne Kahan acted as gatekeepers in two directions: mediating Israeli musicians' access to advantageous exposure and regulating the editor's access to the Israeli scene. Others were involved, but Yair is the only musician on the album to be acknowledged in this capacity by the compiler.

These multifarious connections exemplify the generalization that in most networks certain nodes are more highly connected than others. Yair is both a hub and a bridge, maintaining an unusually high number of connections within the ethnic music network but also connecting to several others.[25] It is unusual, I believe, that someone so prominent, with such high centrality in one network, should be so obviously and widely involved in bridging networks. Yair appears willing to play with musicians from almost any background, exploiting his networking skills and maximizing his employment potential. But he has also drawn the line on several occasions when organizational efforts threatened to take too much of his time and energy from musical endeavors. After the Oslo peace concert, for instance, he brought the Israeli and Palestinian children's choirs together again for one more performance of "Zaman el-Salaam" in Israel, but "more than that was too hard. . . . You have to give yourself to that completely and do nothing else . . . because the bureaucratic difficulties are greater than the musical difficulties. . . . I felt that I am losing myself. I can't do that. I am a creative person, I've got an ensemble, I want to progress," he told me.[26] A few years later he abandoned a music education program he had instigated in the Tel Aviv area because the bureaucracy was taking too much of his time. Clearly there are limits, perhaps unquantifiable but nonetheless real, on the number of connections a person can sustain.

Mapping the Ethnic Music Network in Israel

Implicit in the preceding discussion of Yair's bridging various networks is the assumption that the ethnic music scene constitutes a discrete network that has a *boundary*, however fuzzy. Yair's many connections call the idea of a boundary into question even as they suggest the possibility of a group of musicians with sufficient compatibility and mutual interests to consti-

25. One far-flung connection is with Sheldon Sands, a musician and concert promoter from Boulder, Colorado, who met Dalal while living in Israel in 1996, produced a Dalal concert in Colorado in 2001 (see Bernheimer 2001), and included Dalal in his CD *Dead Sea Strolls* along with several other Israeli musicians (including Eyal Sela) and Colorado-based players.
26. June 1998, my translation.

tute a field of musical practice, one that is large enough to subsume or link to Bustan Abraham, Alei Hazayit, and similar bands. To map this network we need to consider the boundaries of its membership.

A review of social network studies of boundaries discerned three "definitional foci for delimitation" used singly or in combination: (1) possession of a specified attribute; (2) involvement in a specified type of relationship; (3) participation in a given event or activity (Laumann, Marsden, and Prensky 1983: 23–25). How useful are these three criteria for considering how musicians, music industry, critics, researchers, and other audience members define membership in the ethnic music scene in Israel? The first focus of delimitation is problematic, as some musicians would be judged more likely than others to be members by virtue of particular attributes such as playing an "ethnic" instrument or competence in improvisation that is informed by Middle Eastern practices.[27] The second is not a useful criterion because no relationship is common to the nodes in this network. Moreover, not all the students (or teachers) or coperformers of these musicians are members of the ethnic music scene. Some of the important institutions, such as the Israel Festival or the Arab Music Department of the Jerusalem Academy, have strong affiliations to other types of music, while others such as the Confederation House[28] or the Magda record label are more fully committed to this network. The third focus of delimitation is the most apt. All the people discussed in this chapter have participated significantly in a recognizable field of musical production.[29]

But this brings us back to the defining characteristics of this field. Arguing for a relational approach to sociology, Emirbayer has noted the difficulty of moving from continuity to discontinuity that is inherent to defining boundaries for webs that lack clear-cut, "natural" ones (such as all the residents of a particular town, all the students in a school, or all the workers in a factory). By way of illustration he points to Bourdieu's seemingly circular definition of the limits of a field of practice: "where the effects of the field cease."[30] In the case at hand, such an approach actually is losing utility as the field's effects begin to spread into mainstream Israeli popular music, an area that should be considered a distinct network for many reasons, especially having to do with aesthetics, production, and promotion.

Thus, it is useful to maintain a certain looseness of definition when speaking of the ethnic music scene in Israel as a network in its own right,

27. Some might even consider the musician's ethnicity, though I did not hear mention of that as a criterion for inclusion or exclusion. Comments on individual competence did not pertain to membership in the network.

28. The full name of this institution is The Zionist Confederation House but it is usually called *beit hakonfederatzia* (confederation house), the omission of "Zionist" making it far more acceptable a place for Arab musicians to appear.

29. I say "significantly" to screen out those whose involvement has been as slight as contributing to one track on a recording or a one-time collaboration in performance.

30. Emirbayer 1997: 304, citing *An Invitation to Reflexive Sociology* by Pierre Bourdieu and Lois Wacquant (1992: 100).

containing smaller subnetworks and intersecting with other networks in Israel, the Occupied Territories, and other countries. Some musicians mentioned in the coming pages might not consider themselves members of the same network, yet I argue that there are sufficient similarities in musical resources, processes, marketing language, and overall "sound" to define a shared field of practice. These similarities outweigh considerable differences in goals, repertoire, and approaches to composition, arrangement, and performance. Music critics in the Israeli press recognize the similarities. Beginning in the mid-1990s, they have repeatedly noted the local ethnic music scene, punctualizing it as a single entity despite its stylistic diversity. Some musicians do, too. Shem Tov Levy writes in the liner notes to his *Circle of Dreams*, "While working on the soundtrack I had the good fortune to get to know great musicians and players from the ethnic field [*tkhum*], who gave the music a unique color and style" (Levy 2001, my translation). The English liner notes to that album characterize the participants as "Some of the leading and most creative musicians on the Israeli ethnic musical scene."

What are these people noticing? Bands in this field tend to share an affinity for particular ways of making music: cyclical patterns played on hand drums (usually of Middle Eastern provenance) as a rhythmic foundation; predominantly heterophonic use of melodic instruments, at least some of which are Middle Eastern; the partial adoption of Middle Eastern modal practices, such as certain scales and motifs; and a preference for acoustic instruments. At a micro level the interactive networks of individual bands tend toward similarity due to their approaches to rhythmic foundation and heterophonic textures. The incorporation of some non-Middle Eastern elements is nearly as important but harder to define because this is an area of greater variety that adds to the diversity of the field. These bands also share approaches to representation, to be discussed in chapter 11, including particular tropes such as Israel as a cultural crossroads or bridge between East and West. These affinities aside, the field encompasses considerable stylistic diversity. Jamming "dance bands" such as Sheva, Esta, and Gaya, for instance, sound quite different from the instrumental virtuosity and refined orchestration of Bustan Abraham or the love songs of Alei Hazayit.

Yet even bands that sound quite different may be closely linked through common personnel, recording label, and so on because the field of ethnic music in Israel is a densely interconnected network, far more compact than the six degrees of separation usually cited as characteristic of a small world[31] phenomenon. Most participants are no more than two steps apart. If A and B have not actually met or worked together they will almost certainly each have had some significant professional connection with C, where A, B, and C all stand for musicians or other nodes in the ethnic music network in Israel. Figure 8.6 represents many, though by no means all, of the important musicians and bands in that scene and some of the less-known

31. Cf. the small, closely connected network described by Regev and Seroussi at the beginning of their history of the Israeli rock scene (2004: 138).

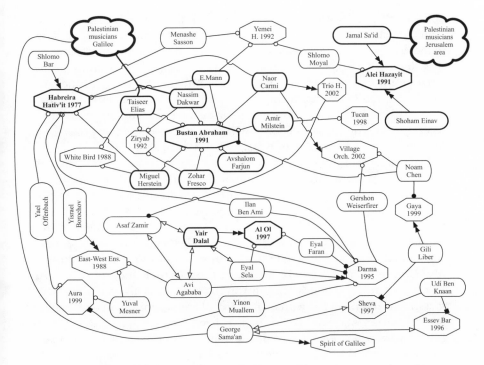

Figure 8.6　Performance links of selected bands and musicians in the ethnic music scene in Israel. Key: 1992 = year of founding or first recording; Trio H. = Trio Hamaalot; Village Orch. = Village Orchestra, Yemei H. = Yemei Habeynatayim. The main subjects of this study are set in boldface within thicker borders.

ones as well in order to demonstrate this point. In addition, two "clouds" represent Arab music networks that will be discussed below, under "Intersections." To maintain legibility the diagram does not include any of the support personnel or institutions. Since the layout of the diagram could not represent chronology while also showing other characteristics I wished to highlight, the year each band was founded or issued its first recording is indicated to add that dimension.

The seminal role of Habreira Hativ'it in the scene is evident from the many links leading to other parts of the network. It has served as a de facto gateway to the network since many of its members have left to found or join other bands in the scene. Of the original four band members, two went on to make their mark with other ensembles: Bassist Yisrael Borochov founded the East-West Ensemble, while Miguel Herstein founded White Bird with Taiseer Elias, then joined Bustan Abraham.[32] More recent members of Habreira Hativ'it have joined Bustan Abraham, Yemei Habeynatayim, Aura,

32. Before founding Bustan Abraham, Avshalom Farjun worked with Bar not as a musician but as the producer of some of his concerts.

and a number of other bands and projects within or closely related to the ethnic music scene. These are mainly asymmetrical connections, tending to move away from Habreira Hativ'it and its leader Shlomo Bar.[33] None of these figures have replicated the sound of Bar's band, which is strongly centered on his impassioned singing and drumming as well as his penchant for Jewish and Moroccan musical and textual references, yet even musicians such as Yair Dalal who were never members of Bar's band point to its early importance as evidence of what was possible in mixing the many musical resources available in Israel.

Also apparent in figure 8.6 is Bustan Abraham's far higher degree of centrality relative to Alei Hazayit. Though both were self-contained ensembles, their position within the scene differed greatly. The only member of Alei Hazayit directly connected to other musicians in the network was the bassist Shlomo Moyal who was, at best, a part-time member of the band and did not serve as a bridge between the band and the larger network as far as I could ascertain. By contrast, various members of Bustan Abraham performed in or with other ethnic bands (only some of which are shown in figure 8.6). Yair's centrality in the network is also apparent. The fact that he has managed a greater variety of connections than most members of Bustan Abraham is less evident here, but was apparent in figure 8.4. The diversification evident in Yair Dalal's roster of offerings is apparent here in Avshalom Farjun's decision to field breakout ensembles Ziryab and White Bird as part of a package to increase performing opportunities and revenue for Bustan's foreign tours.

If we follow the careers and associations of these bands within the larger network of production, including recording companies and performance venues, more connections emerge. A majority of the musicians and bands have recorded on the Magda label, while many others have recorded on Avshalom Farjun's Nada Records. Magda asserts its centrality on its Web site with a 1999 quote from the press: "16 CDs is still a small and modest catalog but compared to the Israeli marke[t] who does not have one label focusing soully [*sic*] on ethnic music Magda is a dominant factor."[34] It also claims a political stance:

> The **Magda** label is an ethnic music project identifying with the idea of the new Middle East. Its existence is based on the welcome possibility of Jews and Arabs of the region coming together in peace. The label's aim is to combine the musical expression of different cultures in this same geographical sphere. The human and political reality existing, the merging of worldwide ethnic groups and the meeting of the three major religions is conducive to a rich and fascinating musical expression. The process of conciliation and tightening of ties is the essence behind the artistic and creative inspiration of all Magda artists.[35]

33. Some musicians have stayed with him for decades.
34. The quote is attributed to Haaretz, without author or specific date.
35. See www.magda.co.il (accessed July 25, 2006).

Many of the musicians recording on Magda do not fulfill this mission statement. Recordings of current groups such as the Ochestre Andalou d'Israel and the Kol Oud Tof Trio represent efforts by Israeli Jews to continue traditions brought to Israel from North Africa, Central Asia, and the Middle East, but they involve no Arabs. Meanwhile the Nazareth Orchestra, also recording on Magda, consists solely of Israeli Arabs playing Arab art music. A third area of publishing consists of reissues of recordings by older and deceased Jewish musicians from Arab countries (such as Maurice El Medioni and Filfel Gourgy), which demonstrate the historic connections of Jews to Middle Eastern and North African music. But the label also publishes collaborations of Jews and Arabs, such as those led by Yair Dalal and Sameer Makhoul. It is a sense of affinity for Middle Eastern music, broadly defined, rather than the proclaimed political stance that lends coherence to the label's roster.

The quality of prominence and the phenomenon of hubs offer means for elaborating the analysis of this network. It is instructive to compare how Yair Dalal and Shlomo Bar, for instance, have achieved prominence. Each has numerous connections and appears as the featured performer, backed by other instrumentalists, but Bar has not moved from band to band or one type of association to another; nor does he tend to appear as a guest on other musicians' projects. His prominence derives from his pioneering status both in ethnic music and in the self-assertion of North African Jews in Israel. He is a hub in that many musicians have entered the network through his band. By contrast, Dalal owes much of his prominence to bridging different networks and thereby reaching a wider public and more professionals.

The ethnic music network includes hubs other than musicians. As sound man at concerts and recording engineer in the studio, Uri Barak is one of the more highly connected individuals. He has worked with most of the musicians in this scene, including Bustan Abraham, Habreira Hativ'it, Yair Dalal, The East-West Ensemble, Essev Bar, Gaya, and Sheva. His high degree of centrality is apparent in the fact that he is credited as principal or sole recording engineer on more than a quarter of the commercial recordings I surveyed.[36] Because these groups play acoustic instruments almost exclusively—electric bass being the most common exception—and prefer hand drums to sticks, they require a different approach to amplification and recording than that used for most Israeli popular music. Uri Barak has developed the expertise and connections to dominate this aspect of the network.

The Israel Festival is also an important hub in the ethnic music network, a venue at which various groups have performed and collaborated with foreign musicians as well as a site for listeners to hear new acts that they might otherwise not hear. For many years the festival has had a mutually beneficial relationship with Avshalom Farjun, who has supplied

36. This is based on a sample of seventy-two compact disks issued mainly by Hed Arzi, Magda, and Nada.

foreign musicians, usually from some part of Asia. It was at this festival that Farjun organized the jam session that brought Elias and Herstein together, planting the seed for Bustan Abraham, which in turn had its most prominent "debut" at the Festival and appeared there in subsequent years with prominent foreign guest artists.

The relationship between the ethnic music scene and the Israel Festival is asymmetrical. Despite the festival's importance for musicians in the ethnic music scene, only a small portion of its program has ever been devoted to such music. By contrast, the Confederation House, also located in Jerusalem, is a self-proclaimed center for the ethnic music scene, producing two annual music festivals in addition to individual concerts. It serves as a meeting place, fostering circles of musicians that differ considerably but have in common ethnic music performance. This is certainly not the only venue for such music, nor is it solely dedicated to music (also hosting poetry events), but it is unusually prominent in the field, particularly in Jerusalem.[37] Moreover, its artistic director has explicitly worked to foster musical and social connections between Jews and Arabs in his programming decisions.[38]

Intersections

Through such festivals and other frameworks, the ethnic music network has intersected with other types of music, including mainstream Israeli popular music, mainstream Arab music, Israeli jazz, Western art music, and Jewish religious music.[39]

Israeli popular music: The ethnic music network exists in the shadow of the far larger popular music network. Some of its musicians left that network, a few participate in it in a limited fashion to make a living, but most have never tried to be a part of it. The most significant links between these two networks are created when figures central to the pop world invite musicians to add "ethnic" flavor. This is an important form of professional recognition for the individual from the ethnic music network, who may gain prestige by association with a star,[40] experience working with bigger record labels, a higher pay scale, more frequent performances, and exposure to larger audiences. This was the case for Zohar Fresco when he

37. Other examples could be drawn from venues in Tel Aviv and Haifa. This is mainly an urban-centered phenomenon, although some festivals occur in rural settings.

38. For instance, according to Fiske 2007, "Artistic director Effie Benaya has given numerous interviews where he has put forth his vision for the festival as a return of sorts to the Golden Age of Spain, when Jews, Christians and Muslims enjoyed widespread dialogue and collaboration."

39. In addition, musicians in the ethnic music scene have participated in recordings by performers such as Ensemble Esfahan, Ilana Eliya, and Shmuel Ruzbahan who take a more traditional orientation toward various types of Central Asian music.

40. Cf. Saada-Ophir, who gives examples of unknown musicians getting a boost from established musicians in the *musika mizrahit* scene (2006: 221–222).

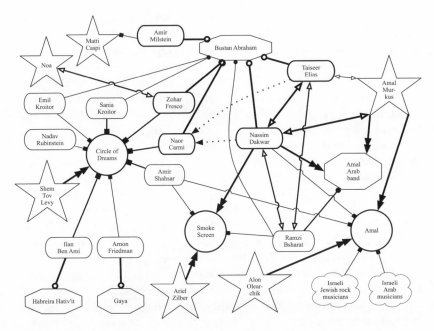

Figure 8.7   Bustan Abraham's connections to popular music in Israel

began to work with Noa. Invitations from mainstream pop figures also demonstrate that the ethnic music scene itself has attained recognition and independent status rather than cooptation into the much larger and commercially more important local pop scene. Figure 8.7 is a selective representation of connections of members of Bustan Abraham to projects by stars in Israeli popular music.

A fixture on the Israeli popular music scene of the 1970s and 1980s, Ariel Zilber reemerged from relative obscurity in the late 1990s with his album *Smoke Screen* (*Masakh Ashan*, 1998). Zilber hoped to attract attention through his new interest in Arab music, expressed through the involvement of Arab musicians and several Zilber compositions informed by aspects of Arab music. He wrote "Sama'i," an instrumental named for a classical Arab musical genre that used the ten-beat meter and formal scheme of that genre but featured his non-Arab trumpet playing. Well into the project he called on Nassim Dakwar of Bustan Abraham to request his help in polishing the Arab aspects. According to Dakwar, a lot of help was needed. His presence in the band also authenticated the Arab aspects of Zilber's project.

Shem Tov Levy's *Circle of Dreams* (2001) is similar in some ways: A middle-aged musician, who rose to prominence in Israeli popular music in the 1970s, attempts a comeback by turning to "Eastern" sounds for a new twist. Invited to write the soundtrack for a film about a poor, mainly Sephardic neighborhood, he created the CD as an extension of the soundtrack by jamming with musicians over several months. But rather than bringing in Arab musicians to polish his compositions as Zilber had done, Levy turned to Zohar Fresco who served as the bridge to the ethnic music network. The partners Fresco engaged—characterized by a music critic as "a kind of ethnic music super group" (Davis 2001d)—included his fellow Bustan Abraham member Naor Carmi and three other active members of the ethnic music network: Ilan Ben Ami (guitar and 'ud), Sania Kroitor (violin), and Amir Shahsar (Persian ney). Kroitor had performed with Bustan Abraham, while Ben Ami was a member of Habreira Hativ'it and had performed with other "ethnic" bands. Shahsar's extensive links in the ethnic music network (including participation in Zilber's project) will be discussed presently.

These moves toward the local exotic by Zilber and Levy were strategically publicized in relation to some element in the performer/composer's background. Zilber's mother, Bracha Tsefira, was a famous Yemenite singer who played a pioneering role in bringing a strongly non-European voice to popular and folk music in the years before the state of Israel was founded. Levy authenticates his excursion by referring to the Middle Eastern sounds that filled his childhood in a predominantly Yemenite neighborhood. But in the same interview (Davis 2001d) Levy claimed, "You can hear all the influences I have been exposed to in *Circle of Dreams*. They all flow through me" and listed musicians he listened to, from the Beatles to Stevie Wonder, Joni Mitchell, Led Zeppelin, John McLaughlin, and Frank Zappa—hardly a Middle Eastern list, but not too surprising for a cosmopolitan Israeli fundamentally oriented toward the West.[41]

What was the impact of these attempts? Zilber's fan base is loyal but not large enough to change the public's taste at this point. In fact, the fans may be part of the problem, because they relate to his long-established identity. This was obvious on the *Masakh Ashan* tour where Zilber began with his Arab-influenced pieces. At a concert I attended, the audience responded politely, but only rose to dance and display excitement when he shifted to his old pop hits. Afterward both Nassim and Zilber told me that the concert would fail if they did not play the old hits because the public was not yet ready for the Arab-influenced work.[42]

Levy may have a more lasting effect, not least because he has not espoused extremist right-wing positions as Zilber did shortly after his "Arab" excursion. Critic Barry Davis sought to single out Levy by writing that "In recent years increasing numbers of commercial artists have tried their hand at the ethnic variety of music, and there has been criticism of some trying to make a fast buck while the trend lasts" but "Levy denies any such intent on his part" (Davis 2001d). A few years later, Jamal Sa'id underscored Davis's assessment of the trend when he noted disparagingly that Arab music was the flavor of the moment that every musician suddenly

41. He did say that he had listened to Turkish and Persian recordings before contacting Zohar.
42. July 23, 1999.

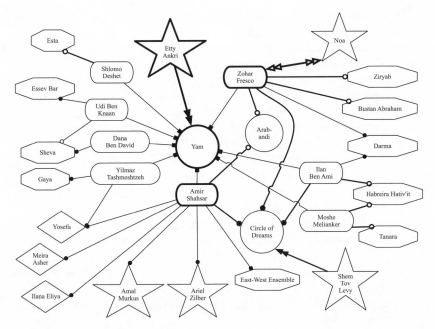

Figure 8.8   Etty Ankri's CD *Yam* as a hub in a network of musicians

wanted to add. This can be understood as yet another effort to create something uniquely Israeli and lay claim to Israeliness, following Regev and Seroussi (2004), but more important for our purposes is the mainstream popular music network's recognition.

Another intersection between Israel's ethnic and popular music, centered on an album by singer Etty Ankri, is depicted in figure 8.8, which includes some of the same connections as figure 8.7 and some very different ones. Ankri has made several pop albums with generic instrumentation (such as keyboards, guitars, and drum set) and sound that only hint at her North African heritage. On her album *Yam* (Ocean), however, she worked with a large cross-section of the ethnic music scene. Figure 8.8 is incomplete, but full enough to make the point that the Israeli ethnic music scene is represented on this album by a musician or two from nearly every band in the scene, including the standard bearers (Habreira Hativ'it, the East-West Ensemble, Bustan Abraham) and bands of the second generation (Darma, Gaya, Sheva, Essev Bar and Esta). It is particularly significant that despite differences in sound and orientation among these bands, not to mention the stylistic differences of the singers strewn around the diagram, shared understandings support this confluence.

The structure of the diagram also emphasizes the betweenness centrality of Amir Shahsar. As the preeminent Persian *ney* player in Israel, he is the first call for anyone desiring the distinctive sound of that end-blown flute. He also plays other Persian instruments such as *zurna* (double reed) and *kamanche* (bowed lute) and has worked with the East-West Ensemble and on numerous "solo" projects by other artists, especially singers. He was also part of the Arabandi project, a concert recording featuring Zohar Fresco and Taiseer Elias of Bustan Abraham with the Indian *sarod* player Krishnamurti Sridhar. Shahsar's centrality derives not only from his competence but also from lack of competition. I have found no evidence of another player of the Persian *ney* in Israel in the 1990s, a period when competent players of the Arab *nay* were also rare and Albert Elias, an old Iraqi Jewish musician, dominated that market.[43]

Connections to several other Israeli pop stars as well as less known singers are also shown in figure 8.8. I have singled out Shem Tov Levy's album *Circle of Dreams* because it connects several of the musicians in this diagram. Their connectors are thicker and end in dots rather than squares because Levy spoke of this album in terms of joint creation evolving from lengthy collaboration, i.e., greater involvement than we might expect from the contributions to Ankri's *Yam*. The connections between musicians and bands along the right side of the diagram emphasize, once again, the density of links among musicians in this scene. Had I included all of the relevant musicians and their other working relationships the diagram would have been illegible.

Mainstream Arab music: The ethnic music network has several important connections to performers of mainstream Arab music, indicated schematically in figures 8.6 as two geographically distinct networks of Palestinian performers of Arab music, one from the Galilee and the other from the Jerusalem area (see chapter 2). Taiseer, Nassim, and Jamal have connected these networks with the ethnic music scene. The right side of figure 8.7, the diagram of Bustan Abraham's connection to popular music, represents efforts that involve Arabs and Arab music centrally or exclusively. The membership of this network has shifted several times in the past decades with more musicians, ensembles, and formalized instruction now than at any time in recent memory. It remains predominantly Arab, although the old Jewish musicians from Arab countries (principally Iraq, see figure 8.4) who have retired or died are beginning to be offset by the entry of young Jews, who are not exclusively of Middle Eastern descent.

The performers of Arab music indicated in these diagrams have played a very wide array of music, but recent developments in Arab musical performance in Israel have enabled musicians like Taiseer and Nassim to move to the art end of the spectrum (see chapter 2) and it was this kind of music that they contributed to Bustan Abraham. Yet Nassim was also centrally involved in Amal Murkus's pop-oriented CD, which was an unusual confluence of forces, produced by one of the leading veterans of Israeli rock, Alon Olearchik, and performed by a mixture of Jews and Arabs in a rock-

---

43. *Nay* and *ney* are distinct enough in sound and playing technique that they might not directly compete.

tinged style.[44] For simplicity these groups of musicians are represented as two "clouds" in figure 8.7 with the exception of Ramzi Bisharat, an Israeli Arab musician who was involved in the first days of Bustan Abraham and had connections with both Nassim and Taiseer. The diagram shows his work with musicians as radically different in musical and political terms as Zilber and Murkus.[45] Murkus parted ways with the Jewish musicians and Nassim became her music director, reworking her repertoire for an Arab ensemble and adding his own instrumental compositions to her concerts.

George Sama'an, positioned at another intersection of Arab and Jewish musical networks, is an activist for peaceful coexistence. His joint choir for Israeli and Lebanese children was mentioned in chapter 7. His other efforts at bridging the divide between Jews and Arabs include a conservatory program that brings underemployed Russian Jewish immigrant musicians from the nearby town of Carmiel to teach European classical music to Arab children in his hometown of Rame. George has appeared frequently with Ehud Banai, member of a Jewish family prominent in Israeli entertainment for decades. In a duo with his longtime partner, Arab drummer Salem Darwish—who appeared on Amal Murkus's *Amal* and is subsumed in the cloud of Israeli Arab musicians in figure 8.7—Sam'an has performed in government-sponsored cultural programs. Although he has played Arab art music with Taiseer Elias and others in that circle, Sama'an appears in figure 8.6, rather than figure 8.7, linked to two Israeli "ethnic" bands, Essev Bar and Sheva. George is not a member of either, but has appeared with both (I was lucky to see him do so in two concerts in one evening). The following newspaper notice positions George's own band well:

Arab-Jewish sextet Galilean Spirit [*Ruah Glilit*], which will precede the Gipsy Kings, is a permanent fixture on the Bereshit-Boombamela-Shantipi festival circuit. In these troubled times of security problems, and heightening inter-ethnic tension, the existence of groups like Galilean Spirit is heartening. (Davis 2001a)

The three festivals mentioned feature bands that favor Middle Eastern grooves, along with drum circles and alternative medicine, in an atmosphere reminiscent of hippy "happenings." When Sama'an took me to a late night concert in the heart of the Galilee the audience looked as if it had fallen through a time warp from Berkeley in the 1960s, but the music that he played with Salem Darwish and members of Sheva—one of the leading bands in the ethnic scene whose members have spent considerable time in India—owed more to Arab musical practices than anything else.

44. Amal had also worked with Taiseer Elias in performances of Arab music for broadcast on Israel Radio, but the two were never close associates, hence their thin link in figure 8.7.

45. Bisharat's link to the East-West Ensemble (see figure 8.6) is not shown here because he played on just one track of their *Imaginary Ritual* (1998).

Israeli jazz: The network of musicians and institutions involved in various aspects of jazz intersects the ethnic music network in several ways. The improvisatory skills of several of the key players in the ethnic music network were shaped through formal instruction or performance experience in some type of jazz. Bustan Abraham members Amir Milstein and Naor Carmi exemplify this well, but are far from unique in this respect. The Rimon School of Jazz and Contemporary Music is peripherally linked to the ethnic music network by virtue of the world music performance that Yair Dalal has taught there. Jazz musicians flow steadily between Israel and the U.S., particularly New York and Boston (because of the Berklee School with which the Rimon School is affiliated). Perhaps because of their struggle to survive or their need to create a unique artistic identity, many musicians in the Israeli jazz scene appear to search for relevance and local roots by incorporating 'ud (as Avishai Cohen did on several albums) or other aspects of Middle Eastern music.

Such initiatives also come from promoters. For instance, the Jewish-Arab Festival in Jaffa initiated the Minuette Quartet's engagement with Egyptian composer 'Abdel Wahhab's music, which later appeared on *The Eternal River* (1996). A decade later, the Israel Festival staged a jazz marathon that included a section in which "Daniel Zamir represents Jewish-Israeli jazz, while Eli Benakot, together with Yair Dalal, integrate Middle Eastern and ethnic elements with jazz."[46] And sometimes the initiative comes from the "ethnic" side. When Bustan Abraham went through a brief transformation to a quartet at the end of its career, Amir Milstein, Taiseer Elias, and Zohar Fresco turned to an Israeli jazz pianist to refresh their music,[47] and Yair Dalal has begun to perform "ethno-jazz."

Western art music: Composers of European-derived art music have also searched for local relevance, either through Arab or Middle Eastern Jewish motifs, since the days of the British Mandate in Palestine. This history, too long to recount here, intersects with the ethnic music scene through Taiseer Elias and Yair Dalal, among others, who have each collaborated with composers of such music. Elias has performed with orchestras and chamber ensembles in Israel and abroad, principally in pieces composed for him by Menahem Wiesenberg, head of the department of jazz and interdisciplinary music at the Jerusalem Academy. Dalal was involved in the recording and subsequent tour of *Sheshbesh*, which featured a number of composers, including works by Albert Piamenta, a veteran member of the Israeli jazz scene who is known for his interest in Middle Eastern

46. www.israel-festival.org.il/english/more_text_eng.html, accessed April 2008. This was not a unique occurrence. For instance, in 2004–5 the department of jazz at the Jerusalem Academy offered a series of concerts that paired jazz ensembles with "world music" ensembles, with one evening featuring an Arab music trio—Taiseer Elias, Zohar Fresco, and Sami Khashiboun—opposite Esta, a band of Israelis founded in New York that has developed a particular fusion of jazz, rock, Balkan, and Middle Eastern elements (Shalev 2004).

47. Amir Milstein, 2003. One track can be heard on Bustan Abraham's *Live Concerts* (2003).

musical resources (see figure 8.4). The connections between jazz, European-derived art music, various types of Middle Eastern music, and the ethnic music scene are manifold and deserve fuller investigation as a locally specific nexus of bodies of musical knowledge and practice whose boundaries are increasingly blurred.

Jewish religious music: Adding to the complex intersections with existing musical networks is the emergence of another network alongside the ethnic music network. It consists of young orthodox Jewish men who perform a repertoire of religious music in both traditional and new arrangements. Much of the music is North African or Middle Eastern in origin, but Eastern European klezmer is also an important resource. Naor Carmi, bassist in Habreira Hativ'it and then Bustan Abraham, has played key roles by leading ensembles and by playing in others' projects. The night I saw his Village Orchestra, billed as a combination of religious and secular Jews, Carmi and band member Gershon Weiserfeier stopped in the middle of the concert to debate questions of religion and national unity on the stage.[48] Other musicians from the ethnic music scene who have joined Carmi in these efforts include Asaf Zamir (a frequent collaborator of Yair Dalal's) and Noam Chen (who substituted for Zohar Fresco in Bustan Abraham). Joining the turn toward religious material, Eyal Sela, who is secular but has played klezmer for ultraorthodox Jewish celebrations, issued *Call of the Mountain*, a contemporary arrangement, complete with electronic loops, of repertoire from the pilgrimage site on Mount Meron. Avshalom Farjun's Nada Recordings and Productions produced the album and ensuing tour. Clearly Carmi is not alone in spanning the religious and ethnic networks.

These two networks overlap in infrastructure as well as personnel. Carmi has performed with other young orthodox men in presentations of the repertoire of North African and Middle Eastern Jewish singer poets, under the auspices of *Kehilot Sharot* (singing communities), a program in which Yair has also been involved, that seeks to reinvigorate communal knowledge and singing of such music.[49] One of the lead figures in this project, Ron Ish Ran, studied Arab modal theory in Taiseer Elias's program at the Jerusalem Academy, just as Naor Carmi did. Other participants studied at the Center for Classical Oriental Music and Dance, Bar Ilan University, or the Rimon School.

Two possible intersections are notable for their absence from this survey. Just as difference is a basis for individual and group identity, the boundaries of a field of practice are defined by distinction from others. Musicians in the ethnic music network have distanced themselves from *musika mizrahit*, voicing protestations of difference from this music far more often than other distinctions. They appeared to fear association with

---

48. The band issued a CD, *Tizmoret*, in 2005. Carmi's Trio Hamaalot, an ensemble of orthodox musicians, is named after a concept central to Jewish mysticism.

49. See Dardashti 2008.

this music both for its banality (in their eyes) and the superficial similarities in name and sound that lead the ignorant to assume a link.[50] The desire to be seen and heard as distinct from *musika mizrahit* may actually be the most salient trait common to Alei Hazayit, Bustan Abraham, and Yair Dalal. Shoham Einav made particularly strong statements in this regard, perhaps because she was most "at risk" of being miscast, but members of other bands were also adamant on this point. Early in their career the members of Bustan Abraham turned down a request for collaboration by a *musika mizrahit* star who wanted to put lyrics to one of their pieces and sing it with them.[51] Yair Dalal tells of "converting" a young man who approached him for singing lessons so that he could be a successful singer of *musika mizrahit*. After hearing his rendition of a classical Arab song Yair convinced him to deepen his knowledge of that practice and then engaged him as a singer for his projects.

Political antipathy rather than distinctions of social class or musical value bar the intersection with another network, which is closely related in some ways but remains virtually sealed off from all of the above. Consisting of Palestinian musicians centered around institutions such as Yabous in Jerusalem and the Edward Said National Conservatory in Ramallah,[52] this network discourages ties with any of the other networks mentioned here because it is strongly associated with Palestinian nationalism and resistance to Israeli domination. Yet a few musicians, principally Palestinians, have crossed even this divide.

The larger picture that emerges from this survey of intersections is one of numerous connections, captured well in a festival advertisement:

> The Pe'imot shebang will close with [Zohar] Fresco leading a percussion-visual extravaganza at Beit Shmuel on April 2. Fresco will share the stage with tabla player Erez Monk, [cajon] (South American box drum) specialist Sasson Levy, ethnorock Esta band drummer Shlomo Deshet, former Riverdance troupe percussionist Abe Doron, fiddler Gal Shahar and singer-castanet player Yarona Harel. Flamenco dancer Sharon Saguy will add some visual aesthetics, with soft rock singer Etti Ankari [*sic*] filling the guest spot.[53]

This world music sampler shows that institutions, too, may be positioned in several networks. This festival and the Jerusalem Academy of Music and Dance link to several different networks including classical, jazz, and Arab. This complicates the typology of mediation or brokerage proposed by Gould and Fernandez (1989), which assumed for the sake of theoretical

50. *Musika mizrahit* literally means Eastern music, which also labels one of the dominant threads in the fabric of the ethnic music scene. The superficial similarities include use of Middle Eastern drumming and melodic resources.
51. I heard about this incident from several of the members of the band.
52. Their Web sites are ncm.birzeit.edu and www.yabous.org, respectively.
53. See www.confederationhouse.org/english/festivals/peimot.

clarity that each party involved in mediation was only a member of one network. This is not necessarily the case even in the business organizational structures that they studied, but in a music world as diverse as Israel's it is far less likely. Avshalom Farjun may be an extreme example of an actor mediating within and between networks from many different positions, but numerous others work in two, three, or more networks. Moreover, the mere fact of belonging to two networks does not necessitate brokering exchanges between them. Multiple memberships have other effects. For instance, the conventions and assumptions of one field of practice may be transferred, consciously or unconsciously, to other fields of practice.

Such convergences raise questions regarding musicians' attitudes toward the skills they have acquired and the musical practices in which they are involved. Do they maintain some separation, compartmentalizing their competences in two or more musical practices, or do they combine them? Are certain elements likely to dominate in such combinations? These are questions of enormous scope, capable of generating massive new research. They will be touched on in the next chapter with regard to the musicians central to this book.

One must also ask what benefit musicians derive from belonging to several networks. To address this it is instructive to survey some of the engagements of one leading musician in the ethnic music scene, Amir Milstein. While still a member of Bustan Abraham he formed a trio, Tucan, devoted to Brazilian music. He played with Matti Caspi, the pop icon who made Israelis aware of Brazilian music in the 1980s by arranging and recording Hebrew versions of Brazilian hits (see figure 8.7). He also was a member of a flamenco group, alternating with another flute player whose own stylistic affinities, aside from flamenco, were for Irish music. In the flamenco group Amir interacted with percussionist Sasson Levy (mentioned in the Pe'imot Festival ad cited above), who also plays *cajon* with Joseph and One and other ensembles. The connections are seemingly endless and point to a fairly large number of serious, dedicated, and talented musicians who are fluent in certain "world" styles and flexible enough to adapt to others. They form numerous links, some ongoing, some project-based. Milstein underlined the prevalence of this phenomenon in Israel when we spoke in June 2003, asserting that the economics of the Israeli musical world favor the *kolboinik* (jack-of-all-trades).[54]

Connecting to networks with Jewish musicians who perform other types of music holds the promise for Arab musicians of access to a new market that they would not reach otherwise. That it began at the time of the first Palestinian uprising, when work was very scarce for West Bank

---

54. Cf. the flexibility required of studio musicians in centers such as Istanbul or London. See Bates 2008 regarding the expectation that Istanbul studio musicians play a dizzying variety of musical styles (2008). Gordon Thompson found that London studio musicians' relative importance depended on the number of distinct niches they could fill, their adaptive abilities, and the variety of styles, instruments, and sounds they could deploy (2002).

musicians, is hardly surprising. At the same time that the number of musicians was increasing, the market for live Arab music contracted dramatically as the underground leadership of the *intifada* banned celebrations in the West Bank. This led to intense competition, which worsened due to technological changes that further lowered the bar to entry into the field of *haflah* bands. Synthesizers enabled young musicians with relatively little training to form small, cheap bands that could undercut the larger, more experienced ones (see chapter 2). One outlet for Arab musicians feeling this pressure was the nascent ethnic music scene where Arab musicians were in demand because they added authenticity to predominantly Jewish bands playing Middle Eastern tinged music. This was clearly the case when Shoham Einav approached Jamal Sa'id and when Ariel Zilber asked Nassim Dakwar to work on the *Masakh Ashan* album and concert tour. It was less obvious in a group like Bustan Abraham, where members of the band insisted that ethnicity had not been a factor in selecting the original musicians. Since financial reward was hardly a certainty when the ethnic music scene arose—and is still in doubt—economic considerations have hardly been the only motivation. Curiosity and desire for new sounds and creative freedom (a relative term, of course) must also be considered as motivations.

Legitimacy is at stake in these intersections. It is sought by many who cross stylistic borders and called into question by that very act. Leading participants in ethnic music have gained cultural capital through recognition of their bands and the scene as a whole. The caliber of Bustan Abraham not only inspired other musicians to form their own ensembles and experiment in similar directions, but also brought prestige to the scene as a whole. It helped so-called ethnic musicians to distance themselves and their music from *musika mizrahit*. As Howard Becker observed, such boundaries must be maintained in order not to squander cultural capital: "aspirants to the status of art have to dissociate themselves from related crafts or commercial enterprises . . . aspirants construct histories which tie the work their world produces to already accepted arts" (1982: 339). These assertions are borne out by publicity and other discourse surrounding ethnic music in Israel.

Another observation by Becker is pertinent to the connections I have shown between the ethnic music network and the much larger popular music network in Israel:

> Art worlds typically have intimate and extensive relations with the worlds from which they try to distinguish themselves. They share sources of supply with those other worlds, recruit personnel from them, adopt ideas that originate in them, and compete with them for audiences and financial support. (1982: 36)

The ethnic music network has yet to grow big enough and strong enough to challenge the popular music network for audience and financial support. It may never achieve that status, but it does offer an alternative to audiences looking for novel music with local ties and the potential to project authenticity and integrity.

From Isolated Clusters to Art World

Relying on the reader's familiarity with colloquial usages such as "jazz scene" or "folk scene," I have used the expression "ethnic music scene" to refer to a network of musicians and people closely affiliated with them. This is common usage among Israeli music critics writing in English. Scene implies a certain looseness of organization and affiliation that seems fitting for the early years when a network of performers was beginning to form.[55] It is less clear that music critics such as Barry Davis or institutions such as the Jerusalem Academy of Music and Dance or the Israel Festival are encompassed by that term. Howard Becker's concept of art world is useful for including such components in a comprehensive understanding of the interactions among individuals, groups, and institutions.

Becker proposed the art world as the "unit of analysis" for theorizing the production of art. Taking examples as diverse as jazz and stereo photography he demonstrated that a network of people is always involved in the production of art, although only a few of those involved are generally considered "artists" (1982: 35). His approach deserves greater attention from music scholars, as it offers a means of integrating network analysis of the people and processes that go into making music.[56]

Both scene and art world focus on relationships between actors and are therefore instances of networks, but they are neither equivalent nor diametrically opposed (Straw 1991: 252). Straw saw "the role of affinities and interconnections which, as they unfold through time, mark and regularize the spatial itineraries of people, things and ideas" (2002: 253) as important to understanding a scene. Becker defined an art world as "the network of people whose cooperative activity, organized via their joint knowledge of conventional means of doing things, produces the kind of art works that art world is noted for" (1982: x). Scene implies a relatively loose form of affiliation, diffuse in organization, whereas an art world rests on an extensive support system for the production and distribution of art. This distinction may also have a temporal dimension, an art world tending to be established over longer periods of time than scenes. Straw saw a danger of reification in the identification of art worlds (2002: 252) but Becker forestalled this: "The [art] world exists in the *cooperative activity* of

---

55. See Straw 1991 for a widely cited theorization of scene. He contrasted scene with musical community, which he took to denote locally rooted musical traditions. Straw later rethought the term but continued to advocate for it because it avoids the rigidity associated with other concepts in sociological morphology (2002: 250), but he also recognized the different ways in which the term can be deployed.

56. As I was completing this book, Peter Martin published an article arguing for the utility of this model for musical studies (2006).

those people [the entire network], not as a structure or organization, and we use words like those only as shorthand for the notion of networks of people cooperating" (1982: 35, emphasis added). Mapping the stages and people involved in the production of the work of art[57] he underlined the mutability of an art world when he observed that the boundary between artist and nonartist may change and the "bundle of tasks" associated with a given role is also open to change.

I contend that the relatively loose ethnic music scene in Israel—recognized by music critics, record companies, and many of the musicians involved—had begun to organize as an art world by the end of its first decade of existence through increasing elaboration and tightening of the network of connections. It became better established, with greater public awareness and the beginnings of an infrastructure that included recording labels, performance venues, and circuits (both local and international), as well as programs of instruction that prepared musicians with some of the knowledge central to this music. In the following pages, I elaborate on this assertion and draw on Becker's work to support it. Beginning with aspects of network formation such as catalysts, clusters, and affective links, the discussion proceeds through paired concepts: cooperation and competition, conventions and competence, enculturation and training, and production and distribution.

Becker points to three types of *catalyst* in the creation of art worlds: the invention and diffusion of new technology, the development of a new concept or way of thinking, and new audiences (1982: 311–13). Technological innovation did not play a prominent role in the coalescence of the ethnic music scene, which has made limited use of existing technologies, such as amplification for acoustic instruments. New ways of thinking have been far more important catalysts, as musicians have sought to create innovative combinations of "East" and "West." New audiences have played a role, too, albeit scattered around the world in a distribution just thick enough to enable and require tours abroad in order to sustain a career.

Becker also emphasizes the development of art worlds from localized *clusters* (1982: 320–21), a characterization that matches well the coalescence of the Israeli scene from relatively isolated clusters of musicians who were experimenting in the early 1990s with mixing elements of Middle Eastern and other kinds of music in ways that were similar enough to come to be subsumed under the label ethnic music. This is an important prerequisite for the development of a market and a supporting infrastructure. Prior to the establishment of this recognition, individual bands struggled with the lack of clear stylistic categorization because performance venues hesitated to book acts that they did not know how to characterize for ticket buyers. This problem receded as more musicians began to participate, festivals and other venues began to open their stages, and the audience emerged. The formation or discovery of affinities among performers was also key to this development.

57. Becker 1982: 5–6 in particular.

Affective links among people form the basis for musical scenes and new links form through those scenes. People tend to congregate around a particular set of venues, sounds, and attitudes and behaviors relating to those sounds.[58] Festival directors, producers of concert series, and record companies seek out or create such links to package more product. On a very small scale, Bustan Abraham's formative private jam sessions served as a laboratory for creating affective links and winnowing out the musicians who were not interested enough to devote their time and energy to creating this new music. In essence there were two main stages to the selection of the band: first Farjun drew on his networks of personal friends and of musicians whom he had produced, while Taiseer brought in musicians from his network of Arab musicians. Then the band stabilized through a selection process that was partially self-motivated and partially group-dictated. Some left of their own accord and one or two were asked to leave because others thought their playing did not fit the emerging musical consensus—the seed of a new cultural space (cf. Straw 1991: 372).

Selection of personnel and musical style did not occur in a vacuum, of course. Affective links among members of the ethnic music scene include shared models inside Israel and foreign influences. Habreira Hativ'it had been setting an example for over a decade and musicians also were influenced by foreign sources. By the time Yair recorded his first album, Bustan Abraham had also become a model, with two albums and numerous performances to their credit. Yair was inspired by them and shared an admiration for certain foreign bands that had experimented with fusion, but went in a different direction.[59] Opportunities for affective links increased as more recordings became available in Israel, agents like Avshalom Farjun imported more like-minded foreign musicians, and Israeli musicians began to tour abroad, performing at festivals where they heard other musicians and sometimes played with them. It was a fortunate coincidence that interest in various aspects of Middle Eastern and Asian cultures was growing in Israel at the same time that world music fusions were burgeoning at festivals outside the country, creating the potential for a market for such music.

Becker stresses *cooperation*, maintaining that "an art world is born when it brings together people who never cooperated before to produce art based on and using conventions previously unknown or not exploited in that way. Similarly, an art world dies when no one cooperates any longer in its characteristic ways to produce art based on and exploiting its characteristic conventions" (1982: 310). New cooperative networks that bridge deep social divisions are central to the emerging ethnic music art world in Israel. Collaboration is a touchstone, integral to the creation of trust, the emergent musical language, and, often enough, to marketing.

58. This is true of the musicians and their audiences and perhaps for intermediaries, though profit motives enable some to participate in the mediation without much personal aesthetic connection.
59. See chapter 9.

I would balance this emphasis on cooperation with recognition of the presence and importance of *competition*. Musicians compete for recognition, for insufficient performance opportunities, and sometimes for band members. Yet the emergence of the scene depended on reaching a critical mass to create performance opportunities and broader recognition for all involved. The high degree of connectivity within the network demonstrated above is evidence of a key form of cooperation. Many of the musicians have performed together as guests in one another's bands or by forming new bands. Competition for foreign engagements became politicized after the onset of the second *intifada* in late 2000 according to Yair. He told me of numerous instances in which Palestinian musicians—some of whom had previously collaborated musically with Israelis—and their supporters excluded Israeli performers (including some Palestinian Israelis) or cancelled performances that had already been scheduled.

Cooperation within the ethnic music art world has depended, to some extent, on the emergence of *conventions*. This, too, aligns with one of Becker's main arguments—that the division of labor and all other decisions concerned with the production of art are highly conventionalized in an art world—though he emphasizes that conventions may be changed (1982: 29). I part ways with Becker over his emphasis on the final product, the work of art. This is a limiting view, beholden to romantic (and modernist) ideals. The network of people and institutions involved in making ethnic music and the performance *processes* that constitute this emergent musical practice are far more central to the definition of this field of cultural production than any particular work created in it.

Adaptation of conventions from other art worlds and formation of new conventions have posed substantial challenges for performers in the ethnic music scene, since they did not share an a priori set of conventions. Because Arab and Turkish music are central components of most of the various stylistic mixtures, performers fluent in the conventions of these practices have had a certain advantage and could, if they chose, keep on doing largely what they had been trained to do as long as they were open to learning new melodies and arrangements. The Arab musicians in Alei Hazayit or the Azazme Bedouin performing with Yair did just that. Others, such as Taiseer and Nassim, treated those conventions as a springboard for innovative explorations, using the conventions of Arab music more selectively.

To put it another way, this nascent art world is a *discourse community*[60] in the act of constituting itself. The emergent conventions are the foundation for musical discourse—with its own set of overlapping competences— that has outpaced verbal discourse. The latter still lacks a widely shared terminology, regular press coverage, and aestheticians, criteria cited by Becker as required for art works: "Work that aspires to be accepted as art usually must display a developed aesthetic apparatus and media through which critical discussions can take place" (1982: 339). A few journalists

60. Becker does not use this term.

have written now and then about musicians in this art world—this book is informed by some of their columns—but they have yet to develop a specialized critical language or to write in depth about this music. However, musical *competence* based on fluency in the new musical discourse, has become increasingly widespread.

Musical *enculturation* depends on the growing availability of this music and is aided by increased *training* possibilities ranging from Yair's free-form weekly workshops at his Jaffa studio to the instructional programs discussed in chapters 2 and 3. The Mediterranean Musical Dialogue workshop (see chapter 3) is another key element in this web of educational possibilities, bringing together a significant portion of the professionals and aspiring professionals in the field with select foreign guests. After eight annual workshops, Seroussi, the convener, noted three results (2003):

1. the opening of the Israeli musical world to various traditions in the Mediterranean basin [of] which, until the 90's, they only had second hand knowledge. As a result of this process, some Israeli young people decided to follow their careers with those masters they met at the MMD, especially from Greece and Turkey, two countries with music that has a strong impact on Israeli audiences.
2. the creation of new musical groups including Israeli artists from various styles who met for the first time at the MMD.
3. the knowledge [of] Israeli music acquired by musicians from the most diverse origins. Many of these MMD guests were extremely surprised about the musical richness and diversity of their Israeli colleagues.

It is hardly a coincidence that Turkey and Greece are the two closest Middle Eastern and Mediterranean countries that are non-Arab and therefore impose few restrictions on Israelis wishing to visit or stay for lengthy periods. Note that participants are learning components that they can adopt and adapt for the ethnic music scene rather than the actual music that they play in that scene. The second observation is particularly relevant to this chapter, as it points to the formation of new links and clusters within the network.

A growing competence base enables this network development because it means more musicians can move easily from one band or project to another and band leaders can expect to find replacements for musicians who cannot go on tour or who leave the band. Naor Carmi was able to replace bassist Emmanuel Mann in Bustan Abraham because in addition to his experience playing a different ethnic mix in Habreira Hativ'it, he had listened to Bustan's recordings and had received training in Arab music from Bustan members Taiseer Elias and Nassim Dakwar, among others, at the Jerusalem Academy of Music and Dance. When Zohar Fresco was too busy to tour with Bustan Abraham in 2000 because of his commitment to pop star Noa and her far more lucrative tours of Europe, Noam Chen was able to supply the sort of varied and imaginative hand percussion parts that

Fresco had pioneered because they had become well known.[61] Jamal Sa'id called on a pupil of his from the Center for Classical Oriental Music and Dance to substitute for him in Alei Hazayit and Yair took his pupil Haim Ankri to sing with him on *Asmar*. Teachers and recordings are key agents in transforming a casual scene into a long-term art world.

Ethnomusicologists such as Seroussi have been involved in the formation of this art world in several ways. The influence of Dalia Cohen has been tremendous. She campaigned relentlessly to establish the Department of Oriental Music at the Jerusalem Academy, overcoming years of opposition and foot-dragging by an entrenched opposition.[62] The Workshop for Non-Western Music, which I directed at the Jerusalem Music Center, was her brainchild, intended to give musicology students the experience of bimusicality and acquaint composers with source materials. No less important was her influence as a professor at the Hebrew University and the Jerusalem Academy (at that time the Rubin Academy) where her students have included central figures in the ethnic music scene, such as Taiseer Elias, Amir Milstein, and Nitzan Peri (founder of Joseph and One). She imparted theoretical tools for comparison of scales and rhythms while opening her students' ears to a wide variety of music from around the world. She integrated Arab *maqamat* in her theory classes, wrote *East and West in Music* (1986), and taught a course with that title. She did not advocate mixing elements of different musical practices or have in mind bands such as Bustan Abraham or Joseph and One at that time, but these may be the most influential result of her efforts.

Dalia Cohen's students included ethnomusicologists who assumed mediating educational roles. Edwin Seroussi, Amatzia Bar Yosef,[63] and I have taught ethnomusicology in Israel and have been involved in other ways in the emerging ethnic music world, through activities such as Seroussi's Mediterranean Musical Dialogue, Bar Yosef's classes on *maqam* theory at various institutions, or educational concerts that presented the Israeli public with various kinds of music that they were not accustomed to hear. When I initiated these concerts in 1986 at the Jerusalem Music Center, there was nothing comparable. By the late 1990s, the situation had changed dramatically, with festivals, concert series, and workshops on various Middle Eastern, Mediterranean, and Central Asian musical practices increasingly common.[64] All of these efforts contributed to spread competence in listen-

61. Like Carmi, Chen would have known Fresco's recordings with Bustan Abraham.
62. She was frustrated that when this finally bore fruit, the Center for Classical Oriental Music and Dance opened, splitting the market and public attention.
63. Bar Yosef applied Cohen's theoretical framework in a dissertation comparing melodic and rhythmic organization in European classical music, Arab classical music, and Central Javanese gamelan (1997).
64. Note that some types of music presented at these early concerts, e.g., Javanese gamelan or Ugandan music, were not incorporated into the ethnic music scene.

ing and performance, make connections between performers, and lay the groundwork for the establishment of an art world—a professional network that is robust enough and productive enough to sustain and disseminate particular types of musical performance.

Coordination of the numerous tasks involved in the *production* of art and its *distribution* to consumers is a key organizational challenge for an emerging art world. It can remain a matter of dispute and negotiation in established art worlds as well—witness the struggles between unions and producers on Broadway or in Hollywood over the number, types, and qualifications of personnel required to produce a show or film.

Musicians creating a new kind of music and searching for new means of expression, as well as audiences and performance opportunities, must identify or create a support structure for production and distribution. Avshalom Farjun did this by establishing a record label and production company, in addition to creating and managing Bustan Abraham. For many of his projects, Yair Dalal has also taken on a very large "bundle of tasks," to use Becker's term. Others in the scene have attempted a do-it-yourself approach to recording. But none of these can successfully remain one-man operations. Farjun realized this when he signed distribution agreements with European and American companies (see chapter 5).

Many roles may be involved in the production network for recordings, for instance. The elaborate, arty booklets inserted in Yair's CDs are an excellent example of the involvement of image-makers—photographers, translators, and graphic designers. One of the signs of the establishment of this scene as an art world is centralization: A handful of individuals are involved in the production of a significant portion of the recordings. For instance, a few graphic designers have put their stamp on a large percentage of the ethnic music albums.[65]

The emergence of recording companies such as Nada or Magda and festivals such as the Confederation House's annual Oud Festival and Pe'imot Festival (featuring percussion) bears out another of Becker's observations: "The development of new art worlds frequently focuses on the creation of new organizations and methods for distributing work" (1982: 129). None of these differed radically in organization from established channels of distribution, except that they were devoted to this new field of musical activity. Perhaps the musicians might have enjoyed greater recognition and income if the methods of distribution had been revolutionized. Still, the success of these companies and festivals in persisting over a decade is not insignificant. Neither is the decision of most of the musicians in this art world to stay with the small labels. That may seem a natural choice now that these labels have a considerable stock of recordings, but it was neither the obvious choice nor the easy path in the 1990s.

65. E.g., Morel Derfler provided the cover art for most Bustan Abraham albums and Aliza Hayon designed most of the pamphlets for CDs produced by Magda through 2007.

An art world's geographical extent is rarely congruent with political borders.[66] Both Israeli and Palestinian societies are deeply fractured, as I showed in the first chapters of this book, and each has extensive transnational connections to diaspora communities, as well as complex mutual ties within the confines of Israel and the occupied territories. The emergent art world of ethnic music spans some, but certainly not all of those divisions. The bridging of networks of Arab and Jewish musicians that had been almost completely independent and unlinked before the 1990s is one of the more important changes wrought in the ethnic music scene in Israel, contributing to the emergence of new social relations across boundaries.[67] On its way to becoming an art world this network has also branched out to involve other locations and people of other nationalities. The network of production and distribution has become more international over the past decade as musicians like Dalal have recorded in Israel and abroad with foreign musicians and technicians for Israeli and non-Israeli labels.

Conclusion: Network Dynamics

If musicians are unlikely to apply network theory to their own careers, they still must use some networklike understandings of structure and dynamics in order to navigate relationships with other musicians, intermediaries, and the public, to insert themselves into new sets of connections, link to hubs, identify gatekeepers, and so on. A large part of Yair Dalal's success must be attributed to his canny self-insertion into existing networks and creation of new links. Avshalom Farjun also has exploited many types of connections and positions in several networks to various ends. Many of the musicians discussed here have used their networklike understandings to help others, too, by providing other musicians points of entry into the network. Taiseer Elias brought Nassim Dakwar to Bustan Abraham. Yair Dalal told me that he led Zohar Fresco to the circle of old Iraqi Jewish musicians where they learned much of their craft, while Yinon Muallem said that he followed Zohar Fresco into the ethnic music scene.[68] Each of these moves opened doors to other connections and possibilities.

As these developments show, networks are rarely static. They expand or contract as new members join and links are formed or people leave or break off connections. Networks change not only due to these internal dynamics, but also in relation to their sociocultural environments. The impact of political events such as the Oslo Accords or the Palestinian uprisings on the ethnic music network has been considerable. The ethnic music

66. See, e.g., Jocelyne Guilbault's analysis of the circuit of production for calypso that is not confined to one nation state or society (2001).
67. I develop this point in chapter 12. This intersection differs greatly in nature from occasional joint performances prior to the 1990s by Jewish immigrants from Arab countries with Arab musicians in Israel.
68. Feb. 28, 2002 and Mar. 16, 2006, respectively.

scene arose in the midst of the pressures of the first *intifada*, which began in 1987, and flourished during the mid-nineties when the Oslo Accords were seen by many as a basis for peaceful resolution to the Israeli-Palestinian conflict. The second *intifada*, beginning in 2000, directly affected parts of the network by making collaborations between Israelis and Palestinians from the West Bank nearly impossible due to military closures. It also weakened external links to international networks by causing a drop in European invitations to perform and in the number of foreign artists willing to risk a trip to Israel at a time of numerous suicide bombings.[69] At roughly the same time, a slump in the Israeli music business tied to a downward economic spiral had a tremendous impact by reducing cultural subsidies, performance opportunities, and profits. That the ethnic music network survived is evidence of its robustness.

Questions of robustness and vulnerability that are of great concern in the analysis of large networks such as the international banking system or the Internet are also valid for the much smaller ethnic music network. Robustness is usually attributable to high connectivity as measured by the number and strength of connections (Barabasi 2002: 111): Many nodes can be removed randomly without significantly hampering a network's function because the probability of many hubs being in this random sample is low. But if the hubs disappear from the network—if, for instance, Avshalom, Taiseer, and Yair all were to decide to disconnect from the rest of the network, the likelihood of failure would increase.

The ethnic music network's considerable robustness appears to be attributable to its high connectivity. Most of its nodes—both people and institutions—have many links, which directly and dramatically lowers the degree of separation within the network. High connectivity manifests in the prevalence of guest appearances, ad hoc formations, and shifts in band memberships, as well as the relatively small number of performance venues, recording companies, and educational institutions that serve nearly everyone in this network. This has implications for the rate at which people influence one another and for the ease with which musicians can find like-minded partners for special projects or new ensembles. That such a high degree of connection does not necessarily lead to stylistic homogeneity can be ascribed to the distinctive abilities and tastes of these musicians.

This discourse community has grown and matured through the development of shared or overlapping competences and comfort with ways of making music pioneered by musicians such as Bustan Abraham and Yair Dalal. The growth of the pool of competent replacements has contributed to the network's robustness by making it easier to find partners for new bands or projects. When Yair Dalal decided to record his album *Asmar* with a more varied group of musicians than his band Al Ol, he had little trouble assembling a rather large slate of participants (some of whom are

69. For instance, Joseph and One were fortunate to be signed by WOMAD for a tour in the summer of 2003. This sort of outside intervention could really have helped the band, but due to the Iraq war the tour was greatly curtailed.

shown in figure 8.4) that was enabled by the growing labor pool in this emergent art world. At this point the chief threats to its sustainability would appear to be lack of sufficient employment and decrease in audience interest.[70] The former is only partially dependent on the latter since invitations to perform outside Israel have already proven to be strongly influenced by perceptions of the political situation in the Middle East.

In the smallest network, a musical ensemble, the departure of a single member may lead to the disintegration of the band. But this is not true for every band member or every band. It is difficult to conceive of Habreira Hativ'it without Shlomo Bar, but every other member of that ensemble has been replaced with only minor changes to function and style. Likewise, Alei Hazayit saw tremendous turnover among the instrumentalists but without Shoham it would surely have been a very different ensemble because so much of the social and musical "work" of the group was built around her as both singer and, in many ways, sponsor. Bustan Abraham also survived various absences and substitutions, most of them temporary. Nassim Dakwar's departure in 2002 may have precipitated the end (which will be discussed below) but this must be seen in the context of the near collapse of the Israeli music business during a larger economic downturn and the dearth of touring opportunities abroad, i.e., the failure of connections to a larger network of sponsors, venues, and other elements of the music industry. These affected musicians deeply but clearly not enough to stop people from pursuing their musical careers, as none of the musicians I studied gave up their profession during this period.

Network analysis of a musical scene should aim to discover the reasons that musicians and other members of a scene or art world move from one set of associations to another. In theory the possible motivations are endless. Common ones include boredom or frustration with current associations, the lure of greater creative freedom or monetary return, abandonment by one's fellows, or the departure of a key member of the subnetwork. The following comparison emphasizes the importance of interactive structures and processes for the character of individual pieces, the overall shape of a performance, and even the career of a band.

In 1998, I had the good fortune to interview Naor about his role in Habreira Hativ'it just before he was invited to fill Emmanuel Mann's place in Bustan Abraham. He said that he was ending his membership in Habreira Hativ'it because "I want to go to ensembles . . . where I'm a more important part" (June 29, 1998). This underscores a fundamental difference in organization between Bustan Abraham and Habreira Hativ'it, one that has not been explored sufficiently for other musical practices, although it exists in many. Where Habreira Hativ'it was the prototypical autocratic organization, Bustan Abraham was resolutely egalitarian. Shlomo Bar has run Habreira Hativ'it as a vehicle for his singing, drumming, and compositions, with a hierarchy that was apparent in the physical positioning and musi-

70. See DeWitt in forthcoming article in *Music and Sustainability: Special Issue of the World of Music*.

cal prominence of Bar relative to the rest of the band (see chapter 3). One of the outcomes of this interactive network has been a relatively high turnover of musicians. Of his original band only Indian musician Samson Kahemkar stayed with Bar until old age and illness forced him into retirement. Despite the high turnover, Bar seems never to have lacked for new musicians and has maintained enough popularity to keep his band performing in Israel and abroad for three decades, longer than Bustan Abraham lasted. Yet bands based on cooperative networks like that of Bustan Abraham appear to predominate in the field of ethnic music. Why should this be the case?

I suggest that in addition to a greater sense of control and fulfillment, egalitarian bands offer musicians greater initial excitement. But over time the musicians may drift apart in interests and levels of competence, the initial excitement may wear off, and interaction within the network may fall into well-worn patterns. Without a major shift in power relations no member of the band has the authority to lead the band out of its troubles or replace players. A strong leader might have caused several members to leave Bustan but would presumably have found replacements. As it was, three of the best musicians took a different approach, dissolving the band, then reconstituting it as a quartet with one new musician and none of their former colleagues.

Naor's desire to be a "more important part" of a band is but one of the centrifugal forces that may be part of the dynamics of a network. Other factors that have the potential to tear the fabric of a cluster within the network include multiple allegiances, conflicting commitments, and differing aesthetic and economic goals. As nodes become hubs or are drawn to other hubs, the network is strained and its internal connections may be overpowered by more powerful external attractions, ranging from shared musical tastes to complementarity, from friendship to economic interest.

The intersection with mainstream popular music has benefited the ethnic music scene by elevating its visibility and it has benefited individual musicians by offering new employment opportunities. This has also had a negative impact when better pay and more frequent performances of the popular music work interfere with band rehearsals, concerts, and tours. Zohar Fresco's tours with Noa took precedence over Bustan Abraham engagements even though he remained loyal to the band in all other ways and always returned to play in it after those tours. Similar conflicts had existed from the beginning for Arab musicians who had to choose between lucrative wedding gigs and the more tenuous benefits of involvement in the ethnic music scene. Solving this was largely a matter of self-selection, although the synthesizer player in Alei Hazayit tried to have it both ways, forcing Jamal and Shoham to fire him when he skipped one of their concerts to play a wedding.

The intersection of two networks can also increase an individual's prominence. To illustrate this I return to Taiseer Elias, whose prestige, I argued earlier, exceeded Avshalom Farjun's despite the latter's centrality to the network. Like stars in other networks, Taiseer is the object of numerous unidirectional links, i.e., far more people wish to link to him than he can reciprocate. He has had more potential connections than he could possibly pursue, perhaps exceeding Yair Dalal in this regard. During his twelve years in Bustan Abraham, he became increasingly selective regarding performance opportunities. Dalal has not ascended to similar positions of institutional authority despite his many activities. While this has left him freer to pursue a variety of connections, one could also suggest that it has required that he do so in order to promote himself.

Taiseer's rising prestige illustrates one of the dynamic effects of a network. Before ascending to positions of authority he was already connected to a wide variety of musicians due to his playing ability and his work on television and radio. These positions have magnified his prestige and multiplied the number of connections. Being perceived as a hub increases one's desirability—many want to connect to a hub because others have done so[71]—and reinforces the position of prominence, enabling greater selectivity by providing more opportunities to choose the best connections from among a larger than normal assortment.

But increasing prestige can also be a liability. Unlike airports and other major institutions, which maintain their status as hubs by upgrades and repairs, a musician can call on few external resources and has to have the energy, time, and desire to maintain numerous links. This is a balancing act. Elias extracted himself from the network of Arab wedding musicians as he established himself in the ethnic music network. By the end of 1993, he could maintain his career without performing contemporary Arab popular music at *haflat*. Thus, it was interesting to find him in December of that year at the Shefa'amr rehearsal described in chapter 2. Discussing this involvement, Elias explained that he felt compelled to agree to the invitation despite his distaste for the music because the leader of the band was his student[72] and they were both members of the local Christian Arab community that was sponsoring the celebration. In other words, when a social network overlapped several musical networks, the social ties trumped musical distaste, drawing Elias into temporary association with a musical network in which he had ceased to be active. Conversely, associations that began for professional musical reasons have led to personal connections among people from social circles so different that the likelihood of interacting without the musical link was close to nil. This was obviously the case in the relationships that developed between Shoham and the Palestinian members of Alei Hazayit, but that is hardly a unique example.

Two particular network issues affected Alei Hazayit: a long-running struggle over leadership within the band and failure to find a manager. Without delving too deeply into personal dimensions of the leadership struggle, it is possible to point to certain structural problems. Jamal's prominence in decisions over arrangements was unusual for a drummer within

71. Barabasi aptly terms this phenomenon "the rich get richer" (2002).
72. In reciprocal fashion he invited this student to perform popular music on one of his television programs.

the ethnic music scene and other affiliated networks, such as that of Arab music. On various occasions he told me that he was considering starting to sing lead or take up the *'ud*, which I took as indications not only of a desire for direct melodic expression, but also as options intended to create greater congruence between his position in the musical interactive network and his leadership position in rehearsal. This might smooth his interactions with Omar, with whom he often clashed over musical decisions. Shoham clearly occupied a position of leadership in practical matters—essentially managing the band, arranging concerts, and providing funding—but this did not carry over smoothly into musical domains where she often debated with Jamal and Omar. These interactions generally had positive musical outcomes but the confusion in hierarchies was also evident and produced considerable strain.

Alei Hazayit was not well connected to the professional, commercial musical networks in Israel. Only Shoham and Jamal used professional connections on behalf of the band. The other members of the group seemed to have no hand or interest in obtaining gigs and little say in programming decisions, although some of them contributed to the musical decisions crucial to the shaping of a song. Because she took up her musical career relatively late in life, Shoham did not have a large number of professional musical connections, depending rather on her well-developed social network that included people in important positions, a tried and true Israeli method for getting along in the world. These connections led to many of the band's performance engagements inside Israel, but they were haphazard and, in the absence of a manager or agent, appeared to be insufficient for launching a successful career.

Jamal was used to operating as a musician in a world of pickup bands, wedding engagements, and gigs at restaurants and hotels. He had connections in the media through his work as an actor, and knew a vast and highly varied array of Jews and Arabs in all professions. As long as he played conventional Arab music he did not need a manager because word of mouth sufficed in his core sociocultural world;[73] nor did he need an intermediary to form Alei Hazayit because he had direct connections to numerous musicians. But once he formed the band his network was not useful (or perhaps he did not use it well) for political and sociocultural reasons. For instance, the Hakawati Theater to which he was well connected was associated with strongly nationalist Palestinian policies and performances.[74] He was also hindered by the dearth of frameworks in local Palestinian society for concerts other than fundraisers and celebrations of particular occasions.

73. Recall that Jamal disparaged local musicians who put out cassettes of their own music since he saw this self-promotion as evidence of low prestige (see chapter 2). The lack of a gatekeeper to check the quality of Arab music recordings reduced the desirability of the product because it meant that anyone could produce a cassette.

74. Although some members of Bustan Abraham did perform there together with Palestinian expatriate Simon Shaheen, it was not a likely venue for either Bustan Abraham or Alei Hazayit.

Shoham and Jamal were aware that a good manager could advocate for them, but told me that the candidates they interviewed immediately wanted to alter the band's sound. This was not the service or relationship that Shoham and Jamal sought. They wanted someone to mediate the practical aspects of their relationship with the industry and the public, not take the role of a producer.[75] Whether or not the rehearsals those prospective managers heard were flawed, it is safe to say that in the mid-1990s there was a dearth of managers with an understanding of what Alei Hazayit was trying to accomplish.

By the turn of the twenty-first century there was no lack of intermediaries who knew the music. Magda Records and Avshalom Farjun's Nada Records had each signed an impressive roster of musicians. Yvonne Kahan, who had managed Yair Dalal's career through Najema Productions, has gone on to run the Olamale[76] agency where she has assembled an eclectic list of clients who straddle the borders between the ethnic music scene and other types of music. A few examples from that roster will give an idea of that variety: Esta, an Israeli band formed in New York that has established a strong identity through its mix of rock and jazz with Middle Eastern elements; rocker turned ethnic musician Shem-Tov Levy (see above); the Alaev family, originally from Tajikistan; Yiddish singer Bente Kahan; and Sameer Makhoul, an Israeli Arab who will be discussed in chapter 12. The rosters of the Nada and Magda labels are at least as varied.

Bustan Abraham's structural problems differed from those affecting Alei Hazayit. There was never any doubt that Avshalom was the manager, but other members of the band were quick to emphasize (without any solicitation on my part) that this did not confer upon him any right to musical leadership. That he was also a musician—and sometimes limited in that role by musical illiteracy—created conflicts with the others concerning his promotional desires. But after the band's demise, individual members of the band blamed that process on a different structural problem, the conflict between the musical desires of two classes of band members: those with Eastern or Western musical orientations. Without questioning the basic assumption that the band was dedicated to bridging the East/West divide, each one identified those who "pulled to the West" and others who "pulled to the East," exacerbating the divide and preventing them from continuing to address the challenge that had given birth to the band and served it well throughout its career. When Bustan disbanded it left a legacy of highly respected recordings. It had set the standard for virtuosic solo and ensemble playing. It had also explored numerous ways of combining musical elements from diverse resources. These explorations in composition, arrangement, and improvisation are the subject of the next two chapters.

75. In terms of Gould and Fernandez's mediation typology (1989), Shoham and Jamal were seeking a representative, not a coordinator. See also Hennion 1989.

76. This is an elision of Hebrew words meaning "a world full of"; see www .olamale.com/htmls/about.htm.

PART III

New Forms of Musical Expression

9

Musical Mixtures—Fusion of Styles
and Styles of Fusion

Combining elements from two or more distinct types of music is characteristic of Israel's ethnic music scene, no matter how different the approaches and the results. The chapter title indicates both the centrality of this activity (fusion of styles) and the diverse ways in which musicians have undertaken it (styles of fusion), while foregrounding a problematic label. Fusion denotes the combination of disparate elements into a whole, but for some musicians it connotes shallowness due to the popularity of the term in world music circles and the perceived superficiality of much of the music advertised as fusion. Common criticisms of rival musicians within the ethnic music scene in Israel, as well as foreign musicians in the international world music scene, include insufficient knowledge of the musical elements that are being combined (often expressed as a lack of roots), unsuccessful merging of these elements, and exploitation of novel combinations purely for commercial gain. We can infer then, that the musicians who voice these criticisms prize deep knowledge of musical sources, demonstrated through well-conceived, meaningful syntheses that privilege aesthetics over commerce and artistic integrity or vision over popularity.

I use the term *fusion*, nonetheless, both to highlight these issues and for lack of a better brief alternative. The term *hybrid* is an unattractive substitute in the eyes of musicians whom I have queried and its biological connotations are problematic for the analyst, particularly due to links to racialized discourses that assume certain "essences" to be mixed through interbreeding.[1] Given the extensive discussion of cultural hybridity in recent

---

1. Ingrid Monson raises a similar terminological issue with the challenge "postmodern concepts of multiplicity and hybridity need a distinction analogous to that between groove as a noun . . . and groove as a verb," which she equates to distinguishing "the constellation of interlocking parts defining a style" from "how the pastiche gets used and acquires meaning" (1999: 60). The distinction is useful but *pastiche* is inappropriate as an umbrella term for the music considered here. See the last section of this chapter.

decades, we cannot ignore this term, but it clearly does not resonate with the goals of the musicians whom I studied. Miguel Herstein explicitly rejected both fusion and hybrid as labels for Bustan Abraham's output because he felt that the band had sought and achieved an organic integrity that these terms fail to convey. Yet no alternative term has gained wide acceptance. Both Taiseer Elias and Yair Dalal use *shiluv*, a Hebrew word meaning combination, blend, or integration, and Yair has also used "multi-ethnic" in keeping with his advocacy of multiculturalism in Israel.[2] Bustan's original press release used the word *synthesis*, a relatively neutral term. Alei Hazayit's press releases and program blurbs tended to name the sources on which the band drew, but not the process by which they were combined.[3]

That things cultural involve process, not just product, is especially important to keep in mind when discussing musical fusion or synthesis. Listening to mixing of resources we need to ask what the musicians are doing and how they do it.[4] Recordings give only a partial impression: Some of the most interesting and significant negotiations of diverse musical resources take place in rehearsal and performance. The members of Alei Hazayit clearly sought to bridge cultural and sociopolitical divisions through the processes of performance, not just to create musical artifacts, and spent many hours of rehearsal honing these processes. For Jamal Sa'id and Shoham Einav, the songs were merely the framework, the canvas on which they painted. Yair Dalal and Bustan Abraham also emphasized process. Creating the permanent record of their collaborations was a long process of intense interaction, motivated mainly by the need for material to perform at their numerous concerts. Some compositions were created outside of this context,[5] but the bulk of the work was composed both to create a specific product, an album, and to provide frameworks for performance, to serve as the basis for further creation and re-creation in performance.[6] These musicians had their greatest impact on stage, in the exploration of new ways of bringing together musical elements from different sources and enabling musicians of diverse backgrounds to make music together.

The four sections of this chapter address stylistic mixture from different perspectives. In the first two, I discuss methods of combination (styles

2. See Coleman 1998. Palestinian musician Nabil Azzam, who holds degrees from Israeli conservatories and universities, named his ensemble Multi Ethnic Star Orchestra (www.mesto.org).

3. See program book for Children of the Millennium, a September 2000 concert in Jerusalem. The Asia Festival program book (for their concert in Hong Kong) speaks of a "combination of music from Arab lands and Israel."

4. Hannerz calls attention to this difference regarding hybridity (1987: 550). Steven Pond, writing about Herbie Hancock's *Headhunters* makes this point for fusion (2000) and Kevin Fellezs, also writing about jazz-rock fusion, takes it further: fusion-ing is "hybridity in action" (2004: 39).

5. Miguel Herstein, Avshalom Farjun, and Yair Dalal all mentioned older compositions that they had "taken out of the drawer" to have performed. Others may also have composed some pieces not specifically for a given CD or concert.

6. See chapter 10 for discussion of the relationship between composition and improvisation.

of fusion) and the sources from which elements are drawn (fusion of styles). The third section surveys prior attempts at mixing Middle Eastern musical elements with other musical ideas and practices before turning to analyses of the music of Alei Hazayit, Yair Dalal, and Bustan Abraham that show how they have dealt with the challenges of mixing distinct means of musical expression. Finally, to balance the critiques of fusion in world music that have focused on power relationships, ownership, and meaning in a globalized economy, I argue that a synthesis of musical styles that exceeds the bounds and idiosyncrasies of a single work is likely to involve emergent forms of musical competence that deserve further attention.

Styles of Fusion

The possible ways to combine elements from different musical practices are so numerous, perhaps infinite, that it seems unlikely one could devise an overarching set of principles to foresee or account for every type of juxtaposition, fusion, or synthesis. Yet if we are to go beyond the simplistic statements typical of press releases and liner notes—the recipes that enumerate the ingredients of a particular musical stew—we need to delineate the space of possibilities in which musicians work when they combine stylistically varied resources. The three dimensions of comparison proposed here—contrast, dominance, and blend—describe important aspects of musical fusion and give a sense of the conceptual space within which the work of mixing is done without bogging down in details.

Contrast: How different are the musical elements or processes that are being combined? Some styles[7] share less common ground than others. For instance, while both Arab *maqam*-based melody and blues guitar styles may make use of pitches that are "outside" the chromatic scale, they do so in markedly different ways. When they are juxtaposed—as they are in Bustan's "Jazz Kar-Kurd" (● audio track 6)—they are likely to signify the musical complexes from which they have been taken rather than sounding a new synthesis. By contrast, combinations that draw on Persian, Turkish and Arab musical practices share enough commonalities that they are likely to be less contrastive than a combination that includes elements of frailing banjo, funk bass, and "Arab" violin and drumming.[8]

Dominance: Are the different styles accorded roughly equal attention or are some subordinate to others? Arab musical practices dominated much of the music performed by Alei Hazayit even when the compositions themselves were Israeli songs based on harmonic progressions, melodies, and rhythms that were decidedly atypical of Arab music. In Yair Dalal's work, Arab music is always present but sometimes shares equal "space"

---

7. I use "style" here in an encompassing sense, as shorthand for the more unwieldy expression "musical practice."

8. The labels Persian, Turkish, and Arab are problematic in themselves for the differences and the similarities that they hide.

with Indian, Persian, or Jewish musical elements (labels that will be problematized shortly). In "Dikklat Nour," for instance, he adds his violin to a track that otherwise derives mainly from Hindustani musical practices. The balance in Bustan's music varied greatly from one piece to the next, with Middle Eastern (Turkish and Arab) elements dominant in some pieces and subordinate or absent entirely in others. The group set out to achieve balance overall, if not in each piece—recall that the mission statement on their first CD critiqued other attempts at East-West fusion for favoring one side or the other—but ultimately fell apart over precisely this issue of dominance.

Blend: Are the different musical resources blended or kept separate? Answers to this question generate a spectrum from contrastive to integrative, from stark juxtapositions of musical styles that foreground differences to seamless integration, where difference is elided in a synthesis. Within the repertoire under discussion, certain pieces, such as Avshalom Farjun's "Black Seagull," evoke a single mood while others, such as Taiseer Elias's "Jazz Kar-Kurd" or "Metamorphosis," evoke two or more. Among the latter, one can distinguish simultaneous combination, stark juxtaposition, and more gradual metamorphosis. Similar contrasts abound in Dalal's work. That performers recognize varying degrees of blend or distinctiveness is evident in their explicit attempts to control the degree of blend as a compositional device. Examples include Taiseer's "Metamorphosis" and "traveling" pieces, such as Yair's "Bagdad-Barcelona" and "The Perfume Road."[9]

These questions concerning contrast, dominance, and blend may be posed at various levels, from moments within a piece, to entire pieces, recordings, or concerts.[10] Alei Hazayit's concert programming highlighted the band's contrasting resources by alternating Hebrew and Arabic songs. Both the clash and the double accessibility were important. The band also combined elements within individual songs. Most of Bustan's albums were highly eclectic, including Arab or Turkish pieces alongside original compositions that represented varying blends or juxtapositions of resources. With the exception of his debut album, Yair Dalal has tended to produce recordings that are stylistically more uniform. Among the subjects of this study he was the only one to create an album-length work.

Diverse stylistic resources can be combined simultaneously or consecutively, posing different challenges and experiences for performers and

9. Examples by other musicians in the ethnic scene include "Bharat—Middle Eastern Raga" and "Dublin, Bukhara" on Eyal Sela's *Darma,* "Middle Eastern Polka" by the Israeli Celtic group Black Velvet, "Musicelty" by Sheva, and "Turkish Western" by Essev Bar.
10. I wish to acknowledge and then sidestep the fact of different perspectives and responses. The performers and their audiences are privy to different sorts of information and bound to have differences in knowledge of particular types of music. This is especially true when musicians tour away from their home base. Even at home, there is a strong likelihood that some in their audience will make different associations and identifications on hearing particular sounds.

listeners. This brings us back to the distinction between texture and form, simultaneous and consecutive dimensions of interactive structure, discussed in chapter 6. In simultaneous combinations disparate elements are being performed and experienced together in the moment, while in consecutive combinations we move from one sound world to another, changing orientation and, perhaps, aesthetic sensibility. Numerous pieces by Bustan Abraham and Yair Dalal involve a sequence of solos in disparate styles on different sounding instruments. These have the potential to remain compartmentalized, invoking separate semiotic fields. Pieces such as "Jazz Kar-Kurd" and "Dub Dulab" feature extensive improvisations by Taiseer Elias and Amir Milstein on 'ud and flute that differ greatly, not only in instrumental sound but also in musical style. Similarly, Dalal's *The Perfume Road* includes 'ud, clarinet, and *sitar* improvisations that are idiomatically distinctive. Yet there are convergences, too, such as similar rhythmic manipulations of brief motifs by Taiseer and Amir (see chapter 10). Similarly, Yair Dalal and Eyal Sela have achieved stylistic convergence in some of their joint recordings.

These solos generally are played out over a third type of interactive structure, one that has both simultaneous and consecutive aspects and therefore mediates that binary distinction. A significant element in many of the pieces performed by Bustan Abraham, Yair Dalal, and Alei Hazayit, this is a repeated complex made up of a drum pattern and melodic pattern, often played on a bass or in the lower registers of various melodic instruments, to be repeated and varied in small ways. Thus, at least two simultaneous elements in a vertical relationship also have a horizontal—i.e., formal —aspect because they impel the music onward even as they repeat numerous times, creating the possibility of both energy and stasis.[11] This supporting rhythmic-melodic matrix, or groove, often involves significant fusion in its own right. The integration of bass and percussion as a backing to solos in Bustan performances, for instance, creates a field of musical experience and potential that is neither neutral nor directly derivative of one particular musical practice, having an emergent character of its own that is synthesized from sources as diverse as Arab, Indian, African American, and European musical practices.

Texture and form take on new importance in stylistic fusions. The distinction becomes highly significant for both performers and listeners because the disparate elements call on different competences for the performers and presumably evoke different associations for listeners. For instance, a distinctively Arab modal improvisation (a *taqasim*) on a melodic instrument can be performed prior to or simultaneously with an Israeli song that is not "Arab" at all in sound or conception. This creates contrasts in many dimensions. Improvising the *taqasim* prior to the song the musician will have a significantly different experience than doing so simultaneously with the singer (as in "Erev Shel Shoshanim," 🔊 audio track 1). In the latter instance, the musician's knowledge of Arab modal practice is

---

11. Several examples of such patterns will be discussed in the next chapter.

likely to be affected—to what degree it is difficult to say—by the contrasting musical context of the Israeli song. Instances of this juxtaposition in Alei Hazayit's arrangements will be discussed in the third section of this chapter. Other simultaneous juxtapositions present different challenges, but the principle remains the same: producing something in a new context makes demands that differ from the culturally specific musical competences these musicians acquired.

Combinations of disparate musical styles often relate directly to the combination of instruments in an ensemble, each player continuing to play the style "native" to his or her instrument. Native is obviously a problematic concept, particularly for instruments such as the violin and guitar, which have become central to the performance of many different musical practices. The concept is clear enough, however, by contrast to the transfer of "foreign" styles to instruments on which they are not usually heard. Some transfers are relatively seamless or "natural." Others sound awkward or force their novelty upon us. The uneasy performance of arpeggiated chords on 'ud and *nay* in Alei Hazayit's "Erev Shel Shoshanim" (🎵 audio track 1) stands out as a relatively unsuccessful example, not because of the idea itself, but because of the less-than-fluid execution and the failure to follow the song's harmonic progression.[12] For the most part, the musicians in Alei Hazayit did not venture far from the idiomatic playing that they had learned performing mainstream Arab music. A more successful blend, to my ears at least, is the transfer of the Arab *sama'i thaqil* rhythmic mode to Indian tabla in Dalal's "Adon Haslichot" (🎵 audio track 4).

Fusion of Styles

Stylistic distinctions are central to the ethnic music scene. This section takes stock of the array of musical resources used by Alei Hazayit, Bustan Abraham, and Yair Dalal and problematizes the labels used to describe them. Of these groups, Bustan used the most varied stylistic palette, Alei Hazayit the least. The basic choices can be characterized in terms of playing styles, repertoires, formal structures, textures, and melodic, rhythmic, and harmonic "vocabularies" and "grammars." It would be tedious to catalog all of the elements or the source styles. Far more pertinent is a discussion of the categories invoked in the discourse of the musicians, their record labels, concert promoters, and the press.[13] Most of the texts that

12. See the discussion of this piece below. Chords have become more common in contemporary 'ud playing, but playing them in harmonic progressions did not appear to be part of the competence of most 'ud players I encountered in Israel and the West Bank. Taiseer Elias is exceptional for the facility with which he plays chords and blues licks on the 'ud (e.g., in "Jazz Kar-Kurd") but to my ear they still stand out as transfers referencing another instrument and idiom.

13. Conversations with musicians and the various texts produced in and around this scene provide the data for this analysis. A study of reception would

they generate—including liner notes, press releases, and reviews—list the types of music from which the musicians draw their material. They map many distinctions onto geocultural entities, i.e., styles associated with particular nations, peoples, or areas of the world. Other distinctions are class and consumption based. All of these associations are problematic in one way or another yet, as Jocelyne Guilbault has argued, they do cultural work whether or not they are historically accurate or informed.[14]

In the discourse surrounding this field of musical production, the array of musical materials is almost always characterized either in terms of a binary opposition—usually East and West—or as a list of ingredient styles. The binary opposition reproduces a trope fundamental to Orientalist perspectives that must still resonate widely given its ubiquity. The list appears to serve two main functions, demonstrating the musicians' versatility and appealing to the broadest possible taste community. Despite their popularity, both of these formulations are highly problematic.[15]

Discursive Binaries

Binary oppositions presume identity or similarity within the cluster on either side of the divide and a high degree of contrast across it. In other words, we are predisposed to expect two types of relationship: likeness vs. radical, perhaps irreconcilable, difference. Such expectations ignore heterogeneity within a category, such as the infinite diversity within either "West" or "East," just as they ignore similarities between the supposed opposites. The very definition of the contrasting terms is problematic. Stating sources in terms of an East/West dichotomy overlooks not only the enormous diversity subsumed under each of these two labels and the numerous connections between them, but also the very ambiguity of the territories covered by the terms.

A sampling of reviews and publicity shows that the East/West dichotomy is cited frequently and in relation to a wide array of music. Bustan "plays original, authentic music that combines East and West," according to Lior Peri (1992). Yoav Kutner, the dean of Israeli rock critics, sketched Bustan's connections to Habreira Hativ'it and the East-West Ensemble, noting that these groups create a "non-commercial synthesis which sounds 'eastern' to the rock public and 'western' to the eastern audience" (1992). A third early review quoted Avshalom Farjun as saying that Habreira Hativ'it

---

be a useful complement as musicians' stylistic distinctions may not be fully congruent with listeners' cognitive mappings.

14. "What is at issue in examining music labels is not to try to find the 'right' definitions for each of them and subsequently their 'correct' uses . . . to talk about music labels . . . means to talk about the promotion of a philosophy, the vindication of a principle, or the claim to a public space; and that, through the expression of these various positionings" (1997b: 1–2).

15. Ingrid Monson discusses some of the limitations of binaries, suggesting the multiple layered riffs of Afrodiasporic music as a better metaphor (1999: 49, 57).

emphasizes the East and the East-West Ensemble emphasizes the West, but Bustan tries to work with both and "go outside all the categories" (Kaspi 1992). These were the terms with which the band was primed to present itself. An undated sheet of talking points on Nada Productions letterhead stated, "Bustan Abraham . . . has succeeded in pioneering a unique form of instrumental music which combines elements of both Eastern and Western forms without sacrificing the musical integrity of either."[16] Avshalom and his band mates succeeded in conveying this message. When Bustan appeared in Germany, for instance, the program book promised that their music was not just a mix, but rather a unique synthesis of Eastern and Western music culture (Schwitz 1995). But some saw beyond this formulation. As the band marked its first decade a reviewer wrote, "To say that Bustan Abraham is a synthesis of East and West is to belittle the results," and proceeded to list the band's various influences and albums (Harsonski 2001). The reviewer concluded that the band went far beyond such a mix as a result of daring experimental musical work reflecting the musicians' openness and education.

The East/West trope is by no means restricted to Bustan's reviews. For example, the description of the music of another ethnic band, Shotei Hanevua, as "a hybrid of traditional Israeli music, fusing both Eastern and Western sounds over a foundation of modern dance beats" (Chasnoff 2001) is typical of reviews in the Israeli press. But perhaps the best evidence of the centrality of the East/West dichotomy for cognitive mapping of cultural and social knowledge is the way musicians riff on it. When bassist Yisrael Borochov left Habreira Hativ'it, he named his new band the East-West Ensemble. Avshalom Farjun chose a play on words when he gave the subtitle *East Meets East* to the *Arabandi* concert and recording for which he had brought together Indian, Persian, and local Israeli (Jewish and Arab) musicians. I encountered a different twist on the expression at a concert of North African Jewish hymns (*piyyutim*) in Jerusalem called *mizrah uma'arav* (East and West). The organizers had reinterpreted this dichotomy by claiming both sides of it for those Israeli Jews who normally fall solely under the Eastern label. They did so by equating the West, the *ma'arav*, with *Maghreb*, the cognate Arab word that designates North Africa, the western end of the Arab world. For centuries North Africa and Spain were the "West" for the Jewish world, too. But to make such a move now, in the early twenty-first century, is a strong political statement, one that resonates with a fundamental frame of thought and challenges it at the same time.

The East/West binary is a deep-rooted dichotomy fundamental to general Israeli discourse. Many who would agree on little else share the rarely questioned assumption that the world—and Israel in particular—is divided on this principle.[17] For decades debate has raged over the position of Israeli

16. Courtesy of Amir Milstein.
17. East and West is the theme and title of Dahlia Cohen's *East and West in Music* (1986) and the epilogue to Peter Gradenwitz's survey of Jewish music (1996).

society and culture relative to this imagined polarity. Many in the Israeli establishment have seen Israel as part of the West and have nurtured ties to Europe and the United States.[18] The perceived superiority of Western institutions of education, governance, and industry have served both as models and as excuses either to "elevate" or to exclude that which is not Western: not only Palestinian Arabs, but also Jews who came to Israel from Muslim countries in North Africa and Asia. One of the starker examples, dating to the early years of the state of Israel, is to be found in the introduction to *Israel Between East and West:* "the question is whether the *successful acculturation* of the Oriental population groups can be accomplished by the Western element in Israel before it becomes numerically too weak to impress its own imprint on the Oriental parts of the population" (Patai 1953: 6). It is against this stance that North African and Middle Eastern Jews have battled through social, political, and cultural activism since the 1970s. For many Israeli Jews, the East/West distinction continues to mark a fundamental sociocultural divide within the nation despite several generations of intermarriage and cohabitation in Israel.

For some Israeli Arabs, the distinction is a source of tension between "forces of progress" oriented toward the West and pride in tradition that exalts the heritage of the "Orient." As with Jews, this tension exists not only among members of the Arab community, but also within a single individual, and may lead to a strong urge to combine the best of both worlds. Palestinian musicians are not inherently or wholly "Eastern." Some have extensive training in European music and stronger allegiance to European musical aesthetics of the classical and romantic eras than do many of their Jewish colleagues. Likewise, Israeli Jews, even those of European ancestry, should not automatically be considered "Western."

Complicating matters, many Jews who have a fundamentally Western orientation consider Israel to belong to the "Orient." One position within the early Zionist debate over cultural formation argued that the new Jewish homeland—and therefore the culture to be produced there—was in and of the East rather than an extension of Europe, although the primary agents of this proposed change were of European origin (Hirshberg 1997). In the field of music, Edwin Seroussi notes

> the latent state of the "East and West" issue, which since the 20's has been the object of debate between Jewish music educators, composers and journalists in Palestine. Most of them aspired, to one extent or the other, to turn the new Israeli culture into a *sui generis* synthesis of such opposed approaches. It is evident that this debate reflects the essentialist and stereotyped concepts [of] the primary qualities of "Western" and "Eastern" music that prevailed at that time.[19]

18. Other English-speaking countries, especially Canada and South Africa, are included but less frequently mentioned.
19. Seroussi 2003, translated from Spanish by Francisco Susena.

I would add that these concepts continue to prevail, despite the far greater availability of music from almost anywhere in the world and growing knowledge about that musical diversity. The aspiration to create a new, unique cultural synthesis also persists, evident in the promise made in the liner notes of Bustan's first recording (see chapter 5).

Such ambiguity regarding Israel's location in relation to the East/West divide would seem to weaken the usefulness of a dichotomy that nevertheless refuses to leave the stage. The situation is reminiscent of Russian Orientalism. Richard Taruskin ends his discussion of this phenomenon by recounting the irony of Diaghelev's success in Paris: Russian Orientalism came to represent Russian music as a whole and Russia came to represent the East for Parisians (1992). Born & Hesmondhalgh adduce this as an example of the "relativity of Orientalist positioning" (2000: 10). One could argue that when Avshalom promoted Bustan to audiences in Hong Kong, Europe, and North America as a successful bridging of the gap between East and West, he was, intentionally or not, blocking such an interpretation. How could Israel represent the East if it is itself a blend of East and West? Rather than positioning themselves against an Orientalist construction of the East as a fictionalized Other, the members of Bustan were bringing East and West into dialogue on equal footing as people who were simultaneously of the East and West.

Contestation of Israel's situation in the East or the West does not prevent members of the ethnic music network from gushing about the aptness of Israel as a site for East/West musical fusion, and musicians from strategically deploying different identities depending on context. Israeli Jews of "Eastern" ancestry who consider themselves to represent the East may also situate themselves in the West. Yair Dalal was candid about this when discussing *Music Channel,* his collaboration with Norwegian and Palestinian musicians (see chapter 8).[20] Yair said that the producer had particularly sought out Israeli musicians "who have both sides. They knew that Israelis ought to be the bridge."[21] Yair saw himself as the one who connected East and West in this gathering both because of his linguistic skills (speaking Hebrew, Arabic, and English) and because of his musical experience. He grew up immersed in Anglo-American rock—a background he shared with the Norwegians—as well as Middle Eastern music, which he had in common with the Palestinians. He expressed this musically by choosing the Beatles' song "We Can Work It Out." He selected the song because the title was appropriate for a collaborative project involving Palestinians and Israelis. Thinking about how to bring it closer to Arab musical practice, he asked, "What do you do with the harmony? So, I thought 'ud—I don't know how to play chords on the 'ud, so let's do it without chords. . . . I took it

20. Shoham Einav also situated herself in various ways in her interactions with Arab members of Alei Hazayit. Fluent in several European languages and at ease in "Western" settings she could also be "Eastern" in her speech and sympathies, with the lineage to support it: her father had emigrated from Iraq to Israel and her mother was a Sephardic native of Jerusalem.

21. June 21, 1998.

eastward (*lakahkti et ze mizraha*)—no harmony, ethnic melodic lines with *'ud* [and] *darbukkah*."[22] The performance is heterophonic, with typically "Arab" ornaments. When I asked whether there were difficulties of communication in the musicians' interaction during the project, Yair talked about his mutual understanding with Saed, the Palestinian singer: "I could feel Saed from the first day I met him, two Orientals [*mizrahiyim*] who respect each other."

The opposition between East and West also surfaced on numerous occasions in my conversations with the members of Alei Hazayit and Bustan Abraham, as a crucial conceptual division for the kinds of music that they play, value, or reject. It was a useful explanatory device for former members of Bustan when they talked to me individually about the band's breakup. The pull to the "East" did not come from the quarter one might expect, the Arab members of the group. Nassim was quite explicit about this: "I'm not interested and Taiseer's not interested, we won't take the band and 'Easternize' it.[23] It's not possible and if I think or Taiseer thinks in an Eastern direction then we put together a different ensemble. Why [do it with] Bustan?" Such statements notwithstanding—and each of them did indeed form a band devoted to Middle Eastern music—the East/West division eventually contributed to the demise of the group. In a postmortem, Amir Milstein told me that he felt that the group was too heavily weighted toward the East. He pointed specifically toward the lack of sufficient harmonic competence on the part of most of the band.[24] To the extent that we take East and West to refer to entire complexes of ideas about music there is more than a grain of truth in such statements.

Musicians and listeners use East or West as shorthand for a range of phenomena that they perceive as a package. The two sides are usually presented in terms of the absence of some definitive component in one type of music or the other, such as functional harmony or counterpoint in Eastern music and modal nuance and melodic ornamentation in Western music. While much attention is devoted to scales and rhythms in East/West comparisons, musical familiarity or strangeness rests at least as much on intonation, timbre, and texture. For most of the musicians I interviewed, improvisation is a key trait of Eastern music.[25] Nuances of intonation and melodic ornamentation are also associated with this term. This holds true both for performers and for listeners, although the latter are less likely to have the technical language to identify familiarity or strangeness. Nassim Dakwar, for instance, applied the term *Eastern* to a wide range of music without a trace of irony:

any Eastern (*mizrahi*) music, it doesn't matter where it comes from—Iraq, Persia, Turkey—I hear it and I . . . taste it, I know what's going on

22. June 21, 1998.
23. He used the Hebrew neologism *lemazreah*.
24. June 25, 2003.
25. E.g., Naor Carmi said, "it's all improvisation in most of the East" (June 29, 1998).

there. . . . Because it's all connected. All those musics are connected to each other. There are lots of similarities, lots of similar *maqamat*. Sometimes they have a name of a *maqam* that means something different but I'm not talking about names, I'm talking about the music, about the content, what you hear. There are a lot of things there that are similar.[26]

For Nassim, the connections outweigh the differences when it comes to thinking within the largest categories of musical style. Later in the same interview, which was peppered with numerous references to East and West, he praised Amir Milstein's composition "Hamsin" and the solo flute introduction in particular. Nassim noted Eastern influences in this solo, saying that the contact with Eastern musicians "gave Amir the opportunity to hear many musics that came from the East, it doesn't matter which East."

Nassim is not alone in using Eastern (Hebrew *mizrahi*, Arabic *sharqi*) with considerable geocultural looseness to signify music associated with any of the following: (1) everything that is not Western; (2) Asia in general; (3) a more restricted area stretching from South Asia to the Middle East and North Africa; (4) a somewhat smaller scope perhaps excluding anything east of Iran; or (5) at the most restricted, just the Middle East "proper"— Arab countries and Turkey. Musicians, critics, and the public speak loosely of an Eastern sensibility in musical practices of the Arab world, extending it without comment to any of the above spheres.

By contrast, Western connotes a complex of elements including instruments, ensembles and the ways in which they function together, staff notation, concert halls, the elevated status of composers and their works, as well as the equal tempered chromatic scale, polyphony, and functional harmony. West as applied to popular music is perhaps even more problematic than it is as a label for the high culture of Europe due to the predominant role of African and Afrodiasporic elements and influences. For the musicians under discussion here the term can range from bluegrass banjo through flamenco guitar to jazz and ideas that have their roots in the works of Bach, Mozart, and Beethoven.

Whatever the definition of West and East, the basic problem of glossing over both musical difference and similarity remains in any version of this dichotomy. Note that sub-Saharan Africa, Oceania, and Latin America are completely absent from all of these distinctions. The East/West dichotomy steers the mind away from huge swathes of the world, while building up artificial walls and unities in the rest of the world.

The dichotomy between Jewish and Arab music also figures in some descriptions of the music of these groups and several similar bands. Since Jews and Arabs are involved in making music together, many assume that they are engaged in a fusion of Arab and Jewish music. Sometimes—as in a few of Yair Dalal's pieces—this is the case but often it is not. All of the Arab musicians involved in this scene play Arab music, but most of the

26. July 16, 1999.

Jews do not perform Jewish music. While more restricted in scope than East/West, the Arab/Jew binary is also rife with ambiguity, both with regard to people and to music. For the most part it does not coincide with a West/East binary since much of Jewish music is understood to be Eastern.

Defining Jewish music is a challenge that evokes very diverse responses and has engendered several books.[27] Jewish communities around the world have created and transmitted many traditions of song in Hebrew, Yiddish, Ladino, Arabic, and other languages. Some of it is religious, some secular. Musically, these songs are often related closely to practices of the surrounding community or to other non-Jewish musics, either as a result of integrationist tendencies and or due to the involvement of Jews as musicians serving the broader public as well as their own community.[28] Because Jews in various Arab countries were musically active in the performance of both specifically Jewish and more general repertoires, there can be considerable overlap between Jewish and Arab music. Eastern European klezmer music, one of the few instrumental styles commonly identified as Jewish, is more European in its instrumentation, ensemble style, and use of harmony than many other types of Jewish music, but with its varied roots it is also related, via Balkan and Turkish musical practices, to the Middle East. This is apparent in melodic modes and additive meters. Yair Dalal and his frequent partner Eyal Sela, an expert klezmer clarinetist who also specializes in Turkish folk music, have exploited this connection as they combine elements of klezmer with Middle Eastern elements.

Arab music as a category is widely used and understood. It is not as debatable a term as Jewish music but is nonetheless problematic as a broad label that covers not only numerous regional styles but music that has been performed by many non-Arabs: by Jews, Turks, Armenians, Greeks, and members of other ethnic groups throughout the Middle East. Scott Marcus notes that only in the twentieth century did Arabs begin to use the label *musiqa 'arabiyya* (Arab music) instead of *musiqa sharqiyya* (Oriental or Eastern music), a label that is still in use (1989a: 27). He links this change to the rise of Arab nationalism.

In short, the Arab and Jewish musics that musicians like Alei Hazayit and Yair Dalal set out to blend are constructed categories. They are elusive and not nearly as unrelated as some might assume. But as mutually distinctive conceptual categories they carry weight, particularly because of the associated political baggage of the ongoing Israeli/Palestinian conflict. In the case of Alei Hazayit's songs, the contrasts are made clear by language, Hebrew vs. Arabic, but this is precisely the boundary that the band then blurs by combining languages within a song. With the exception of "Shabehi Yerushalayim," their repertoire has been completely secular, the traditional Jewish songs being Hebrew translations of Ladino ballads. By contrast, Yair has taken two Iraqi Jewish hymns, "Ya Ribon Alam" and

27. In an early example, Idelsohn wrote "Jewish music is the song of Judaism through the lips of the Jew" (1967 [1927]: 24).
28. See, for example, Bohlman 2000 and Shiloah 1992.

"Adon Haslichot," as the basis for lengthy pieces. Bustan Abraham, with its focus on instrumental music and on bridging the East/West divide, steered clear of religious music and the Jewish/Arab musical division.

Lists of National, Regional, and Ethnic Ingredients

Listing musical styles like ingredients for a recipe is the other organizing principle in the discursive formation of the ethnic music scene. The descriptive labels most commonly used in liner notes, promotional materials, and interviews are national or ethnic attributions, often modified by words such as improvised, classical, ethnic, and folk. The following excerpt from a concert review is representative: "The Dem Ensemble, playing music written in the Middle East, Iran, Turkey and the Caucasus, performs an evening of eastern improvisations" (Ajzenstadt 1998). Note that this appears in a column bearing the title "Critics' Choice: Classical Music," implying music on a par with European art music, although one wonders how well the tools and standards the critic brought to the task actually fit the job. Among the terminological problems in this excerpt is the apparent contradiction between written and improvised music. The phenomenon of improvisation, with associated questions of aesthetic standards and the relation to composed material, is a matter of novelty and, perhaps, insecurity for critics and other listeners coming from a background in European art music.

The title of this review is geographically ambiguous. "Middle Eastern" is difficult enough to pin down, but "eastern" is truly amorphous. The list "Middle East, Iran, Turkey and the Caucasus" seems to set both Turkey and Iran outside the Middle East. This is not so uncommon for Iran, but Turkey is generally considered to be part of the Middle East and there are certainly convincing grounds to consider it so from a musical point of view. But the assumption underlying Ajzenstadt's geographic list (assuming that there was a conscious decision) appears to be that the Middle East consists of Arab lands while Turkey and Iran lie across the border of this area and beyond them is the Caucasus. This is even more restrictive than the narrowest definition of East cited earlier.

Another *Jerusalem Post* journalist, who usually covers pop, rock, and jazz, offers a more detailed list in an accounting of the origins of Bustan Abraham's members and their musical resources. In a review titled "Around the World in 180 Days," he characterizes Bustan Abraham as

> something of a musical League of Nations. Qanoun player Avshalom Farjun's family has been living in these parts for over 200 years, oud player Taiseer Elias and violinist Nassim Dakwar add Arabic influences, flutist Amir Milstein was born in Brazil, Miguel Herstein adds a touch of Spanish guitar, while percussionist Zohar Fresco's parents hail from Turkey. "Yes, there are Turkish influences in my music, but I also take things from Eastern Europe, and the Middle and Far East," Fresco explains. "All the band members come from different cultural backgrounds, and that also has a direct effect on how I play my own

instruments. When I play with Taiseer and Nassim, I bring in Arabic sounds, then I play more jazzy and Brazilian strains with Amir or more flamenco-influenced material with Miguel." (Davis 2000a)

Davis proceeds to quote Zohar regarding the Israeli musical melting pot as an inspiration and his attempts to "synthesize all the influences that exist here."

Reviews such as these by Ajzenstadt and Davis, never intended as definitive scholarly statements, are easy targets for critique. They are worth our attention because they are representative of widespread conceptualizations and usages at the center of a discourse in which musicians, intermediaries, and general listeners all partake. Such statements are ubiquitous and musical maps characterized by fuzzy, overlapping territorial labels are the rule rather than the exception. This is just as true of most musicians. The Web site of Trio Hamaalot, one of the bands formed by Naor Carmi after the demise of Bustan Abraham, characterizes its music as "roots music from Jewish diasporas, and Greek, Turkey, Kurd, Indian, Armenian, Caribbean, African and Latina [sic] music."[29]

Arab music and other Middle Eastern musics enjoy a place of privilege within the musical mixtures of the ethnic music scene. This is evident in a widespread preference for modal orientation to the composition and elaboration of melody and a taste for textures that feature heterophonic variation of a melody played over rhythmic modes performed on hand drums. Specific Arab *maqamat* are used in some compositions and musicians may play *taqasim*-like solos that would not be out of place in standard Arab practice. Turkish, Persian, Indian, and Azerbaijani music are all listed among the ingredients in the dishes cooked by Bustan Abraham or by Yair Dalal and his collaborators. The *baglama-saz* that Yehuda Siliki, an immigrant from Turkey, brought to Bustan is emblematic of Turkish folk and folk-derived musics. Avshalom Farjun's Turkish connections and interests were fundamental to the band, too, and both Taiseer Elias and Nassim Dakwar have taken considerable interest in Turkish music.

Indian music is particularly prominent in Yair's work with his band Al Ol because most of the other members of that band have studied Hindustani music. They draw on but are not bound by the conventions of Hindustani music, evoking various *rags* and *tals* (melodic and metrical modes) without playing them in full.[30] Several people versed in Hindustani music have commented that they do not hear Hindustani music in Al Ol's performances, but that was not Dalal's intent. Such music has also figured in the work of Bustan Abraham, and not just because the group emerged out of a jam session with *sarod* player Krishnamurti Sridhar and later hosted

29. This Web site, accessed in June 2004, is archived at http://web.archive .org/web/20040110110009/www.triohamaalot.com/aboutus_eng.html.

30. My thanks to Matthew Rahaim, an ethnomusicologist specializing in *khyal*, for his analyses of several recordings by Dalal and Al Ol that feature Hindustani elements.

Hariprasad Chaurasia and Zakir Hussain. The members of the band absorbed elements of Indian practice into some of their other work, evident in rhythmic play (see chapter 10) and some of the slides and figuration in Taiseer Elias's *'ud* improvisations. His slides and ornamentation in "Pictures Through the Painted Window," for instance, are reminiscent of *sarod*, an association strengthened by the use of a *tambura* (a long-necked, fretless lute) to supply a quintessential Indian drone in this piece.[31]

The presence of Persian music as an influence in Israel's ethnic music scene owes much to the ubiquity of Amir Shahsar, who immigrated from Iran and has played in numerous bands and special projects (see chapter 8), but he is not alone. Menahem Sasson, a Persian *santur* player has been a member of Shlomo Bar's band for years and played in Yemei Habeynatayim with Emmanuel Mann (see figure 8.6). Dalal teamed up with a young Israeli singer of Persian descent, Maureen Nehedar, for his album *Asmar.*

In addition to this strong "Eastern" presence, members of Bustan Abraham drew on or referenced musical styles from various European regions and practices, including art music, flamenco guitar, and the additive meters common in various Balkan practices. Miguel Herstein's range of guitar styles, including virtuosic flamenco runs, has been woven into the textures of ethnic mixtures in Israel since the early days of Habreira Hativ'it when he evoked Spain in dialogue with Indian musician Samson Khamkar's *sitar* and violin. Conversely, Spanish guitar playing has also been influential on Middle Eastern *'ud* playing, and Taiseer Elias pointed to the Spanish guitar virtuoso Paco de Lucia and his band as an admirable model for fusion.[32] Amir Milstein's "Seven Eleven" features Moldovan guest artists playing accordion and violin, who give a decidedly Eastern European "flavor" to this piece that sets it apart from the rest of Bustan's repertoire.[33]

American vernacular musics have also been influential. This is hardly surprising given the strong presence of American recordings on Israeli airwaves since the 1960s. Miguel Herstein introduced elements of American guitar- and banjo-based folk music traditions into Bustan's mix, as he had in Habreira Hativ'it fifteen years earlier. Taiseer Elias picked up on this when composing "Jazz Kar-Kurd" and "Sireen," which reference blues and hoedown, respectively. Musicians and promoters frequently cite jazz (that overworked signifier) as an element in Bustan Abraham's music, as in many other cases of fusion. In the work of Bustan, its presence is clearest in the playing of Amir Milstein and Emmanuel Mann. Emmanuel had also played bass in a funk band in Paris before immigrating to Israel in the 1980s. Yair Dalal mentioned rock and blues as early influences, as types of music that occupied his attention as a teenager, but this is not readily apparent in most of his recorded output.

31. E.g., at 7:46.
32. Taiseer had the chance to appear in concert with de Lucia and his band when Avshalom Farjun brought them to the Israel Festival, one of many examples of Avshalom's mediation.
33. Eyal Sela has also brought Balkan musical elements to his frequent collaborations with Dalal.

Although the result of these experiments in mixing musical elements is often called Israeli, the label rarely figures in lists of ingredients. The *shirei eretz yisrael* (Songs of the Land of Israel) that were the mainstay of Alei Hazayit's repertoire are quintessentially Israeli. While European elements, especially Central and Eastern European folk song, are undeniably central to this body of songs, to set it in opposition to Arab music as a genetically distinct type of music is to ignore the important influence of Arab music on some of the composers of Israeli song.[34] Yet that opposition is generally taken for granted and served as a main premise for Alei Hazayit's originality.[35] When the band performed one of these songs in a markedly Arab manner they were innovating, catching the audience's attention precisely because prevalent essentialized notions of these musical practices are conceptually so distant.

Why Essentialize?

Given the problematic nature of these labels, why do musicians and others continue to use them? What motivates such gross essentialism? To say that a certain band or musician bridges East and West is to pose a challenge, a seemingly irreconcilable difference, and thus to elevate the achievement of the musicians who meet that challenge while providing the grounds for criticizing those who do not. Besides, these highly problematic labels continue to be meaningful to musicians and their audiences, a shorthand for affective similarities and differences used repeatedly by those involved in this musical scene. There is little point in taking musicians to task for sloppy geography or imprecise notions of the relationships between, say, Azerbaijani and Hindustani music. Richard Taruskin's comment on contemporary Russian composers is apropos: "if any cliché, however disprovable, is accepted by artists and embodied in their art, then it has indeed become a stylistic determinant. And the art it determines is in no way necessarily condemned to banality" (2000).

It is crucial to bear in mind that people from both sides of the East/West and Jew/Arab divisions essentialize when they use these terms. There is mutual awareness of difference from the Other, but the heterogeneity of that Other is often ignored. The status difference is not fixed: West may sometimes be held up as superior; at other times East is given preference, and sometimes there is no overriding value judgment. Nor is "Eastern" necessarily Other—that depends on speaker, audience, and sociocultural context. The positions, in any case, are substantially different from those attacked by Edward Said in his classic work on Orientalism (1979).

The achievements of these musicians warrant listening beyond facile labels to discover what they have actually cooked up with the ingredients in their recipes. Alei Hazayit developed a particular way of performing their

34. See, for instance, *Nights in Canaan*, a documentary recording that demonstrates some interesting connections (Mazor 1998).

35. From the perspective of song texts and national histories, it is a valid premise.

songs that varied somewhat over time, but stayed fairly close to the model of a small Arab ensemble, a *takht* (see chapter 6). Aside from Shoham's singing, the only significant difference from the dominant Arab sound was the addition of a jazz-oriented bassist. Emphasizing blend over juxtaposition, the band aimed for originality in the details of particular arrangements, striving for dramatic interpretations of the song texts. By contrast, the composer-performers of Bustan Abraham varied the recipe (and the dominance of particular elements) from one piece to the next, sometimes in highly distinctive ways. In some cases this meant juxtaposing starkly different resources, while other compositions were more homogenous in sound or involved blurring the contrasts. From one album to the next the band members retained a recognizable sound even as they mobilized a plethora of musical resources in numerous ways, rather than varying one or two arrangements. They also achieved variety by augmenting the ensemble with guests in a few pieces and performing with a reduced ensemble in others. Yair Dalal also varied arrangements considerably, but through different means. With his band Al Ol, he developed a distinctive sound within which he achieved variety by having his musicians switch instruments from one track to another or even within a track (e.g., on "Adon Haslichot," 🔊 audio track 4). For greater variety, he has worked with different musicians, while his own sound on *'ud* or violin changes little from one setting to another. Despite the greater span of partners, his stylistic palette has tended to be more restricted (or less contrastive) than Bustan Abraham's.

Musical Mixtures

To contextualize these musicians' claims to originality—made largely on the basis of the novelty and quality of their musical mixtures—we must look at precedents, locating this moment in a larger history. As Hirshberg, Seroussi, and others have shown, European Jewish composers were already attempting "fusion" in Palestine in the 1930s.[36] Some of their efforts were directed toward the concert hall; others were intended as contributions to the growing body of songs of the Zionist community in Palestine. These compositions generally incorporated specific Middle Eastern tunes, scales, or rhythmic patterns into a European-derived field of musical practice. Collaborations between male European immigrants and female Yemenite Jewish singers that introduced a few non-European voices to the mix were influential, but Hirshberg concludes that, "despite ideologically motivated attempts at merging east and west, compartmentalization won the upper hand" (1997: 5).

Recordings from the early 1960s featuring Shoshana Damari, one of the most famous Yemenite Israeli singers, display an eclectic program that was clearly a response to and part of an early "world music" phenomenon—

36. Hirshberg 1984, 1995, 1997, 2002; Seroussi 2002c.

the international folk song movement in which performers like Pete Seeger, Theodore Bikel, and the Weavers were highly visible and audible. Like these performers, Damari sang songs in several languages (including Hebrew, Turkish, Yiddish, Arabic, Romanian, and Spanish).[37] Most of her recordings feature orchestral accompaniment, but a few song settings attempt to meld aspects of Middle Eastern performance practice in rather unsatisfying ways. The Yemenite Jewish hymn "Im Nin'alu" (later turned into an international dance hit by Ofra Haza) is accompanied by very plain *darbukkah* playing and a guitar strummed percussively in a manner that sounds unlike the techniques common for *'ud* or other Middle Eastern string instruments. Similarly, a Bedouin song "Dahla Ayunik" is given a heavy-handed and modally unsatisfying treatment. Despite Damari's spirited singing, these treatments sound forced and anemic in comparison to efforts by Alei Hazayit, Bustan Abraham, and Yair Dalal. This may be due to the top-down production model, based on scores created by the conductor-arrangers (Gershon Kingsley and Elyakum Shapira) for European orchestral instrumentalists, rather than the cumulative input of musicians with Middle Eastern musical competences. The network and processes of performance would have been radically different from those of the current ethnic music scene.[38]

Jo Amar, a popular singer who immigrated to Israel from Morocco in the 1950s, also participated in mixing European, Arab, and specifically Jewish musical elements. Unlike Damari, who came to Palestine as an infant, Amar had already enjoyed success as a singer of popular and religious songs in Morocco. Some of his recordings subsequent to immigration followed the conventions of mid-twentieth-century Moroccan music, combining North African and Middle Eastern music with aspects of European light music (Morocco had long been exposed to French and Spanish culture). Other recordings use much the same choral and orchestral settings that were employed at that time for Israeli music with European roots.[39]

Beginning in the days of English and French colonial rule in the Middle East, musicians made numerous attempts at combining Arab music with elements drawn from European art music and international popular music ranging from tangos to Hawaiian guitar. Among those most influential for the musicians in this study were the renowned Egyptian singer, *'ud* player, composer and actor Muhammad 'Abd al-Wahhab and the Lebanese

37. Reissued on CD, Damari 1995.
38. Kingsley, born in Germany (1925), immigrated to Palestine in 1938 before moving to the U.S. after WWII where he worked for Vanguard, arranging albums of Greek, French, and Israeli folk songs. He also worked on Broadway, composed theatrical works, and pioneered electronic pop and the use of the Moog synthesizer (see www.spaceagepop.com/kingsley.htm and www.kingsleysound.com/frameset.html). Shapira also worked on Jewish records for Vanguard.
39. See Shiloah and Cohen 1983 and Cohen and Shiloah 1985 for discussion of such combinations in a matrix of possible attitudes toward traditional music exhibited by Jews of North African and Middle Eastern origin after immigrating to Israel.

Rahbani brothers, whose songs and musical plays were made famous by the singer Fairuz. 'Abd al-Wahhab experimented with instruments and forms taken from non-Arab sources and indulged his taste for melodies from nineteenth-century European symphonies and operas. The Rahbani brothers showed how one might blend the chords and orchestration of light popular music with melodies drawn from or sounding like the folk music of Lebanon, Syria, and Palestine.[40]

Musicians in Israel's ethnic music scene did not emulate these examples directly. While Shoham sang songs that Shoshana Damari and Jo Amar had recorded, her performances of "Sheharhoret" and "Shir Hashikor" differ greatly from theirs. Nassim Dakwar and Taiseer Elias have both composed pieces that combine harmonic progressions and Western instruments with aspects of Arab music, but the connections to earlier syntheses by 'Abd al-Wahhab and the Rahbani brothers are tenuous. Again, the differences are due to the relatively egalitarian collaboration among musicians who generate innovation through their cross-cultural encounters with one another, driven by their multiple competences rather than imported foreign concepts.

The first Israeli group to actually do something akin to the work later produced by Bustan Abraham and Yair Dalal was Habreira Hativ'it (see chapters 3 and 8). Several members of Bustan came from this band (see chapter 8) and Yair Dalal said that the band had opened his ears to the potential of this kind of fusion and to the possibility that a non-European Israeli Jew could make a career with music drawn from his roots. The constant in the band's sound is Bar's exuberant and idiosyncratic playing on a variety of hand drums. The rest of the mixture has depended on who was playing in the band at the time, usually including Indian, Persian, and Moroccan music brought by musicians from those countries, and various other styles and instruments, such as flamenco guitar, double bass, and oboe.

Among the foreign bands cited by Yair Dalal and members of Bustan Abraham as inspirations for cross-cultural encounters, the most frequently named was Shakti, which was formed in 1974 by English jazz guitarist John McLaughlin and several prominent Hindustani and Carnatic musicians, including a very young Zakir Hussain who would perform with Bustan Abraham many years later.[41] Shakti was an inspiration because of its virtuosity and the appearance of equality and mutual respect,[42] but it also offered a negative example of directions the musicians in Israel chose not to take.[43] Israeli musicians also cited Oregon, an American group that

40. For analyses of the music of 'Abd al-Wahhab and the Rahbani brothers, see Azzam 1990 and Habib 2005, respectively.
41. Just as the Beatles' *Sgt. Pepper* opened things up for John McLaughlin and many other musicians (Fellesz 2004: 154), McLaughlin's Shakti opened up new vistas for musicians in Israel (and elsewhere).
42. This is discussed at length in Fellezs 2004.
43. I could not elicit a clear explanation of musicians' negative judgments of what they called McLaughlin's fusion. McLaughlin himself rejected the pos-

mixed Indian music and musical instruments and influences from other cultures with jazz and Western classical music, and Night Ark, a U.S.-based band that mixes Armenian music and jazz elements.[44]

Alei Hazayit

Shoham and Jamal characterized their collaboration as unprecedented. Socially speaking it certainly was. In musical terms their originality lay in the mixture of elements they assembled for well-known songs. Their arrangements of "Erev Shel Shoshanim" and "Ro'e vero'a" are characteristic of their early work, while "Lamidbar" (🔊 audio track 3) and "Shabehi Yerushalayim" are later additions to their repertoire that exhibit some changes. The first three are classic *shirei erets yisrael*. Arab musical practices were dominant in most aspects of their arrangements, with other elements added in ways that aimed to blend more than contrast. Thus I will discuss only one Arab song, "Balla Tsoubou Hal Kahwa," since their treatment of such songs was innovative chiefly because of who they were rather than how they combined disparate elements.

"Erev Shel Shoshanim," a love song by Yosef Hadar and Moshe Dor (🔊 audio track 1), is addressed by a man to a woman, extolling the fragrances of an "evening of roses" (*erev shel shoshanim*). Its melody in "modal" minor (the seventh degree is never raised),[45] goes with a chord progression that typically is played on guitar or accordion. There are no particular introductory or transitional melodies associated with the song, nor is it generally associated with drumming. The rendition by Alei Hazayit applies the conventions of an Arab *takht*. The way Omar Keinani slides into some notes, ornaments others, and alters timing and dynamics are all part of an Arab musical episteme that has little if anything to do with that of the original song. The same is true of the drumming, though in a less subtle way. After each vocal phrase, the melodic instrumentalists respond with brief melodies much as they would for an Arab song.

One might expect the introductory arpeggiated minor chord to change to suit the harmonic progression of the song, but the *nay* player continues to repeat it as the song progresses, probably not as a conscious decision but through lack of understanding of harmonic conventions. When the bass player, an accomplished jazz musician, added his part he followed the chord changes implicit in the melody. Since harmonization of the song requires at least three chords[46] this creates an oddly bitonal effect. When Shoham begins to sing, the *nay* and *'ud* players finally abandon the repeated

---

sibility of an East-West fusion: "I don't believe one can talk about east-west fusions in music. . . . If you try to make an east-west fusion you're going to be a miserable failure right away" (Stephen 1979).

44. The founding members of Alei Hazayit knew nothing about these bands and operated with rather different models in mind.

45. A variant of the melody, which can be sung alone or as harmony to the first, includes both raised and lowered forms of the sixth degree of the scale.

46. The i, iv, and VII chords are basic to the song.

arpeggio and when she moves to the fourth degree they circle and emphasize that pitch rather than clashing with it as they did during the violin solo. At several junctures the instrumentalists go back to playing arpeggios as filler.

Shoham ends the first verse by gliding up to the fifth degree rather than staying on the tonic. Omar takes that as the starting pitch to play what would be an acceptable *taqasim* (solo instrumental improvisation), an impression enhanced when he flattens the fifth degree to hint at a modal change. Here, however, the improvisation serves to set the atmosphere for Jamal's declamation of an Arabic text he wrote, a decidedly unconventional usage. Shoham joins them, wordlessly crooning the song's melody while Omar continues to improvise in a fragmented fashion and the other instrumentalists provide much the same background that they had played earlier. The aggregate effect is unlike any standard Arab or Israeli performance.

Shoham sings the song with few deviations from the standard melody. Her wordless rendition alongside Jamal's recitation departs from the composed melody only in nuances of timing and prolongation of the pauses between phrases. But these are important, contributing to a sensation of timeless floating. Her most striking move comes at the end of the vocalise when she extends the pentatonicism of her first phrase by singing 4 7 5 rather than simply ascending to the fourth degree of the scale (see figure 9.1, measures 20–21). This opens up a fifth with the sustained 1 (C) that Omar has reached on the violin via a cadential melody that would not be out of place in a *taqasim*. Jean Claude complicates the tonal space by abandoning his rhythmic bass plucking to bow a 4 (F) throughout this passage. While Jamal concludes his declamation, we are left suspended in a hybrid musical space—Arab drumming and the echo of a conventional Arab violin cadence set against open-throated vocalise and bowed bass that outline the interval of a ninth and point in other stylistic directions. It is Omar who brings the ensemble back to the composed song by playing its concluding phrase and leading back to the tonic.[47]

Returning from the interlude to the song, the musicians treat the melody more freely. Shoham alters it in fairly dramatic ways, Omar adds pyrotechnics on the violin, and Jean Claude bows an ascending bass line that creates a counterpoint. The coda, twenty seconds long, leaves an unsettled feeling as the singer and violinist cadence on the fifth rather than the tonic while the *nay* player adds a few parting wisps. To end a song so vaguely was highly unusual for Jamal, who directed this arrangement. As a powerful, flashy drummer he tended to bring every song, in Arabic or Hebrew, to a rousing finish, marked by a loud slap on the drum.

---

47. The transcription in figure 9.1 is rhythmically more straightforward than the subtleties of timing performed by Shoham and Omar as they avoid coincidence with the beat. Adding to the difficulty of transcription is the fact that Omar's violin improvisation is far back in the mix, which is dominated by Jamal's speaking voice, with Shoham's vocalise a close second. This difference in prominence reflects their relative dominance in the group at that time.

Figure 9.1 "Erev Shel Shoshanim" excerpt (2:51 to 3:37): Shoham Einav (vocal) and Omar Keinani (violin)

This recording is useful here precisely because it was one of the first songs that the group arranged and recorded, one of four tracks on their demo CD. While some of the musicians—Jamal, Shoham, Omar, and the second drummer, Walid—had worked out the song and figured out how to work together, the others lacked this common ground and brought to the task basic competences that really did not overlap. The 'ud and nay players at the recording session were not regular members of the group, though both had worked extensively with Jamal in local Arab bands. The nay player seems to be trying to figure out when to play the arpeggio and when to focus on the main melody. The bassist, called in to add his part to the mix, had never played with Arab musicians before and had to be coached by Jamal, who told me that he stood in the control booth of the recording studio and gestured high and low through the window to show the basic drum pattern. The bassist picked up that rhythm and chose pitches to fit the inherent harmonies of the song, his greater understanding of harmony offsetting his lack of knowledge of Arab music. For all these reasons the parts are not as well integrated as they might be and there are some intonation problems.

For all its flaws, this recording should be viewed as a daring departure from what these musicians were accustomed to do. Although some Palestinian musicians are well trained in harmony, none of the musicians involved in this band had that kind of competence so they dealt with the harmonic implications in an idiosyncratic manner. The setting was also quite different from anything that Israeli audiences might expect for this song. Shoham's rendition did not go completely unnoticed. It received modest airplay and might have become a hit were it not for the lack of professional management and a commercial release of the recording. Hora Yerushalayim, the preeminent folk dance troupe in West Jerusalem, chose to accompany dances with this song and "Ro'e vero'a" from the same demo recording. Shoham claimed that after this song aired on the radio, several people had stolen two key aspects: the use of Arab instruments and the recitation in Arabic.

Although "Ro'e vero'a" (Shepherd and Shepherdess) makes no explicit reference to Israel, it is a pastoral love song like numerous other *shirei erets yisrael*.[48] The instrumental parts conform to contemporary Arab practice, providing a strong rhythmic foundation and heterophonic treatment of the melody before Shoham begins to sing. Much as they would for any number of Arab songs, the instrumentalists punctuate the pause at the end of each vocal phrase in the verse with a burst of sound: a scalar run played on *nay* and violin, while a drum roll on the *darbukkah* ends with a slap on the next downbeat. The bass doubles the drum pattern on the tonic, occasionally alternating with the fifth degree of the scale. After two fast, highly rhythmic verses, the instrumentalists go into a holding pattern, the violinist starts to improvise, and Shoham launches into a rhapsodic vocal improvisation that is quite foreign to her two main repertoires. It is not an imitation of conventional Arab vocal improvisation (in *layali* or *mawwal*), but neither is it completely alien to that aesthetic. Shoham succeeds in singing against the grain, relating to the underlying rhythm (the syncopated *maqsum*) in subtle ways as she stretches the words almost to the point of perdition. A few rapid bursts of text emphasize the otherwise glacial pace of delivery over the driving bass and drums. The vocal quality is anything but icy, peppered with intense vibrato and burning dissonance, heightened by complex relationships with the violin—sometimes hetero-

48. From the 1930s to the 1950s Matityahu Shelem, the composer and lyricist (1904–1975), wrote a number of pastoral songs, such as "Shibolet basade" (a sheaf in the field), "Se ugdi" (goat and kid), and "Rikud hakotsrim" (dance of the harvesters), and created new secular ceremonies for the traditional Jewish holidays (Shahar 2004).

Figure 9.2   "Ro'e Vero'a" Excerp (2:01 to 2:19): Shoham Einav (vocal), Omar Keinani (violin), Jean Claude Jones (bass)

phonic, at other times polyphonic. The version that Shoham recorded has no Arabic but in rehearsal I recorded Jamal declaiming in Arabic while Shoham rhapsodized and Omar improvised his own prolonged lines mixed with short rapid bursts of notes. In other words, they applied the same procedures that they had used in the middle of "Erev Shel Shoshanim." The effect of these multiple layers is exhilarating (see figure 9.2). The combination of elements in this song is typical of Alei Hazayit's arrangements.

"Lamidbar" (to the desert), recorded about seven years later, offers a different take on this basic formula. In general, the band became more adventurous in orchestration and arrangement the longer they worked together.[49]

49. "Reyakh tapuakh," for instance, features a bass solo and an unusual use of tambourine jingles.

The personnel had changed: the bassist Shlomo Moyal had performed with the band for some time and the regular *'ud* and *nay* players were available so no substitutes were needed. Finally, Jamal used the studio to compile several tracks of drumming as a foundation for the song. For all of these reasons this song has a much fuller sound than the earlier recordings. It also enjoyed greater circulation than some of the band's other pieces. A video of desert scenes set to the recording aired on television.

At seven minutes in length, "Lamidbar" is more ambitious in structure than earlier songs, which lasted four to five minutes. Extra-musical sounds set the scene and paint a more evocative picture. The extensive introduction and coda feature a howling wind and the bells of a herd of goats or camels, evoking the atmosphere of the song's subject, the desert. As in several other songs, this arrangement is enriched by a simple but effective instrumental interlude, invented by the musicians, that is related to the song's melody but goes beyond mere elaboration. Shoham builds a contrast between prolonged phrases and ones sung at the band's rapid pace. The tension works well and exemplifies both the support that Shoham craved from the musicians and the freedom she felt when given that support.

The song's longer duration allows for solo improvisations on *'ud* and *nay* in addition to violin. Before the last verse, Shoham declaims a text in Arabic, with violin and *nay* improvisations swirling above her voice. The rhythmic matrix of bass and various drums continues throughout this interlude. Although the Hebrew song text is ungendered and consists of a command ("Take us to the desert on the humps of camels") and a description of the desert replete with stars, camels' bells, and shepherds' flutes, the declaimed Arabic text, written by Jamal, differs, featuring a female voice that begins as a personification of aspects of nature (seasons, the river) and ends by asking a man to take her with him on a camel.

The band's most ambitious undertaking was "Shabehi Yerushalayim," two verses of Psalm 147 set to music by Avihu Medina, leading composer and spokesman of Israeli Mediterranean Music (his upscale term for *musika mizrahit*), and popularized by Daklon, another pioneering figure in the field of *musika mizrahit*.[50] Various artists have recorded this song but never in so dramatic an arrangement. While Alei Hazayit sometimes connected a few pieces into short medleys, this was their most extended arrangement. Here Jamal and Shoham moved farthest from the strophic structure common to all their songs. This is also the only song in their repertoire bearing any religious connotations. Jamal and Shoham indulged their imaginations with a range of recorded sounds to evoke the soundscape of a city holy to three religions. The results are provocative, not only because of the mixing of church bells, the Muslim call to prayer, and the blowing of shofars, but particularly because a Jewish song that celebrates Jerusalem and can easily be heard as highly nationalistic has been "repurposed" to em-

50. See Regev and Seroussi 2004: 221.

phasize the importance of Jerusalem to Jews and Arabs, whether Muslim or Christian. No political symbol is more hotly contested than Jerusalem in the Israeli-Palestinian conflict. This arrangement thrusts it to center stage as Jamal and Shoham preface the singing by calling out epithets for the holy city alternately in Arabic and Hebrew. Because this was such a potentially explosive arrangement Shoham did not release it, waiting for the right time, for fear of the consequences for the Palestinian musicians and theft of the group's original ideas.

Most of the band's arrangements were more predictable than this one, based on a small stock of drum patterns and patterns of orchestration that varied little, giving the songs an overall stylistic unity. The drumming for a given song was the topic of discussions in rehearsals more often than any other aspect of arrangement and rehearsal. Jamal was particularly adept at finding the right drum patterns to suit the character of the Israeli and Ladino songs. He and Shoham both placed great importance on finding the appropriate match of melody, text, drum rhythm, and mood. It is here, too, that they most often clashed, which I take as a sign of the vitality of this connection. Shoham explained the procedure of working on a new song thus:

> I talk about it in terms of feelings, when I hear his rhythm. For instance, how was "Lamidbar" born? With that rhythm I said, "That's wonderful!" . . . it went together beautifully . . . there are things that I don't like. But he is an artist in these things. I enjoy how he takes a song and I never play it for them in someone's cassette. I sing it clean, like that . . . otherwise what's the point? (3/1/95)

She wanted the musicians to respond to the unadorned melody of the Hebrew songs she introduced, not to prior arrangements of these songs. While Jamal had a dominant role in the arranging, several of the others contributed. Omar and the 'ud player (either Ghidian al-Qaimari or Fu'ad Abu Ghannam) added melodic introductions and interludes, drawing on short Arab pieces (particularly the genre of *dulab* that is traditionally played at the beginning of a suite of pieces) and inventing new phrases as preludes and interludes.

Declamation of a poetic text in Hebrew or Arabic to complement a text sung in the other language is one of the most striking aspects of the arrangements by Alei Hazayit. In response to selected Hebrew songs, Jamal wrote texts in poetic Arabic, which either he or Shoham would declaim. For "Erev Shel Shoshanim," for example, Jamal eschewed a paraphrase and instead wrote a text that spoke of the dawn and the dew, evoking the magic of the morning after the romantic, rose-scented evening stroll in the garden. For certain Arabic songs, Shoham prefaced a Hebrew declamation that distilled the meaning or atmosphere of the song's text.

Shoham recited such a preface for "Balla Tsoubou Hal Kahwa," a song popularized by Jordanian singer Samira Tawfic about Bedouin preparing to honor their guests with coffee.[51] The Arabic text commands one to salute the strong men on horses by pouring them coffee with cardamom. It invokes custom and honor, tried and true tropes associated with Bedouin. This song exemplifies the great importance that Shoham and Jamal placed on creating a unique atmosphere with each song. They departed from the short, relatively monochromatic pop rendering of the song, which served as their source, to create a rich play of moods and sounds.

As with the Arabic texts declaimed for Hebrew songs, Shoham's Hebrew text was written to create a mood and set the stage for the song rather than to translate its text:

> And the desert is big and wide / and the night seems enveloping.
> The moon looks at you as if he were talking to you. / The coals whisper
> and the fire, like a lighthouse /for those who wander on the road.
> And the smell of the coffee seems to strike like waves. / And here they are.
> The horse riders have come galloping / handsome and daring.
> Pour the coffee and add cardamom![52]

In rehearsals that I attended Shoham declaimed this dramatically, while two musicians sustained a drone on violin and synthesizer and Rajay improvised a *taqasim* on *nay*. The free-flow of the *taqasim* is not based on the same sense of time as the dramatic recitation, creating a challenge for the *nay* player. Because Rajay did not understand Hebrew, he had great difficulty when Shoham was nearing the end of her text so they had to rehearse this several times. To help him and to add drama, Shoham tried ending with a shout that cued the instrumentalists to begin the song itself.

Jamal and Shoham sought emotional impact through their choice of songs and the foregrounding of texts and the human voice, richly supported by melodic instruments over a solid foundation of drums and bass. The juxtaposition of Hebrew and Arabic, in various combinations, heightened this, as did the combination of Arab musical tools and Israeli songs with diverse stylistic roots. Some of the musical juxtapositions were straight analogies to the linguistic contrasts; others were not so clear, a musical stew of ingredients that did not contrast as starkly as the two languages. Among their songs are numerous examples of the simultaneous layering of contrasting musical styles like the interlude in "Erev Shel Shoshanim." Such mixtures, based on a relatively restricted mixture of musical practices, are open to interpretation depending on the listener's experience and interests.

51. This is the transliteration of the title on Tawfic's recording. A more standard transliteration is "Balla Tsubbu hal-Qahwa" (A. J. Racy, personal communication, 2009).
52. My translation.

Yair Dalal

Yair Dalal has experimented with mixing musical materials in a wide variety of settings. Some of the pieces created with his band Al Ol had significant input by band members, with multiple composers or arrangers credited for certain pieces. Although this appears to match and even exceed Bustan Abraham's multiple authorship and collaborative editing, Yair has maintained a strong authorial voice, as a composer, an improviser, and the director-producer of his concerts and recordings. As with Alei Hazayit, Arab musical practices are dominant, but other elements, such as Hindustani music and klezmer, can be quite strong, too, lending a greater range of possibilities in his oeuvre and greater contrast between the elements in some pieces and projects.

"Adon Haslichot" is a good example of the synthesis Yair created in working with Al Ol (🔊 audio track 4). This group arrangement of a traditional song incorporates recognizable elements from several distinct cultural sources, but creates a convincing unity of mood. Based on the melody of a Jewish hymn, the piece consists of two movements. There is no real break between the two and they are thematically tied to one another, though distinct in character. I enumerate the variety of sources used here not to predict what a person should or might hear, but to delineate which materials the musicians chose and how they combined them.

Indian elements dominate at the start, when only *sitar* and *tabla* are heard. The piece then proceeds with melodic improvisation on violin and clarinet in alternation as the *sitar* player, Eyal Faran, drops back to sound a sporadic drone. It is not until the middle of the piece that he surfaces again, playing the main melody alone to create a bridge between first and second movements. Yair plays the violin with many slides, subtle ornaments, and free rhythms that do not lock into Nurit Ofer's drum pattern. These characteristics stem from Yair's experience playing Arab music. Sela's experience as a performer of klezmer and Turkish clarinet is evident in his improvisation and later in his handling of the melody, though he is not given the scope for the virtuosity he displays in other pieces. Yair and Sela employ playing styles that differ considerably from Faran's *sitar* playing, yet the shared melodic material and the underlying drum pattern hold things together. The sparse pattern Ofer plays throughout the first half is not Indian, as one might expect since she is playing *tabla*, but the ten-beat *sama'i thaqil* usually associated with more serious pieces in Arab and Turkish music.[53] Here it is played unusually slowly, at forty beats per minute, transformed by the *tabla*'s timbre and playing idiom, which offers different ways of filling in the space between the main strokes of the pattern. One of the oddities of using this pattern for this song is that the juxtaposed melody and meter do not align. The clarinetist starts the melody in sync with the *tabla*, but most of his downbeats do not coincide with hers, a relatively rare instance of asynchrony in Yair's work.

53. See discussion of Taiseer Elias's composition "Hamsa" in chapter 10.

The second half of "Adon Haslichot" contrasts with the first in many ways. Most obviously, it is much faster, it includes singing, the four-beat drum pattern aligns with the melody, and the instrumentation changes. Yair switches from violin to 'ud, Sela from clarinet to flute, and Ofer from *tabla* to singing, while Eylon Nufar drums on *darbukkah*. Faran continues to play *sitar* throughout the piece, maintaining continuity between the two halves. Several of the men add soft, open-throated, textless singing of the melody of "Adon Haslichot," repeating it several times. Ofer joins them in a similar singing style, then after an Arab-style improvisation on the *darbukkah*, she sings in a far more intense voice, improvising in a style that shows clear Indian influence, replete with ornaments unlike anything performed in Arab or Jewish music.

This confluence of Indian, Arab, Turkish, and Jewish music revolves around the song. At the time, it was relatively unusual in the Israeli ethnic music scene to make use of religious music. Performed here without its text, "Adon Haslichot" is not readily identifiable as a Jewish hymn in praise of God. Yet the slow, expressive beginning and the numerous iterations of the melody convey a prayerful attitude. Field recordings of the same hymn sung by Iraqi and Turkish congregations in prayer[54] show that the experience of the song in its religious context is not nearly so contemplative: the tempo is faster, the voices may be raucous and are heterophonic to the verge of polyphony (or chaos). Yair and friends have "rescued" the tune from an "every man for himself before God" approach to performance and given it a setting that can, in the course of twelve and a half minutes, transport the listener first to a meditative state and then toward a more ecstatic one as tempo and intensity are raised. This suits contemporary seekers of spirituality who seem to be attracted to music like Yair's.

The members of Al Ol mix instruments and styles of vocal and instrumental performance in a variety of textures that draws on each of the practices in which they have trained. There is a tendency to build in intensity over fairly long stretches by increasing tempo and volume and by adding layers. In "Adon Haslichot" this intensification is reinforced by transposing the main melody up a fourth toward the end of the piece. Compared with most of the longer pieces by Bustan Abraham (see chapter 10), this piece is less complex, with fewer sections, fewer changes of meter, and no changes of mode. On the other hand it creates an expansive sense of time and convincingly integrates diverse musical resources to create a particular atmosphere.

Yair's most ambitious composition to date is "The Perfume Road," highly pertinent to a discussion of fusion because its programmatic concept demands such music. Yair introduces this piece in six movements as his "symphony." At seventy minutes in length it far exceeds the scope of other works by any of the musicians under consideration here. Portraying the ancient caravan route over which spices and perfumes were brought across the Arabian Peninsula from the Indian Ocean to the shores of the

54. Included in the cassettes accompanying Shiloah 1985.

Mediterranean, "The Perfume Road" is intended to evoke the different atmospheres, landscapes, peoples, and musics one would encounter along the way. The concept emerged from a peace trek from Jordan through Israel to Gaza in which Yair participated. He imagined the traders who made the trek along the Perfume Road, how they would tire as they neared the end of their eighty-day journey, increasingly missing their girlfriends or wives. Yair found in such imaginings an excuse (if not a historical reason) to mix Indian, Persian, Arab, and Turkish elements, because he saw this as a leg on the trip from India to Turkey and onward to Europe. "It's no coincidence that the piece begins with *dashti* [a Persian mode] and ends with clarinet playing [*maqam*] *nakriz*. There's even a little bit of klezmer," he explained to me.[55] Sela's clarinet does double duty here, representing both Turkish and European Jewish cultures. The different *maqams* and meters (*iqa'at*) that Yair combines are supposed to represent the mixture of men from different tribes who participated in these caravans. The sections in *maqam bayyati* symbolize the desert because Yair feels that that is the mode of the desert, noting that there are many Bedouin songs in *maqam bayyati*. Whether an audience perceives the details in this representation of a series of cultures is questionable. The more knowledgeable will note Indian, Arab, and European instruments but may be harder pressed to tease out the constituent elements blended in this music.

Although the program of "The Perfume Road" would seem to demand it, identifying the ingredients that went into the stewpot is not necessarily the point. The power of some of these collaborations between musicians who perform in traditions that overlap or have similar possibilities and constraints lies in the synergy created by the discovery of common ground and the exploitation of different nuances, as in the Arabandi project, which brought together two of Bustan Abraham's members with musicians from India and Iran. Yair's more recent recording, *Asmar*, in which he teams up with Maureen Nehedar, a Persian-Israeli singer, succeeds in this regard.

A comparison with *Sheshbesh* is instructive for its contrast to the rest of Yair's wide-ranging endeavors. The project, which included a few concerts but focused on the CD, included works by Yair and five other composers, each relating in some way to the musical traditions of the area stretching from North Africa through the Middle East to Central Asia. Yair found that he had to adapt to a different set of conditions for this project, which was directed not at his usual audience but at one oriented toward Western art music.[56] Two of the three other musicians were highly trained classical musicians, but, unlike Yair's partners in Al Ol and other collaborations, did not know how to improvise. Yair contrasted this with Taiseer Elias's collaborations with composer/pianist Menahem Wiesenberg, whom Yair views as a formidable improviser in a jazz idiom. As in many, perhaps

<hr>

55. February 28, 2002. These are his own characterizations, evocative but hardly historically consistent.

56. June 21, 1998. His parents, whose frame of reference is Arab music (Iraqi and general Middle Eastern), preferred his other recordings to *Sheshbesh*.

most, experiments in mixing different musical styles, Yair felt that the *Sheshbesh* participants pulled in different directions. As an example, he noted that he had to adapt his articulation on the *'ud* to match the flautist's articulation. A moment's attention to any track on the disk and a listener cannot fail to notice the difference from Yair's other work. *Sheshbesh* presents a precisely scored musical environment in which the mix of elements is controlled almost exclusively by the composer rather than emerging from the collaboration of a group of improvising musicians who can each add their own content and shape the work. Player input appears to have been limited to the microcosmic, such as Yair's adjustment of his articulation.

The album liner notes characterize Israel as "a country where the tradition of western classical music at its highest level meets oriental music in its various forms" and makes the valid point that "with immigrants from all over the world living in Israel, this country is the natural meeting point for all these kinds of music, and thus the perfect place for *Sheshbesh* to start from" (*Sheshbesh* 1998). This is a product of ENJA, based in Germany, whose Web site promises that *Sheshbesh*'s music will invite "the listener to a journey through mid-eastern and oriental areas offering ethnic authenticity on a classical level." This Orientalist view, that European classical music can mine the Orient for its gems, then polish and elevate them to a higher status, has been expressed by others in Israel, but has failed to yield an audience sufficient to sustain a steady flow of such collaborations.[57] That this project fell between the chairs is evident in the following review from Rootsworld, an internet site that characterizes itself as "a network of culture, art and music on the web" and titles its review section "listening to the planet." After praising the music for being carefully worked out by excellent players, the reviewer concludes "But for me the passion inherent in much Middle Eastern traditional music (or jazz, for that matter) is here stifled by the too-polite approach. Group interplay and precision are the main qualities in evidence, and while the CD succeeds on its own terms, it's a little too restrained overall."[58] It is precisely this "interplay" that differs from the norms of Yair's other interactions where greater flexibility ranges from small momentary decisions to larger scale improvisation.

Great differences in musical competence and difficulties in communication surfaced in the three-way *Music Channel* collaboration noted earlier.[59] This meeting of two Israelis (Yair and Eyal Sela), two Palestinians, and a Norwegian progressive rock quartet took place over a two-week period in Norway in the mid 1990s. Yair reported that the Norwegians had trouble with the Arab drumming. The bass player heard the *maqsum* rhythmic mode backward with the heavy *dumm* as upbeat rather than

---

57. This project did give rise to an Israel Philharmonic offshoot, Sheshbesh: The Arab-Jewish Keynote Ensemble of the Israel Philharmonic Orchestra.

58. Joe Grossman, www.rootsworld.com/rw/reviews2.html

59. Yair told me, "even with the Norwegians [there was communication] it's a cosmopolitan language" in the same conversation that he related these difficulties.

downbeat, causing a lengthy argument. The musicians also brought very different sorts of songs to the project, adding elements that were stylistically foreign to the original song. "There's one song in Norwegian that in the middle we bring in a really Arab *mawwal* (vocal solo). We stop, make a break, leaving the drum machine, and add *'ud* and Arab vocal. Suddenly from Norway it lands in the Middle East, without any preparation."[60] The process of working out how to put these elements together was laborious. Dalal said that starting with the Beatles's "We Can Work It Out" helped because most of them knew it.

Despite the frustrations and misunderstandings, this experience encouraged Dalal to dream big. He envisions rerecording his "Mantra for Peace," a setting of a poem by the late Israeli poet Yehuda Amichai, with greater forces—including Ladysmith Black Mambazo—and "to take Saed and Anna [the Palestinian and Norwegian singers on *Music Channel*] or some other female singer, maybe a famous singer from the U.S. The song is a bit Indian, a bit Arab, a bit America, a bit of everything." He characterized this song as "something much more *cosmopolitan*. . . . I want to do something really big with it, something *cosmopolitan* . . . but I don't have the means . . . sort of "Give Peace a Chance" for now, for the year 2000" (emphasis added). This dream has yet to come to fruition, but the desire expressed is just as important for our purposes as it shows a musician who has tried out various positions in the world music scene, figuring out what resources he would like to tap to make a splash and get his work the attention he believes it deserves. Yair is open to juxtaposing all sorts of musical styles, his imagination limited only by the available resources.

Bustan Abraham

Bustan Abraham rose quickly to prominence in the nascent field of ethnic music due to the masterful integration of a diverse array of musical resources in compositions and improvisations that were performed with multistylistic competence. They quickly became the gold standard that other groups in Israel attempted—and usually failed—to match. Appraisals such as "world music at its best" (Nave 1997) and "without a doubt the most consistent and highest quality band in the field of ethnic music in Israel" (Efrati 2000) are typical of their reviews. In the space of ten years and five CDs they amassed an impressive catalogue of work, too much to discuss here in the detail that it deserves. A few composed and improvised sections from this corpus will serve to demonstrate their methods for combining a truly diverse array of musical resources, ranging from juxtaposition through seamless blend.[61] They argued over the dominance of Eastern or Western elements in their work, but this tended to vary considerably from one piece to the next and sometimes from one moment to the next.

60. Dalal, June 21, 1998.
61. Taiseer Elias's compositions predominate in this discussion to give a sense of one composer/performer's breadth and because he was one of the most prolific composers and soloists in the band.

Certain moments in the band's work explicitly referenced established musical styles. Miguel Herstein's guitar flourishes at the end of "In the House of Maimonides" are immediately recognizable to anyone who has heard flamenco and his quoting of "Oh Susannah" on banjo in the introduction to "Tini Mini Hanem" elicited a laugh from the audience at every concert I heard live or on tape (🔊 audio track 8).[62] In this introductory solo, Miguel toyed with his listeners' associations as he passed from one style to another. In a performance taped in St. Louis,[63] for instance, Miguel plays an extended pentatonic section, with many hammer-ons and pull-offs, which sounds initially like Appalachian banjo, but he then employs elaborating techniques more reminiscent of Chinese *p'ip'a*. This flows into a flamencolike cadenza, returning from the pentatonic to A major. Lowering the second and sixth degrees, he creates a scale like *maqam shahnaz* (on A). The motivic treatment at this point is reminiscent of an Arab *taqasim* until Miguel piles up harmonic clashes. After another cadence, he works his way subtly back into an American fingerpicking style, hinting gradually at the melody of the Turkish piece that he is to introduce. From one performance to the next, Miguel worked his magic differently while following a similar path. He usually changed modes several times, going into a markedly Middle Eastern sound world, but I also heard him quote the American tune "Old Joe Clark."[64] In the recorded version (*Bustan Abraham*, 1992) he uses some of the same elements, but does not change mode or otherwise reference Arab music.

"Oh Susannah" is a blatant quote, well known to most listeners, and the sound of flamenco guitar is also widely recognized. The juxtaposition of references such as these with a Turkish melody or Arab violin borders on pastiche. It stands out (to my ear, at least) as something quite different from much of the band's material—enjoyable, but pulling the listener away from any new sound world the band might have created by referencing familiar ones. Which moments in a Bustan Abraham performance will trigger associations to other musical styles must depend to a great degree on who is listening. Members of the group cited this variability of response as a strength, claiming that there was something for everyone in their music. In an interview, Avshalom was quoted as saying "the music consists of so many different elements and the public is also not homogenous so each person finds something interesting. Some like jazz, others prefer flamenco. All that is in our music." Taiseer Elias says, "Through fusion of different music styles we're creating a new universal musical language" in the same article.[65]

62. These were American and French audiences. Unfortunately, the concerts I heard in Israel did not include Miguel for various reasons.
63. I am indebted to Taiseer Elias for giving me a copy of the tape. As the recording quality is poor I have not included it on this book's Web site.
64. Berkeley, November 17, 1994. In the version of "Tini Mini Hanem" recorded on the band's *Bustan* album, Miguel inserted this quote much later when he took his solo turn in the body of the piece.
65. Kaatz 1995. My translation.

Stylistic juxtapositions as a result of individual band members' improvisational choices characterized "Tini Mini Hanem," one of the few non-original compositions in their repertoire. The band arranged the piece to showcase the individual musicians, each solo ending by returning to the tune, as Miguel did at the end of his introduction. Each musician tended to improvise in a distinctive style for this piece. Particularly striking was the duet between drummer Zohar and bassist Emmanuel, who applied techniques of hammering and picking the electric bass that he had mastered in the 1980s while playing funk, but never applied to other Bustan pieces. His dynamic duet with Zohar was often one of the highpoints of the piece and the show. At a Paris concert, for instance, this portion of the piece outweighed all the other solos, lasting five and a half minutes out of a total duration of fourteen.

Like "Tini Mini Hanem," several other items in Bustan Abraham's repertoire ran through a series of stylistic contrasts, either in stark contrast or ongoing blends. The title of Taiseer Elias's "Metamorphosis" points directly to stylistic contrasts joined by transitions (🔊 audio track 7). The piece begins and ends with a lilting, pastoral flute melody with harmonic accompaniment consisting of guitar arpeggios over bass guitar with supplementary tremolos and arpeggios on *qanun* and *'ud*. This section draws stylistically on European classical music and is diametrically opposed in manner and mood to the rest of the piece. A transition for *'ud* and bass guitar leads to a faster section in a contrasting meter (4/4 instead of 3/4), with different orchestration and a rhythmic drive supplied by percussion and reinforced on other instruments. The Middle Eastern feel here stems from the entrance of the *qanun* and the foregrounding of the *'ud*. But this theme, like the first, is built on a harmonic progression. It also involves exchanges between a soloist and the ensemble reminiscent of much Arab composition in the twentieth century (see figure 9.3). The second theme then serves as the springboard for an extended *'ud* solo in the course of which Taiseer further transforms melodic material, finally coming to the third theme, which the ensemble plays seven times. They pause, shout "hey," and shift the tonal center up a step from F to G, playing an ostinato at a faster tempo in an additive 4/4+6/8 meter. This serves as the basis for improvisations on *'ud*, flute, drums, and bass guitar in turn. When Emmanuel takes the final solo on bass guitar most of the ensemble fades out, abandoning the ostinato. Zohar maintains the metrical framework on percussion, but in the absence of the ostinato, Emmanuel is freer to wander as he improvises on the scale of *maqam hijaz* (on G). He concludes by ascending this scale three times toward a deft modulation that takes him back to the transition to the second theme. The rest of the ensemble joins in, playing the second and first themes. As its title promises, the piece undergoes a number of metamorphoses, returning to the point of departure in a classic arch form. The mixture of compositional styles and elements reflects the multiple competences and interests that Taiseer Elias has acquired as a performer and scholar of Arab and European art music, as well as the input of other members of the band.

Figure 9.3   Exchanges in "Metamorphosis" by Taiseer Elias, beginning at 1:53 and 2:35

The opening of Taiseer Elias's "Jazz Kar-Kurd" offers an intense example of juxtapositions of styles (🔊 audio track 6). Miguel's flamenco chords and rapid runs alternate with Taiseer's blues-tinged 'ud playing while the ensemble melodies that follow have little to do with either style. In this introduction, Taiseer plays on the possibilities of similarity and difference that the guitar and 'ud offer, an area of experimentation he and Miguel explored in White Bird. The title of the piece indexes its hybridity. *Maqam hijazkar kurd* is similar to Phrygian based on C, but the rhythmic drive and blue notes of Taiseer's part reveal some of the "jazzy" reasons he might have invented the punning title. The piece contains two long improvisational segments highlighting the flute and then the 'ud. Taiseer juxtaposes contrasting styles on a larger scale in the settings for these solos. Highly rhythmic bass and drum parts accompany the flute, with the bass outlining a descending melodic progression with harmonic implications, while the 'ud solo is set to an atonal, loosely organized texture in free rhythm with extensive contributions from the flute, percussion, bass, and violin that would not be out of place in a concert of art music from the 1960s and 1970s.

Taiseer continued to work with contrasting musical materials, creating varying degrees of blend in compositions on later albums. These pieces exhibit a fertile imagination that is not restrained to one direction of musical exploration or dominance of one particular style. His light piece "Sireen" exhibits considerable affinity for American vernacular styles—a Middle Eastern hoedown of sorts—while "Hamsa" makes greater use of Middle Eastern melodic, rhythmic, and formal conventions, such as the ten-beat *sama'i thaqil* rhythm. Yet it is in no way a conventional Arab piece. Even if one sets aside Amir's intense flute solo, the orchestration and the metric manipulations (see chapter 10) are not easily attributable to anything other than the new language that the band promised.

Juxtapositions and blends of various sorts are also evident in compositions by other members of the band, as the following brief analyses of compositions by Miguel and Avshalom show. These pieces differ in style at least as much as Taiseer's compositions do, but composers' individual preferences are attenuated by the contributions of other band members to the arrangements and performances. These selections also demonstrate the breadth of the musical language that the band developed. Despite developing conventions of ensemble style they maintained sufficient "space" for individual expression, particularly but not only in featured solo passages. This is evident, for instance, in Miguel's "Shazeef" and "In the House of Maimonides," which showcase his two instruments, banjo and guitar.

"Shazeef" is a catchy tune in Dorian mode (on C) that starts out with frailing banjo, an Appalachian playing style that differs markedly from the bluegrass fingerpicking that Miguel plays in other pieces. But once the band enters, the syncopated *maqsum* drum pattern doubled by bass, the timbres, and the ornaments make it clear that we are not in Appalachia. After several iterations of the first theme and its variations, a new melody, also introduced on banjo, introduces a modal shift followed immediately by a downward modulation. Over a simple bass and drum ostinato, Nassim plays an extended violin solo, touching on several modes, most notably by flattening the fourth degree to give a taste of *maqam saba*. He ends by leading into the second theme. As foreign as this solo and the opening banjo melody might seem if juxtaposed, the passage from one to the other and back again is seamless rather than jarring, a tribute to the maturity and versatility of the composer, the band, and the soloist, as well as the band's integration of diverse musical elements.

Inspired by a visit to Spain, Miguel's "In the House of Maimonides" is programmatic, changing textures, moods, and tempi many times. At nearly nine minutes it is the longest piece on *Hamsa*. The beginning features Spanish guitar and involves harmonic complexity and flamenco runs, chords, and rhythms. In a live performance that I heard shortly after this was released, Naor and Amir clapped an interlocking pattern during Miguel's final solo, reinforcing the reference to flamenco. But the composition is not completely "Spanish" as it involves a lengthy *'ud* improvisation in the middle in which Taiseer follows his "muse" into various *maqamat* whose main pitches are not congruent with the guitar's F minor chord accompaniment. The sense of contradiction is heightened when the flute enters with a lyric melody, but the strands begin to come together when Taiseer doubles this melody with tremolos on *'ud*. In the ensuing passage Nassim plays the violin with "Western" timbre and intonation, aligning himself with Amir's flute, and Taiseer interjects a few brief passages that show the *'ud* in a more typical light as they play with the possibilities of stylistic reference.[66] Throughout this piece the musicians manipulate the degree of blend or distinctiveness, creating stark juxtapositions at some points only to ease into a more unified musical language at others.

Avshalom Farjun is, by his own admission, one of those who pulled the group to the "East." This is evident in his compositions, such as "Black Seagull," which features Turkish-Arab modal scales and gestures. Unified in mood and conveying a melancholy beauty without any striking contrasts, it serves as a vehicle for a long, leisurely violin improvisation by Nassim with subtle responses from other members of the ensemble. The

66. The *'ud* solo begins at 3:47, the exchange with the flute and violin at 5:21 on the CD.

a.

b.

Figure 9.4   Melody and ostinato from "Bustan" by Avshalom Farjun
with Shimon Ben Shitrit

melody, drumming, and solo are all well within the parameters of Arab and
Turkish musical conventions. The most unconventional aspects are the
final fade out and Zohar's use of a rain stick to evoke the wash of the waves
on the shore.

Avshalom's composition "Bustan" is less resolutely "Eastern." Composed together with Shimon Ben Shitrit before Avshalom founded Bustan,
the piece is a kaleidoscope of sections, colors, and patterns. It is an early
example of the band's fascination with complex meters. While the first section is in 4, the middle switches to 3+3+4 with the melody from the first
section overlaid (see figure 9.4, ◉ audio track 9). There's something mesmerizing and off-balance about this section due to the combination of the
relentless, asymmetrical ostinato and the timing of the overlaid melody that
was in 4/4 and is now stretched to 5/4. An extensive violin solo is followed
by brief contrapuntal sections. The orchestration varies considerably while
the same melodic material is repeated numerous times. All of these elements came to be hallmarks of the group's collaborative arrangements.[67]

Because "Bustan" was later recorded by a jazz combo headed by Avshalom's co-composer, Shimon Ben Shir (formerly Ben Shitrit), it offers a
good means to underscore the difference in performance possibilities between the ethnic music field and jazz and to explore one of the paths not
taken by Bustan Abraham.[68] Most of the basic melodic material is the
same in the two performances, but the rhythmic feel differs greatly. In-

67. See chapter 10 for further comments on "Bustan."
68. Ben Shir 2003.

stead of Bustan Abraham's even subdivision of the beat, Ben Shir's combo plays a heavy swing and remains in 4/4 throughout, without the long middle section in 10 (3+3+2+2), which was a later addition by Avshalom.[69] The original melody implies certain harmonic possibilities, but Bustan Abraham did not develop them. In Ben Shir's version, a chord progression is played as an underpinning to the improvised solos. Each member of Ben Shir's band takes a solo, following standard jazz practice. The Bustan Abraham performance of this piece (as in most of their other pieces) does not follow this practice, limiting solos to some subset of the band and sometimes to as few as one or two members. In Ben Shir's performance, the only striking deviation from jazz conventions lies in the piano solo, which ends the piece in a rhythmically free fantasia. In Bustan Abraham's performance, there is a free rhythm section in the middle in which Taiseer improvises on the 'ud, with light touches from the other instrumentalists as accompaniment. These are nonharmonic in nature, basically extending the concept of drone, but in unusual ways. Nassim Dakwar's violin solo, on the other hand, is played over a complex accompanying texture consisting of several shifting layers derived from the preceding asymmetrical ostinato and melody.

Nassim Dakwar's composition "Dub Dulab" (on *Hamsa*) offers a similar opportunity to contrast Bustan's integrated manner of composing and performing to a jazz-oriented fusion project. Simon Shaheen's "Waving Sands" (on *Blue Flame*) uses the same melody played with a completely different feel (actually several different rhythmic grooves in succession) and division of labor. Not only does Shaheen employ a standard jazz rhythm section, but the solo improvisations are much closer to standard jazz practice.[70]

This raises an important connection between Bustan Abraham's musical innovations and the band's interaction with its audiences. The conventions of a musical practice apply to the listeners as well as the performers, governing their expectations and accepted modes of interaction with the performers. The conventions associated with small group jazz provide the most likely model for Bustan Abraham's audiences outside the Middle East because the long improvised solos in most of their compositions are more similar to jazz than to chamber music, rock, or pop, for instance. But many of these compositions have not been structured to leave "space" for audience applause. At the first Bustan concert I attended, in Berkeley in 1994, it was clear that the audience was responding in jazz mode by applauding after each solo. They expected discrete solos so when

---

69. Avshalom gave the following account of the genesis of this work: "The collaboration on 'Bustan' was during the first gulf war in my house near the *heder atum* [sealed-off room]. We started together the first and last melody until it was formed. Each of us brought a sentence [phrase] after improvising around . . . then he left to the U.S. and I continued all the middle part of the composition" (e-mail communication, June 24, 2004).

70. See the comments on "Dub Dulab" in the next chapter.

Miguel played a response in the middle of one of Taiseer Elias's improvisations they took that to mean that Taiseer had finished, applauding and obscuring most of Miguel's brief contribution. Again and again the music following a solo was obliterated in this manner. A few months later when I asked Emmanuel and Zohar about this they laughed and answered:

EM: We don't wait for the audience.
ZF: because there are instances where [applause] doesn't come.
EM: and it doesn't fit the music [to wait] whereas in jazz . . .
ZF: personally it doesn't bother me, on the contrary, it's great.
EM: me either. Sometimes in "Gypsy Soul" after Nassim's solo Miguel has a part there which enters during the applause so he waits a bit. But the audience is giving its praise, that's very important for a musician. So even if it comes into the arrangement while things are continuing, it's nice.[71]

Note that they interlocked with one another in speech as smoothly as they coordinated bass and drums on stage.

Mixing musical practices risks mismatching audience expectations and performers' intentions. Who is to say which of the corresponding aesthetic expectations and behavioral patterns are to be brought along into the mix? Jazz-related responses predominated in the interactions that Emmanuel and Zohar reported and that I observed. Drawing markedly on Arab (and Turkish) musical improvisatory practices, as Taiseer, Nassim, and Avshalom did, Bustan Abraham might as easily have encountered the sorts of interjections of praise and encouragement that Ali Jihad Racy has theorized in his ecstatic feedback model (2003). In mainstream Arab music, singers and instrumentalists expect such feedback from the audience during solo improvisations and often leave spaces for it, but I never heard the audience call out in the middle of an improvisation at Bustan Abraham concerts I attended, as they might during a *taqasim*. These were precisely the spaces that were often filled with musical or vocal interjections by other members of the group.

Performer-audience interaction can involve singing, dancing or clapping along in time to the music. Expectations regarding such activities are just as much a matter of cultural convention as any other part of the performance, sanctioned or even expected in some contexts and grossly out of place in others. Most of Bustan Abraham's music was highly rhythmic, featuring exciting drumming. This rarely evoked dancing but many tried to clap along. The band did not appreciate this because it obscured the music and because their music involved so many tempo changes, meter changes, and complex meters that the clapping was bound to fall out of sync with the music. I heard such failures in numerous performances. But even when the beat was steady, some members of the group disdained clapping.

71. Dec. 28, 1994.

When people clapped to the beat at a Berkeley concert and Nassim wanted to begin his solo he looked at the audience—the only time during the entire evening that I noticed him acknowledge their presence—and arched an eyebrow in disdain. This brought almost immediate silence, demonstrating that the audience was highly attentive but simply did not know the appropriate conventions. This is one of the dangers in staking out new musical territory. When Avshalom tried to convince the other members of Bustan Abraham that they needed to play more pieces that were as easily assimilated by listeners as "Tini Mini Hanem," he warned the band that promoters were saying their music was too serious. The audience, he claimed, needed something lighter to leaven the preponderance of rhythmically, melodically, and texturally complex pieces.

"Sireen" by Taiseer Elias was just such a piece, first offered to the group at the very rehearsal where Avshalom argued with other members of the band over the need to please the crowd. In the published recording of "Sireen," Miguel starts with a line that would not be out of place in a Bach invention, the banjo sounding almost like a harpsichord. But as he accelerates the mood changes and he is replaced by Taiseer's rapid-fire, highly percussive 'ud. The other musicians then enter in a flurry, the bass playing a line that flings the piece into the orbit of hoedowns and polkas. In a call and response section, Taiseer bends blue notes while in the next short solo Miguel comes to the fore again, this time plucking bluegrass banjo rolls. Next up Emmanuel is featured playing a descending bass line to which Taiseer adds ascending counterpoint while Miguel continues to roll out a background. The contrapuntal lines move inexorably to the tonic where Nassim and Amir await with trilled V-I cadences taken straight from eighteenth-century common practice (European, that is). All of these changes follow in quick succession during the first minute of this brief piece (which lasts 2'39" on the CD). Supporting this tapestry, Zohar lays down a subtle but persistent beat on shakers that wafts "Latin"-ness through the air. This is picked up by Amir in a brief solo more reminiscent of Cuban flute than anything Middle Eastern or European. The piece continues at a dizzying pace of exchange between the members of the ensemble and ends with a play on minor and major versions of the third degree of the scale, yet another reference to blues-based Americana. It offered a highly varied representation of the band's resources in a rhythmically straightforward manner that allowed people to engage through clapping while thrilling to the speed and brilliance of execution.

Musical Competence as a Perspective on Hybridity

"Sireen" is probably the most pastiche-like piece in the Bustan oeuvre, a piece of showmanship saved from chaos and kitsch only by shared virtuosity and the rondolike recurrence of the theme. In most respects—other than that virtuosity and tight ensemble coordination—it was not a particularly good representation of the band's artistic aspirations. But its accessibility and stylistic patchwork accentuated, perhaps unintentionally, the complex synthesis more typical of the band's work.

This brings us back to the very nature of fusion or musical mixing. How might we best understand the mixing and melding of musical practices exemplified in the works of Alei Hazayit, Yair Dalal, and Bustan Abraham? Are synthesis and pastiche two ends of a spectrum? At what point does a combination of elements from disparate sources become a style in its own right, the sources receding from dominance? I have argued that Bustan Abraham achieved significant integration of disparate resources into a musical means of expression—what they called a language—that was both original enough and sufficiently describable to be instantly recognized as stemming from this band, yet affording scope for considerable diversity from one piece to the next. But I have also demonstrated that stark stylistic contrasts could be juxtaposed in a single piece.

Pastiche has a long and generally negative history in European arts.[72] Though its usage varies considerably, the term generally denotes a mixture of sources and a lack of authorial integrity, either because the work was created by multiple authors or because it draws on multiple authors, flouting, in either case, a fundamental assumption of Romantic notions of art—the primacy of a single creative genius. But collective authorship, as we have seen, is common in the ethnic music scene in Israel, and does not appear to be disdained despite the persistence of other Romantic ideals. Frederic Jameson criticized pastiche for its attenuation or severing of links to sources, to history, to older idioms of expression. Ingrid Monson makes two points about pastiche that are relevant to my argument when she critiques Jameson's statement that pastiche is "heaps of fragments" characterized by "waning historicity." Monson faults him for failing to distinguish "between amalgams of incongruous elements and the network of social interactions, which they may or may not set off" and points to his failure to distinguish between "unsynthesized collections of borrowed elements which lose their historical referentiality, and those which do synthesize, develop a social base, and become themselves models for borrowing and reinterpretation."[73] She implies that the requirements for authenticity include maintaining historical referentiality, developing a social base, and creating or becoming a model that is borrowed by others. Bustan Abraham and Yair Dalal answer these requirements, though in somewhat different ways. They have a sense of historicity, not randomly plucking bits and pieces from here and there, shorn of all roots and relations. And they have become models for others, both through direct teaching and through more indirect emulation.

A negative example will serve to highlight the degree of integration achieved by these musicians in their development of new forms of musical expression. In 2005, Dalal gave a solo concert at Ashkenaz, a folk club in Berkeley that caters particularly to dance music ranging in "flavor" from

72. See, for instance, Price's entry on *pasticcio* in *Grove Music Online*.
73. Monson 1999: 59; see also Erlmann 1996a: 483.

Afrobeat to Appalachian clogging by way of Reggae, Cajun, and Balkan dance music. He invited three local "world music" performers to join him on stage for a rendition of his composition "Al Ol." He had rehearsed briefly with the drummer, who accompanied him in other parts of the concert, but the didjeridu and soprano saxophone players had not rehearsed with them and may never have heard the composition prior to the concert. The group succeeded in establishing a driving groove before Dalal began the melody but their efforts were otherwise solipsistic, indicating, by way of contrast, how successful Dalal has been with his regular partners—the band Al Ol, the Azazme Bedouin, or duos or trios with drummers like Avi Agababa, Asaf Zamir, or Erez Mounk—at integrating disparate sound worlds, melding instrumental idioms and approaches to melody making.

Even if we discount such unprepared improvisations, it is evident that there are different styles of fusion, some more integrative and others more like a montage (or pastiche). That such distinctions are not necessarily simple or straightforward emerges from the typology proposed by Georgina Born and David Hesmondhalgh. In an essay that is otherwise a model of clarity, they propose distinctions between pastiche, parody, juxtaposition, and montage but fail to disentangle these categories satisfactorily (2000: 39–40). Far more useful is their proposal of "intermusical representations figured intramusically" as a third type of signification to add to the widely accepted binary distinction between asemantic and semantic significations (2000: 41). I would argue that much of the music produced by Bustan Abraham consists of elements well enough synthesized to be heard as an integrated musical style, but that certain moments—or, in the case of "Sireen," entire pieces—stand out because they reference other widely known musical styles. Passages such as Miguel's introduction to "Tini Mini Hanem," discussed above, are "intermusical representations" of various styles of music likely to be recognized as such by many in the audience. As in Born and Hesmondhalgh's examples, these disparate styles of musical expression are juxtaposed and thus create "perspectival distance, fragmentation, and relativism between each musical object alluded to" (2000: 40). In Dalal's work with Al Ol, the integration is not always as complete as in Bustan Abraham's music—the Indian, Turkish, and Arab elements more often retaining something of their source identities rather than merging into a new musical language. Nonetheless, Dalal and associates have also crafted their own characteristic form of expression.

These new means of expression are a bricolage, cobbled together from bits of various preexisting practices. Using this term to interpret Paul Simon's work with Ladysmith Black Mambazo on the much-critiqued *Graceland* album, Veit Erlmann argues that bricolage "cannot recapture the experience of a local world, firmly framed by the clear-cut binary relation between signifier and signified" (1994: 179). But I would argue that for Bustan Abraham and others, bricolage may actually capture the local quite well because of the mosaiclike nature of musical practices in Israel (see chapter 12). Long-established local musics are strongly associated with one segment of society or another but not with society as a whole, while bricolage assembles bits and pieces from various groups. This is part of the appeal of ethnic music in Israel: its potential to reach many "sectors" of Israeli society—especially including Western and Middle Eastern orientations —without indexing one in particular, which might put off people from other social groups.

Analyzing the power relations at work in the culture contact that produced *Graceland,* Erlmann maintains that First World hegemony persists and the album represents "a global soundscape in which the boundaries between the symbols, perspectives and interpretations of culturally distinct spheres have become almost seamlessly enmeshed with each other to produce a post-modern space littered with semiotic debris without any referent to authenticity" (1994: 179).[74] Apt as it may be for *Graceland,* this characterization hardly applies to Bustan Abraham's work or to most of Dalal's. For an analogous example we can turn to the album *Seven Times Seven,* by Oliver Shanti (1998), a project that incorporates tracks recorded in isolation by Dalal, Eyal Sela, and Amal Murkus (among many others) into a postmodern collage that does indeed appear to "lack any referent to authenticity." This rootless assemblage stands in sharp contrast to the success of Dalal, Bustan Abraham, or Alei Hazayit in creating the sense of a local world, "reflecting" and perhaps shaping the cosmopolitan reality of contemporary Israel, with its plethora of cultural resources, affiliations, and tastes.

Scholars trying to come to terms with hybridity have deployed two other concepts, transculturation and creolization. Fernando Ortiz proposed transculturation to denote the convergence and mutual influence of European and African culture he discerned in Cuba (1995 [1940]). Convergence and mutual influence are easy to find in ethnic music in Israel, in the mixing of Middle Eastern musical practices with ideas from Europe, America, and South Asia. But the encounters in Israel are demographically and culturally far more complex, as I showed in previous chapters, than the stark binary opposition between two peoples with two radically different cultures that Ortiz analyzed. Creolization is also a less than satisfying match for the situation at hand. The subjects of this study are not as marginal as those studied by Ulf Hannerz in his seminal application of that concept (1987). Despite the undeniable existence of striking power imbalances in Israel, the role of the subaltern, whose identities and cultural practices have been described in terms of creolization, applies to few of those involved in the ethnic music scene. The sociocultural terrain in which Israeli ethnic music arose goes far beyond underlying Jew/Arab or Israeli/Palestinian binaries (see chapter 3). Unlike the European/African cultural binary central to the theories of Ortiz and Hannerz, the diverse musical traditions accessed by musicians such as Bustan Abraham do not map onto prevalent sociopolitical divisions in straightforward, mutually exclusive ways. The lack of clear homologies between the relevant musical practices and social groups

74. This analysis is reiterated in Erlmann 1996b: 309-312.

defined by ethnicity, language, class, or religion complicates the socio-political interpretation of these musical mixtures.

Musical competence offers an important perspective for understanding what is involved in these particular mixtures and what their impact might be. It affords a basis for differentiating the ethnic music scene, in general, and the subjects of this book, in particular, from the earlier Israeli attempts at mixing East and West (surveyed above) and from much of what is marketed as world music. Rather than touching on the exotic now and then (though some of them undoubtedly do that, too) the musicians in this scene have engaged deeply with differing types of musical competence and developed new forms of competence suited to handling the demands of particular syntheses that they have created. To conclude this chapter, I draw several conclusions regarding musical competence from the examples analyzed above and discuss the emergence of new forms of competence.

The root competences of the musicians involved—their musical "first languages"—matter a great deal. Bustan Abraham gained extensive resources and integrity from the diverse root competences of its members. Their exploitation of areas of compatibility between different musical practices enabled them to create smooth transitions as well as stark juxtapositions. Miguel's banjo introduction to "Tini Mini Hanem" and his composition "In the House of Maimonides" exemplify this. So does the interplay between musicians in "Adon Haslichot" by Yair Dalal and Al Ol. Multiple competences are assets, to be deployed according to the needs of the moment. This is apparent in Nassim's comments on different approaches to violin playing: "For instance, Miguel brings things that are Western. We [Nassim and Taiseer] played Western music so we fit in quickly and I—or Taiseer—I know immediately what sound he wants on the violin . . . when I should give the Oriental sound and when I should play the Western sound—I've got both of them."[75] Speaking about "Nedunya," by Naor Carmi, Nassim called it "a really beautiful piece. I play a solo there—in fact a thoroughly Arab solo." When I asked whether Naor wrote the solo, Nassim responded that it was his own, reiterating that it was "a completely Arab solo without any influence of another music." When I commented that that was rare in the opus of Bustan Nassim, he answered, "Yes, usually we try to combine [leshalev] but there I felt that I have to play really 'orientale'," inserting the French equivalent for "Eastern" into our conversation in Hebrew. This exchange, similarly to those I had with other members of the band,[76] shows that the multiple competences were often managed with conscious decisions rather than intuitively. This band maintained conscious control over the minutiae of its stylistic choices.

By exploring overlaps and meeting points in the area of modes, instrumental techniques and timbres, rhythmic organization and feel or groove —what Jason Toynbee has termed "cross-cultural reusability" (2000: 168)—

75. July 16, 1999.
76. E.g., Nassim told me that on "Gypsy Soul" his solo is in Gypsy style. One can hear that he played with far more portamento.

the musicians of Bustan Abraham and Al Ol have laid the groundwork for new types of musical competence. The solutions that they discovered early in their explorations came to be part of their stock in trade, an emergent competence. This is especially true of Bustan Abraham, not only because it rehearsed and performed together over a longer period, but because it was as close to a perfect democracy as possible rather than representing the dominant influence of a single composer and leader who calls on others to make their contributions to his project. On the other hand, Dalal's projects with Al Ol tend to have a more unified sound precisely because most of them are guided by one mind rather than seven (as in Bustan). The success of both bands in finding listeners in Israel and abroad indicates that performers' new competences are forming new audience tastes and, perhaps, expectations or ways of listening.

The fluency with which Bustan Abraham exploited overlaps between established musical styles supports their claim for forging a new musical language. For example, Taiseer Elias made frequent use of the flatted fifth and third degrees of the scale in his improvisations, pointing toward a blues idiom. In many cases it was not the pitch alone that stood out, but the emphasis that Taiseer gave it through articulation, dynamics, and repetition. Sometimes he played these as "bent" notes in contexts that unequivocally evoked a blues sound, while at other times his sound was closer to an Arab modal aesthetic—*maqam shuri*, for instance, has a flatted fifth degree while the raised fourth degree is characteristic of *maqam nakriz*, among others. Taiseer's improvisation in "Suite for Deizy" displays the polysemy that can arise at such moments of heightened intensity (🔊 audio track 10).[77] The ensemble melody preceding his solo uses the scale A B C D-sharp E F-sharp G, the core of *maqam nakriz* transposed from C to A. Taiseer takes these notes and works them hard in various combinations. After exploring the characteristics of the *nawa athar* pentachord on A (A B C D-sharp E) and a *hijaz* tetrachord on E (E F G-sharp A), he reinterprets the D-sharp as an E-flat, the flat fifth, which allows him to explore a bridge to a blues modality. This double interpretation is emphasized by interaction with Nassim, who responds on violin in Arab style, and then with Miguel's blues guitar interjection. Taiseer's motivic manipulation at the beginning of the solo is quite different from a typical Arab *taqasim*. This becomes apparent later in the solo—the precise moment differs in the three performances I have compared—when he switches to a *taqasim*-like cascade of modal invention, moving from one *maqam* to another and finally to a conventional Arab cadence (*qaflah*). Such skillful melding of musical sources can be found in the playing and composition of other members of Bustan Abraham, demonstrating the scope of the musicians' capabilities and interests as well as their spirit of experimentation. In Alei Hazayit, Omar Keinani approached such fluency, but other instrumentalists in his band did not, continuing to stay close to the conventions of Arab music.

77. See also chapter 10.

While other Israeli bands, such as Al Ol, Darma, Sheva, and Essev Bar, often achieve variety within and between pieces by exploiting their abilities as multiinstrumentalists, most members of Bustan Abraham focused their energies on stretching the limits of conventional techniques and playing idioms associated with their main instruments.[78] Much of the band's innovation in this area began by emulating sounds, techniques, and instruments they encountered in other musical practices. Miguel wrote me that he has been emulating other instruments on his guitar and then on the banjo since childhood.[79] He described the process and the motivations eloquently:

> While attempting to create such a varied palette of sounds from which to draw it became clear that traditional banjo techniques were sometimes inadequate. After much experimentation I discovered various combinations of picks, fingernails (both sides), skin (at numerous points on fingers and thumb—and even knuckles!) coupled with different left-hand techniques. This variety provided opportunities to include the banjo in a number of pieces where it might not have otherwise contributed.

The casual listener may not notice when Miguel borrows 'ud techniques of elaboration, transformed by the tone of the guitar, in the solo that introduces "In the House of Maimonides." This is but a moment in a long history of interaction between players of guitar and 'ud. Miguel has been interested in such mutual influences throughout his career. When I asked him what he played as a solo guitarist opening for Laura Nyro on a U.S. concert tour in the 1970s, he said

> Not exactly flamenco—my own stuff which was a little of everything basically, like I do now. Because I was into Indian music, also American Indian music and also flamenco and also I knew a little bit about Arab music. . . . I liked 'ud. It wasn't easy to get that kind of music in those days. But I found a record by somebody named Berberian, an Armenian player who played 'ud and I really liked it . . . the stuff that I was composing used elements from various things (interview, January 2002).

This experience and his fundamental openness to different musical practices and to experimentation served him well when he participated in the formation of Habreira Hativ'it with Shlomo Bar in 1977, White Bird with Taiseer Elias in 1987, and Bustan Abraham in 1991.

---

78. The exceptions to this generalization are Miguel Herstein, who played banjo and guitar, and Zohar Fresco, who amassed a varied collection of drums, shakers, bells, and cymbals, and developed techniques for playing several at once. He has been highly influential in the Israeli ethnic music scene in this regard.

79. June, 2004.

Other members of the ensemble experimented with their own instruments, too, although not necessarily as extensively as Miguel. In his solos Amir came to employ a wide range of flute timbres, moving away from the "sweet" and "cool jazz" sounds of the early recordings to an array of edgier, more percussive sounds. He enriched his timbral palette with flutter tonguing, humming, attacks which range from strong to violent, simultaneous octaves and hints of other multiphonics.[80] Taiseer combined a highly percussive approach to the 'ud with dramatic leaps and slides into and away from notes, and a variety of unconventional ornaments to create a personal style that is instantly recognizable and well integrated, yet bears traces of Indian *sarod* and American blues guitar. Emmanuel also developed a highly individual, easily recognized composite approach to the bass. He crafted his parts from a judicious mix of doubling the melody, holding a drone or chord root, and contrapuntal lines. He could maintain the rhythmic groove, leaving Zohar free to improvise more complex rhythms, or he could hold back and emphasize only the downbeat. This flexibility suited the band well. They had rejected the first bass player they auditioned because his jazz orientation was too strong.[81] When Naor Carmi came in as the group's last bassist, he had already learned Emmanuel's parts from the band's recordings, but he brought an individual "voice" to the ensemble, usually playing double bass rather than electric bass and exhibiting a sensibility formed by his extensive study and performance of Arab music. In this progression of three bassists there is a subtle shift in orientation from "West" to "East."

The competence that the members of the band developed owes much to their prolonged interaction with one another. Despite mutual criticisms and different strengths and weakness associated with particular types of music, they all developed a common understanding and the ability, built up over years of shared experience, to know where a solo was heading, when to respond to the soloist or support him in some other way, exactly what the next groove was going to feel like, and so on. The development of common understandings did not mean a homogenizing of individual differences. These were maintained and exploited selectively in the band's arrangements.

Countering the integrative tendencies of an emergent competence, certain aspects of a given musical practice may exert a force akin to a gravitational pull, enhancing the notion of dominance suggested at the beginning of this chapter. Musicians may be willing to forsake those aspects altogether in certain pieces, but if a piece sounds close enough to a familiar model it will be drawn into the orbit of that model and expected to conform. Carmi's "Nedunya" is composed in a scale based on C in which E half-flat, *sikah* in Arab music theory, is a prominent pitch. But musicians

80. There is a taste of this in "Metamorphosis" on Bustan Abraham's first recording, but it becomes much more prevalent and varied in later recordings.
81. Amir Milstein, Jan. 15, 1997.

who are fully competent in Arab music distinguish three slightly different intonations of that note. Nassim recounted the following genesis story:

In Naor's piece he wrote it in *[maqam] sikah* and *[maqam] rast*. Now I'll tell you what happened at the last rehearsal. On the *qanun*, there's the quartertone, the E half-flat, and there are the levers that can raise or lower it one eighth [tone].[82] And it remains a quarter tone, you still call it that, but it's not the same thing. The quartertone in *sikah* is not like in *rast* and not like in *bayyati*. Taiseer and I know immediately how the E [half-flat] is supposed to sound. What Naor plays is a bit low, Avshalom is a bit high. Naor says he wants it one way and we argue, tell him that it's not correct. He says "no, it's pretty." For us it sounds out of tune in the modal framework. . . . So Taiseer and I immediately . . . put the finger down [on the neck of the violin or *'ud*] according to your feeling and it's in the right place. So I said, "Naor, listen, you gave the piece, but in this matter trust us. This is what's right. Both Eastern and Western ears will be able to hear it. A Western ear will hear that it's a bit higher or lower, but the Eastern ear will immediately say— that's not correct, it's out of tune.

BB: So did he accept that?

Yes. And that's the piece that he wrote! He hears that he wants a quarter tone there, but not our quarter tone that we hear.[83]

A complex interplay of authority and ownership informs this account. Because "Nedunya" bears most of the characteristics of two Arab *maqamat* (*rast* and *sikah*) Nassim assumes that it is *in* those two modes and must therefore be played with the appropriate intonation. The possibility that Naor, the composer, could want something different was not valid once he entered the domain of *maqam*. He must surrender to the authority of the *maqam* system, a core concept of Arab music that is not open to negotiation even though Nassim is fully willing to mix and match many other musical characteristics and to play pieces that are not based on a *maqam*. In a sense Nassim is complimenting the composer, implying that Naor succeeded in creating a piece so convincingly *maqam*-based that the authorities on *maqam* within the band insist that it conform to *maqam* practice.

Aspects of one musical practice may actually hinder acquisition of another. Amir felt that it was difficult to communicate the nuances of a sense of swing to the members of Bustan Abraham who were steeped in Middle Eastern music because they were so accustomed to hearing a heavy drum stroke on the downbeat.[84] I had encountered an analogous problem

---

82. The actual microtonal intervals available to the player depend on the setup of the instrument.

83. July 16, 1999.

84. Analogous examples with regard to chordal harmony are not hard to find.

years earlier when I taught several Israeli Arab musicians to play Javanese gamelan. They commented on the disorientation they felt when the low strokes on the Javanese drum did not coincide with the main melodic accents. This is not a question of root competences that must either be acquired through enculturation from an early age or not at all. Numerous musicians have demonstrated, particularly in the past few decades, the ability and dedication necessary to excel at making music that differs radically from their root competence. However, Amir's comment regarding swing points to a conflict between core conceptual and perceptual aspects of two musical practices that requires some form of accommodation. That Bustan Abraham rose above such conflicts demonstrates that musicians can collaborate without gaining full competence in the same musical practices. The key is to find compatibilities that enable interaction.

In addition to learning new ways of making music individually, these musicians modified prior models of interaction in order to work together. They did not play like an Arab *takht*, a rock band, a jazz combo, or a Western chamber ensemble. They combined elements of the ensemble workings of all of these and more, developing new solutions to the new problems they created with their particular confluences of diverse musical discourses. If Middle Eastern musical practices appear to enjoy a certain pride of place, improvisation within composed frameworks is a defining component of this ethnic fusion, although it is certainly not limited to improvisation of the sort commonly practiced in the Middle East. And the innovation in interaction is nowhere more apparent than in the relationships constructed among musicians in the course of improvisation. This is the subject of the next chapter.

10

Bustan Abraham's Approaches to
Composition and Improvisation

𝕿he repertoires performed by Alei Hazayit, Bustan Abraham, and Yair
Dalal differed with regard to the length and structural complexity of
the pieces and the relative weight accorded to composition and improvisation. These differences relate directly to each ensemble's division of labor,
attitudes toward innovation, and expectations about audience reception.
Underlying this variety are shared musical resources, the integration of
improvisation into every piece, a common preference for collaboration in
composition and arrangement, and the fuzziness of the boundaries that
demarcate the domains of composition, improvisation, and arrangement.

Given the prevalence of this type of creative terrain in many of the
world's musical practices today—including much of the world music scene,
but also various other popular musics and even, I suspect, an increasing
portion of the new music produced by and for art/serious/elite contexts—
the relationships among the domains of composition, arrangement, and improvisation deserve more attention. The analysis of Bustan's work offered
in this chapter is organized around those relationships. Based on their
recordings, but informed by observation of performances and conversations with band members, I begin with general remarks on approaches to
composition and arrangement, then focus on how the compositions and
arrangements enabled improvisation. This leads to analysis of featured improvisations in relationship to their ensemble contexts.

Composition and Arrangement

Bustan Abraham's compositions were notable for their number, extent, variety, and quality. By the time they disbanded in 2003 they had issued five
recordings and a compilation, comprising thirty-eight distinct pieces of
which twenty-seven were original compositions by band members, six were
by other composers, and five were traditional tunes arranged by the band

TITLE	NC	ND	TE	AF	ZF	MH	EM	AM	YS
Abadai								X	
Black Seagull				X					
Bustan*				X					
Canaan				X					X
Dub Dulab		X							
Fanar			X						
Fountainhead						X			
Gypsy Soul							X		
Hamsa			X						
Hamsin								X	
In the House of Maimonides						X			
In the Name of the Children						X			
Jazz Kar-Kurd			X						
Journey						X			
Mabruk			X						
Metamorphosis			X						
Nedunya	X								
Pictures through the Painted Window				X					
Pinar					X				
Sama'i Kurd		X							
Seven Eleven								X	
Shazeef						X			
Sireen			X						
Solaris							X		
Suite for Deizy									X
The Walls of Jericho						X			
Wallah									X
TOTAL	1	2	6	4	1	6	2	3	3

Figure 10.1 Composition credits in Bustan Abraham's repertoire. Key: TE = Taiseer Elias; AF -= Avshalom Farjun; YS = Yehuda Siliki; MH = Miguel Herstein; AM = Amir Milstein; NC = Naor Carmi; ZF = Zohar Fresco; EM = Emmanuel Mann; ND = Nassim Dakwar; * = with Shimon Ben Shitrit

(see figure 10.1).[1] Taiseer Elias and Miguel Herstein contributed the most compositions to the repertoire that emerged from the band's tough, selection process.[2] Each of the others, with the exception of the drummer, Zohar Fresco, contributed several compositions.

1. *Live Recordings,* issued in 2003 after the band's demise, contained another ten tracks, eight of which had appeared on earlier albums.
2. In concert the band tended to play everything on their CDs. Although pieces recorded with guest artists were unlikely to be played without those guests, I did hear "Fanar" once without the Indian solosits for whom Elias had

To put this achievement in perspective, compare it to the output of two other groups in the field of ethnic music that specialized in instrumental music. Over a similar time span (1988–1998) the East-West Ensemble recorded three albums on which fourteen pieces were credited to the leader, Yisrael Borochov (including one shared credit with Amir Shahsar), while five were composed by musicians not in the group (including Peter Gabriel and two leading mid-twentieth-century Arab composers).[3] None were credited to other members of the band, which changed personnel from one album to the next.[4] Between 1995 and 2003, Yair Dalal led or contributed substantially to nine albums, which included twenty-eight pieces credited solely to him, four joint compositions, and three joint arrangements. As with Borochov's East-West Ensemble, no pieces were credited solely to any member of the band other than the leader. The contrast between Bustan's varied composer roster and the auteur model espoused by Shlomo Bar in Habreira Hativ'it and perpetuated by Borochov and Dalal is striking.

The attribution of Bustan's original pieces to individual composers belies the extensive group involvement in the shaping of many of these pieces. Modification and arrangement through group debate were the norm. Some compositions were rejected and most underwent substantial revision, particularly in the early years when the band rehearsed several times a week for many hours at a time. Nassim Dakwar commented on what I had heard from other band members about group involvement:

> Some bring a finished piece, some don't. And sometimes someone brings a finished piece but the others don't agree. For instance, there's a new piece by X. He brought a piece that's three pages long. We played half a page and said that's enough, we don't need all the rest. And we arranged it here and there and a piece emerged from that. So it varies. Sometimes someone brings one line and we develop and make it into a big piece. (July 16, 1999)

By their last album this practice had abated as members brought finished products to the relatively infrequent rehearsals. To some extent this was due to their busier schedules, but the years of intensive group editing and arranging contributed to the formation of a common language and must have helped each individual to create pieces better suited to the strengths and preferences of the band.

This emphasis on collective production contributed to the stability of the band's membership, and therefore to its success. It gave members a larger stake in the repertoire and allowed a great variety of approaches from different authorial voices while ensuring integration through the inclusion

---

composed it. I never heard Bustan play a piece in concert that did not appear on one of their CDs.

3. These were Farid al-Atrache and Muhammad al-Qasabji.

4. Besides Borochov only one other musician played on all three disks and only two others played on two disks.

of other views. Nassim noted that "everyone intervenes, everyone gives his own opinion."[5] Amir's recollection of the development of Avshalom's composition "Bustan" seems to typify their process. Avshalom had wanted everyone to play the melody so that it would be strong, but Amir suggested a background that would strengthen the melody.[6] On the recording one can hear a sophisticated, shifting orchestration, particularly in the middle section (● audio track 9).

Based on such statements and similar evidence, we can conclude that the boundaries between composition and arrangement were fuzzy for this band. The general outline of the piece with its specific progressions (rhythmic, melodic, and so on) constituted the composition while some of the details of who played what were matters of arrangement (or orchestration) that might enhance the piece but not alter its basic identity. On the two occasions that I heard Bustan perform without Miguel, they adapted to his absence by adjusting each piece, either by dividing his part among the others or by omitting it. This produced different arrangements, but essentially the same compositions.

The band quickly fulfilled Avshalom's vision of a superstar ensemble through complex compositions that balanced the display of individual virtuosity with tightly coordinated and highly responsive ensemble playing. The complexity of their music gained them loyal fans and glowing reviews, but probably limited their popularity. Failure to achieve major success led Avshalom to try various strategies for producing and marketing recordings (see chapter 5 and chapter 8), which affected composition in various ways. When renowned Indian musicians were to perform with the band, for instance, Taiseer composed "Fanar" as a framework for this interaction. Most relevant for the present discussion, however, is the debate within the band over Avshalom Farjun's pressure to create lighter music (see chapter 5). In response to booking agents' claims that the band had a reputation for playing music that was too serious, Avshalom wanted to add more pieces like "Tini Mini Hanem," the band's standard encore. This is when Taiseer introduced "Sireen," which was well suited to that role. When I asked Nassim about this a few years later he said, "We can have one or two light pieces, but on a [high] level," agreeing with me that "Sireen" fulfilled that requirement and adding "and the new piece by Miguel is also light and beautiful. But we won't turn Bustan into a band of light music that you can dance to."[7] He did not mention his own "Dub Dulab," which fits this category, too. Despite the opposition to "lightening" their repertoire, the musicians were probably happy to have these new pieces as substitutes for "Tini Mini Hanem," which they had played for years at almost every concert.

The band members also resolutely opposed accompanying vocalists, recording only two songs. When they appeared on a variety show on Israeli

5. July 16, 1999.
6. Jan. 3, 1997.
7. July 16, 1999.

television[8] the host asked, "Why aren't there singers?" Taiseer replied, "We've performed with Achinoam Nini. . . . We love all the singers but prefer to make good instrumental music, which is too rare in Israel and the world." The host insisted that he wanted to have them back again on the show with singers, "just a one-time thing. Do you all agree?" The band's silence was eloquent. According to Amir they could afford to maintain these standards because they no longer had to rely on Bustan for their main income.[9] Similarly, Miguel said that they could reserve Bustan for playing what they really wanted—challenging, sophisticated music.[10] Nassim summed this up, "In a lot of pieces there's complexity in the rhythm and the structure of the pieces. We devote a lot of time and a lot of thought to constructing the pieces: how a piece will develop, where we want a piece to go."[11] Complexity was cited repeatedly in commentary on the music by critics and musicians.

Rhythmic complexity: The band seemed to revel in rhythmic complexity. They generated tremendous drive and excitement in many ways, ranging from Zohar's powerful drumming on a battery of hand percussion through the percussiveness of Taiseer's 'ud and Amir's flute to the precision of fast ensemble passages. Counterrhythms complicated the rhythmic texture in composed and improvised sections. Some of the rhythmic complexity derived from the musical resources themselves, such as asymmetrical meters, and some from the way that the musicians combined those resources, both in simultaneous textures and in forms that were often considerably more complex than the music of other bands at home and on the international world music circuit. While others in the ethnic music scene, such as Eyal Sela, incorporated Balkan additive meters, sophisticated metric schemes set many of Bustan's compositions apart from the rest.

They were inspired by, but not limited to, the traditional resources they brought to the band. Nassim said, "we try not to play conventional things or rhythms that are common in Middle Eastern music." He noted that for "Sama'i Kurd," which he composed in a traditional Turkish/Arab form, he felt he had no choice but to use the conventional ten-beat pattern associated with that form, "but we try as much as possible to create new things, new rhythms in Bustan. So that it will be interesting . . . all the time we're searching."[12] He innovated by omitting the drummer from most of that piece, so that the meter was implicit in the melody. When Zohar entered for the contrasting final section, Nassim had him play a seven-beat pattern rather than the triple or compound meter most common for that section.[13]

8. *Reakh Menta*, taped in December 1998 and broadcast July 1, 1999.
9. Jan. 15, 1997.
10. Jan. 6, 2002.
11. July 16, 1999.
12. July 16, 1999.
13. Nassim said that the drum pattern differed from the seven-beat pattern played for some *sama'i* compositions. Several nineteenth-century Turkish *semais* use a seven-beat meter according to Eliot Bates, personal communication.

Figure 10.2   Ostinato from "Fanar" by Taiseer Elias

Taiseer's "Fanar" uses additive meters so complex and rapidly shifting that when I showed him my transcription he was not sure whether it was correct. "Rhythmically I thought about syncopations. I didn't think about metric patterns and making it complex," he explained, "and after I thought of [Fanar] it came out in all sorts of meters."[14] The beginning of the piece can be represented as 16/8 divided into 9+7, followed by a section in 14/8, that is internally divided into 6 and 8. Other complications arise later in the piece. It ends, for instance, with alternation between a pair of measures sub-divided 4+3+9 (the 9 sometimes a rest and sometimes filled with a scalar run that implies 2+2+2+3) and a single measure subdivided 3+3+3+3+4. Much of the time Taiseer's syncopations do seem to be a more important organizing principle than any underlying metrical scheme. In some sections, however, the bass player sustains a rhythmic groove over a considerable span as support for improvisation by soloists.[15] Yet here, too, the composer complicates the rhythmic organization by layering conflicting additive rhythms (see figure 10.2, 🔊 audio track 11).

Taiseer's "Metamorphosis" (🔊 audio track 7) moves through a series of meters and tempi (see figure 10.3 and chapter 9). Early in the piece a metrical modulation leads from the first theme to the second. The tempo is increased by roughly 4/3 so that the new measure of four beats is equal in length to the old measure of three. Toward the end of the piece this process is reversed as the musicians move from the second theme back to the first. But Taiseer combines this cyclical return with a linear tempo progression. While the musicians work their way back to the point of origin, completing the arch form of the piece, the tempo is considerably faster when the second and first themes return.

14. June 28, 1998.

15. Here and elsewhere I use the word *solo* as it is used in jazz discourse to indicate the featured player whether or not other musicians are playing less fore-grounded roles.

Time	Meter	bpm	Section
0:00–1:24	3	138	introduction and first theme
1:25–3:56	4	170	second theme, 'ud solo
3:57–4:01	seven groups of 2		transition
4:02–8:39	4+3	196	four solos (on 'ud, flute, drums, bass) over ostinato played on drums and bass
8:40–9:13	4	210	transition and second theme
9:14–10:02	3	152	first theme

Figure 10.3 Meter and tempo changes in "Metamorphosis" by Taiseer Elias

Figure 10.4   Metrical modulation in "Hamsa" by Taiseer Elias

In "Hamsa" the shift in meter is accomplished by a metrical modulation that reinterprets both the beat and the grouping of the beat. The first theme is based on the traditional ten-beat Turkish/Arab *sama'i thaqil* drum cycle[16] (figure 10.4, audio track 12). After three iterations of the theme, with more instruments added each time, the beat subdivides into triplets during a brief transition. These subdivisions then become the new beat, which effectively triples the tempo to an extremely rapid 338 bpm.[17] But not everything triples because the note values of the first theme are doubled in relation to the beat. Note that while the theme looks virtually the same, the beat has changed from a quarter note to an eighth note and the melody now flows over the metrical framework and accompaniment in a different manner. Rather than reverse this metrical modulation at the end of his flute solo, Amir joins the other members of the ensemble in emphasizing the *sama'i* rhythm (3+2+2+3) and then countering it with unison accents that go against the grain (see figure 10.5). This brings the piece to a temporary halt before the *qanun* pulls the first theme out of the silence (audio track 13).[18]

16. This is the same cycle transferred to the *tabla* for Al Ol's "Adon Haslichot" (see chapter 9).

17. Since the ensemble also accelerates, this is more than three times as fast as the initial tempo of 101 bpm.

18. Note a metrical modulation of a different sort in Emmanuel Mann's "Gypsy Soul." In the four-beat meter of the opening section the Emmanue

Figure 10.5   Rhythmic break in "Hamsa" by Taiseer Elias

A barrage of metrical complexities features at the climax of Em-manuel's "Solaris." In a rapid-fire exchange between flute and *'ud,* Amir and Taiseer play sixteenth-note runs in 4/4 against the ensemble's 6/8. Cross-rhythmic groupings complicate this further and the melody is treated somewhat like a Hindustani *tihai* (cadential phrase), which is played three times to resolve on the downbeat. This leads back to the original theme in 6/8, which undergoes further rhythmic variations (see figure 10.6, ◐ audio track 14). Such pyrotechnics tended to enthrall the audience at the con-certs I attended and the abrupt ending, perfectly coordinated, was an au-tomatic trigger for applause.

A far more relaxed but no less complex layering of conflicting rhythms is integral to the basic structure of Amir's "Hamsin." Considerable syncopa-tion in the melody and bass line rides over the 3+2 grouping of the five-beat meter in this sophisticated adaptation of a twelve-bar blues. Amir compli-cated this further by composing a passage in 3 against 4 that runs across the bar line for the third phrase of each "chorus" of this blues (see figure 10.7, ◐ audio track 15). Additional examples abound in the band's com-positions, but this should suffice to demonstrate the complications of meter and rhythm that appealed to these musicians at the compositional stage.

Scales and modes: Perhaps Nassim did not include scales or modes when he listed complexities because the Arab *maqam* system that he has mastered is more complex than Bustan's melodic experiments, but for a listener (or performer) coming from a non-Middle Eastern background the melodic resources employed by Bustan's composers exhibit consider-able variety and a strong affinity for scale structures found in Arab music. Alongside major and minor, scales featuring *hijaz* and *kurd* tetrachords pre-vail. The *hijaz* tetrachord is formed by the interval sequence minor second-major third-minor second (e.g., D E-flat F-sharp G or G A-flat B C), while the *kurd* tetrachord comprises the sequence minor second-major second-major second (e.g., D E-flat F G or C D-flat E-flat F).[19] Other aspects of Arab *maqam*s are evident in some pieces, but most composed sections

---

Mann reiterates the tonic in a long-short-long rhythm (4+1+3). This trans-forms into a nine-beat pattern (2+2+2+3) but the long-short-long reiteration of the tonic is still audible, though transformed to 6+1+2 (figure 10.9b, audio track 19).

19. In Arab *maqam* theory *hijaz* and *kurd* also refer to modes built on these tetrachords. See Marcus 1989.

Figure 10.6   Excerpt from "Solaris" by Emmanuel Mann

avoid intervals based on quarter tones because Amir and Miguel would have difficulty matching the pitches on flute, guitar, or banjo. Exceptions to this generalization include Naor Carmi's "Nedunya" (see chapter 9) and the traditional Iraqi melody arranged as "Igrig," which both feature the pitch E half-flat prominently. Amir and Miguel simply sat out those pieces. In other pieces Nassim and Taiseer featured or made passing reference to a wide assortment of Arab modes—including ones that use quarter tones—in solos and briefer interjections. Their arrangement of the widely performed Arab song "Lamma Bada" (which they titled "Muwashshah") exemplifies such compartmentalization, with quarter tones used only for a long interpolation that features Miranda Elias singing to the accompaniment of her husband Taiseer's 'ud after the third verse. Freed from the constraints of

Figure 10.7   Cross-rhythms in "Hamsin" by Amir Milstein

the band, Miranda and Taiseer are able to modulate from *maqam nahawand* (which is congruent with minor and therefore playable on flute and guitar) to *maqam saba*, which uses E half-flat.

Even without quarter tones the band's composers used quite a few scales that differ greatly from major and minor. For example, Avshalom's "Black Seagull" is based on the scale G A-sharp B C D E-flat F-sharp and several accidentals further enrich the tonal resources in the course of the tune.[20] Taiseer's "Fanar" also uses an unusual scale.[21] In "Abadai," which begins with C minor, Amir alternates between a *hijaz* scale on D (D E-flat F-sharp G A) and a *nakriz* type on C (C D E-flat F-sharp G). This pendular motion between the two tonal centers introduces an element of harmonic tension in keeping with the tendency of the composer, Amir, to advocate for harmonic and contrapuntal elements in the band's work.

Harmony: The issue of harmony, like mode, is too complex to address comprehensively here. In many pieces the composers focus on melodic, rhythmic, textural, and timbral elements of composition, avoiding harmonic elements or leaving them in the background. But chords and functional harmony play important roles in a substantial portion of Bustan's repertoire, most explicitly in the works of Miguel and Amir. There are moments in the solo guitar sections of "In the House of Maimonides," for instance, that are just as harmonically conceived as anything in the guitar repertoire. Given the strong influence of flamenco guitar, it is hardly surprising that chordal passages alternate with melodic runs or that dissonant suspended chords (such as D-flat major over C) and a descending progression over a Phrygian bass line (F E-flat D-flat C or A G F E) are a central part of his vocabulary.

During their early collaboration in White Bird, Miguel and Taiseer began working on a practice-based theory of harmonization for *maqam*-based melodies that included quarter tones. Although they never articulated this in print, it was evident in Miguel's use of the guitar that went beyond or sidestepped triadic harmonies. The difficulty of picking out what he is actually playing in some of the more complex ensemble textures is a measure of his success.

20. E.g., A-natural and B-flat in the upper register and E-sharp leading to F-sharp.
21. According to Matt Rahaim, the pitches E F G A-sharp B C D-sharp E are congruent with both Raga Todi and Raga Multani (personal communication). Taiseer told me that an obscure Arab *maqam* also uses this pitch set.

One of the ways in which Nassim broke with convention in composing his "Samaʻi Kurd" was to integrate harmonic and modal thinking in
the framework of the venerated *samaʻi* form. At times this is explicit, with
chords played on the guitar or compiled from the blended notes of other
instruments. At other times it is implicit in the progression of the melody
or the short responses that fill the pauses in the melody. This half-explicit,
half-implicit approach to harmony is evident in other pieces, lending a
subtlety that would be lost if the piece were either harmonized throughout
or played without chords altogether.

Structure: The invention of large musical structures is surely one of
the bigger challenges in forging a new mode of musical expression. Bustan diverged not only from the songs favored by Alei Hazayit, but also from
the majority of pieces by Yair Dalal and other musicians in this scene. While
other bands favored strophic structures, basing a piece on many iterations
of a single tune or other framework, the members of Bustan explored a
wider range of options, by borrowing forms from other musical practices
and inventing various multisectional frameworks.

Amir and Nassim made distinctive additions to the band's repertoire
by modifying existing forms. They followed many of the conventions associated with the form they chose, but integrated elements quite foreign
to the source practice. Amir disguised the twelve-bar blues harmonic progression underlying "Hamsin" by giving it a dissonant bass line based on
the tritone interval and an unusual meter played on frame drum, while integrating Arab melodic influences into the chromatic melody played over
"cool" jazz chords on the guitar.[22] When Taiseer added an *ʻud* improvisation to this, he created an especially striking juxtaposition of musical
styles, not a blend but a mind-tickling clash. In his "Samaʻi Kurd," Nassim
honored most of the conventions associated with the Turkish-Arab *samaʻi*
form, but filled that form with content that linked it convincingly to other
pieces in the Bustan repertoire. Besides employing a richly chromatic
melodic language that implied harmonic progressions, he orchestrated the
piece—probably with contributions from other members of the group—in
a manner atypical for a *samaʻi*.

Most Bustan compositions were invented without such clear precedents and tended to be multisectional.[23] These structures can be described
in terms of the same structural characteristics of repetition, variation, and
contrast that are manifested in forms such as the *samaʻi* or rondo. Compared to other ethnic bands, they tended to apply an unusual degree of invention to varying repetitions through changes in orchestration. Zohar's
colorful use of a broad array of percussion contributed greatly in this regard.
Although a few pieces, such as Miguel's "In the House of Maimonides," are

---

22. He exploits intervallic congruences between the Arab *maqam saba zam-
zama* and scales commonly used for playing blues. This piece is discussed further in the section on improvisation below.

23. Even the strophic blues form of "Hamsin" is offset by a lengthy introductory flute solo.

Time	Meter	bpm	Section
0:00–1:21	4	176	first theme
1:22–2:28	0	0	'ud solo in free rhythm
2:34–4:34	10 (3+3+2+2)	170	qanun initiates an ostinato
4:35–4:46	4		transition
4:47–7:47	10 (3+3+2+2)		ostinato & melody transposed up a fourth
5:35			texture thins, violin solo over ostinato
7:4–8:47	10 (3+3+2+2)	330	'ud restarts ostinato faster, add melody
			8:27 drum break, 8:34 ostinato back to tonic
8:48–9:39	4	170	first theme with rhythmic transformations

Figure 10.8 Meter and tempo changes in "Bustan" by Avshalom Farjun with Shimon Ben Shitrit

through-composed, many more are based on establishing an idea, moving away from it to one or more contrasting ideas and returning in the end to the first idea, as in "Metamorphosis" (figure 10.3). "Bustan" does not involve as many dramatic changes, but it too follows an arch form and involves additive meter as well as a more standard 4/4 (see figure 10.8). Several of the transitions in this piece are abrupt compared to pieces composed later in the band's career. Rather than modulate back to the original key, for instance, they insert a drum break and the melodic instruments simply re-enter in the old key. Over their career these musicians learned how to fashion more sophisticated transitions.

More minimal in composition than either "Metamorphosis" or "Bustan," Nassim's "Dub Dulab" consists of a symmetrical pair of phrases, each lasting four measures of four beats and played three times, with varying orchestration (🌀 audio track 16). The ensemble then switches to a "holding pattern," a short melody repeated until the soloist enters. All of this takes scarcely half a minute. Taiseer's 'ud solo lasts nearly two minutes, accompanied by bass and drum. As he reaches his final cadence, Amir begins a flute solo lasting over one and a half minutes. Amir ends his solo by playing the original theme once, before the others join him to play it twice more. In such a straightforward piece where over three quarters of the material is improvised, the solos matter a great deal and the two solos by Taiseer and Amir are so powerful that we will turn to them shortly.

The theme of "Dub Dulab" is typical of the symmetrical phrasing that seemed to serve as a counterbalance to Bustan's penchant for complex meters and metrical schemes. Much of their repertoire is consturcted from even-numbered groups of phrases of equal duration. Miguel's "Shazeef" exemplifies such symmetry: The main theme consists of two phrases, each four measures long and played twice. As the piece proceeds, however, the apparent symmetry is disrupted in various ways—including insertion of a drum break and extension of a phrase beyond its expected length—that make "Shazeef" more than just a catchy little tune. Miguel changes the melody and mode incrementally, and introduces a modulation, too, before starting a second theme that sets the stage for a solo improvisation. "Shazeef" demonstrates what the members of Bustan were able to do in developing an ostensibly short, simple piece.

Structuring albums and concerts: Considerable variety is also apparent in the internal sequence of Bustan's five studio albums and their concerts. Unlike Dalal's *The Perfume Road*, which was conceived as a single work consisting of six movements, Bustan's recordings were not concept albums, with the possible exception of *Hamsa*, the last album. Its name comes from the Arabic word for five, which also denotes the hand symbol that wards off the evil eye and is a ubiquitous item of ornament in houses and as jewelry. This was the band's fifth album and the number five figures in the title or the composition of several of the works.[24] Recall that Taiseer's piece titled "Hamsa" is based on a meter of 10 or two pairings of 5 (3+2, 2+3) and Amir's "Hamsin" is based on a meter of 5. The title of the piece is also related: *Hamsin* (Arabic for fifty) refers to a particularly hot, dry desert wind that settles on Israel periodically, hence the English subtitle of the piece, "Desert Wind."

More important than any of these numerical connections is the mature sound of the ensemble in each of the pieces. While each of the earlier albums had its odd juxtapositions between and within pieces, *Hamsa* seems to flow in a manner that reflects the ensemble's experience and the coalescence of certain ways of doing things without becoming too formulaic. Miguel's "In the House of Maimonides," which begins and ends with clear Spanish guitar influences, contrasts strongly with his own "Shazeef," that leans toward old-time Appalachian banjo picking. Both pieces contrast with most of the other pieces on the disc. Yet there is greater "crosstalk" between the pieces on this album than on the group's earlier albums. In part this is due to the avoidance of guest artists, in part to the mastery of compositional techniques that integrate the ensemble and utilize its resources to maximum effect, creating optimal frameworks for improvisation.

A tour followed the release of each album, featuring new pieces, but always including older ones, too. Clear tendencies emerge from a comparison of six concerts that took place between 1994 and 2000.[25] "Suite for Deizy" was the opening piece for every concert but the last. There it was replaced by "Mabruk," the opening piece on *Hamsa*, the new album that they were touring. At the end of every concert "Tini Mini Hanem" served as an encore. Avshalom introduced this at the concert described in chapter 1 as the song that the audience does not want them to stop playing and the crowd did indeed go wild, dancing along to the music. At other concerts,

24. The least likely connection I found was the five-fold iteration of the slow melody that serves as a cantus firmus for "Nedunya," the last piece on the album.

25. At four of these concerts I took notes. Taiseer Elias gave me complete recordings of the other two, including applause and announcements.

where dancing was not feasible, the straightforward duple meter of the piece, coming at the end of a concert characterized by complex, odd, and shifting meters, enabled the audience to clap along.

Other perennial favorites included "Canaan" (played in all six concerts), "Fountainhead" (five out of six), and "Jazz Kar-Kurd" and "Longa" (each was played in four of six concerts). Some pieces were played less frequently and several from the first two albums were not played in any of the concerts for which I have data, even though three of those concerts were restricted to music from those albums. The other concerts analyzed took place after the release of four albums, yet pieces from the first two albums continued to constitute at least a third of the program. These choices demonstrate a cumulative attitude toward albums and repertoire. Rather than simply sweeping aside the old pieces, they added new pieces selectively, a good way to please a loyal fan base. Considerable variation in the improvised solos ensured that there was always something new even in the older pieces, such as the ones that served as bookends to the evening.

Framing Improvisation

The considerable improvisatory skills of the members of the group set Bustan apart from many other ensembles just as their compositions did. Each musician was capable of playing long, varied, and convincing solos. Several were truly outstanding, even judged on an international level. Improvisation accounted for a large portion of each performance—some solos lasted as long as four or five minutes—and had tremendous impact on audiences. Jason Stanyek has noted the prevalence of improvisation in intercultural collaborations, giving as reasons expediency and "the dictates of temporary relationships" (2004: 95). Of course, Bustan's in-group relationships were anything but temporary. When they did host guest musicians they took it very seriously. Avshalom had Taiseer compose "Fanar" specifically as a vehicle for the improvisations of their guests Hariprasad Chaurasia and Zakir Hussain. This emphasizes the integral relationship between improvisation and composition in the band's repertoire. Stanyek makes a useful distinction between improvisation used for sonic generation —e.g., Paul Simon putting Los Lobos in a studio and telling them to play, without score or other guidance so that he could use their improvisations— and that which is constitutive (2004: 94–95). During Bustan's career, improvisation passed from being generative in the early jam sessions to become more constitutive thereafter.

Framing improvisation: The relationship between composition and improvisation is one of the distinctive features of this band, particularly as it is expressed in the profusion of patterns that support solos and in other interactions between soloist and band. Bustan explored possibilities that included improvising between iterations of a single theme, alternating improvised sections with several contrasting composed sections, and rapid alternation between members of the ensemble. The resources used in compositional settings for improvisation included drone, short repeated pattern (which I will call an ostinato), background melody, and chord progression. Comparisons to performance practices associated with Arab music and jazz appear in the following discussion because these are the musical practices among the band's sources that feature lengthy instrumental improvisation and were thus most likely to provide models and set expectations (keeping in mind that members of the band were not equally familiar with each).

Some pieces were composed to provide spaces for brief improvised interjections, a common feature in Arab performance practice. Two of the best examples were the band's regular opening and closing numbers, "Suite for Deizy" and "Tini Mini Hanem" (🔊 audio track 8), probably because this structure gave each musician an opportunity to introduce himself at the beginning of the concert and have a final moment in the spotlight at the end. In "Suite for Deizy" the second theme (starting at 1:33) consists of four-measure phrases, each ending in a sustained note or rest, during which one of the musicians can play a brief solo. "Mabruk," which replaced "Suite for Deizy" as the concert opener on the tour promoting the *Hamsa* album, also has this feature (beginning at 3:26). Each iteration of the theme in "Tini Mini Hanem" features a window for a brief "announcement" by the upcoming soloist, who is then joined by the rest of the band to complete the melody before he launches into a lengthy solo. Each soloist ends by playing the theme again, which cues the others to return.

"Tini Mini Hanem" was exceptional as the only piece to feature an extended solo by every member of the band. For most pieces the choice of soloists was a compositional decision. The band did not adopt the model that has dominated jazz since the 1940s in which each member of the band takes a turn improvising in the spotlight. For instance, the lengthy improvisation on violin was an integral feature of "Gypsy Soul"—no other instrument took the lead there. Many of the other pieces included only one or two solos. Note also that the composer of the work often was not featured as a soloist. Like the group revision process, this is evidence for the relative suppression of ego within the group.

Solo and composed accompaniment: The accompaniments composed for improvisations were a significant area of innovation for this band. In standard Arab musical practice the options accompanying lengthy instrumental improvisations (*taqasim*) are a drone on the tonal center or an ostinato that reiterates that center in alternation with a secondary pitch in a characteristic rhythm (see figure 10.9a).[26] Only a few minor variations on this pattern are common. While Bustan made use of this ostinato in some pieces, many of their compositions featured unique patterns. A few examples will demonstrate the scope of their explorations.

26. Such patterns can be called *'ardiyya* or *asas,* but most commonly *wahda,* after the name of an accompanying drum pattern (Taiseer Elias, April 26, 2008). Usually a fourth lower, this auxiliary pitch is a third lower in certain *maqamat;* the pitch a whole step below the tonal center is also commonly used.

Figure 10.9   Ostinato patterns. a. two variants of ostinato typical in Arab Music; b. "Fountainhead" by Miguel Herstein; c. "Gypsy Soul" by Emmanuel Mann; d. "Dub Dulab" by Nassim Dakwar; e. "Jazz Kar-Kurd" by Taiseer Elias

The ostinato from Miguel's "Fountainhead" includes the bass part transcribed in figure 10.9b, and the guitar's relentless repetition of a drone that subdivides the beat (⬤ audio track 17). Reminiscent of a European ground bass, it outlines an extended progression that has melodic and harmonic implications, ascending by step from the tonic to the dominant.[27] Other bass patterns, such as those in "Gypsy Soul" and "Dub Dulab," have more clearly defined rhythmic character and do not imply any melodic or harmonic movement. Rather, they function as rhythmic elaborations on a drone, reinforcing the tonal center with neighboring tones (in "Gypsy Soul," figure 10.9c, toward the end of ⬤ audio track 19) or the fifth degree of the scale ("Dub Dulab," figure 10.9d, ⬤ audio track 20). The bass line that underlies the flute solo in the first half of "Jazz Kar-Kurd" combines both attributes. It delineates a clear harmonic progression and a rhythmic groove (see figure 10.9e). These patterns most often were played by the bassist in conjunction with the drummer, but every member of the ensemble took this sort of supporting role at some point. Some ostinato melodies were repeated precisely (e.g., in "Gypsy Soul") while others were varied with each repetition (e.g., "Jazz Kar-Kurd"). I have not indicated the drum parts in these examples because they tended to vary considerably while

27. The doubling of the harmonic rhythm in the final measure gives a sense of acceleration.

remaining congruent with the rhythmic character of the ostinato (similar to typical Arab musical performance).

Bustan achieved complexity in this area, too. Taiseer's impassioned 'ud solo in "Pictures Through the Painted Window" unfolds over a mesmerizing texture gradually woven by the other string players. They build toward a bit of counterpoint from the preceding, composed segment of the piece, varying their overlapping iterations of a brief phrase almost imperceptibly (⬤ audio track 18). The ostinato in the middle of "Bustan" layers an ingenious reworking of a fragment from the first theme (figure 9.4a) stretched from a four- to a five-beat meter, shifted in relation to the downbeat, and combined with an ostinato based on an additive meter (figure 9.4b). Several members of the band played these parts, varying them in small ways to provide a kaleidoscopic backdrop for Nassim's featured violin improvisation (⬤ audio track 9).[28]

These ostinato patterns offer a soloist rhythmic, melodic, and (in some cases) harmonic frameworks for his ideas. They maintain the tonal center and a rhythmic groove to which the soloist can relate in various ways. In their solos on Nassim's "Dub Dulab," Taiseer and Amir play with locking into the groove and playing against it. Taiseer begins with forceful rhythms that run counter to the metric framework, generating tremendous drive from the rhythmic conflict as well as pitch clashes with the tonic (see figure 10.10, ⬤ audio track 20).[29] By contrast, he plays the end of his solo in free rhythm, represented somewhat awkwardly in the transcription in order to show how far he moves from the bassline for most of this segment (see figure 10.11).

Following immediately after Taiseer, Amir takes the cross-rhythm idea and works it out in myriad ways (see figure 10.12), ending his solo with further rhythmic play that runs against the underlying meter (see figure 10.13). Some of this is instigated by the drummer, Zohar, who suggests a triplet subdivision that Amir picks up. However, Amir makes this into a 3:2 cross-rhythm by repeating each pitch, playing pairs across the triplets. Next he takes a type of rhythmic play central to Hindustani music (the *tihai* mentioned earlier) and works it into his solo by repeating a descending scalar passage every one and a half beats. This creates a larger cross-rhythm, which he resolves by reversing the scale, ascending to hit the tonic on the downbeat. The numerous iterations of pitches G and A that end this example lead to the return of the theme in the next measure (not shown in figure 10.13).

Amir, Taiseer, and the other members of the band took various approaches to building a coherent statement over the span of several minutes. One favored technique, evident in the "Dub Dulab" solos, involves reiterating distinctive fragments while manipulating their metrical placement or their rhythmic and melodic contours. Polyrhythmic play served as a

28. See also the double ostinato from "Fanar" (figure 10.2).
29. Zohar repeats a drum pattern throughout this excerpt that is not fully represented here.

Figure 10.10   Beginning of Taiseer Elias's 'ud Solo on "Dub Dulab" (1:00 to 1:18)

Figure 10.11   End of *'ud solo* by Taiseer Elias in "Dub Dulab" (2:23 to 2:41)

Figure 10.12   Beginning of Amir Milstein's flute solo on "Dub Dulab"
(2:40 to 3:10)

Figure 10.13   End of Amir Milstein's flute solo on "Dub Dulab"
(2:34 to 4:04)

common thread to join the solos by Taiseer and Amir in "Dub Dulab."
But on other occasions, such as Taiseer's composition "Jazz Kar-Kurd,"
they took fundamentally different approaches to improvisation (🔊 audio
track 6).

Some improvisations build to a climax then fade away, perhaps repeating that progression once or twice. Others build to a climax at which

point the rest of the ensemble enters or another soloist enters. Cueing the return of the ensemble likewise is accomplished in several ways, including visual cues or switching from highly melodic, rhythmically free playing to regular reiteration of a single pitch (as Taiseer does at the end of his solo on "Suite for Deizy" at 6:23 on the CD *Bustan Abraham*). The most straightforward method, used by Amir at the end of his solo in "Dub Dulab," is to return to the composed melody. Many solos end in this manner, often preceded by repetition of a motif that brings the improvisation to a close. There is no direct analog to this in Arab musical practice nor is it precisely the same as the common methods of ending an improvisation in other musical practices that these musicians have learned. But it is similar enough to create broad compatibility and intelligibility for performers and audiences.

Some improvisations clearly reference other musical practices these musicians know. Miguel's ever-changing introduction to "Tini Mini Hanem" is a case in point (see chapter 9). Parts of solos by Nassim and Taiseer would not be out of place in an Arab *taqasim* and many of Amir's flute solos would fit comfortably into a jazz-oriented performance devoid of Middle Eastern elements. But in each case the improvisation takes on new meaning in the context of the band's particular stylistic blend.

Each member of the ensemble had a different "voice." Even Taiseer and Nassim, longtime musical partners who have almost the same musical backgrounds, differed strikingly in the way they improvised with this band, despite the fact that they came into contact with the same influences through recordings and great musicians from other countries and cultures whom they met in Israel and on tour abroad. Styles of improvisation changed over the years, too, as one might expect, especially given the lack of conventions to constrain such change. Since I have known him the longest, I take Taiseer as my example again.

Taiseer was already experimenting with incorporating ideas from his European art music training in *taqasim*[30] when I first heard him in 1986, five years before Bustan Abraham was formed. His solos have changed dramatically since then, as he has expanded his technique and discovered ways of integrating influences from the various musicians and types of music that he has experienced in the ensuing years. Arpeggiated chords and other gestures that once sounded out of place have been integrated fluently. The slides, pitch bends, leaps, and percussive playing style that are integral to many of his most striking improvisations seem to have emerged from his exposure to Indian *sarod* gained through performance with Krishnamurti Sridhar, to American blues and bluegrass through long association with Miguel, and to the Spanish guitar virtuoso Paco de Lucia, with whom he has performed. His admiration for the pioneering twentieth-century Iraqi *'ud* player Munir Bashir and collaborations with contemporary Israeli composer Menahem Wiesenberg have also broadened his artistic palette.[31]

30. References to Bach stand out in my memory.
31. Changes in improvisational style were also particularly evident in Amir's flute solos.

Ensemble interaction: Without a conductor Bustan Abraham achieved an unusually high degree of coordination for an ensemble of this size. The precisely synchronized, off-balance bursts at the end of "Bustan" are a good example of their virtuosity as an ensemble (🔊 audio track 21). The band developed an optimal stage seating that they maintained throughout their career: an arc stretching from Avshalom through Nassim, Amir, Zohar, Emmanuel (later Naor), and Miguel to Taiseer. Placing Zohar in the middle ensured rhythmic precision. Leadership was shared among several members of the band, with cues coming most frequently from Taiseer, Zohar, and Amir (standing just to Zohar's right). This also put the musicians who constituted the "engine" of the ensemble close to one another, beginning with the tightly linked pair of bass and drum, adding the 'ud and often the guitar, too. Although roles constantly shifted within the ensemble, these players provided the rhythm and harmonic underpinning for most pieces most of the time.

Aside from their featured solos, the musicians had many other opportunities to improvise in every piece they played. They paraphrased the melody played by others or responded to the lead player of the moment and subjected many of the composed parts to variation, including the ostinato patterns discussed above. The interaction between Zohar and Amir shown in the first line of figure 10.13 is a particularly clear instance of mutual responsiveness. Their studio and live recordings abound with instances in which players who are not playing the featured solo or the accompanying ostinato "chime in" to interact with the soloist. Some of these interjections are composed in the sense that they belong to the piece either as the composer envisioned it or as the group arranged (or recomposed) it, but their details may not be fixed. The responses that Nassim and Miguel play during Taiseer's 'ud solo in "Suite for Deizy" exemplify this. Just as the solo differs in each of the three performances available to me (the album *Bustan Abraham* and two concert tapes) so do the contributions by Nassim and Miguel differ both in timing and content (🔊 audio track 10). A particularly striking example of the variability of such interactions is available for "Bustan." The free-form atonal responses by band members to Taiseer's 'ud solo on *Live Concerts* (from a performance in 2000) differ substantially from the original recording released eight years earlier on *Bustan Abraham*.

Such responsiveness was facilitated by the nonhierarchical seating arrangement with its open sight lines. In concerts this also facilitated looks of encouragement and smiles of appreciation in response to others' solos. This was a band that was truly enjoyable to watch and consistently elicited enthusiastic responses from the audience.

Freedom of improvisation: Members of the band valued the freedom of improvisation even at the lowest "level" where they could change the details of parts that the composer had prescribed. Early in the band's career, when I interviewed Zohar and Emmanuel, they contrasted their relative freedom to the work of orchestral musicians, expressing disbelief that a musician would consciously choose a role in which he or she must play only what is written. Zohar had become aware of the tension between that position and his own when he played in the backing orchestra for popular singer David Broza. He felt that members of the orchestra either resented his freedom or looked down on him for not reading the notes.[32]

Improvisation should not be seen as completely distinct from composition for this band. The same could be said of numerous other musicians working in other styles, but it bears repetition since the terminology conveys too sharp a distinction.[33] For instance, some of the players developed improvisations that they liked and repeated, thus in effect adding another fixed element to the composition. But even the most fixed improvisations were probably never as fixed as the compositions themselves. They consisted, instead, of a sequence of ideas that the musician had settled on as optimal for that spot in the piece. Musicians differed in their views of what was fixed and what was not. A conversation with Taiseer and Nassim in 2000 ranged over these possibilities. When I asked which pieces changed most from one performance to another, Nassim said that "Solaris" was not a good example because the solos by Amir and Taiseer were fairly fixed and short. Taiseer contradicted this, but Nassim argued back that Taiseer started each solo the same way in that piece. Taiseer countered by saying that everything changes, even the composed parts. They agreed that sometimes an idea surfaces in an improvisation that is never repeated; in other instances they remember such ideas and make them a regular part of improvisations for that piece.

Years earlier Taiseer explained to me that most of the band's solos were almost fixed, in the sense that they had certain beginnings, stations along the way, and motives that recurred from one performance to the next.[34] But he said this in the context of waxing rhapsodic over the last concert of the tour they had just completed where he felt so free that he played a solo that was completely different from the ones he had done before and did not make use of the motives that he usually played for that piece. On another occasion, Nassim spoke to me at length about improvisation and the difference between recordings and live performances:

> In Bustan what you hear on the disc is not what you hear in performance . . . a piece that is built on improvisation takes a long time until you crystallize, as a player, exactly what you want to play in this piece. We talked about this subject a lot: let's play the new material for a long time before we record it. . . . And whatever you do on the recording . . . won't come out like in performance . . . we give a large proportion to improvisation in this ensemble . . . you can't ask a player, tell him "take your instrument and improvise." You need atmosphere, good

32. Dec. 28, 1994.

33. See Benson 2003 for a philosopher's analysis of the terms composition and improvisation and the acts that they misrepresent.

34. Dec. 27, 1994. This formulation probably reflected his ethnomusicological training. He had just completed dissertation research on improvisation in Arab music (Elias 2007).

"sound," a good audience—all this influences the musician on the stage, what he can create on the stage and what he can give the audience. Sometimes you don't have this in the studio, you miss it on the disc. I, for instance, really regret things I did on the discs, because I know that I can do something several times better and all the time I say "halevai" [if only] I'll have luck and I'll have the right "head" [frame of mind] and it will come out like I play in the performances. It doesn't come out exactly. . . . Take "Gypsy Soul" by Emmanuel—what I play in performance is completely different . . . with time I developed a solo there. (July 16, 1999)

Four years after my interview with Nassim, Avshalom released *Live Concerts*, which includes a performance of "Gypsy Soul" well worth comparing to the version that appeared on *Pictures Through the Painted Window* in 1994. The first, most striking difference is that the piece starts off considerably faster (206 vs. 175 bpm), but more important is the fact that instead of slowing down to play the additive ostinato (2+2+2+3) that supports and motivates Nassim's solo Emmanuel and Zohar actually speed up (273 vs. 183 bpm). Nassim could not possibly have "fit" the solo he played on the original recording to this accompaniment. The band had altered the shifts in meter and tempo that are basic compositional aspects of "Gypsy Soul." Thus from improvisation we arrive back at composition. The two are entwined in the works of Bustan Abraham, seemingly separable at times, yet feeding into each other in countless ways.

PART IV

Roots and Routes

11

Representations of Place and Time

W ith music, words, and images, the musicians in Israel's ethnic music scene map the past, present, and future of their cultural terrain. They refer to places, times, and heritages through their choices of titles for compositions, albums, and ensembles. The images in their publicity and CD covers are tools for evoking particular historical, geographical, and cultural associations, while the texts of publicity materials and liner notes convey more explicit messages that reiterate or augment these images. Together with their new musical mixtures, offered as prototypes for locally rooted expression, these packages of words and images point toward a better future in which ethnic, national, and religious divisions are bridged rather than deepened into abysses that threaten to swallow all else.

There is, of course, no single vision of the future. Rather, presentation and representation are evocative of particular worldviews and involve symbols that have multiple meanings.[1] A book less concerned with musicians and musical processes might profitably center on such questions of representation as who is saying what to whom and for what purpose. Here I can only sketch this mapping out of place and time, pointing to some of the more common public meanings of these symbols, while assuming that other meanings exist,[2] some exclusive to small groups or even to individuals, such

---

1. Surveying the challenges that world music poses for popular music studies, Jocelyne Guilbault has called for attention not only to the possibility of multiple meanings but also to the fluidity of meanings (1997a).
2. The possibilities for differing interpretations were abundantly clear at a performance by Amal Murkus that I attended in Tel Aviv in 2003. A Jewish audience member who understood some Arabic heckled Amal for singing a song that she understood to be anti-Jewish because it talks only about those who pray on Friday and Sunday (i.e., Muslims and Christians). A lengthy debate ensued in which Amal insisted that she intended nothing of the sort. Arab musicians whom I have asked about this song by Ziad Rahbani explain it as an attack on religious hypocrites whose show of piety stands in contrast to their amorality in the face of economic inequalities in Lebanon and elsewhere.

as the composer of a song or an audience member for whom a particular sound or image evokes personal associations. More research remains to be done, particularly concerning reception.

Compared to Alei Hazayit and Bustan Abraham, Yair Dalal has deployed the richest array of symbols with his lushly illustrated, multipage CD booklets, his numerous referential composition titles, and the press materials that adorn his Web site. Yair offers a particular view of the Middle East past and present, his place in it as an Israeli Jew of Iraqi descent, and his hopes for a better future based on peace with the Palestinians. Shoham and Jamal also deployed an array of potent symbols in the staging of Alei Hazayit performances to enunciate their views. Although in comparison to Yair they did not promote themselves quite as actively as representatives of peaceful coexistence between Jews and Arabs, they did perform that role both at home and abroad.

By contrast, members of Bustan Abraham were strikingly wary of political interpretations. Concerned that they be perceived as opportunists, they stated repeatedly, in public interviews and in private conversations, that the music was the end and any message of peaceful coexistence was serendipitous.[3] Taiseer Elias summed it up well when he said, in response to a spate of overtly political musical endeavors, that Bustan Abraham is not associated with the "kitsch of a band that arises in order to bring people together and while waving slogans loses its music" (Bar On 1997). But Bustan Abraham's work is not completely devoid of references to the circumstances of its production. Their *Live Concerts*, issued two years after the group's demise, bears the trace of that sociopolitical reality on the band's oeuvre. It is dedicated to the memory of the artist who created the covers of their other CDs, noting that he was killed in a terrorist bombing. What journalists, sponsors, and the general public have read into their work is significant, too. While their emphasis on a more abstract vision of music for music's sake means that some of the symbolism is less overt and thick on the ground, the work of Bustan Abraham also offers fodder for an analysis of representation.

Place and Music: Claims to Canaan

Arjun Appadurai's oft-quoted observation that "the landscapes of group identity—the ethnoscapes—around the world are no longer familiar anthropological objects, insofar as groups are no longer tightly territorialized, spatially bounded, historically self-conscious, or culturally homogeneous" (1996: 48) has sparked considerable rethinking, not only of the contempo-

3. See chapter 5. The denial of overt political intentions is reminiscent of white South African musician Johnny Clegg: "I don't see myself as an ideologist; I'm not propagating a particular political system or philosophy. I see myself as a cultural activist, committed to mixing cultures and trying to find a common ground. Unfortunately, in my country, that is considered to be a political act" (Van Matre 1990).

rary world but also of the basic tenets of anthropological and ethnomusicological research and teaching. From this observation, Appadurai derived the question "what is the nature of locality as a lived experience, in a globalized, deterritorialized world?" (1996: 52). Continuing in this vein half a decade later, Akhil Gupta and James Ferguson summarized a trend in anthropological critique that focuses on the deterritorialization of cultural difference produced by the mass migrations and transnational culture flows of a postcolonial world. Pointing to an accelerating "global cultural ecumene" and a "world in creolization" they asked how questions of identity and cultural difference are spatialized in new ways and set out to explore the intertwined processes of place making and people making in the complex cultural politics of the nation-state (1997a: 4).[4]

These statements apply to some aspects of the world in which Israelis and Palestinians live, informed as it is by numerous transnational links and flows, but the Israeli-Palestinian conflict is intensely territorialized: every square centimeter of land is noted and disputed. The basic purpose of the Zionist project is to bring Jews back to work and live in the land of Israel.[5] Palestinians' common goal is to reclaim control of that same piece of land from the Jews and to return the millions of Palestinians who live in exile. In the very period discussed by Appadurai, Gupta, Ferguson, and others, the emphasis on territoriality has heightened, if anything, even as transnational flows of people, capital, and ideas have indeed lowered certain barriers and brought people into ever more complex juxtapositions, complicating identities in the process. Hyper-connectedness does not "signal the erasure of local difference or of local identity, but rather revalidates and reconstitutes place and presents new challenges for how places and people give, and are given, meaning" (Watts 1992: 122). Work by Ted Swedenburg and Semadar Lavie on the *interzone*, the cultural space in which Arabs consume Israeli music, actually underscores difference even as it demonstrates cross-border flows.

Both Palestinians and Israelis mobilize poetry and song to stake or strengthen claims and emotional ties to the land as a whole and to specific sites within it. The genre of "songs of the land of Israel" (*shirei erets yisrael*) so central to Israeli cultural life in the formative decades of the state is predicated upon the notion that the nation state can be sung into being through the naming of its most beautiful or significant places.[6] A similar belief motivates the use of song by Palestinian nationalists.

While songs about the land are prominent in Palestinian political activism,[7] for many Israeli Jews analogous songs have entered the realm of nostalgia rather than political action. Other outlets for longing have surfaced, born of the geopolitical isolation within which Israelis live. In the

4. They referenced the work of Appadurai and Ulf Hannerz, among others.
5. The exact borders of this biblical land to be reclaimed were a matter of dispute. See below.
6. See, e.g., Regev and Seroussi 2004 or Seroussi 2002a.
7. See, e.g., Oliver 2002. The concert at the Hakawati theater recounted in chapter 2 drew heavily on such songs.

early years of the state, various Israeli adventurers attempted to penetrate Jordan in order to see the fabled Nabatean city of Petra, carved in the red stone of the southwestern Jordanian desert. The lure of this forbidden fruit, and the failure of the adventurers to return are hauntingly retold in "Hasela Haadom" (The Red Rock), popular in the 1950s and 1960s. In the 1960s, the song "Mahar" (tomorrow) expressed hopes for a world with open borders, ships sailing freely from Eilat to the Ivory Coast, naval destroyers converted to the export of oranges. In the late 1970s, the immensely popular musician Yehuda Poliker evoked Israel's earlier isolation in "Radio Ramallah," remembering the sound of Jordanian radio easily received a few miles away in pre-1967 Israel—the other side so close, yet impossibly remote for an Israeli. Once travel to Egypt and then Jordan became possible, the yearning for the unattainable was transferred to places such as Syria. The vaguely ludicrous Israeli entry in the 2000 Eurovision contest expressed this longing with a young Israeli woman singing about making love to her boyfriend in Damascus.[8]

The musicians discussed in this book play on the longing for the sounds of elsewhere in a nonconfrontational manner. Positioning themselves as artists they are suspicious of the aesthetic value of enterprises that are motivated primarily by a political end, whether it be peace or the overthrow of the state. Some of them would argue for the autonomy of art, but even those who acknowledge art's political aspects, distinguish the music they value from that which is explicitly political. Some Palestinian members of Alei Hazayit have performed political songs that are allusive in nature,[9] but they did so in other contexts, not through Alei Hazayit. Others avoided such music altogether. To my knowledge none of the Israeli Jews central to this scene have been involved in anything analogous.[10]

Regardless of their identity and political beliefs each of these musicians feels deeply connected to his or her homeland. A few express this directly in song as Shoham and Jamal did when they chose "Shabehi Yerushalayim." Others express it in the themes that they choose to evoke through the titles of their instrumental compositions. Yair Dalal has made the land and surrounding parts of the Middle East the subject of individual pieces and of entire albums. His large work *The Perfumed Road* is an

8. Performed by Ping Pong, the song finished twenty-second in a field of twenty-four entries. See www.eurovisiondatabase.co.uk/2000/2000.htm for reports of Israeli critics of this selection as well as the performers' somewhat clueless responses. A video clip included in *Israel Rocks!* (Abraham and Erga, 2000) shows the beautiful lead singer holding a cucumber, while the geekier male member of the group wears a checkered Arab headcloth and waves a Syrian flag.

9. For instance, at the Hakawati concert described in chapter 2.

10. However, just a few years after collaborating on the recording and tour of *Masakh Ashan* with Nassim Dakwar and other Israeli Arabs, Ariel Zilber veered to the right end of the Israeli political spectrum, even writing a campaign song for an extreme Jewish nationalist. See chapters 8 and 9 for discussion of his peripheral involvement in ethnic music.

excellent example of this, but before discussing it the terms of contention should be reviewed.

At the root of the Israeli-Palestinian conflict lie conflicting claims over land. To support one's claim and motivate one's cohort it is necessary to define and naturalize a particular vision of the land. Maps and other means of representing and communicating the extent of domain play a central role in efforts of this sort, as historian Thongchai Winichakul has shown in *Mapping Siam*. Several competing geobodies[11] figure in the Israeli/Palestinian dispute:

- Israel within its pre-1967 borders (the "Green Line," named for the color of the border demarcation on maps)
- Israel and the territories presently under its control (which might be subject to negotiation, depending on one's political view)
- Greater Israel based on an interpretation of the Bible to include a considerably larger territory than modern Israel has ever comprised, which has motivated the right end of the Israeli political spectrum
- Palestine as a state alongside Israel in the West Bank and Gaza Strip
- Palestine as a state replacing Israel, binational in its citizenship
- Palestine as a state erasing Israel and all its non-Arab citizens, as called for in the founding documents of the Palestine Liberation Organization and in the Covenant of the Islamic Resistance Movement (Hamas).

Just as visions of Palestine differ with regard to the makeup of its citizenry, the images of Israel may further be differentiated based on whether one sees Israel as a Jewish state or as a state for all its citizens, albeit dominated by the symbols and hopes of Jews. These viewpoints, ensconced in maps published by their adherents, are mutually exclusive.[12] Many weapons are deployed in the battle over the future shape of nations in this conflict, but the representations produced and disseminated by the musicians under discussion here are not clearly linked to any of these views.

If any one geopolitical image emerges from the ethnic music scene in Israel it is one that minimizes political borders and divisions between peoples. Congruent with their figurative border-crossings in music, these musicians argue, sometimes in subtle ways, for a breaking down of boundaries. For instance, "Canaan," the first piece that Bustan Abraham worked out, references the ancient past and the land before it was named Israel or Palestine

11. This term was invented by Thongchai Winichakul to comprehend the "territoriality of a nation" (1994: 17).

12. Reporting on the Jerusalem Project, a historic joint undertaking of Palestinian and Israeli researchers planning an exhibit of Jerusalem for the 1993 Smithsonian Folklife Festival, Amy Horowitz chronicles the difficulties that nomenclature and boundaries presented to the folklorists and the government agencies with which they interacted (2000).

and became the object of conflict between Jews and Arabs. But this is just one reading. Since some Palestinians now claim Canaanites as their ancestors, this symbol can, like most symbols, be read in very different ways.

A wealth of geo-historical references marks Dalal's projects, particularly in *The Perfume Road*, one of the most explicit musical calls for breaking down borders in the Middle East. The title refers to a trade route that was in active use for many centuries, traversed by caravans bearing perfumes and other goods from the Persian Gulf and Indian Ocean across the Arabian Peninsula to the Mediterranean. Dalal is clear about the symbolism he sees in this route:

> The perfume routes that in the past linked peoples and cultures once again link people of different nations, religions and cultures. But . . . peace does not yet reign in the Middle East and a complete journey along the Perfume Route from the shores of the Indian Ocean to the Mediterranean coast remains a Utopian dream. However, the Perfume Road can be transformed into a peace road, a route of brotherhood between the peoples living in the region because PEACE is the most precious merchandise of all. (1998)

Photos augment the text in a lavish CD booklet. The cover of the album shows ancient petroglyphs and the centerfold of semi-transparent parchment overlays images of the musicians on a background photo of open desert.[13] Among the credits is one for "historic survey," surely an unusual item on anything other than an ethnographic or archival recording. But this is no ethnography or historical document. It is a creative imagining in the service of a political ideal, as well as Dalal's own aesthetic and career goals. As far as Dalal is concerned, music and musicians should lead in the dismantling of borders and other restrictions on the free movement of people and ideas. Journeys, which imply motion across or in spite of borders, figure on most of Dalal's albums in one way or another and surface in numerous compositions performed by other groups.

If unrestricted travel through the Middle East is the main theme of Dalal's *The Perfume Road* then the arduous passage across the desert is the subtext, while the link between music and the identities of the different people along the route is the countertheme. Conceived as a suite, the individual movements bear titles marking stages along the caravan route, moving westward from "El Halidg (The Persian Gulf)" to end with "Shalomediterranee," a play on words that conjoins peace and the Mediterranean, the caravan's destination.[14] The implication, whether intentional or not, is that the riches of the East come to the West. But Dalal is neither colonizer nor victim in this scenario. If anything, he stresses the debt of the West to

13. The cover image is available at www.yairdalal.co. The booklet centerfold is reproduced in Brinner 2004.

14. Brief samples can be heard on Dalal's Web site. One movement, "Jethro," predates the album by many years, going back to one of Dalal's first bands, Midian. In the Bible, Jethro is a Midianite priest and the father-in-law of Moses.

the East, portraying the good things in life—music, perfume, spices—that traversed the Middle East en route to Europe. This is consonant with the vision of Israel put forth by the architects of the Oslo Accords, whereby the advent of peace and the demilitarization of borders would see Israel and a Palestinian entity playing pivotal and integral roles in an economic area spanning the Middle East.

The lack of explicit reference to Jewish or Arab aspects of local history in *The Perfume Road* is striking and an interesting choice for an Israeli musician. Sidestepping the claims of any current nationalism, Dalal celebrates a past epoch of (imagined) free movement through the Middle East.[15] This suits his political leanings well, by setting aside the Israeli-Palestinian conflict and turning a spotlight on the mixing of peoples for mutual benefit. However idealized this view of the past may be, it does serve to reorient the attentive viewer and listener to a radically different mapping of the Middle East, predicated on the movement of people, goods, and song along trade routes that traverse expanses of land, rather than on compartmentalization within strictly policed borders. And it stresses the position of this part of the world in a continuum that stretches from India (and points east) to Europe through a series of links: sea-faring traders on the Indian Ocean hand off their goods to a caravan that crosses the desert to pass its goods along to other ships waiting to sail from the southeast coast of the Mediterranean for other points across that sea.

The marketing appeal of this erasure of divisions and conflict aligns with the position of Magda Records, the label on which Dalal records. Magda proclaims itself to be "Israel's Leading Ethnic and World Music Label" and sports a sun-shaped logo, resplendent on the home page of the company's Web site over the motto "Sounds from another Middle East."[16] This can be taken as an invitation to imagine an alternative and presumably better political reality. It can also imply that there already is a different reality, one that does not foreground war and other acts of violence. The motto appears in Hebrew and French in addition to English. The absence of Arabic, an official language of the state of Israel that appears on government documents and currency is disturbing.[17] Whether it is motivated by a desire to lessen the Arab presence or by fear of putting off some Israeli buyers, it undercuts the political potential of the motto and is particularly strange considering that many native speakers of Arabic—Jews as well as Muslims, Druze and Christians—have recorded on this label.

The Mediterranean as geographical motif deflects attention from Israel's isolation among Arab neighbors and repositions it in a more welcoming web of connections. Recall that Dalal concludes *The Perfume Road* with "Shalomediterranée," combining tropes of place and peace. Ethno-

---

15. He ignores the many conflicts over the centuries in which powers such as Egypt, Assyria, Greece, and Rome vied for control of this area.

16. See www.magda.co.il.

17. Amal Murkus accomplished a reciprocal erasure on *Amal*, which does not include any Hebrew writing despite the central role of Israeli Jewish musicians and production by an Israeli company.

musicologist Edwin Seroussi characterized his annual Mediterranean Musical Dialogue[18] as "a series of interrelated workshops which aim to create an exchange of ideas among musicians who perform in a 'Mediterranean' spirit." A music critic noted that this "allows the event organizers to stray far beyond the physical borders of the countries around the Mediterranean. In previous years there have been musicians from places like Azerbaijan and Iran. This year, one of the foreign teachers is . . . from Bombay—not exactly in our geographical locale" (Davis 2002b).[19] Seroussi himself ends an article on this musical trend with the conclusion "musical Mediterraneanism in its different manifestations was always a strategy to avoid full-fledged Arabiness [sic] while at the same time to develop a sense of belonging to the blurred, and yet not 'all-European'," Mediterranean cultural area" (2002c: section 7). Analogous representations exist in other parts of the Mediterranean. Describing collaboration between Italian and Tunisian musicians, Goffredo Plastino writes that it "delineates an imaginary Mediterranean without explicitly quoting Tunisian or Sicilian musical forms, but rather suggests an open, Mediterranean space. . . . Poetry and music are here two Mediterranean lingua francas that mirror and lead back to each other" (2005: 189).

A third way to deflect attention from borders—favored by musicians, publicists, and critics alike—is to cite Israel's location at the intersection of Asia, Africa, and Europe. This method tends to hyperbole with expressions such as "crossroads of the Middle East," "navel of the world,"[20] and "cradle of civilization" that point to the ancient roots of local culture and to earlier configurations of space and cultural identity. Participants in the "ethnic music" scene in Israel cite their special position as a strength—they sit at the intersection of complexly intertwined roots and routes. "Israel is truly the center of the world," Shlomo Bar told me, in a context that implied spiritual as well as cultural and geographic centrality. "It's so small yet it touches four [sic!] continents. It is truly the border of East and West" (June 24, 1998). Similar imagery appears in the liner notes to Sheva's *Day & Night:*

> Israel, and the Galilee in particular, is an oasis, a green island in the great desert, at the crossroads of the ancient king's ways between Africa, Europe and Asia. On this mysterious ancient and renewing land grew many movements of light throughout human history. Here they dug wells and watered caravans on their way from Ophir in Africa to China, the land of silk. The fruits of this oasis are tangible in their

18. See chapter 8.

19. The renaming of the popular *musika mizrahit* (eastern music) as *musika yamtikhonit* (Mediterranean music) is a similar attempt at repositioning and it is similarly problematic since Yemen and Iran are both important sources for this music but neither is a Mediterranean country.

20. This label has been applied to quite an array of places, ranging from Baghdad to Rome to Rapanui. It appears in Jewish rabbinical literature, in the Midrash Tanhuma, which likens the postition of the land of Israel in the world to the navel in the body.

cultural value. Israel is a meeting place for many cultural landscapes. (1999)

After the breakup of Bustan Abraham, bassist Naor Carmi and his new partners in Trio Hamaalot argued for the authenticity of their band in a similar manner:[21]

> Over two millennia or more, the historical role of Israel was to be a bridge between the civilizations of Africa, Asia and Europe. With this ancestry across continents and its geographical setting, Israel has always occupied a favored place at a crossroad of civilizations and a meeting point of many races and influences.[22]

Such statements serve a purpose similar to the emphasis on Mediterranean location, though they put Israel more unequivocally at the center of things.

The centrality of Jerusalem is a point on which Zionists and Palestinian nationalists can agree and yet forever remain at odds. Both sides believe it to be of the utmost importance; neither is willing to cede it to the other. Nowhere is the politics of representation more strenuously contested. Perhaps because of the highly divisive potential of this symbol, Jerusalem does not figure in the titles of pieces by musicians discussed here with the exception of "Shabehi Yerushalayim."[23] When Shoham Einav and the members of Alei Hazayit decided to arrange this song, they were making a far stronger statement than singing about Tel Aviv, Paris, or Rome. This song in praise of Jerusalem is in Hebrew, derived from the Bible, and is easily associated with a Jewish nationalist claim to Jerusalem. It was exceptionally audacious to transform it into an ecumenical representation of the city replete with sonic emblems of Judaism, Christianity, and Islam (see chapter 9), fraught enough to cause Shoham to delay release.

Place and Music: Roots and Authenticity

Nature imagery is as important to creating a sense of roots and belonging as the cities and borders over which people vie. In a comparative analysis of Israeli and Palestinian discourses, Carol Bardenstein has shown that trees, the Jaffa orange, and the prickly pear cactus are potent symbols and weapons in the Palestinian-Israeli conflict,[24] used to inculcate a sense of

21. See chapter 8.
22. The Web site, accessed in June 2004, is archived at http://web.archive .org/web/20040110110009/www.triohamaalot.com/aboutus_eng.html.
23. But note that Nasser Al-Taee analyzes songs by popular Arab and Jewish singers about Jerusalem (2002).
24. The prickly pear was also key to Jews' efforts to distance themselves from their Diaspora legacy when establishing the Israeli state.

rootedness in this contested homeland.[25] Those who would resolve the conflict use it, too: Witness the band names Bustan (orchard or garden) and Alei Hazayit (olive leaves).

Even more prevalent in the ethnic music scene than such symbols of growth and fertility are desert motifs. Alei Hazayit's demo recording cites "sounds of the desert" as characteristic of their music (see chapter 1). The desert looms large in Zionist history and mythology as a site of redemption, a barren wilderness to be made fertile.[26] But this is not the desert that interests Yair Dalal, who is drawn to its essential difference from other landscapes. Professing a preference for the desert over the city Yair spent his early adulthood living and wandering in the deserts of Israel and Egypt.[27] Ehud Tomalak's hour-long film—"I Got No Jeep And My Camel Died" (2006)—focuses attention on this aspect of his life, including footage of a small desert whirlwind. Yair has named a composition, an album, and a band after this whirlwind, which the Bedouin call al-'ol. To introduce the composition in concerts he sometimes tells a Bedouin story about the whirlwind. Thus "Al Ol" comes to represent the desert, the Bedouin who live there, and their folklore. The music spins obsessively, like the whirlwind it depicts (🔊 audio track 5)—an apt metaphor for Dalal's busy life on and off the road. He also evokes the desert through photos on several of his recordings and through the titles of pieces such as "Ein Radian" (an oasis) and "Shacharut" (the community where he resided in the southern Negev).[28] He went so far as to perform *The Perfume Road* suite with sand strewn on the stage and colored stage lights. "When the yellow lights came on it really felt like the desert," Yair claimed.[29] He is sincere about his love of the desert, but the pervasiveness of the desert in his work and its appearance elsewhere is also symptomatic of a romanticization that can easily be read as self-orientalization.[30]

25. See also Parmenter 1994 for an analysis of place and identity in Palestinian literature.

26. David Ben Gurion, the first Israeli Prime Minister made a point of living in the Negev and led a campaign to make the desert bloom.

27. Personal communication on several occasions.

28. See illustrations in Brinner 2004 and at www.yairdalal.com. Other instances of titles associated in some way with the desert include: Bustan Abraham's "Hamsin" (Desert Heat); Dalal's "Min Hamidbar" (From the Desert), and "A Voice in the Desert" and "Desert Winds" on Dalal's Norwegian collaboration *Music Channel*; Alei Hazayit's "Lamidbar" (To the Desert, see ch. 9). Others in the ethnic music scene have recorded "A Troll in the Desert" (Eyal Sela), "Sinai Memories" (East/West Ensemble), and "Shayeret Gemalim" (Caravan of Camels, by Gaya).

29. Personal communication.

30. Uniting two of the symbols discussed here, Guy Kark's *Canaan* features photos of Kark and his band, Yemei Habeinatayim, in the desert. Other works by Yair also evoke locality. Like *The Perfumed Road*, "Bagdad-Barcelona" (on *Samar*) gives a sense of geographical sweep from East to West within the confines of a single piece. "Acco Malca," recorded on both *Silan* and *Shacharut*, refers to the ancient port city of Acco (Ar. Akka, Engl. Acre).

Romanticizing roots, hardly unique to the Middle East, is widespread among Israelis and Palestinians alike. Writing on Palestinian refugee identity, George Bisharat notes, "Imagery that contrasts the purportedly natural serenity of indigenous Palestinian life, allying it with the earth and elements, against the unnatural, artificial Israeli intrusion is a common theme in Palestinian cultural expression . . . the hyperemphasis of the pastoral connections of Palestinians to the land is reflective not of genuine rootedness but of an intellectualized, stylized assertion of place under conditions of rupture and threat" (1997: 225).[31] Similarly, Mauro Van Aken analyzes the emblematic status of the village *dabke* dance and its music for Palestinian refugees living in Jordan (2006). Nationalist initiatives in music that focus on promoting Palestinian village traditions—e.g., by El Funoun, a folk music and dance troupe—are part of a larger nativist impulse that seeks to anchor Palestinian history and identity.[32] This gives rise to an intriguing clash of meanings in a video clip on the enhanced CD of Ariel Zilber's *Masakh Ashan*,[33] which shows an Israeli Arab folk troupe dancing a *dabke* to playback of one of the tracks on the CD and Zilber engages in desultory conversation with a member of the troupe regarding the suitability of the dance for his Hebrew song. No mention is made of the ambiguities of the dance as a Palestinian nationalist signifier that has long since been appropriated for Israeli folklore.

Palestinian members of Alei Hazayit, who had performed such village music in other circumstances,[34] did not find a place for it in their work in this band, perhaps precisely because it is so strongly linked to the Palestinian cause. The song "Balla Tsoubou Hal Kahwa," which Jamal arranged and staged for Shoham and Alei Hazayit, did not pose this problem, probably because for Jamal and many other urban Palestinians the Bedouin are an exotic Other not directly associated with Palestinian nationalist aspirations. When Jamal decided to teach Shoham this song about Bedouin warriors and hospitality, he had a clear ethnic stereotype in mind, including an ideal of manliness, a particular way of speaking quite different from urban Palestinian Arabic, and a set of attitudes about hospitality that are emblematic of Bedouin. He coached Shoham to produce a more masculine delivery of the text, pushing her across both ethnic and gender boundaries. By contrast, he told her to sing "Til'it Ya Mahla Nurha" (a pastoral song by Egyptian composer Sayyid Darwish) like a little girl woken by morning's

31. Bisharat cites the work of scholars such as Ted Swedenburg and Barbara Parmenter on the celebration of peasant and village as the essence of Palestinian identity and Lisa Taraki on the museumization of Palestinian culture.

32. Note that El Funoun's CD (1999) is produced by a company named Sounds True. See Williams and Chrisman for a brief summary of attacks on nativism by Said, Appiah, and others (1994: 14).

33. See chapter 8 for a discussion of this project, which featured significant musical involvement by Nassim Dakwar.

34. See chapter 2 for discussion of my recording session that involved such "folklore" and Ghidian's request for the lyrics to sing for Palestinian students in Germany.

first ray of sunlight.[35] For their appearance at the Festival of Asian Arts in Hong Kong, Jamal staged "Balla Tsoubou" with props to represent a Bedouin encampment. How different from Yair Dalal's performances with the Azazme Bedouin Tarab Ensemble where actual Bedouin performers presented themselves on stage!

It is a small and easy slippage from the rootedness of nature imagery to roots music and musicians. Included in their self-presentation, performers' personal roots shape audience perceptions of authenticity. Bustan Abraham and Alei Hazayit emphasized the distinctive origins of their members not only to provide a menu of the ingredients in their "stew" but also to demonstrate their genuine rootedness in particular musical practices. The involvement of "native-speakers" of the various musical practices accorded each of these bands a sense of authenticity. By contrast, many in the ethnic music scene have learned to perform particular types of music as adults. A few, such as Eyal Sela, Zohar Fresco, and Yinon Muallem, gain acceptance from the "native" speakers as full-fledged professionals in the ethnic music scene.[36] A discourse constructed around roots is also evident when musicians critique others engaged in combining musical idioms for lacking deep understanding of a given musical practice.[37] This roots discourse privileges Middle Eastern musical idioms over the other styles performed in this scene.

Past and Future in the Here and Now

Rootedness implies a connection to a particular place and set of cultural practices over time, often a very long span that reaches back into the realms of legend and myth. Time entwines with place and particularly with place names. Bustan Abraham's "Canaan," as noted earlier, referenced the earliest biblical name for this much-disputed land. By naming a piece "Ararat," Dalal evoked a biblical past that is deeper still, referring to the supposed resting place of Noah's Ark. Inclusion of "Lamma Bada Yatathana" on Bustan Abraham's second album indexed a more recent but still remote past, as the poetic form of the *muwashshah* evokes medieval Spain.[38] By performing the song in Arabic, Hebrew, and Spanish, the band underscored the shared heritage of Muslims, Jews, and Christians that dates back to the so-called Golden Age of medieval Spain.

Yair Dalal keeps the Iraqi Jewish musical past alive through the curatorial role that he has adopted. He also presents Iraqi Jewish culture and

35. Shoham recounted this when she introduced Darwish's song at a private party (recording courtesy of Shoham Einav).

36. Taiseer Elias and Nassim Dakwar both consider Zohar to be an excellent drummer for Arab music. Yinon Muallem plays with the Istanbul Saz Endeleri, an ensemble supported by the Turkish Ministry of Culture.

37. Various musicians volunteered such evaluations.

38. However, this song is of relatively recent origin and its poetic form differs from the medieval muwashshah (A. J. Racy, personal communication).

his own roots through arrangements of traditional hymns ("Adon Hasli-chot" and "Ya Ribon Olam"). His album *Asmar* commemorates this past with old photos from Iraq and inclusion of an instrumental composition by the Iraqi Jew Salim al-Nur. The title "Samai Wachi Al Naharein" refers to the two great rivers of Iraq, as the liner note relates: "the Euphrates and Tigris, which have flown [sic] through Mesopotamia—ancient Babylon and today's Iraq—since time immemorial. This region is the cradle of human-kind's earliest civilization. It is the birthplace of Abraham, the prophet of the monotheistic faith and the home of the Jews during their exile from the Land of Israel for 2,500 years" (2002). While presenting the work of a liv-ing composer, he deftly establishes the great antiquity of his own roots. In *Asmar*'s handsome booklet a sense of the past is conveyed visually by the use of black and white photos, evoking a nostalgia that blends images from the recording sessions with archival ones taken before Yair's parents and the rest of the Jewish community fled Iraq in the early 1950s. He is more explicit about his roots than most, but he is hardly exceptional in assert-ing rootedness.

These representations of place and time should be understood in the context of various efforts to make sense of the past and exploit it while stak-ing claims in the present and shaping the future. The past, caught up in the present, is a premise for the futures envisioned by Israelis and Palestinians. To capture such a sense of enmeshed times, Eric Hirsch and Charles Stew-art have proposed redefining the term *historicity* to describe

a human situation in flow, where versions of the past and future (of persons, collectives or things) assume present form in relation to events, political needs, available cultural forms and emotional dispo-sitions. This usage . . . capture[s] the reflexive, mutual conditioning that occurs between objects and subjects. . . . Historicity in this sense is the manner in which persons operating under the constraints of so-cial ideologies make sense of the past, while anticipating the future. . . . [It] concerns the ongoing social production of accounts of pasts and futures. (2005: 262)

Seen in this light both Yair's *The Perfume Road* and Bustan Abraham's "Canaan" are a part of the social production of historical awareness, taking different routes toward a similar goal. Yair references a historical connec-tion across borders, when movement was less constrained, and he educates his reader-listeners with text and images. Bustan Abraham merely cites a distant past through its band name and the title of a signature piece.

Despite their ancient references, the primary thrust of such works, I argue, is not retrospective, but future-oriented, fostering visions of a dif-ferent Middle East. Citing Zimbabwean musician Thomas Mapfumo as an example, Veit Erlmann distinguished music that reappropriates the past as part of a new historical consciousness from the average world music recording, which he characterized as having the "pseudohistorical sound of pastness" (1996a: 483). He comments on the assemblages of musical fragments that characterize a considerable portion of recent world music and the seeming lack of historical awareness of producers and consumers of this music.[39] The music of Dalal, Bustan Abraham, and others in the ethnic music scene in Israel may not be as directly message-oriented as Mapfumo's, but neither is it as ahistorical as the bulk of world music. The musicians and support personnel involved in the production of performances and recordings are acutely aware of local histories and manipulate symbols to produce a particular sort of time-space through allusion and direct reference. When Yair Dalal organized the "Zaman el-Salaam" extravaganza in Oslo in 1994[40] he hoped to bring a future "time of peace" (*zaman el-salaam*) into the present. While reaching back into the past for musical resources, symbols, and authenticity, he and his fellow musicians have their sights set on the future.

39. In this he is joined by Ingrid Monson (1999). Both cite Frederic Jameson, see chapter 12.
40. See chapter 7.

12

Roots in the Past, Routes to the Future

> World music is a new aesthetic form of the global imagination, an
> emergent way of capturing the present historical moment and the
> total reconfiguration of space and cultural identity characterizing
> societies around the globe.
>
> —Erlmann 1996a: 468

If this ethnic music scene in Israel is a local manifestation of world
music, how does it capture its present historical moment? What is its
significance for Israelis, Palestinians, and others? In chapter 11, I pointed
to some of the ways that musicians contributed to a particular sense of historicity, the "ongoing social production of accounts of pasts and futures"
(Hirsch and Stewart 2005: 262). In this final chapter, I argue that two
seemingly distinct answers to these questions—sociopolitical and musical
—are, in fact, intertwined. Despite the seemingly endless, cyclical nature
of conflict in the region tremendous change has occurred since the early
1990s, much of it outside the spotlight of news coverage. Alongside the
hardening of divisions, such as the rise to power of Hamas and the en-
trenchment of Jewish settlers in the West Bank, there have been signs of
readiness to compromise, to enter into meaningful relationships across
deep divisions. Musicians in the ethnic music scene in Israel are participating in Erlmann's "reconfiguration of space and cultural identity." They
are not miracle workers; their powers are limited in many ways and every
new outbreak of violence jeopardizes the public's receptivity to the possibility of coexistence, even as it makes the necessity of coexistence more evident. Yet at some level, people who see and hear these musicians become
aware of possibilities for other ways of being within the Israeli/Palestinian
sociocultural sphere.

I propose that the collaborations analyzed in this book have laid the
foundation for an inclusive music culture that can appeal to people from
different sociocultural backgrounds within the highly diverse life experiences of Jews, Arabs, and others within Israel and beyond, through the
combining of the familiar and the unfamiliar in musical sound and, in some
cases, in language. The "musical imaginary" offered by the musicians I
have presented here alters the boundaries between social categories and
"prefigures emergent, real forms of socio-cultural identity or alliance," to

use a formulation proposed by Georgina Born and David Hesmondhalgh.[1] Many aspects of this phenomenon are unique to the social, political, and cultural situation in Israel and the Palestinian territories at the turn of the twenty-first century, requiring that we take stock of the conditions that have enabled, even favored, the emergence of this musical scene at this particular time and place. Other aspects are closely linked to contemporary transnational phenomena, to the "new aesthetic forms" cited by Erlmann, and thus require consideration of the ethnic music scene's transnational facets in the second section of this chapter. I conclude with a discussion of the transformative power of this musical scene and what its emergent forms of alliance and musical expression may mean for the future.

Why in Israel? Why in the 1990s?

To answer these questions is to examine the conditions of possibility from which the Israeli ethnic music scene—and, more specifically, musical collaborations between Arabs and Jews within that scene—emerged and the reasons this began in the last decade of the twentieth century. When I ask what is specifically "Israeli" about this phenomenon, I am asking not what represents or supports the Israeli government and nation, but what is uniquely attributable to the confluence of people, ideas, cultural attitudes, and musical competences found in Israel. Israeli society and culture affect the lives of all inhabitants of the state, whether or not they accept the state's authority and legitimacy, and influence those adjacent to Israel, increasingly so as political, economic, and technological changes have made national borders more permeable.[2] None of the main musicians discussed in this book were responding to directives issued by the government or any other political organization when they embarked on their various experiments in musical collaboration. Their efforts must, nonetheless, be considered in relation to long-standing imperatives and debates regarding the creation and promulgation of an Israeli national culture.[3]

The contrast of East and West dominates these debates as it dominates many other discourses in Israel. The denotations and connotations of these two terms are dynamic, shifting with speaker, context, and purpose as I demonstrated in previous chapters. The country's location with regard to these essentialized polar opposites is a matter of contention in any number of arenas, ranging from politics to social conduct to culture. Far less

---

1. This is the second of four relationships between music and identity outlined by Born and Hesmondhalgh. The others are: purely imaginary identification, which they characterize as psychic tourism; the reproduction or reinforcement of extant sociocultural identities; and a reflexive reinsertion of musical representations of identity into a changing sociocultural formation (2000: 35–36).
2. See, e.g., Swedenburg 2000 or Swedenburg and Lavie 1996.
3. See Foster 1991.

controversial than Israel's location between East and West is its central role for world Jewry.

The centrality in the Israeli psyche of the "ingathering" of the Jews is crucial to an understanding of the ethnic music scene.[4] Ideologically, this phenomenon derives from the idea of national redemption for a dispersed people returning to its ancestral homeland, a place that has been commemorated, worshiped, and longed for throughout the millennia of exile. Zionist ideology centers on the birth of a new nation from the dispersed remnants of the old. The vitality of this rebirth has been argued in tractates and celebrated in speeches, textbooks, and festivals for the past century, suffusing Israeli consciousness. The idea that a nation needs a national culture, and that a secular Jewish nation-state needs something more than or different from traditional Jewish practices has motivated considerable creative activity over the decades. It helped to foster a mentality that sees the musical traditions of various ethnic groups (Jewish and non-Jewish) as resources at a composer's disposal, an outlook for which figures such as Bartók and Kodály serve as models. It is not difficult to find traces of this ideology in the ethnic music scene as well, with the key difference that many in this scene are expressing a different national body, not the Jewish nation-state, but a post-Zionist entity that includes Arabs as well as Jews.

The ingathering of Jews, achieved jointly by Zionist organizations and the nascent state of Israel, brought together musicians from places as disparate as Yemen and Europe, Morocco and Central Asia, or the United States and India, creating a highly concentrated and diverse cultural resource pool.[5] During the first decades of the state, however, many of the customs, languages, and musical practices brought to Israel by immigrants were disdained and repressed as incompatible with the creation of a new Israeli culture.[6] A countercurrent, weak at first, sought to collect, preserve, and rework aspects of these diverse cultural heritages, most prominently in folk dance troupes that performed for domestic and foreign consumption.[7] Musical endeavors included a massive documentation project at the Ethnomusicological Institute for Jewish Music (founded 1948).[8] The Renanot Institute for Jewish Music, another institution created to "preserve, teach and create Jewish music," justifies its mission in terms of the potential of

4. This is considered a homecoming, too; see Lomsky-Feder and Rapoport 2001 on national ethos and homecoming with regard to recent Russian immigrants.

5. I expand here upon the account given in chapter 3.

6. Only a few practices, such as Yemenite dance, gained exposure and support. See Roginsky 2006 for an analysis of the cultural politics involved.

7. Barbara Kirshenblatt-Gimblet recounts her clash, in 1976, with the Israeli Foreign Ministry over the performers to be sent to the Smithsonian's Folklife Festival (1998: 71).

8. Working under the auspices of the Ministry of Culture and Education, this institute continued earlier scholarly collection efforts. The National Sound Archive, founded in 1964, became the premier institution for documentation of Jewish musical traditions. See Shiloah and Gerson-Kiwi 1981.

"musical dialogue" to overcome social differences (within the Jewish population) and provide cultural enrichment through exposure to the music of other Jewish communities.[9] But such ideas were seldom heeded in the mainstream of Israeli musical life that ran through the educational system, central broadcasting, and the main recording companies.

Internal challenges to the Zionist program of creating a unitary Israeli identity have come from various directions. Inherent to this program are tensions between old and new, and among the various traditional practices that constitute the old. As Eastern European Jews numerically dominated the early Zionist establishment and Central European Jews came to dominate cultural life from the 1930s onward, the masses of immigrants who arrived from North Africa, Iraq, and Yemen after the founding of the state of Israel found themselves and their ways of life excluded from mainstream Israeli culture and society. Some of these immigrants and their children mounted protests in the 1970s, a moment and movement in which Shlomo Bar first made his mark as a musician. The popular music known originally as *musika mizrahit* emerged from the social margins early in the next decade, its supporters fighting exclusion from radio broadcasts and other media. These developments coincided roughly with the ascent of the right-wing Likud Party under Menahem Begin in a 1977 electoral upset often cited as a watershed moment in the struggle of North African and Middle Eastern Jews to gain a political voice in Israel.[10] The ensuing culture wars, which have continued into the twenty-first century, involve demands for state funding and recognition of culture practices transmitted, adapted, or invented by members of this aggrieved population. More recent Russians and Ethiopian immigrants have also demanded recognition. Multiculturalism has gained currency as a concept, to the point that the Web site of the Israel Ministry of Foreign Affairs sports an article on the topic (Melcer 2001).[11]

Growing awareness of cultural diversity among the Israeli public in the late 1970s and early 1980s was linked to shifts in national sentiment with regard to diasporic roots, Israeli culture, and the very idea of what it meant to be an Israeli. By the 1990s, elements of many of the musical practices brought from the Diaspora were woven into the fabric of the ethnic music scene and negative attitudes toward Middle Eastern musics had abated noticeably.

9. www.renanot.co.il/about.htm, accessed June 13, 2004. While neither fusion nor hybridity is mentioned, the idea of creating something new is intimated in a prefatory quote "The new will be sanctified, and the old will be renewed" attributed to Rabbi A.Y. Hacohen Kook, who was adopted posthumously by religious Zionists as a leader.

10. A significant portion of Begin's support came from these groups.

11. This is all the more striking given that the article ends by declaring that Israeli society faces the greatest challenge yet in coming to terms with multiculturalism that extends to the numerous foreign nationals (from places such as Nigeria, the Philippines, and Colombia) who now live and work in Israel. This exceeds the demands of most activists for multiculturalism.

Calls for multiculturalism have also come from Israeli Arabs, who have protested various forms of discrimination, including the long-established practice of allotting far more government resources to the Jewish sector than to Israeli Arabs. In the early 1990s, Taiseer Elias, who later wielded considerable power within government-sanctioned or supported organizations such as the Israel Broadcasting Authority, complained to me about the lack of support for the Arab orchestra he had established. A few years later, Nassim Dakwar voiced similar concerns regarding the lack of concert halls in Arab communities. Responding to such grievances in 2007, Adalah, The Legal Center for Arab Minority Rights in Israel, proposed a constitution that would guarantee recognition and support for Arab culture within the framework of the Israeli state. This was answered indirectly, in 2008, by a policy proposal from the council of the World Zionist Organization, recommending a multicultural Jewish state with cultural autonomy and proportional funding for Israeli Arabs on condition of loyalty to the state.[12] These are the latest shots in an ongoing battle, but they mark a significant break from the past in that the different parties recognize one another and promote a policy of multiculturalism.

Despite this seeming convergence on multiculturalism, it is important to note that different issues are at stake and the effect on the ethnic music scene is not uniform. Israeli Jews of North African and Middle Eastern descent are almost certain to see themselves as Israelis while Palestinian Arabs vary greatly in this regard. Israeli Jews also have greater access to governmental support—the Israeli Andalusian Orchestra is the most striking result in this regard[13]—though this may vary considerably from one ethnic Jewish group to another. Palestinian efforts at defining and presenting a national culture have not directly affected the ethnic music scene. They constitute an alternative, peripheral path for musical expression (see chapter 2).

Palestinian Arabs born in Israel have taken three distinct approaches to coping with their problematic situation: flight, resistance, and accommodation. Musicians such as Simon Shaheen and Bassam Bishara have rejected the possibility of life in Israel, emigrating to other Arab countries, to Europe, or to North America. Others, such as Amal Murkus and Khaled Jubran, have remained in Israel or the Palestinian Territories, but take explicitly critical stances toward Israel. The musicians who have figured prominently in this book, however, have chosen a third path, a form of accommodation, accepting the fact of Israel and making their way in it as best they can. It is difficult for a person to nuance these categorical divides and mutual evaluations can be harsh. Those who resist may view the accommodators as traitors to the Palestinian cause. They, in turn, may see the resisters as hypocrites, enjoying the educational and economic opportunities

12. For the text of Adalah's proposed constitution, see electronicintifada.net/v2/article6606.shtml and for an article about it, see Stern 2007 (Feb. 28). See Stern 2008 (Feb. 19) for a report on the WZO proposal.

13. See chapter 3.

of Israeli citizenship, including occasional government support for performances at home and abroad, while projecting an image of fierce independence that denies the Israeli part of their personal histories. Israeli Jewish musicians face no commensurate existential dilemma, though some choose to live abroad for political reasons.

Regardless of the success or failure of multiculturalist policies, the musicians involved in the ethnic music scene often cite the cultural diversity of Israel as an inspiration and primary motivation for the ethnic music scene. Miguel Herstein told a reporter: "A confluence of culture exists here [in Israel] because of the geographics and demographics. You've got immigrants from all over, it's the ingathering of the exiles" (Steinberg 2001).[14] On his CD *Darma* (1999), Eyal Sela also points to the ingathering of exiles as motivation for the emergence of new musical mixtures in Israel, citing "a daily interaction between different nations, religions and ethno-musical cultures" that "offers an opportunity to create a musical mosaic in which the west and the east can live together in peace." He hopes that "the mosaic that we present to the listener will contribute to the tranquility, color and joy which is found in the Israeli musical experience created here." The liner notes of *Joseph and One* (1999) cite a similar sentiment: "Whether Joseph is Jewish or Arab, native born or an immigrant—his personality is an intricate mosaic of all the cultures, societies and landscapes living here side by side. The resulting music strikingly reflects the many-sided personality of Joseph."

Mosaics are potent symbols of antiquity and Jewish heritage, marking the sites of synagogues with Hebrew inscriptions and Jewish iconography that provide archaeological links to ancient Jewish presence in the land, where few other traces remain. As a metaphor for cultural diversity, the mosaic contradicts the various types of homogeneity that the state has encouraged with its melting pot approach to the absorption of immigrants, its policy of Europeanization of immigrants from "non-Western" countries, and its ongoing disregard for the Israeli Arab minority as a source of difference. A reversal in the attitudes of the Israeli government and public would be too big a burden to place on the passage quoted from Joseph and One's liner notes. But the text does bear witness to emerging alternatives to once dominant attitudes in Israel and it is far from unique in this regard: "Anyone who tours Israel, if only for a few days, or who reads an Israeli newspaper, even an English one, knows that the country is a mosaic of cultures" according to the Ministry of Foreign Affairs Web site (Melcer 2001).

This multiculturalism should not be confused with widespread cosmopolitanism (see chapter 3), particularly with regard to political implications. Activists for multiculturalism strive for official recognition, representation in sociocultural decision-making, media exposure, and financial support

14. Members of Bustan Abraham complained to me that journalists twisted their words, so this statement should be read as a combination of what Herstein had to say and what Steinberg wanted to hear.

on behalf of divergent cultural identities and practices, challenging both the theory and the praxis of a unified nation state. Cosmopolitanism, on the other hand, looks outward, assumes cultural links to other countries—generally, but not exclusively, Euro-American—and looks to those countries for standards by which to judge social, political, and cultural aspects of Israeli life. This difference has musical ramifications. Music based on a cosmopolitan perspective is likely to be aimed at listeners outside of Israel as much as at those inside; a multicultural perspective is likely to aim at the Israeli market or a segment thereof. An individual may subscribe to both these outlooks—Yair Dalal is a case in point—and may even combine them by citing multiculturalist movements and policies in North America or Europe as examples for Israel to follow.

Although it is now common in many quarters to revile the Oslo Accords due to the failure to achieve a lasting peace and a Palestinian state, the initial optimism of that period should not be forgotten. From the despair of seemingly endless confrontation emerged hope for a genuine change. The Accords do not explain the establishment of Bustan Abraham or Alei Hazayit, which predate the signing in Oslo, but they do explain the fertile grounds for such efforts in the mid-1990s. Israeli-Palestinian collaborations were viewed in a favorable light both at home and abroad, drawing audiences and financial backing from various sources.[15] The opening of the border with Jordan and the thawing of icy relations with Egypt and various countries beyond the immediate line of confrontation (in Asia and Africa) gave access to new experiences, musicians, and performance opportunities.

The increase in access has several causes and manifestations. Major political changes in Israel have included a shift from a predominantly socialist economy to one in which capitalism and consumerism predominate and the gap between rich and poor has increased dramatically. Like people in many other parts of the world, Israelis have enjoyed the increased mobility and connectivity of late twentieth-century globalization, albeit with restrictions peculiar to Israel's geopolitical situation. As noted in chapter 9, Israelis have gained access to an ever-wider array of music, apparent in the broader selection of recordings for sale (at high prices), the greater frequency of travel to other countries, and more numerous performances by visiting artists from other countries. The styles of music broadcast are also more numerous, partially due to the proliferation of stations. Kevin Fellezs's observation that the "first wave baby boomer" fusion musicians in the U.S. and U.K. took access to a wide variety of musics on record for granted (2004: 20) is pertinent here.[16] However, Israel in the 1990s differed from those countries in the 1970s and the emerging network of ethnic music contributed to that difference, particularly due to the growing availability

15. Al-Taee writes about the growing openness to coexistence among Israelis and Palestinians in contrast to earlier decades (2002).
16. I saw the effect of this firsthand. When I first began bringing gifts of CDs it was relatively easy to find something unknown for these musicians, but by the end of the 1990s this was becoming significantly more difficult.

of instruction in relevant musical practices and the ensuing incorporation of teacher-student links to the network.

Transnational Circulation

The localized nature of this musical scene, which is produced by and caught up in the specificities of Israel and the Palestinian territories, with their particular political and social problems, wealth of cultural practices and peculiar institutions, has been the focus as I sketched the internal reasons (i.e., events and attitudes within Israel) that this musical phenomenon arose at a particular time in a particular place. But to leave it at that would be to ignore the fundamental importance of connections to the outside world and to the world music phenomenon cited by Erlmann in the epigraph to this chapter.

To state that this musical scene would not exist without circulation across state boundaries is no exaggeration. All the musicians with whom I spoke were well aware of this. When foreign invitations to perform were scarce, due to political or economic considerations, their very livelihood was in danger because the local market was just too small to sustain them. Beyond this, the ethnic music scene must also be seen as a localized manifestation of an international (if not global) phenomenon in terms of aesthetics and the circulation of musicians and their music. It differs from world/ethnic/roots music elsewhere due to the sociocultural connections and divisions among the people involved in its production and consumption (which needs no further comment at this point) and to the particular transnational patterns of circulation. A few observations will have to suffice concerning transnational circulation, a topic that deserves further research.[17]

Most of the musicians involved in Israel's ethnic music scene have tapped into several loosely connected networks of music venues and sponsors, including music festivals in North America and Europe,[18] and events produced by Jewish organizations such as community centers and the Hillel Houses adjacent to college campuses. The latter network has been particularly important for performances in North America. Israeli embassies and consulates have given support sporadically by funding airfare or accommodations or producing a single concert, but never sponsoring or organizing a tour outright. As far as I could ascertain, Palestinian organizations and other Arab groups have not been involved in direct sponsorship

17. Whoever undertakes this will need to cover numerous sites in Europe and North America.
18. Performances in the Middle East (outside Israel) have been very rare, primarily for political reasons. Recall that Shoham and Jamal created Alei Hazayit for a concert in Libya that was cancelled. They did perform in Jordan and individual musicians from several bands—including Shoham Einav, Taiseer Elias, and Nassim Dakwar—have performed in Egypt, but these are exceptions to a circuit that runs mainly through Europe and North America.

of any of the groups I studied. However, when Bustan Abraham performed at a Palestinian/Israeli peace festival in Europe in 1995, the program book included letters of sponsorship from both Palestinian and Israeli government officials. In other words, it would be a mistake to see this solely as a Jewish and/or Israeli phenomenon. While there is a preponderance of Jews in the scene, Arab musicians have also initiated bands and recordings and the audience has included many non-Jews even when the venues or sponsors have been associated with Jewish organizations. Bustan Abraham's foreign engagements, for instance, included numerous appearances at world music festivals and individual concerts that had no connection to Jewish or Israeli organizations. Some festivals had specific themes, such as music of the Mediterranean, the legacy of medieval Spain, or Middle East peace, while WOMAD and others were more general in scope. Since most annual festivals will not invite the same band back year after year, musicians and their managers continually seek new venues. Conversely, annual festivals may invite a different musician or band to represent Israel each year, expecting them to fit expectations as to what an "ethnic" band from Israel ought to be.

Given the importance of the foreign market it is little wonder that some musicians have stayed outside Israel for various periods of time. During the period of my research, Yair Dalal became a frequent visitor to California, although he rarely stayed more than a few weeks. Yinon Muallem, who performed alongside Yair Dalal with Eyal Sela's band Darma, is perhaps the most successful ethnic music transplant to date. Members of Bustan Abraham have spent time abroad, too. Due to a lack of sufficient professional work in Israel in the late 1990s, Emmanuel Mann moved to New York where he joined bands that were stylistically not too dissimilar from Bustan Abraham.[19] Zohar Fresco studied briefly in New York with frame drum virtuoso Glen Velez, forming a partnership that has continued on Velez's visits to Israel, where they have conducted workshops for local drummers and given concerts.

Other foreign musicians besides Velez have ties to the ethnic music scene in Israel. One of the more prominent is the Turkish American multi-instrumentalist Omar Farouk Tekbilek who has performed in Israel several times, in collaborations such as the CD *One*, a joint project of expatriate Israeli composer Yuval Ron that also involved Yair Dalal.[20] Bustan Abraham's work with Ross Daly offers another instance of links to an international performance network. Yinon Muallem, an Israeli who moved to Istanbul and established a musical career there, has toured Israel with Turkish musicians. I first met Yinon when he appeared at the Berkeley Jewish Music Festival in 2006 with the band Yahudice, which is a prime

19. During a Bustan Abraham tour in the U.S. Emmanuel filled in on bass for the newly orthodox Naor Carmi when a concert fell on the Sabbath.

20. For a list of Yuval Ron's considerable accomplishments in scoring films and television shows, see www.yuvalronmusic.com. Tekbilek also has a Web site: www.omarfaruktekbilek.com.

example of the spread of a transnational web of affiliations that would have been difficult to imagine fifteen years earlier. Led by an Israeli singer, the band is a collaboration of Israeli musicians, who have studied in Istanbul, and Turkish musicians.

Dependence on the international circulation of people, goods, and money lends tremendous weight to foreign markets or, more accurately, to the perceptions of foreign markets formed by performers, managers, and agents. Such considerations certainly played a part in the shaping of Yair Dalal's offerings and at least some of the albums by Bustan Abraham. Shoham Einav and Jamal Sa'id also attempted to cater to their audiences when they prepared foreign concerts, but their lack of professional management connections to the world music network meant that this really was guesswork.

The urge to satisfy presumed foreign desires for exotic evocations of the Middle East can lead to self-orientalization. The performance staged by Alei Hazayit at the 1998 Festival of Asian Arts in Hong Kong offers a good example. Shoham and Jamal dramatized the band's repertoire using a Bedouin tent and various other symbols of the Middle East.[21] Within this explicitly "Asian" context, Israel represented "Middle Easternness" because most of the other artists represented countries located in South, East, or Southeast Asia.[22] For this performance male members of Alei Hazayit wore a uniform costume of patterned vests and white shirts (see figure 4.3) while Shoham used several changes of costume and props to suit particular songs. Shoham often performed in flowing Middle Eastern dresses with large bracelets and buckles as part of her self-constructed identity: being *of* the Middle East, not just *in* the Middle East. Yair Dalal also performs in a costume that can be read in various ways: as a symbol of humility, purity, or simplicity, perhaps as a loose reference to piety were it not for the lack of head covering, but almost inevitably as "Oriental" (see chapter 7). By contrast, the members of Bustan Abraham shunned such symbolism, usually performing in casual dress, never in a uniform costume. This focus on musical quality rather than pseudoethnic dress was implicit in one critic's praise: "In an era when 'world music' or 'ethnic music' are entrusted in our country to the hands of every runny nosed [child] who wears a *galabiya* [a long, loose-fitting robe worn by Egyptian men, adopted by some in the ethnic music scene as a symbol of "ethnic" authenticity] and plays two chords on the 'ud, the band Bustan Abraham remains the Mercedes of the genre."[23]

Just as Leo Ching has shown that "Asianness" has become a commodity that circulates globally (2000: 257), it is not difficult to see "Middle Easternness" as a commodity that circulates through a variety of channels

21. See chapter 4 for a list of the groups from Israel that preceded Alei Hazayit at this festival.
22. From 1976 to 1998, the only other Middle Eastern countries represented were Syria and Turkey and not as frequently as Israel. I do not know whether this was due to a lack of invitations or interest.
23. Lahav 2001, my translation.

ranging from music festivals through Web sites to restaurants. This is not the place to determine precisely how this differs from the Orientalism identified by Edward Said and his followers. Clearly there is a connection, but significant differences, too, beginning with the fact that it is people from the Middle East who are performing and manipulating these representations in a far different historical moment from the painters and authors first critiqued by Said.

"Middle Easternness" is but one of several recurring tropes that musicians and intermediaries trade as commodities on the world music market. Others include bridges between East and West, collaborations between Jews and Arabs, and concerts for peace. The East/West trope is certainly not unique to this scene, though Israeli musicians have attempted to stake a claim by promoting their unique qualifications and position, as I shall show in the next section. The same is true of Jewish/Arab collaborations. Although Bustan Abraham arose for musical and entrepreneurial reasons, Farjun recognized the value in the image of Jews and Arabs making music together when he approached the Abraham Fund for support (see chapter 5). Yair Dalal genuinely believes in working for peaceful coexistence, but he too has gained from the marketability of this image. These musicians are hardly the only ones to satisfy foreign interest in manifestations of Palestinian-Israeli collaboration.[24] That the musicians recognize this is clear from their critique of others for collaborating solely on such grounds rather than for musical aesthetic reasons.

The promise of peace can move musical product. The notice for a San Francisco concert instigated by Dalal is typical of the promotion for such events: "For a brief few days, a quartet of well-known master Middle-Eastern musicians, known for their peace work and contemplative, heartfelt music will be in the Bay Area. They have played together many times, but for them to come together at this moment is a testament to their commitment to be spokespersons for the greater peace movement within their communities and the world."[25] The moment in question was the 2006 war between Israel and Hizbullah in Lebanon and the principal musicians who joined Dalal were an Israeli, a Lebanese, and a Palestinian Jordanian, all resident in the U.S. The numerous sponsors included San Francisco's Episcopalian Grace Cathedral, in which the event took place, and a large, varied audience purchased tickets to attend. Wishes for peace and Jewish, Christian, and Muslim benedictions prefaced the performances of music and dance.

Events of this sort that commodify musical expressions of peaceful coexistence exemplify the "politics of empathy" (Born and Hesmondhalgh 2000: 41). The desire to see peace in the Middle East must rank high among the motivations of people attending such concerts. The perceived impossibility of personally making a difference makes support for artists who represent such hopes a means of discharging one's moral or civic "duty."

24. If this book garners attention it will be partly attributable to this interest.
25. Jewish Music Festival e-mail bulletin sent Aug 6, 2006.

Steven Feld critiqued a related pattern of consumption with regard to the world music sub-genre he calls "pygmy pop," noting that "concern for the future of the rain forests and their inhabitants is now central to the genre" (1996: 26).

But there are at least two crucial differences between the "pygmy pop" phenomenon and Jewish-Arab, Israeli-Palestinian musical collaboration. For one, the political issue itself differs: Few would express opposition, in principle, to saving rain forests and safeguarding their inhabitants, but a similar consensus regarding the Israeli-Palestinian conflict is distinctly lacking. Even if the majority of consumers who patronize this music would like to see a peaceful resolution of this conflict, their views on the right solution differ greatly. Beyond that, the parties concerned are directly involved in the performance and recording of ethnic music in Israel, not in exploiting recordings of a disempowered people who have little say in the manipulation of their performative culture. In other words, this is not a case of schizophonic mimesis, a concept proposed by Steven Feld (1996) to denote music that has been separated from its context through imitation or sampling of recordings rather than unmediated engagement. Grappling with the implications of various types of involvement in cross-cultural music, Born and Hesmondhalgh implied a moral high ground when they called for "developing relatively unmediated and social engagements with the 'musical other' through attention to modes of performance and practice, and even to playing with those musicians, as opposed to sheer musical results and sound surfaces" (2000: 41). This is a fairly good description of what Yair Dalal, his various collaborators, and the members of Bustan Abraham and Alei Hazayit have done. That they could make a career out of it owed much to the possibilities afforded by overseas travel and circulation of their music for capitalizing on the market for symbols of hope.

Musical and Social Transformations

What of the future, then? Peaceful resolution of the Palestinian Israeli conflict seems as distant as ever. This is evident, for instance, in the severe curtailment of Dalal's performances with Palestinians. What has been the impact of the musicians profiled in this book? What have they performed into being and what does it portend for the future? They have been key actors in a growing musical network (chapter 8). They have developed ways of juxtaposing and synthesizing elements from a wide array of musical resources (chapter 9), and novel approaches to creating music that range along the spectrum that encompasses composition and improvisation (chapter 10). They have mobilized an array of visual, verbal, and musical symbols that stake claims to the past and can also be read as statements about the present and visions for the future (chapter 11). By bridging deep social, cultural, and political divides, these musical collaborations between Jews and Arabs have also called into question the formations of identity, affinity, and distance along ethnic, religious, and political lines that dominate interactions and worldviews in the Israeli-Palestinian arena. In doing so they subvert social norms and conventional ways of thinking about Israelis and Palestinians or Jews and Arabs.[26]

A growing number of musicians and listeners have been drawn to the art world that has begun to emerge as the loosely defined ethnic music scene has undergone several forms of institutionalization. These include the establishment of related instructional programs, recording companies such as Magda and Nada, and promotional agencies such as Nada and Olamale that feature these musicians. The success of these endeavors and festivals, such as those presented annually by the Confederation House in Jerusalem, bears witness to changing tastes and attitudes in the Israeli public.[27] Indicators of the vitality of this field of musical activity include the longevity of certain ensembles, the ongoing careers of pioneers in this musical field—most of the members of Bustan Abraham, for instance, maintained high profiles after the band's demise—and the enlargement of the network through proliferation of affiliated musicians and bands within the field. These are not limited to bands that include both Jews and Arabs, but such bands are central to the scene.

Formalized programs of study created since the mid-1990s for various Middle Eastern and Central Asian musical practices have had both musical and sociomusical repercussions. They provide teaching opportunities for established musicians such as Taiseer Elias, Yair Dalal, or Jamal Sa'id that supplement their performance income and provide some stability of employment. Some programs foster experimentation, either explicitly or by the fact that they bring together like-minded people, forming a hub in the network that steadily renews the supply of potential recruits for projects or bands. Younger musicians, such as Naor Carmi or Sameer Makhoul, have found both a framework to acquire competence relevant to this scene and access to some of the best musicians as potential partners. For instance, Makhoul's acclaimed 2004 album *Athar* brought together some of the best Arab and Jewish musicians, many of whom have studied and/or taught at the Jerusalem Academy of Music and Dance.

This is significant not only at the level of particular individuals, but also in terms of bridging networks of musicians, promoters, and audiences that would otherwise be unlikely to intersect. Consider the number of links to musicians and programs in this partial biography of Makhoul, diagrammed in figure 12.1: graduate of the Jerusalem Academy of Music and Dance where he studied with Taiseer Elias; soloist with the orchestra in Tarshiha founded by Nassim Dakwar; musical director of the Arab-Jewish orchestra at Joret al-Enab music center in Jerusalem; and teacher at the School of Ethnic Music at Bar Ilan University and at the Center for Oriental

---

26. To keep in mind the complications associated with these overlapping but nonequivalent terms (see chapter 1) I will continue to mix them here.

27. Gorenberg 2007 attests to this.

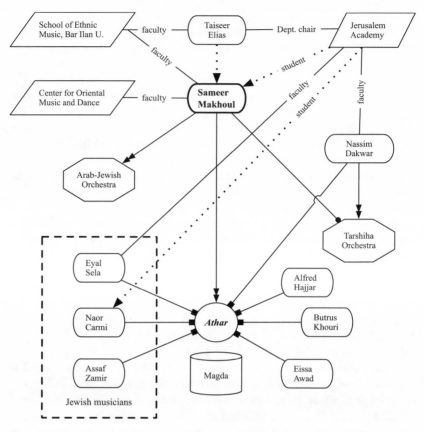

Figure 12.1　Network diagram of Sameer Makhoul's professional activities

Music and Dance in Jerusalem.[28] Such an array of connections and activities bridging Jewish and Arab musicians and musical worlds was unimaginable when Taiseer Elias and Avshalom first drew on their separate networks to form Bustan Abraham in 1991, but now it is not even unusual.

　　Most of these indicators of the health of the ethnic music scene and the persistence of Jewish-Arab collaboration were in evidence at a graduate recital I attended in 2007 at the Jerusalem Academy of Music and Dance. The young Arab *qanun* player drew on fellow students and a couple of outside musicians. That one of the outsiders was Jamal Sa'id's son Raed (see chapter 2), who does not generally move in these circles, was indicative of the extent of the network of connections. The seemingly unproblematic and natural mixing of Arabs and Jews on stage and in the audience struck me as a sign of hope for the future. But beyond this, I was impressed by the

28. Most of this information is taken from www.magda.co.il/sameer.html, Magda's Web page for *Athar*, which also lists a selection of Makhoul's activities abroad.

inclusion of two pieces from the Bustan Abraham repertoire that demonstrated that band's lasting impact. One might dismiss these choices as mere gestures made toward the two composers, Taiseer Elias and Nassim Dakwar, who are teachers at the Academy, if it were not for the new arrangements and the fact that these musicians were as adept at performing and improvising within these compositions as they were for the standard Arab repertoire that formed the bulk of the recital.

The vitality of the ethnic music network is evident in the clustering and reclustering of musicians for single projects and new bands. The numerous performing associations that Naor Carmi formed after leaving Bustan Abraham are particularly striking (see chapter 8). Joseph and One is remarkably close to the model of Bustan Abraham in its membership, its music, and even in its choice of a band name that references the Bible and combines words that are virtually the same in Hebrew and Arabic.[29] The biblical Joseph was Abraham's great-grandson. Appropriately, he became an integral part of Egyptian society, though the Bible does not tell us whether he formed a fusion band to influence Pharaoh's dreams. Multilingual compatibility carries over into the liner notes to the band's recording, however the outer cover is only in English, evidence of the power of the international market. Reviewers in Israel raved about the quality and originality of the music, but also noted the realization of coexistence as a vital act: "How refreshing to discover that someone still remembers 'coexistence' is not just some hackneyed expression, and that music is a wonderful way to express it."[30] One member of this band went on to found another, AndraLaMoussia, whose MySpace profile puts Bustan Abraham first in the list of bands that they sound like.[31]

Perhaps because they failed to achieve fame commensurate with that of Bustan Abraham and remained peripheral to the ethnic music network (see figure 8.6), Shoham and Jamal feared that they were being ripped off as others emulated the basic components of their sound. Despite these suspicions I cannot point to direct influence by Alei Hazayit on any particular band. Yet it is undeniable that their combination of *shirei erets yisrael* and Ladino ballads with a small ensemble consisting mainly of Arab instruments was an innovation in the early 1990s. Yasmin Levi has been far more

29. See www.josephandone.com/inside.html for the band's explanation of their name.

30. This excerpt from a review by Shachar Ran in *Bamachane* is quoted, in English translation, on the band's Web site, without publication information (www.josephandone.com/Review/review.html, accessed June 2007). A review by Amit Zvi quoted on the site enthuses about the band in the "list of ingredients" manner critiqued in chapter 9.

31. "ALM sounds like millennium in the desert. like a band of klezmers travelling [sic] on camel back. a mix between Bustan Abraham, Radio Tarifa, Klezmatics, Oi va voi, Anuar Brahem, and more." See myspace.com/andralamoussia. This band has performed with trumpeter Frank London, of the New York-based Klezmatics, thus offering one more instance of collaboration within a transnational network of musicians.

successful than Shoham in this regard, garnering praise from BBC Radio 3 and credit for revolutionizing the performance of Ladino song by "Arabicising" her singing with "oriental trills and slides" and including the 'ud in her ensemble.[32] Levy was nominated for a World Music award on BBC Radio 3 for three years running and has performed extensively abroad, including at WOMAD. Her success shows both the appeal and the normalization of some of the innovations that Shoham and Jamal pioneered. But Levy does not include Arab musicians in her ensemble and she does not combine Arabic with Hebrew, singing in Ladino.

Alongside the all-Jewish ethnic music bands that proliferated from the middle of the 1990s, joint endeavors by Jews and Arabs from Israel and the Palestinian territories sprang up as people caught the coexistence bug. The documentary *Israel Rocks!* showcases two such bands. The Joys, which included one Israeli Arab, are shown singing a song in Hebrew and Arabic about dividing the moon, "half for me and half for you," a clear reference to the Palestinian-Israeli political impasse. The second band, White Flag, consisted of roughly equal numbers of Palestinians and Israelis (including several women) and collaborated across the difficult Gaza border from 1998 until the onset of the second *intifada* in 2000. Though motivated by some of the same concerns as the musicians who are the focus of this book, this band differed musically. Its sound was dominated by rock instrumentation despite the presence of *'ud* and *darbukkah* and its repertoire was linked to both Arab and Israeli popular song styles.[33] Their Web site provides useful evidence of the issues and pressures involved in creating and maintaining a band that has both Israeli and Palestinian members. They also reveal key external interventions, including the seminal role of a joint Israeli-Palestinian organization (Windows - Channels for Communication) and the fact that after the second *intifada* made collaboration between Gaza and Israel impossible they were only able to reunite when the Dutch group that had produced the documentary *Israel Rocks!* invited them to Europe to document their story.[34]

Such sociopolitical engineering by organizations that are neither Israeli nor Palestinian—compare to the Abraham Fund's support for Bustan Abraham—is not at all uncommon in this arena, further evidence of the politics of empathy at work. Collaboration between Israelis and Palestinians and between Jews and Arabs (remember that these pairs are not synonymous) is seen as a highly desirable goal by numerous foundations and by foreign governmental bodies such as the Norwegian Foreign Ministry.[35]

32. See www.bbc.co.uk/radio3/world/awards2005/profile_yasminlevy.shtml, accessed March 2008.

33. Examples are available at www.whiteflagmusic.com/sound.

34. See www.whiteflagmusic.com/html/exile.htm. See www.win-peace.org for information on Windows-Channels For Communication.

35. *Music Channel,* the CD involving two Israelis, two Palestinians, and four Norwegians (see chapter 7), includes acknowledgments to the Norwegian Ministry of Foreign Affairs and three other Norwegian organizations, among others.

Thanks to this support various musicians have gained financial aid, publicity, and—quite literally—a stage. Joseph and One received an external boost when United Colors of Benetton featured them on their Web site alongside photos of Jews and Arabs coexisting in various settings. The members of the band were literally cast as poster children for Benetton's vision of peaceful coexistence—and joint consumption.[36] The Israeli government does not appear to have capitalized on this potential as much as it could have. Aside from sporadic support for concerts and tours or the appearance of a Bustan Abraham song on an embassy Web site, the government has not invested resources in the development or presentation of such groups despite the potential public relations benefit of showing the world that Israeli Jews and Arabs can and do collaborate to mutual benefit.[37]

When Alei Hazayit and Bustan Abraham took the stage they implicitly contested widely held notions regarding the separation and incompatibility of Jews and Arabs in and around Israel. For Palestinians and Israelis to see such mixed groups was to see the possibility of interaction on an equal footing, at least within the field of musical performance. It opened the door to seeing and hearing the humanity of the Other in a country where mutual fear and suspicion are the norm. Every person who has seen and heard these musicians has gained at least one striking impression to counter all the images of violence and intolerance purveyed through the mass media and, too often, experienced first hand. In addition to their humanizing and particularizing effect these collaborations also have presented new possibilities for the future because they produced a new kind of music. Here, they say, is music that draws on melodies, rhythms, textures, and timbres that are near to us and therefore signify something for each of us, although our associations may differ. It is a suggestion for the production of a shared cultural field, one in which people from various backgrounds with conflicting political interests and aspirations can find meaning and enjoyment. Often this is implicit in the performance, but at times the musicians or their presenters may render it explicit.

According to the anonymous liner notes, "The secret 'Oslo Channel'" that laid the foundations for the peace process between Palestinians and Israelis, sparked the idea of establishing a musical collaboration between the same three nationalities that were involved in the political negociations [sic]" (1995).

36. The lead article on the site was titled "Peaceful Co-Existence in Israel is the Theme of the New Benetton Catalogue." See www.benetton.com/wws/aboutyou/peopleplaces, which also includes an essay by renowned Israeli author and peace activist A. B. Yehoshua.

37. When a new, nongovernmental organization was established in 2007 to help export Israeli popular music groups that sing in English, one musician told a reporter, "The government and the Jewish organizations don't recognize the power of the scene yet—we are a powerful promotional tool for Israel . . . people come up to us after shows and say, 'Now I like Israel'" (Jacobson 2008). Note that this message is quite different from that conveyed by Bustan Abraham or Joseph and One.

At a concert shortly after the 9/11 attacks, Avshalom Farjun reportedly said: "On my left hand are the innocent citizens from this (Arab) culture . . . on my right are the innocent children of Israel and the free world. I bring my hands together and we have one human soul. Then we can clap in rhythm." Thus Avshalom brought together speech, music, and the body to form a complex symbol cluster that touches the noncynic on several levels simultaneously.[38] Relating to the present historical moment he continued, "When the twin towers came down, we decided we just have to play more music. . . . Sooner or later the world will have to accept the message of Bustan Avraham and return to the premise of respecting the innocence and dignity of each human being."

I suggest that these performers are helping their audience to envision a shared future by performing two important types of cultural work. Their new musical syntheses demonstrate possibilities of cultural production and consumption that are appealing and meaningful to people of diverse backgrounds and their public performances demonstrate the possibility of building complex interactions on the basis of mutual trust and respect. This is a radical message, given the reality of two peoples locked in a zero-sum contest, the ability of extremists on either side to call the shots and foil attempts at compromise, and the prevalence of mutual fear, distrust, alienation, and a basic lack of understanding.[39] Many Israeli Jews encounter Palestinians in menial tasks such as construction and the low end of service (dishwashing in restaurants, cleaning and carrying in markets), on excursions into Arab towns, or in the course of military service. Many Palestinians encounter Israeli Jews mainly as soldiers at checkpoints. However insiders and outsiders might view differences between Arabs and Jews in Israel—whether as cultural and ethnic, innate and racial, or in terms that are linked primarily to religious or political considerations—the fact remains that for most people, most of the time (and for many people, all of the time), this distinction is fundamental to the matrix through which the Israeli-Palestinian conflict as well as daily life in Israel and the Palestinian territories are understood. Hence the magnitude of the achievement when musicians work together in substantially integrated ways and thereby subvert stereotypes and disprove prejudices.

Judith Butler has argued (1993) that norms such as socially constructed gender roles are reinforced through repetition. This is certainly the case for the prejudices and fears that separate Jews and Arabs in relation to the Israeli-Palestinian conflict. Such reiteration must be broken and replaced by new patterns in order to progress beyond the current impasse. By normalizing rather than fetishizing the appearance of Jews and Arabs to-

38. This was posted at www.infinite-justice-operation.org/bustan.stm and on the Web site of Noble-Eagle-Operation.com (accessed Dec. 12, 2002) a peace organization. Prefix the first URL with web.archive.org/web/20021214085823/ to access it.

39. See Gavron 2006, an op-ed in Israeli's left-leaning Haaretz newspaper, for a recent, post-Lebanon War critique of the Israeli government's failure to confront the inevitable need for a solution.

gether on stage, the members of Bustan Abraham and other musicians involved in similar endeavors have broken one pattern and begun to inculcate a new one. In other words, there is a decidedly performative dimension that extends from, but is not to be confused with, their musical performances.

At the end of "Scenes and Sensibilities," Will Straw tosses off a particularly felicitous observation about urban scenes and "cultural citizenship" that resonates with the Israeli ethnic music scene in ways that he may not have foreseen. "The virtue of scenes is that they offer laboratories for cultural citizenship which are largely untainted by the sense of unfulfilled collective obligation which national cultural policy so often seeks to impart" (2002: 256).[40] The scene I have analyzed in this book arises out of a sense of untapped wealth, of possibilities that are more fulfilling and less transient than the music of the day. It should be noted that Israeli cultural policy was more successful, perhaps, than many other twentieth-century national policies in inculcating a sense of shared musical culture due to the relatively greater social mobilization of the Israeli Jewish public. But by the late twentieth century this sense had fractured (e.g., Regev 1996, Seroussi 2002c), due to the culture wars discussed above.[41] Furthermore, *musika mizrahit*, the music espoused by some as a form of resistance to hegemonic practices heavily dependent on European (and later American) models, did not work for others as an "authentic" form of expression for musical and social reasons: its "cheap" pop sounds, produced with synthesizers and drum machines, its pathos, and its links to a particular social group.

The appeal of this relatively new musical scene in Israel is due, I believe, to the "cultural citizenship" that it offers, a possibility of affiliation that is rooted in the convergence of Middle Eastern and Euro-American cultures but also reaches out to many others, appealing to the cosmopolitan in Israeli society. Political scientists, media scholars, and others have deployed the concept of cultural citizenship in several ways. Toby Miller, perhaps the most prolific writer on this topic, contrasts it to economic and political citizenship as "the maintenance and development of cultural lineage through education, custom, language and religion and the positive acknowledgment of difference in and by the mainstream" (2001: 2).[42] Joke Hermes offers a rather different definition: "the process of bonding and

40. He cites Toby Miller (1993: xi).

41. The American debate on multiculturalism was picked up in Israel by some of those who feel that their cultural heritage has been subject to government-sponsored discrimination. One outcome is the "Singing Communities" project directed by Yossi Ohana (see Banai 2004 and Dardashti 2008). Intended to reintroduce Israelis to their North African and Middle Eastern Jewish heritage of religious song, this program also involves Yair Dalal. It was first discussed by Dalal and Ohana in Berkeley in 1997 when Ohana, then directing Hillel House, asked me to sponsor a workshop by Dalal.

42. In other publications he discerns three sites for the theorization of cultural citizenship (e.g., 2002).

community building, and reflection on that bonding, that is implied in partaking of the text-related practices of reading, consuming, celebrating, and criticizing offered in the realm of (popular) culture" (2005: 10). This appears closer to Straw's usage (despite the fact that he cites Miller) and more apt for the situation I have described, though Hermes focuses on the audience rather than the primary cultural producers and does not touch on music at all. Straw has also observed that "scenes find coherence through the slow elaboration of ethical protocols to be followed by those moving within them. . . . Music scenes ground their distinctiveness in an ethics of cultural consumption (which music to buy, and where?)" (2002: 256). If one thinks that Palestinian-Israeli rapprochement and peaceful coexistence are worthy goals, then supporting musicians who realize these goals by consuming their music in live performances and through purchase of their recordings is an ethical action and another manifestation of cultural citizenship.

Group affiliations are a pressing issue for many in Israel, with numerous conflicting possibilities of affinity and allegiance in play. In this context the significance of the ethnic music scene lies in the opportunity for cultural citizenship that bridges the ever-deepening abyss that separates Jews and Arabs. Where others working toward coexistence might engage in dialogue groups, joint theater productions, political demonstrations, or concrete acts that deal directly with political and military confrontation—such as Israeli Jews volunteering to assist Palestinians pursuing claims against the Israeli border police or Palestinians risking their lives to work with groups that bring Jewish and Arab children together—these musicians have exemplified coexistence as a creative endeavor that need not address the conflict directly. Jewish and Arab musicians on stage together enact peaceful and productive cooperation with mutual respect and the diminishment, though not elision, of difference.

Matters of identity and affiliation are often not simple, of course. One member of Alei Hazayit, who has long been committed to coexistence with Israeli Jews, told me that he had also acted, with his sons and neighbors, in a fund-raising film for a Palestinian resistance organization in which they acted out Israeli soldiers beating Palestinians. This illustrates the complexity of individual positions and agency (and, perhaps, a certain opportunism). It also exemplifies the reality that Palestinians, particularly those who hold Israeli citizenship, are bound up with Israel and other Israelis, whether they hate them or tolerate them (i.e., accept the need to put up with them).[43]

Mixed bands such as Bustan Abraham or Alei Hazayit perform coexistence for a broad public, demonstrating that Jews and Arabs, Palestinians and Israelis not only can live together but can also enrich one another's lives in working together creatively. This sort of self-exposure and opening up to the other demands a distinctly different effort from that which takes

43. Judith Butler addressed this sort of entanglement (1993: 241) in a passage that Rita Lindahl brought to my attention.

place in Palestinian-Israeli dialogue groups.[44] It also differs from Jewish-Arab interactions in the East West Diwan Orchestra founded by Edward Said and Daniel Barenboim. When they brought together young musicians from Israel and Arab countries, Barenboim and Said recognized the transformative potential of collaborative music making. But the principle "texts" they chose—European art music—were not grounded in the Middle East and the musicians' sense of ownership or connection to this music, however much it meant to them on personal level, must necessarily be attenuated by historical and cultural distance. Members of Bustan Abraham, on the other hand, originated almost all of the music that they played, through composition and improvisation. Because such music is a collaborative production that draws heavily on the idioms of the Middle East, I contend that it "speaks" to audiences differently than a Mozart symphony. This is not a question of relative aesthetic value, but of incorporating a broader range of cultural resources, whereas the imposition, by Said and Barenboim, of the classics of European art music reinscribes Western cultural hierarchy.

Creating a new musical field is a way to practice activist cultural citizenship while offering a cultural critique that attempts to subvert the musical status quo by presenting possibilities other than mainstream cultural offerings. By the very act of coming together to create this music these musicians are also resisting political regimes of hatred and violence. Most of them give precedence to the musical goals of this mission over the sociopolitical aims, but they are aware that their musical actions imply a political stance against the hegemony of distrust, recrimination, and despair and in resistance to the dominant paradigms of conflict, separation, and extremism. This is a utopianism to live by, driven by strong motivation for peaceful coexistence both on moral/ethical grounds and because the alternatives are so bleak.[45]

Most Palestinians and Israelis are caught in worldviews where a gain by one side must be a loss for the other. Even schools and communities founded expressly to educate Israeli Jewish and Arab children together as an antidote to hate, fear, and inequality have stumbled over this.[46] The ethnic music scene has not addressed the issue head-on, but its very existence offers a third way, one of mutual benefit. Those Palestinian Arab musicians

44. Various dialogue groups and educational programs offer opportunities for people to engage with core issues of the Israeli-Palestinian conflict under the sponsorship of such institutions as the Jewish-Arab Center for Peace at Givat Haviva (an institute dedicated to fostering coexistence that is directed by an Arab former member of the Israeli parliament) or Beit Hagefen (a Jewish-Arab cultural center in Haifa).

45. See Ben (not Benedict) Anderson 2002 for a discussion of the immanence of utopia in listening practices.

46. Schools and other organizations that serve Palestinians and Israelis jointly encounter difficulties with regard to marking Israeli Independence Day, which is a day of national disaster for Palestinians. See, e.g., Ahmed 2005: 43–44, Frucht 2006, and Shesgreen 2002.

who have chosen accommodation with Israel and with Israeli Jews have found a path that they perceive as honorable, one that puts elements of their cultural heritage stage center, not as a tinge of ethnic color but as fundamental to the grammar of this new music, closely interwoven with other elements in a new synthesis. The Israeli Jews who participate have not lost anything by participating in this endeavor.

These musicians are not, in themselves, the solution to the fundamentally intractable Israeli-Palestinian problem, but if a solution is to be found, to be implemented and to last, it will only hold if there is a modicum of mutual respect and an envisioning of ways to live together. This is so even if one takes the more pessimistic view that the conflict can only be managed, not resolved.[47] These bands provide exactly that, a model of how one might live together not only in peace, but also in mutually beneficial harmony. Rather than confronting directly the pain, inequities, claims, and counterclaims that scar both sides in the Israeli-Palestinian conflict, these musicians are starting from the beginning and showing by example the beauty and mutual benefit of placing trust in one another—for music making relies on particular kinds of trust, the knowledge that one can count on other members of an ensemble to work together toward a common goal. Such trust is of the utmost importance if the Israeli-Arab conflict is to be resolved. It takes a very long time to build and next to no time to undermine as the events of the past few years have shown. Like the music that Bustan Abraham, Alei Hazayit, and others have created, peaceful coexistence is a matter of improvising within compatible frameworks. These must be collectively created and negotiated, not imposed.

47. Tom Segev, Israeli journalist and historian, voiced this view in a talk on the aftermath of the Six Day War (U. C. Berkeley, May 8, 2007).

Audio Recordings

Available online at www.oup.com/us/playingacrossadivide

Recordings by Alei Hazayit (unreleased, used by permission)

1. "Erev Shel Shoshanim" (4:59)
2. "Ro'e Vero'a" (3:40)
3. "Lamidbar" (6:55)

Recordings by Yair Dalal, Najema Music
(used by permission)

4. "Adon Haslichot" from *Silan*, 1997 (12:36)
5. "Al Ol" from *Al Ol*, 1995 (7:43)

Recordings by Bustan Abraham, Nada Productions
(used by permission)

6. "Jazz Kar-Kurd" from *Pictures Through the Painted Window*, 1994 (6:22)
7. "Metamorphosis" from *Bustan Abraham*, 1992 (10:08)
8. "Tini Mini Hanem" (beginning) from *Bustan Abraham*, 1992 (3:44)
9. "Bustan" (excerpts) from *Bustan Abraham*, 1992 (1:05)
10. "Suite for Deyzi" (excerpt) from *Bustan Abraham*, 1992 (0:51)
11. "Fanar" (excerpts) from *Fanar*, 1997, with Hariprasad Chaurasia and Zakir Hussain (0:53)
12. "Hamsa" (excerpt 1) from *Hamsa*, 2000 (0:49)

13. "Hamsa" (excerpt 2) from *Hamsa,* 2000 (0:38)
14. "Solaris" (ending) from *Fanar,* 1997 (0:55)
15. "Hamsin" (excerpt) from *Hamsa,* 2000 (0:38)
16. "Dub Dulab" (beginning) from *Hamsa,* 2000 (0:26)
17. "Fountainhead" (excerpt) from *Pictures Through the Painted Window,* 1994 (0:47)
18. "Pictures Through the Painted Window" (excerpt) from *Pictures Through the Painted Window,* 1994 (2:20)
19. "Gypsy Soul" (excerpt) from *Pictures Through the Painted Window,* 1994 (1:11)
20. "Dub Dulab" (excerpts) from *Hamsa,* 2000 (1:38)
21. "Bustan" (end) from *Bustan Abraham,* 1992 (0:50)

Glossary

baglama-saz	long-necked lute from Turkey
darbukkah	goblet shaped drum
hafla (pl. *haflat*)	celebration, often of a wedding, involving music
layali	vocal improvisation with minimal text
maqam (pl. *maqamat*)	melodic mode
mawwal	Arab vocal solo, often improvised, with poetic text
nay	Arab end-blown flute
ney	Persian end-blown flute
oud	alternative spelling for 'ud
piyyut	Jewish hymn
qanun	plucked zither
sama'i (pl. *sama'iyat*)	form in classical Arab music (based on Turkish *semai*)
shirei erets yisrael	songs of the land of Israel
takht	small Arab musical ensemble
taqasim	solo instrumental improvisation in Arab music
'ud	short-necked Arab lute

References

Ahmed, Ahseea. 2005. "Contesting Discourse: Can Deliberative Democracy Mitigate Protracted Ethnic Conflict in Israel?" M.A. thesis, Political Science, Simon Fraser University.

Ajzenstadt, Michael. 1998. "Critics' Choice: Classical Music." *Jerusalem Post,* June 18: 19.

———. 2000. "The Center of World Music." *Jerusalem Post,* June 10.

Al-Taee, Nasser. 2002. "Voices of Peace and the Legacy of Reconciliation: Popular Music, Nationalism, and the Quest for Peace in the Middle East," *Popular Music* 21: 41–61.

Anderson, Ben. 2002. "A Principle of Hope: Recorded Music, Listening Practices, and the Immanence of Utopia," *Geografiska Annaler* 84B/3-4: 211–27.

Anderson, Benedict. 1983. *Imagined Communities: Reflections on the Origin and Spread of Nationalism.* London: Verso.

Anonymous. 2002. "Unbenign Neglect." *The Jerusalem Post,* January 11, A8.

Appadurai, Arjun. 1996. *Modernity at Large: Cultural Dimensions of Globalization.* Minneapolis: University of Minnesota Press.

Atamna, Nawaf. 1994. "Me'at Ume'uhar Midai [Too little, too late]." *Haaretz,* July 27: 6.

Azzam, Nabil Salim. 1990. "Muhammad 'Abd Al-Wahhab in Modern Egyptian Music." Ph.D. dissertation, University of California, Los Angeles.

Badley, Bill. 2003. "A Tough Call in the Middle East." Available from http://www.bbc.co.uk/radio3/world/awards2003/middleeast.shtml.

Bar On, Yaakov. 1997. "Akordim Etniyim [Ethnic Chords/accords]." *Pnai Plus,* May 29: 51.

Bar-Yosef, Amatzia. 1990. "Hemshechiut Utmurah Basignon Hamusikali Shel Shirat Hahaddai [Continuity and Change in the Musical Style of the Haddai's Singing]." M.A. thesis, Hebrew University.

———. 1997. "Relationships between Time Organizations and Pitch Organizations in the Central Javanese Gendhing in Cross-Cultural Perspective." Ph.D. dissertation, Hebrew University.

Barabasi, Albert Laszlo. 2002. *Linked: The New Science of Networks.* Cambridge, MA: Perseus.

Barzilai, Amnon. 2004. "The Bedouin Intifada: It's Not If but When." *Haaretz*, May 25.

Bates, Eliot. 2008. "Social Interactions, Musical Arrangement, and the Production of Digital Audio in Istanbul Recording Studios." Ph.D. dissertation, University of California at Berkeley.

Bauman, Richard. 1984 [1978]. *Verbal Art as Performance*. Prospect Heights, Illinois: Waveland Press.

Becker, Howard Saul. 1982. *Art Worlds*. Berkeley: University of California Press.

Ben Ze'ev, Noam. 2002. "The Sounds of Palestine." *Haaretz*, April 2.

———. 2004. "Arab Music Hits an Unexpected High Note." *Haaretz*, June 3.

———. 2005. "'I don't really care if they don't know who I am here'." *Haaretz*, February 23.

Benson, Bruce Ellis. 2003. *The Improvisation of Musical Dialogue: A Phenomenology of Music*. Cambridge: Cambridge University Press.

Bernheimer, Kathryn. 2001. "Holocaust Survivor Records Her Memories in Art." *Intermountain Jewish News*, August 24.

Bisharat, George E. 1997. "Exile to Compatriot: Transformations in the Social Identity of Palestinian Refugees in the West Bank." In *Culture, Power, Place: Explorations in Critical Anthropology*, edited by Akhil Gupta and James Ferguson. Durham: Duke University Press. Pp. 203–33.

Bohlman, Philip. 1989. *"The Land Where Two Streams Flow": Music in the German-Jewish Community of Israel*. Urbana: University of Illinois Press.

Born, Georgina, and David Hesmondhalgh. 2000. "Introduction: On Difference, Representation, and Appropriation in Music." In *Western Music and Its Others*, edited by Georgina Born and David Hesmondhalgh. Berkeley: University of California Press. Pp. 1–58.

Boulos, Issa. 2002. "Review of *Traditional Music and Songs from Palestine*." *Music & Anthropology* 7. http://www.muspe.unibo.it/period/ma/index/number7/boulos/palest.htm

Brinner, Benjamin. 1985. "Competence and Interaction in the Performance of Central Javanese Pathetan." Ph.D. dissertation, University of California.

———. 1995. *Knowing Music, Making Music: Javanese Gamelan and the Theory of Musical Competence and Interaction*. Chicago: University of Chicago Press.

———. 2004. "Beyond Israelis vs. Palestinians or Jews vs. Arabs: The Social Ramifications of Musical Interaction," *Music and Anthropology* 8. http://www.levi.provincia.venezia.it/ma/index/number8/brinner/brin_0.htm.

Butler, Judith. 1993. *Bodies That Matter: On the Discursive Limits of "Sex"*. New York: Routledge.

Cashman, Greer Fay. 2001. "East, West Find Harmony in Music." *Jerusalem Post*, July 2.

Castelo-Branco, Salwa El-Shawan. 2002. "Western Music, Colonialism, Cosmopolitanism, and Modernity in Egypt." In *The Middle East*, edited by Virginia Danielson, Scott Marcus and Dwight Reynolds. New York: Routledge. Pp. 607–13.

Chasnoff, Ariel. 2001. "A new prophecy for the love generation." *Jerusalem Post*, July 19.

Ching, Leo. 2000. "Globalizing the Regional, Regionalizing the Global: Mass Culture and Asianism in the Age of Late Capital." *Public Culture* 12/1: 233–57.

Cohen, Boaz. 1992. "Dukiyum Beahava [Coexistence with love]." *Yedi'ot*, July 5.

Cohen, Dalia. 1986. *Mizrah Uma'arav Bemusika* [East and West in Music]. Jerusalem: Y.L.Magnes.

Cohen, Dalia, and Ruth Katz. 2006. *Palestinian Arab Music: A Maqam Tradition in Practice.* Chicago: University of Chicago Press.

Cohen, Effi. 1992. "Kol Ehad Vehakli Shelo [Everyone and His Instrument]." *Kol Hakrayot,* May 29.

Cohen, Eric, and Amnon Shiloah. 1985. "Major Trends of Change in Jewish Oriental Ethnic Music," *Popular Music* 5: 199–223.

Coleman, Sarah. 1998. "Jewish-Arab Ensemble Hopes to 'Open Hearts' Here." *Jewish Bulletin of Northern California,* April 10.

Connelly, Bridget. 1986. *Arab Folk Epic and Identity.* Berkeley: University of California Press.

Craig, Dale A. 1986. "Trans-Cultural Composition in the 20th Century." *Tempo* 156/2: 16–18.

Dardashti, Galeet. 2001. "Muzika Mizrakhit and Muzika Etnit: Discourses of the Israeli Middle Eastern Musical Aesthetic," *Text, Practice, Performance* 3: 99–126.

———. 2008. "The Piyyut Craze: Popularization of Mizrahi Religious Songs in the Israeli Public Sphere." Paper presented at Beyond Boundaries: Music and Israel @ 60, Center for Jewish Studies, CUNY Graduate Center.

Davis, Barry. 1999. "Blues - the Natural Choice." *Jerusalem Post,* Dec. 10.

———. 2000a. "Around the World in 180 Days." *Jerusalem Post,* Oct. 30.

———. 2000b. "Mediterranean Talking." *Jerusalem Post,* Dec. 1.

———. 2000c. "Oud Festival Kicks Off Tomorrow." *Jerusalem Post,* Nov. 28.

———. 2001a. "Green, Calm, and Collected." *Jerusalem Post,* September 18–19.

———. 2001b. "Hearing the World Loud and Clear." *Jerusalem Post,* March 21.

———. 2001c. "Making a Festival Date." *Jerusalem Post,* October 3.

———. 2001d. "Shem Tov Levy." *Jerusalem Post,* June 25.

———. 2001e. "Yemenite Suite Goes Classical." *Jerusalem Post,* November 26.

———. 2002a. "All for One," *Jerusalem Post,*

———. 2002b. "Bridging the Musical Gaps." *Jerusalem Post,* January 23.

de Certeau, Michel. 1984. *The Practice of Everyday Life.* Berkeley, University of California Press.

Degenne, Alain, and Michel Forsé. 1999. *Introducing Social Networks.* Translated by Arthur Borges. London: Sage Publications.

Delgado-Moreira, Juan M. 1997. "Cultural Citizenship and the Creation of European Identity," *Electronic Journal of Sociology* 2/3. http://www.sociology.org/archive.html.

De Vos, George and Lola Romanucci-Ross. 1982. "Ethnic Pluralism: Conflict and Accommodation." In *Ethnic Identity: Cultural Continuities and Change,* edited by George De Vos and Lola Romanucci-Ross. Chicago: Chicago University Press. Pp. 8–24.

DeWitt, Mark. 1998. "The Cajun and Zydeco Music and Dance Scene in Northern California: Ethnicity, Authenticity, and Leisure." Ph.D. dissertation, University of California.

———. Forthcoming 2009. "Louisiana Créole *Bals de maison* in California and the Accumulation of Social Capital." *Music and Sustainability: Special Issue of the World of Music.* Ed. Jeff Todd Titon.

Efrati, Avi. 1997. "Rega Lifnei Hakibush." *Iton Yerushalayim,* May 23.

Elias, Bari. 2001. "Sex Talk." Review of Yahasim Ptuhim. *Jerusalem Post*, August 13.

Elias, Taiseer. 2007. "The Latent Regularity in Improvisation of Instrumental Arab Music (*taqasim*) in Israel, in Terms of Learned and Natural Schemata." Ph.D. dissertation, Music, Hebrew University.

Emirbayer, Mustafa. 1997. "Manifesto for a Relational Sociology," *The American Journal of Sociology* 103/2: 281–317.

Erlmann, Veit. 1994. "'Africa Civilised, Africa Uncivilised': Local Culture, World System and South African Music," *Journal of Southern African Studies* 20/2: 165–79.

———. 1996a. "The Aesthetics of the Global Imagination: Reflections on World Music in the 1990s," *Public Culture* 8: 467–87.

———. 1996b. *Nightsong: Power, Performance, and Practice in South Africa*. Chicago: University of Chicago Press.

Feld, Steven. 1996. "pygmy POP. A Genealogy of Schizophonic Mimesis," *Yearbook for Traditional Music* 28: 1–35.

Fellezs, Kevin. 2004. "Between Rock and a Jazz Place: Intercultural Interchange in Fusion Musicking." Ph.D dissertation., University of California.

Finlay, Victoria. 1998. "Reviews: The Olive Leaves." *South China Morning Post*, November 6.

Fiske, Evan Gavriel. 2005. "State of the Art." *Jerusalem Post*, Nov. 18.

———. 2007. "Ethnic music festival: Songs of the oud." *Jerusalem Post*, Nov. 1.

Flam, Gila. 1986. "Beracha Zefira – a Case Study of Acculturation in Israeli Song," *Asian Music* 17/2: 108–25.

Fleisher, Robert. 1997. *Twenty Israeli Composers: Voices of a Culture*. Detroit: Wayne State University Press.

Foster, Robert J. 1991. "Making National Cultures in the Global Ecumene," *Annual Review of Anthropology* 20: 235–60.

Frucht, Leora Eren. 2006. "When Ahmed Met Avshalom." *Global Democracy*. http://www.zionism-israel.com/log/archives/00000080.html.

Gavron, Daniel. 2006. "The Great Escape." *Haaretz*, Sept. 17.

Gelfond, Lauren. 2004. "All That (Israeli) Jazz." *Hadassah Magazine*, 85/10: 35–38.

Gorenberg, Gershom. 2007. "Tipping the Scales." *Hadassah Magazine*, 88/7: 10–13.

Gould, Roger V. and Roberto M. Fernandez. 1989. "Structures of Mediation: A Formal Approach to Brokerage in Transaction Networks," *Sociological Methodology* 19: 89–126.

Gradenwitz, Peter. 1996. *The Music of Israel: From the Biblical Era to Modern Times*. 2nd ed., revised and expanded. Portland, Oregon: Amadeus Press.

Granovetter, Mark. 1973. "The Strength of Weak Ties," *American Journal of Sociology* 78: 1360–80.

———. 1974. *Getting a Job: A Study of Contacts and Careers*. Cambridge, MA: Harvard University Press.

Grenier, Line. 1989. "From 'Diversity' to 'Difference': The Case of Socio-Cultural Studies of Music," *New Formations* 9: 125–42.

Guilbault, Jocelyne. 1997a. "Interpreting World Music: A Challenge in Theory and Practice," *Popular Music* 16/1: 31–44.

———. 1997b. "The Politics of Labeling Popular Musics in English Caribbean," *Revista Transcultural de Música—Transcultural Music Review* 3.

———. 2000. "Musical Enactment of Social Difference: The Work of Musical Arrangers in Caribbean Calypso." Paper presented at Toronto 2000: Musical Intersections, the 45th Annual Meeting of the Society for Ethnomusicology, Toronto.

———. 2001. "Beyond the "World Music" Label: An Ethnography of Transnational Musical Practices." In *The Cambridge Companion to Pop and Rock*, edited by Will Straw, Simon Frith and John Street, 176–210. New York: Cambridge University Press.

Gupta, Akhil. 1992. "The Song of the Nonaligned World: Transnational Identities and the Reinscription of Space in Late Capitalism," *Cultural Anthropology* 7/1: 63–79.

Gupta, Akhil, and James Ferguson. 1992. "Beyond "Culture": Space, Identity, and the Politics of Difference," *Cultural Anthropology* 7/1: 6–23.

———. 1997a. "Culture, Power, Place: Ethnography at the End of an Era." In *Culture, Power, Place: Explorations in Critical Anthropology*, edited by Akhil Gupta and James Ferguson, 1–29. Durham, NC: Duke University Press.

———. 1997b. "Discipline and Practice: 'the Field' as Site, Method, and Location in Anthropology." In *Anthropological Locations: Boundaries and Grounds of a Field Science*, edited by Akhil Gupta and James Ferguson, 1–46. Berkeley: University of California Press.

Habib, Kenneth. 2005. "The Superstar Singer Fairouz and the Ingenious Rahbani Composers: Lebanon Sounding." Ph.D. dissertation, University of California.

Halevi, Yossi Klein. 1998. "The New Believers." *Jerusalem Report*, April 2: 14–16.

Hall, Stuart. 1997. "The Work of Representation." In *Representation: Cultural Representations and Signifying Practices*, edited by Stuart Hall, 13–74. London: Sage Publications.

Halper, Jeff, Edwin Seroussi, and Pamela Squires-Kidron. 1989. "Musica Mizrahit: Ethnicity and Class Culture in Israel," *Popular Music* 8/2: 131–41.

Handelman, Don, and Lea Shamgar-Handelman. 1993. "Aesthetics Versus Ideology in National Symbolism: The Creation of the Symbol of Israel," *Public Culture* 5/3: 431–49.

Hannerz, Ulf. 1987. "The World in Creolization," *Africa* 57/4: 546–59.

Harel, Amos. 1998. "Brukhim Hashavim." [?]: Musikat Olam, November 19.

Harsonski, Yossi. 2000. "Kur Hitukh Meratek [A fascinating crucible]." *Maariv*, February 27.

———. 2001. "Habustan Hogeg Asor [Bustan Celebrates a Decade]." *Ma'ariv*, March 1.

Hennion, Antoine. 1989. "An Intermediary between Production and Consumption: The Producer of Popular Music," *Science, Technology, and Human Values* 14/4: 400–24.

Hermes, Joke. 2005. *Re-Reading Popular Culture*. Oxford: Blackwell Publ.

Hirsch, Eric, and Charles Stewart. 2005. "Introduction: Ethnographies of Historicity," *History and Anthropology* 16/3: 261–74.

Hirshberg, Jehoash. 1984. "*Bracha Tsfira vetahalikh hashinui bamusikah beyisrael* [Bracha Zephira and the Process of Change in Israeli Music]," *Pe'amim* 19: 29–46.

———. 1995. *Music in the Jewish Community of Palestine, 1880–1948: A Social History*. New York: Oxford University Press.

———. 1997. "Performers between East and West-Ideology and Reality in the *Yishuv,*" *Musical Performance: An International Journal* 1/2: 5–13.

———. 2002. "Musical Life and Institutions in Israel: 1880–1990." In *The Middle East,* edited by Virginia Danielson, Scott Marcus and Dwight Reynolds, 1023–31. New York: Routledge.

Hobsbawm, Eric, and Terence Ranger, eds. 1983. *The Invention of Tradition.* Cambridge: Cambridge University Press.

Horowitz, Amy. 1994. "Israeli Mediterranean Music: Cultural Boundaries and Disputed Territories." Ph.D. dissertation, University of Pennsylvania.

———. 1997. "Performance in Disputed Territory: Israeli Mediterranean Music." *Musical Performance: An International Journal* 1/3: 43–53.

———. 1999. "Israeli Mediterranean Music: Straddling Disputed Territories." *Journal of American Folklore* 112/445: 450–63.

———. 2000. "Living Jerusalem: Cultures and Communities in Contention." Paper delivered at the Association of Israel Studies, Tel Aviv.

———. 2002. "Israeli Mediterranean Music." In *The Middle East,* edited by Virginia Danielson, Scott Marcus and Dwight Reynolds. New York: Routledge. Pp. 261–68.

Hotem, Ron. 2000."*Shiluv Menatseakh* [a Winning Combination]." *Kol Ha'ir,* December 29.

Israel Ministry of Foreign Affairs. 1995. "Shalom-Salaam: Extending the Olive Branch." *Panim: Faces of Art and Culture in Israel.* http://www.mfa .gov.il/mfa/go.asp?MFAH0a580, accessed 2002.

Jacobs, Andrea. 2001. "BMH-BJ Concert Attracts 650." *Intermountain Jewish News,* August 24.

Jacobson, Ben. 2008. "Ripe for Export." *Jerusalem Post.* Feb. 7

Jones, Steve. 1999. "Seeing Sound, Hearing Image: 'Remixing' Authenticity in Popular Music Studies," *M/C: A Journal of Media and Culture* 2/4.

Junka, Laura. 2006. "Camping in the Third Space: Agency, Representation, and the Politics of Gaza Beach," *Public Culture* 18/2: 349–59.

Kaatz, Gudrun. 1995. "Jüdisch essen, was ist das?" taz Bremen. April 25.

Kanaaneh, Rhoda. 2002. *Birthing the Nation: Strategies of Palestinian Women in Israel.* Berkeley: University of California Press.

Kaspi, Alon. 1992. "*Mizrah Umaarav, Lelo Psharot* [East and West without Compromises]." *Davar,* May 12.

Keltch, Gil. [2002?]. *Israel Progressive Rock Overview.* MIO records. [accessed 2003]. Available from http://www.miorecords.com/IsraelProg .html.

Keren, Michael. 2000. "Biography and Historiography: The Case of David Ben-Gurion," *Biography* 23/2: 332–51.

Khazzoom, Loolwa. 2000. "A Big Piece Is Missing in This 'Peace'," *Clamor Magazine,* October–November.

Kirshenblatt-Gimblett, Barbara. 1998. *Destination Culture: Tourism, Museums, and Heritage.* Berkeley: University of California Press.

Knoke, David, and Ronald S. Burt. 1983. "Prominence." In *Applied Network Analysis: A Methodological Introduction,* edited by Ronald S. Burt and Michael J. Minor, 195–222. Beverly Hills: Sage Publications.

Koskoff, Ellen. 1982. "The Music-Network: A Model for the Organization of Musical Concepts." *Ethnomusicology* 26/3: 353–70.

Kutner, Yoav. 1982? "*Bein Gaon Leshigaon* [Between genius and madness]." *Yediot Aharonot.*

———. 1992. "Habreira Haakustit [the Acoustic Selection]." *7 Yamim,* Nov. 13: 44.

Lahav, Shai. 2001. [Tarbut]. *Ma'ariv.* February 23.

Lakoff, George. 1990 *Women, Fire, and Dangerous Things: What Categories Reveal About the Mind.* Chicago: University of Chicago Press.

Laumann, Edward O., Peter V. Marsden, and David Prensky. 1983. "The Boundary-Specification Problem in Network Analysis." In *Applied Network Analysis,* edited by Ronald Burt and Michael Minor, 18–34. Beverly Hills: Sage.

Lausevic, Mirjana. 2007. *Balkan Fascination: Creating an Alternative Music Culture in America.* Oxford, New York: Oxford University Press.

Law, John. 1992. "Notes on the theory of the actor-network: Ordering , strategy, and heterogeneity." *Systems Practice* 5(4): 379–93.

Lee, Vered. 2008. "Conference asks: Iraqi Israeli, Arab Jew or Mizrahi Jew?" *Haaretz,* May 18.

Lemor, Sonie. 2001. "Express Yourself." *Jerusalem Post.*

Lev-Ari, Shiri. 2003. "Know Thy Neighbor." *Haaretz,* February 26.

Lobeck, Katharina. 2003. *Why Awards?* BBC3 [accessed March 13 2003]. Available from http://www.bbc.co.uk/radio3/world/awards2003/why.shtml.

Lomax, Alan. 1976. *Cantometrics: A Method in Musical Anthropology.* Berkeley: University of California Extension Media Center.

Lomsky-Feder, Edna, and Tamar Rapoport. 2001. "Homecoming, Immigration, and the National Ethos: Russian-Jewish Homecomers Reading Zionism." *Anthropological Quarterly* 74/1: 1–14.

Manuel, Peter. 1988. *Popular Musics of the Non-Western World.* New York: Oxford University Press.

Marcus, George E., and Michael M. J. Fischer. 1986. *Anthropology as Cultural Critique: An Experimental Moment in the Human Sciences.* Chicago: University of Chicago Press.

Marcus, Scott. 1989a. "Arabic Music Theory in the Modern Period." Ph.D. dissertation, University of California at Los Angeles.

———. 1989b. "The Periodization of Modern Arab Music Theory: Continuity and Change in the Definition of the Maqamat." *Pacific Review of Ethnomusicology* 5: 35–49.

———. 1992. "Modulation in Arab Music: Documenting Oral Concepts, Performance Rules and Strategies." *Ethnomusicology* 36/2: 171–95.

———. 1993. "The Interface between Theory and Practice: Intonation in Arab Music." *Asian Music* 24/2: 39–58.

———. 2002. "The Eastern Arab System of Melodic Modes in Theory and Practice: A Case Study of Maqam Bayyati." In *The Middle East,* edited by Virginia Danielson, Scott Marcus and Dwight Reynolds. New York: Routledge. Pp. 33–46.

———. 2007. *Music in Egypt: Experiencing Music, Expressing Culture.* New York: Oxford University Press.

Marks, Laura U. 2003. "What Is That *and* between Arab Women and Video? The Case of Beirut," *Camera Obscura* 18/3: 41–69.

Martin, Peter. 2006. "Musicians' Worlds: Music-Making as a Collaborative Activity," *Symbolic Interaction* 29/1: 95–107.

Meintjes, Louise. 1990. "Paul Simon's Graceland, South Africa, and the Mediation of Musical Meaning." *Ethnomusicology* 34/1: 37–73.

Melcer, Ioram. 2001. "Multiculturalism in Israel: The Situation and the Challenge." http://www.mfa.gov.il/MFA/MFAArchive/2000_2009/2001/8/.

Melman, Yossi. 2004. "Even the Shin Bet is against Discrimination." *Haaretz,* May 25.

Meyer, Rainer. 2000a. "Interview mit zwei Mitgliedern der Band Bustan Abraham." *Aufbau* 24.

———. 2000b. "Wanderer Zwischen Orient Und Okzident Jazz, Ethno, Reggae: Die Israelische Gruppe Bustan Abraham." *Aufbau* 24: 9.

Miller, Toby. 1993. *The Well-Tempered Self: Citizenship, Culture, and the Postmodern Subject*. Baltimore: Johns Hopkins University Press.

———. 2001. "Introducing . . . Cultural Citizenship," *Social Text* 69 19/4: 1–5.

———. 2002. "Cultural Citizenship." In *Handbook of Citizenship Studies*, edited by Engin F. Isin and Bryan S. Turner, 231–44. London: Sage Publications.

Monge, Peter R., and Noshir S. Contractor. 2003. *Theories of Communication Networks*. Oxford: Oxford University Press.

Monson, Ingrid. 1999. "Riffs, Repetition, and Theories of Globalization," *Ethnomusicology* 43/1: 31–65.

Nave, Zohar. 1997. "*Musikat Olam Bemeitava* [World Music at Its Best]." *Kolbo*, May 30: 96.

Nettl, Bruno, and Amnon Shiloah. 1978. "Persian Classical Music in Israel: A Preliminary Report," *Israel Studies in Musicology* 1: 142–58.

Nir, Ori. 2002. "There's a Limit Even to Bedouin Patience." *Haaretz*, March 20.

Oliver, Anne Marie, and Paul Steinberg. 2002. "Popular Music of the Intifada." In *The Middle East*, edited by Virginia Danielson, Scott Marcus and Dwight Reynolds. New York: Routledge. Pp. 635–40.

Ortiz, Fernando. 1995 [1940]. *Cuban Counterpoint: Tobacco and Sugar*. Translated by Harriet de Onis. Durham: Duke University Press.

Parmenter, Barbara McKean. 1994. *Giving Voice to Stones: Place and Identity in Palestinian Literature*. Austin: University of Texas Press.

Patai, Raphael. 1953. *Israel between East and West*. Philadelphia: The Jewish Publication Society of America.

Perelson, Inbal. 1998. "Power Relations in the Israeli Popular Music System." *Popular Music* 17/1: 113–28.

Peri, Lior. 1992. "*Bustan Meiniv Peirot* [the Orchard Bears Fruit]." *Kol Haifa*, June 5.

Plastino, Goffredo. 2005. "Open textures: On Mediterranean music." In *The Mediterranean in Music: Critical Perspectives, Common Concerns, Cultural Differences*, edited by David Cooper and Kevin Dawe. Lanham, Maryland, The Scarecrow Press: 179–94.

Poché, Christian. 2001. "Palestinian Music." In *The New Groves Dictionary of Music and Musicians*, edited by Stanley Sadie. New York: Grove. Pp. 935–37.

Pond, Steven F. 2000. "Herbie Hancock's Head Hunters: Troubling the Waters of Jazz." Ph.D. dissertation, Music, University of California at Berkeley.

Price, Curtis. "Pasticcio," *Grove Music Online*, edited by L. Macy (accessed July 30, 2005), http://www.grovemusic.com.

Racy, Ali Jihad. 1976. "Record Industry and Egyptian Traditional Music: 1904–1932." *Ethnomusicology* 20/1: 23–48.

———. 1977. "Musical Change and Commercial Recording in Egypt, 1904–1932." Ph.D. dissertation, University of Illinois.

———. 1981. "Music in Contemporary Cairo: A Comparative Overview." *Asian Music* 13/1: 4–26.

———. 1983. "Music in Nineteenth-Century Egypt: An Historical Sketch." *Selected Reports in Ethnomusicology* 4: 157–79.

———. 1986. "Words and Music in Beirut: A Study of Attitudes." *Ethnomusicology* 30/3: 413–27.

———. 1988. "Sound and Society: The Takht Music of Early-Twentieth Century Cairo." *Selected Reports in Ethnomusicology* 7: 139–70.

———. 2003. *Making Music in the Arab World*. Cambridge: Cambridge University Press.

Radoszkowicz, Abigail. 2002. "For the Love of the Land." Review of Ahavat Ha'aretz. *Jerusalem Post*, February 7.

Rakha, Youssef. 1999. "Home-Made." *Al-Ahram Weekly*, 4–10 November.

Rasmussen, Anne. 1989. "The Music of Arab Americans: Performance Contexts and Musical Transformations," *Pacific Review of Ethnomusicology* 5: 13–32.

———. 1996. "Theory and Practice at the 'Arabic Org': Digital Technology in Contemporary Arab Music Performance," *Popular Music* 15/3: 345–65.

Regev, Motti. 1993. *Oud and Guitar: The Musical Culture of the Arabs in Israel* (in Hebrew). Tel Aviv: Beit Berel/Zmora Bitan.

———. 1995. "Present Absentee: Arab Music in Israeli Culture," *Public Culture* 7/2: 433–45.

———. 1996. "Musica Mizrakhit, Israeli Rock and National Culture in Israel," *Popular Music* 15/3: 275–84.

Regev, Motti, and Edwin Seroussi. 2004. *Popular Music and National Culture in Israel*. Berkeley: University of California Press.

Robinson, Deanna Campbell, Elizabeth B. Buck, Marlene Cuthbert, and International Communication and Youth Consortium. 1991. *Music at the Margins: Popular Music and Global Cultural Diversity*. Newbury Park, CA: Sage Publications.

Roginsky, Dina. 2006. "Orientalism, the Body, and Cultural Politics in Israel: Sara Levi Tanai and the Inbal Dance Theater," *Nashim: A Journal of Jewish Women's Studies and Gender Issues* 11/1: 164–97.

Saada-Ophir, Galit. 2006. "Borderland Pop: Arab Jewish Musicians and the Politics of Performance." *Cultural Anthropology* 21/2: 205–33.

Said, Edward. 1979. *Orientalism*. New York: Vintage Books.

Sant Cassia, Paul. 2000. "Exoticizing Discoveries and Extraordinary Experiences: 'Traditional' Music, Modernity, and Nostalgia in Malta and Other Mediterranean Societies," *Ethnomusicology* 44/2: 281–301.

Sbait, Dirgham H. 1989. "Palestinian Improvised-Sung Poetry: The Genres of Hida and Qarradi Performance." *Oral Tradition* 4/1-2: 213–35.

———. 2002. "Palestinian Wedding Songs." In *The Middle East*, edited by Virginia Danielson, Scott Marcus and Dwight Reynolds. New York: Routledge. Pp. 579–92.

Scherer, Frank F. 2001. "Sanfancon: Orientalism, Confucianism and the Construction of Chineseness in Cuba, 1847–1997." In *Nation Dance: Religion, Identity and Cultural Difference in the Caribbean*, edited by Patrick Taylor. Bloomington: Indiana University Press. Pp. 153–70.

Schwitz, Jürgen. 1995. "Nähostlichen Fusionen [Near Eastern Fusions]." [Festival program booklet.]

Seroussi, Edwin. 2002a. "Israel: An Overview." In *The Middle East*, edited by Virginia Danielson, Scott Marcus and Dwight Reynolds. New York: Routledge. Pp. 1013–22.

———. 2002b. "From 'Morenica' to 'Sheharhoret': Ladino Songs in the Israeli Repertoire" [in Hebrew]. in *A Century of Israeli Culture*, edited by Israel Bartal. Jerusalem: Magnes Press. Pp. 244–50.

———. 2002c. ""Mediterraneanism" in Israeli Music: An Idea and Its Permutations." *Music & Anthropology* 7. http://www.levi.provincia.venezia.it/ma/index/number7/seroussi/ser_00.htm

———. 2003. "International Musical Multiculturalism: A Perspective from the Mediterranean Musical Dialogue in Jerusalem." Paper presented at the General Assembly of the IMC, Montevideo, October 13–19, 2003.

Shahar, Natan. 2004. "Shelem [Weiner], Matityahu." In *Grove Music Online*, edited by Stanley Sadie.

Shalev, Ben. 2004. "Jazz Meets Maghreb." *Haaretz,* December 28.

Shesgreen, Deirdre. 2002. "Arabs, Israelis forge haven of coexistence." *St. Louis Post-Dispatch*, April 28.

Shiloah, Amnon. 1985. *Hamoreshet Hamusikalit Shel Kehilot Yisrael* [the Musical Heritage of Jewish Communities]. Tel Aviv: Open University.

———. 1995. *Music in the World of Islam: A Socio-Cultural Study*. Detroit: Wayne State University Press.

Shiloah, Amnon, and Eric Cohen. 1983. "The Dynamics of Change in Jewish Oriental Ethnic Music in Israel." *Ethnomusicology* 27/2: 227–52.

Shiloah, Amnon, and Edith Gerson-Kiwi. 1981. "Musicology in Israel, 1960–1980," *Acta Musicologica* 53/2: 200–16.

Shohat, Ella Habiba. 1999. "The Invention of the Mizrahim," *Journal of Palestine Studies* 29/1: 5-20.

Shohat, Ella and Robert Stam. 2003. "Introduction." In *Multiculturalism, Postcoloniality, and Transnational Media*, edited by Ella Shohat and Robert Stam. New Brunswick, NJ: Rutgers University Press. Pp. 1–17.

Slobin, Mark. 1993. *Subcultural Sounds: Micromusics of the West*. Hanover, NH: Wesleyan University Press.

Slyomovics, Susan. 1991. "To Put One's Finger in the Bleeding Wound: Palestinian Theatre under Israeli Censorship," *TDR* 35/2: 18–38.

Stahl, Geoff. 1999. "Still 'Winning Space?': Updating Subcultural Theory," *Invisble Culture: An Electronic Journal For Visual Studies* 2.

Stanyek, Jason. 2004. "Transmission of an Interculture: Pan-African Jazz and Intercultural Improvisation." In *The Other Side of Nowhere: Jazz, Improvisation and Communities in Dialogue*, edited by Daniel Fischlin and Ajay Heble, 87–130. Middletown, CT: Wesleyan University Press.

Staring, Richard, Marco van der Land, Herman Tak, and Don Kalb. 1997. "Localizing Cultural Identity," *Focaal* 30/31: 7–21.

Stein, Rebecca Luna. 1998. "National Itineraries, Itinerant Nations: Israeli Tourism and Palestinian Cultural Production," *Social Text* 56: 91–124.

Steinberg, Jessica. 2001. "Three Israeli Musical Groups Create Community And Peace." http://www.beliefnet.com/Entertainment/2000/06/Three-Israeli-Musical-Groups-Create-Community-And-Peace.aspx.

Stephen, Bill. 1979. "The Cultural Improvisation of John McLaughlin," *International Musician and Recording World,* March.

Stern, Yoav. 2007. "Israeli Arab Group Proposes New 'Multi-Cultural' Constitution." *Haaretz,* Feb. 28.

———. 2008. WZO Council: Israeli Arabs Must Be Loyal to State, Condemn Terror." *Haaretz.* Feb. 19.

Stevenson, William B., and Danna Greenberg. 2000. "Agency and Social Networks: Strategies of Action in a Social Structure of Position, Opposition, and Opportunity," *Administrative Science Quarterly* 45/4: 651–78.

Stokes, Martin, ed. 1994. *Ethnicity, Identity and Music: The Musical Construction of Place.* Oxford: Berg.

Straw, Will. 1991. "Systems of Articulation, Logics of Change: Scenes and Communities in Popular Music." *Cultural Studies* 5/3: 361–88.

———. 2002. "Scenes and Sensibilities," *Public Culture* 22–23: 245–57.

Swedenburg, Ted. 2000. "Sa'ida Sultan/Danna International: Transgender Pop and the Polysemiotics of Sex, Nation, and Ethnicity on the Israeli-Egyptian Border." In *Mass Mediations: New Approaches to Popular Culture in the Middle East and Beyond,* edited by Walter Armbrust. Berkeley: University of California Press. Pp. 88–119.

———. 2001. "Islamic Hip-Hop Vs. Islamophobia: Aki Nawaz, Natacha Atlas, Akhenaton." In *Global Noise: Rap and Hip-Hop Outside the USA,* edited by Tony Mitchell: Wesleyan University Press. Pp. 57–85.

Swedenburg, Ted , and Smadar Lavie. 1996. "Between and among the Boundaries of Culture: Bridging Text and Lived Experience in the Third Timespace." *Cultural Studies* 10/1: 154–79.

Tannen, Deborah. 1984. *Conversational Style: Analyzing Talk among Friends.* Norwood, NJ: Ablex Pub. Corp.

Taruskin, Richard. 1992. "Entoiling the Falconet: Russian Musical Orientalism in Context." *The Cambridge Opera Journal* 4: 253–80.

———. 2000. "Where Is Russia's New Music? Iowa, That's Where." *The New York Times,* Nov. 5. Arts & Leisure, Section 2, p. 20.

Taylor, Timothy. 1997. *Global Pop: World Music, World Markets.* New York: Routledge.

Thompson, Gordon. 2002. "A Delhi in London: Networks, Ecology, and the Life of Music in a Sixties Pop Milieu." Paper presented at the annual meeting of the Society for Ethnomusicology.

Toynbee, Jason. 2000. *Making Popular Music.* New York: Oxford University Press.

Tsur, Shai. 1998. "Sabra Sounds: Why People Agree on Zehava." *Jerusalem Post,* Nov. 4.

Turino, Thomas. 2000. *Nationalists, Cosmopolitans, and Popular Music in Zimbabwe.* Chicago: University of Chicago Press.

Van Aken, Mauro. 2006. "Dancing Belonging: Contesting Dabkeh in the Jordan Valley, Jordan," *Journal of Ethnic and Migration Studies* 32/2: 203–22.

Van Matre, Lynn. 1990. "A White South African Superstar Fights the 'Political' Brand," Chicago Tribune: Friday's Guide To Movies & Music, October 26.

Wang, Oliver. 2004. "Spinning Identities: A Social History of Filipino American DJs in the San Francisco Bay Area (1975–1995)." Ph.D. dissertation, University of California.

Wardhaugh, Ronald. 1986. *An Introduction to Sociolinguistics.* Oxford: Blackwell.

Warkov, Esther. 1986. "Revitalization of Iraqi-Jewish Instrumental Traditions in Israel: The Persistent Centrality of an Outsider Tradition." *Asian Music* 17/2: 9–31.

Waterman, Chris. 1990. "'Our Tradition Is a Very Modern Tradition': Popular Music and the Construction of Pan-Yoruba Identity." *Ethnomusicology* 34/3: 367–79.

Watts, Michael J. 1992. "Space for Everything (a Commentary)." *Cultural Anthropology* 7/1: 115–29.

Williams, Patrick, and Laura Chrisman. 1994. "Colonial Discourse and Post-Colonial Theory: An Introduction." In *Colonial Discourse and Post-*

Colonial Theory: A Reader, edited by Patrick Williams and Laura Chrisman. New York: Columbia University Press. Pp. 1–20.

Winichakul, Thongchai. 1994. *Siam Mapped: A History of the Geo-Body of a Nation.* Honolulu: University of Hawaii Press.

WOMAD Festival. 1995. *Official Programme.* WOMAD.

WOMEX. 2001. *Womex Showcases 2001* WOMEX, [accessed 2001]. Available from http://www.mondomix.org/womexshowcases2001/artistes/yairdalal.html.

Yaqub, Nadia. 2002. "The Palestinian Groom's Wedding Eve Celebration." In *The Middle East,* edited by Virginia Danielson, Scott Marcus and Dwight Reynolds. New York: Routledge. Pp. 573–78.

Selected Discography

Alei Hazayit [The Olive Leaves Band]. 1996. *Shoham.* Self-produced demo.
———. 2001 [unpublished master].
Ankri, Etty. 2001. *Yam.* NMC.
Arabandi (Elias, Taiser, Krishnamurti Sridhar, S. Amir, and Zohar Fresco). 2000. *East Meets East.* Nada Records.
Ben Shir, Shimon. 2001. *Shades: Shimon Ben Shir Group.* Nada Records.
Bustan Abraham. 1992. *Bustan Abraham.* Nada Records.
———. 1994. *Pictures Through the Painted Window.* Nada Records.
———. 1996. *Abadai.* Nada Records.
———. 1997. *Fanar.* Nada Records.
———. 2000. *Hamsa.* Nada Records.
———. 2000. *Ashra: The First Decade Collection.* Nada Records.
———. 2003. *Live Concerts.* Nada Records.
Carmi, Naor and the Village Orchestra (*hatizmoret ha'amamit*). 2005. *Tizmoret.* Nada Records.
Caspi, Matti. 1981. *Twilight/Sof Hayom.* CBS.
Dalal, Yair. 1995. *Al Ol.* Najema Music.
———. 1996. *Samar.* Najema Music.
———. 2000. *Shacharut.* Najema Music.
———. 2002. *Asmar.* Magda/Najema.
Dalal, Yair and Al Ol. 1997. *Silan.* Najema Music & TV.
———. 1998. *The Perfume Road.* Magda & Najema.
Dalal, Yair and Friends. 2005. *Inshalla Shalom: Live in Jerusalem.* Najema.
Dalal, Yair and the Tarab Ensemble. 1999. *Azazme.* Magda.
Damari, Shoshana. 1995. *Israel, Yiddish, Yemenite & Other Folk Songs: With Folk Instruments and Orchestra.* Vanguard Classics.
East-West Ensemble. 1988. *Sinai Memories.* More Productions.
———. 1992. *Zurna.* CDI Ltd.
———. 1998. *Imaginary Ritual.* The Third Ear.
Esta. 1996. *Mediterranean Crossroads.*
El-Funoun. 1999. *Zaghareed: Music from the Palestinian Holy Land.* Sounds True.
Gaya. 1999. *Gaya.* Hed Arzi.
Habreira Hativ'it (The Natural Gathering). 1991. *Origins.* Tarbuton.
Hespèrion XXI. 1999. *Diasporá Sefardí.* Alia Vox.
Israel Ministry of Foreign Affairs. 1972. *From Israel with Love. Original Cast Recording.* Hed-Artzi Ltd.

Joseph and One. 1999. *Joseph and One*. J & 1 Joseph and One Productions.
Kark, Guy and Between Times. 1999. *Canaan*. Sufa Personal World.
Levy, Shem Tov. 2001. *Circle of Dreams/Kikar Hahalomot*. Magda.
Makhoul, Sameer. 20004. *Athar*. Magda.
Mashina. 1985. *Mashina*. CBS
Minuette. 1996. *The Eternal River*. MCI
Murkus, Amal. 1998. *Amal*. Highlights.
Music Channel. 1995. *Music Channel*. WEA/Warner.
Nachal Troupe. [1970?]. *Beheachzut Ha'Nachal Be'sinai. 22nd Program*. Hed-Arzi.
al-Qaimari, Ghidian. 1997. *Oud: Klänge aus dem Orient*. Gema.
Ron, Yuval. 2003. *One*. Magda Records.
Rosenberg, Dan. 2006. *The Rough Guide to the Music of Israel*. RGNET 1168CD.
Salman, Avraham. 1997. *Saltana*. Nada Productions.
Sands, Sheldon. 2002. *Dead Sea Strolls*. Avant-Acoustic Records.
Sela, Eyal. 1995. *Hijaz*. MCI. Rereleased as *Sela* by Magda.
———. 1999. *Darma*. Magda.
———. 2003. *Call of the Mountain: The Mysterious Dances of Mount Meron*. Nada Records.
Shaheen, Simon and Qantara. 2001. *Blue Flame*. ARK 21.
Shammout, Bashar and Gidi Boss. 1997. *Traditional Music and Songs from Palestine*. Popular Art Center.
Shanti, Oliver. 1998. *Seven Times Seven*. Sattva Music.
Shesh Besh. 1998. *Shesh Besh*. ENJA Records.
Sheva. 1999. *Yomam valayla/Day and Night*. Lev Haolam.
Tawfic, Samira. 2001. *The Best of Samira Tawfic*. EMI Music Arabia.
Zilber, Ariel. 1998. *Masakh Ashan*. Hataklit.
Ziryab Trio. 1996. *Oriental Art Music*. Nada Records. Rereleased as *Mashreq Classics* by Crammed Records.

Videography

Abrahami, Izzy, and Erga Netz. 2000. *Israel Rocks! A Journey through Music of Visions and Divisions*. Abrahami-Netz TV Productions & ARVO.
Halfon, Eyal. 2002. *Baghdad Cafe*. On All Fours Productions.
Kahan, Yvonne. 1995. *Time For Peace—Zaman El Salaam*.
Kutner, Yoav. 1998. *Sof Onat Hatapuzim*. Episode 10.
Tomalak, Ehud. 2006. *I Got No Jeep And My Camel Died*.

Index

Page numbers in italics refer to figures. The initial article is ignored in alphabetizing Arabic names. Recordings are italicized and precede band names and composition titles.

BBC Radio 3, 161, 320
Beatles, 149, 152, 190, 224, 247
Becker, Howard, 198–202, 205
Bedouin, 18,–19, 22, 47, 68, 150,
153, 155, 241–242, 300, 301,
302, 314 (*see also* Azazme
Bedouin; Balla Tsoubou Hal
Kahwa; Tarab Ensemble)
 music and musicians, 68, 71, 72,
155, 157, *178*, 179, 181, 202,
233, 241, 245
Ben Ami, Ilan, *158, 185,* 190
Ben Shitrit (Ben Shir), Shimon,
252, *266*
Berkeley, 180, 253–254, 256, 313,
323n41
Berkeley Jewish Music Festival,
180, 313
Bible, 124, 295, 302, 319
 as source for song texts, 5, 299
Bishara, Bassam, 38, 39, 41, 51,
54, 56, 58, 91, 101, 309
Bisharat, George, 15, 33, 301
Bisharat, Ramzi, *189,* 193
"Black Seagull," 218, 251, *266,* 274
bluegrass, 136, 226, 251, 255, 284
blues, 113, 136, 217, 220n12, 230,
250, 255, 260, 262, 272, 275,
284
Born, Georgina and Desmond
Hesmondhalgh, 224, 257, 306,
315–316
Borochov, Yisrael, 71, 185, 222,
267
Brazilian music, 136, 197, 229
Broza, David, 85, 176, 285
"Bustan," 252–253, *266,* 268, 276,
281, 284, audio tracks 9 and 21
Bustan Abraham, 4, 5, 27, 31, 33,
102, 113–130, *116,* 121, 196,
208–209, 228–229, 269, 285,
300, 302, 303 (*see also* Naor
Carmi; Nassim Dakwar;
Taiseer Elias; Avshalom
Farjun; Zohar Fresco; Miguel
Herstein; Emmanuel Mann;
Amir Milstein; Yehuda Siliki;
synthesis of musical styles)
 Arab music, 123, 192
 Arab musicians, 6, 129, 168, 171,
192
 arrangements, 4, 114, 123, 125,
134, 138, 140–142, 147, 232,

249, 250, 252, 253, 262,
265–278
 breakup, 128, 212, 218, 225, 229,
230, 292, 299, 317
 blues, 113, 136, 217, 250, 255,
260, 261, 272, 275, 284
 composition, 123, 140, 216,
265–287
 concert programs and venues,
121, 126, 277–278
 counterpoint, 117, 140, 252, 255,
262, 274, 281
 East and West, 123–124, 128,
212, 221–222, 225, 228, 247,
251, 262
 economics and marketing, 118,
121, 122, 269
 egalitarianism, 125, 128, 140,
141, 209, 250, 252, 267–268,
279
 ensemble precision, 141, 255,
268, 285
 festivals, 119–120, 122, 188
 guest artists, 116–117, 268, 277,
278
 harmony, 225, 252, 274–275,
276, 280, 281, 285
 history, 113–121, 128, 187, 207,
212
 impact and legacy, 6, 201, 212,
256, 318–319
 improvisation, 123, 141, 247,
249–251, 253, 254, 265,
278–287
 interaction, 131–149, 208–209,
249, 252, 261–264, 280–282,
284–285
 internal tensions, 120–121, 212
 and jazz, 127, 229, 230, 248,
253–254, 262, 275, 279 (*see
also* Elias, Taiseer; Milstein,
Amir)
 melodic complexity, 254,
272–274
 mission statement and motivations, 7, 34, 123–126, 127–128,
216
 musical competences, 113, 140,
225, 247, 259–264
 network connections and positions, 170, *185,* 186, 189, *191*
 orchestration, 140, 141, 184,
249, 250, 252, 268, 275, 276

Murkus, Amal, 63, 94, 159, *189*, *191*, 192, 193, 257, 291n2, 297n17, 309
Music Channel, 152, *158*, 159, *178*, 179, 224, 246, 247
music critics, 83, 122, 126, 137, 153, 175, 184, 190, 199, 200, 202–203, 228, 292, 298
music industry, 7, 12, 84–85, 89, 124, 148, 161, 176, 212
  Israel, 53, 74, 75, 76, 119, 121, 122, 179, 207, 208
musical form. *See* form, musical
musical competence. *See* competence, musical
musical interaction. *See* interaction, musical
musika mizrahit, 34n39, 56, 75–81, 83, 153, 195–196, 198, 240, 298n19, 308, 323
muwashshah, 39, 108, 123, 133, 273, 302

Nada Productions (or Records), 117–119, 186, 195, 205, 212, 222, 317
Najema Music (or Productions), 180, 181, 212
nationalism, 21, 71, 86, 211, 299
  and music, 22, 64, 196, 227, 240, 293, 297
  and tradition, 30, 196, 301
nay, 40–41, 47, 192
  in Alei Hazayit, 101, 107, 139, 142, 220, 235–238, 240, 242
"Nedunya," 259, 262–263, *266*, 273
Nehedar, Maureen, *158*, *178*, 230, 245
network, 29–30, 312 (*see also* centrality; hubs; interactive network; intermediaries; links; nodes; prestige and prominence)
  Arab music, 63, 80, 115, 138, 192–193, 237
  characteristics, 148, 165–170, 172, 173, 183, 196–197, 207
  dynamics, 206–212
  employment, 63, 95
  ensemble, 29, 59, 131–149, 157, 208–209
  ethnic music, 13, 115, 314
  Israeli popular music, 75, 188–192

multiple memberships, 197, 209–210
  singer-centered, 138, 144–145
  theory, 28–29, 85, 163–176
  Western art music in Israel, 82, 194
  world music, 27, 84, 148, 246, 312, 314
Nini, Achinoam. *See* Noa
Noa, 85, 117, 269
  and Zohar Fresco, 121, *189*, *191*
Nobel Peace Prize, 4, 151
North African music, 51, 80, 136, 155, 187, 191, 195, 222, 233 (*see also* Moroccan music)
Norway and Norwegian government, 4, 152, 159, 167, 175, 183, 246

Ofer, Nurit, *158*, 243–244
Olearchik, Alon, 160, 176, *189*, 192
oriental music, 79, 81n32, 246 (*see also* Middle Eastern music)
Orientalism, 32, 221, 224, 231, 246, 315
  self-orientalization, 300, 314
originality, 7, 123–125, 137, 231, 232, 235, 319
Oslo Peace Accords, 3, 4, 21, 44, 54, 101, 151, 206–207, 297, 311
Oslo Philharmonic, 4, 151, 159
ostinato, 219, 249, 251, 252, 253, 270, *271*, *276*, 279–281, 285, 287
Oud Festival, 80, 153, *181*, 182, 205

Palestinian. *See* identity
  emigration, 58
  folklore, 45, 46, 64, 73, 301
  national culture, 46, 64, 301, 309
  refugees, 19, 21, 33, 92, 293, 301
  religious divisions, 18, 53–54, 240–241
  resistance, 196
  social networks, 210, 211
Palestinian Authority, 3, 21, 104, 120
Palestinian Liberation Organization (PLO), 3, 21, 151
Palestinian music, 26, 30, 37–65, 133